D1002569

Knowledge Representation

WITHDRAWN

Special Issues of Artificial Intelligence: An International Journal

The titles in this series are paperback, readily accessible editions of the Special Volumes of *Artificial Intelligence: An International Journal*, edited by Daniel G. Bobrow and produced by special agreement with Elsevier Science Publishers B.V.

Qualitative Reasoning about Physical Systems, edited by Daniel G. Bobrow, 1985.

Geometric Reasoning, edited by Deekpak Kapur and Joseph L. Mundy, 1989.

Machine Learning: Paradigms and Methods, edited by Jaime Carbonell, 1990.

Artificial Intelligence and Learning Environments, edited by William J. Clancey and Elliot Soloway, 1990.

Connectionist Symbol Processing, edited by G. E. Hinton, 1991.

Foundations of Artificial Intelligence, edited by David Kirsh, 1992.

Knowledge Representation, edited by Ronald J. Brachman, Hector J. Levesque, and Raymond Reiter, 1992.

003.54
K76b

Knowledge Representation

edited by
Ronald J. Brachman, Hector J. Levesque, and Raymond Reiter

A Bradford Book
The MIT Press
Cambridge, Massachusetts
London, England

First MIT Press edition, 1992
© 1991 Elsevier Science Publishers B.V., Amsterdam, the Netherlands

All rights reserved. No part of this book may be reproduced in any form by any electronic or
mechanical means (including photocopying, recording, or information storage and retrieval)
without permission in writing from the publisher.

Reprinted from *Artificial Intelligence: An International Journal*, Volume 49, Numbers 1–3, 1991.
The MIT Press has exclusive license to sell this English-language book edition throughout the
world.

Printed and bound in the Netherlands. This book is printed on acid-free paper.

Library of Congress Cataloging-in-Publication Data

Knowledge representation / edited by Ronald J. Brachman, Hector J. Levesque, and Raymond
Reiter.
    p.   cm. — (Special issues of Artificial intelligence, an international journal)
  "A Bradford book."
  "Reprinted from Artificial intelligence, an international journal, volume 49, numbers 1–3, May
1991"—T.p. verso.
  Includes bibliographical references and index.
  ISBN 0-262-52168-7
  1. Knowledge representation (Information theory) I. Brachman, Ronald J., 1949–   .
II. Levesque, Hector J., 1951– . III. Reiter, Ray. IV. Series.
Q387.K56 1992
003'.54—dc20   91-5050
                                              CIP

CONTENTS*

*Pages 1–60, 97–345, and 361–395 were prepared with L^AT_EX.

CA [Dec 7 '92

11-11-92 FBS 27.26 alden

ALLEGHENY COLLEGE LIBRARY

Artificial Intelligence 49 (1991) 1–3
Elsevier

Introduction to the Special Volume on Knowledge Representation

Ronald J. Brachman

AT&T Bell Laboratories, Murray Hill, NJ 07974, USA

Hector J. Levesque and Ray Reiter

University of Toronto, Toronto, Ontario, Canada M5S 1A4

The idea of explicit representations of knowledge, manipulated by general-purpose inference algorithms, dates back at least to the philosopher Leibniz, who envisioned a calculus of propositions that would exceed in its scope and power the differential calculus he had developed. But only in the last thirty-five years have we begun to design automated systems that perform tasks in part by reasoning over bodies of represented knowledge. Much of the success of today's "knowledge-based systems" is in fact due to the supporting principles and technology developed by researchers dealing directly with the issue of knowledge representation and the processing of representations in logically-inspired ways. In other words, much of AI's success has been made possible by research in the area of knowledge representation and reasoning (KR). And given that we still have a long way to go before fully realizing the dream of Leibniz and others, the contribution of KR will continue to be a central one in Artificial Intelligence for some time to come.

While KR has almost always been thought of as the heart of AI, for most of the field's history, it was nonetheless a backstage activity. For many years, AI systems relied on representation subsystems to support their domain-oriented activities, but usually were more concerned with the application itself. As often as not, a new application came with a new, problem-specific representational component. However, in the last decade things began to change: a growing number of researchers became interested in understanding in a more general way the nature and limitations of knowledge-based systems. The field began to see that many seemingly different task domains shared a common structure. For example, diagnosis, image interpretation, and certain natural language understanding tasks could all be seen as instances of abduction, or more generally as constraint satisfaction and model

0004-3702/91/$ 03.50 © 1991—Elsevier Science Publishers B.V.

construction. Similarly, the frame problem in time-varying domains, inheritance hierarchies with exceptions, reasoning about prototypes, and the semantics of logic programming are all forms of nonmonotonic reasoning. The recognition of such common patterns of representation and reasoning and the growing interest in their analysis in the abstract became the catalyst for a tremendous surge of interest from many corners of AI. The number of papers submitted to the "Knowledge Representation" areas of major AI conferences grew dramatically. Key KR issues, such as nonmonotonic reasoning and qualitative reasoning, became key AI issues. Now a clearly identifiable subfield, in the mid-1980s, KR moved into the AI spotlight.

In the late 1980s, with a burgeoning literature and growing set of interested researchers, KR was ready for a meeting dedicated to its own research issues. KR'89—the First International Conference on Principles of Knowledge Representation and Reasoning—was the natural response. In Toronto, in May of 1989, several hundred researchers gathered for a technically rich and exciting meeting, focusing on key issues ranging from nonmonotonic reasoning to abduction to planning to constraint propagation. This special volume of *Artificial Intelligence* presents expanded versions of many of the best papers from that conference.

KR'89 focused on principles of commonsense reasoning and representation (rather than, for example, implementation issues), and represented a good cross-section of the research interests of the KR community. The conference Call for Papers gives a reasonable picture of the issues of interest. Among the topics explicitly encouraged were the following: analogical reasoning, deductive reasoning, temporal reasoning, evidential reasoning, inductive reasoning, diagnostic and abductive reasoning, nonmonotonic reasoning, qualitative reasoning, planning and plan recognition, knowledge representation formalisms, theories of the commonsense world, belief management and revision, and formal task and domain specifications. As mentioned above, a key ingredient that has caused the field to gel is the recognition of common patterns of reasoning, and how they cut across different application domains. Among the most exciting developments in KR are the recent theoretical and computational analyses of these very general forms of reasoning, many of which are represented in this volume.

The increasing interest in foundational principles of knowledge representation and reasoning has led to a corresponding growth in the breadth and depth of mathematics to which researchers have appealed. Exotic logics, probability theory, techniques from operations research and decision theory, complexity theory, computability theory, and the differential and integral calculi are all important analytic tools of contemporary KR. These provide an essential vehicle for comparing different theories, and for analyzing the consequences and computational properties of theoretical proposals. While this trend towards formalization within KR is bemoaned in some circles, we feel that it is of great benefit to the broader AI community. The formal concepts resulting from these efforts provide broader coverage, a more unifying perspective and ultimately, a simpler, more manageable account than the vague intuitions that preceded them. As a result, they are more easily assimilated, evaluated by the AI community at large, and passed on to the next generation of researchers.

This is not to say that KR itself does not have its detractors. There has been growing interest in the past few years in the possibility of an AI methodology that would somehow bypass symbolic representation and reasoning. For certain tasks this may be feasible, but it is certainly premature at this stage of AI's development to reject the theoretical foundations that underlie so much successful work in natural language, expert systems, diagnosis, databases, and logic programming. For computational theories of high-level cognition, KR remains the only game in town.

Given the important place held by KR'89 in the field of knowledge representation, and consequently its centrality for AI in general, we felt it would be valuable to collect extended versions of some of the better papers in one place. In preparing this special volume, we chose to invite all of our KR'89 authors to consider submitting extended versions of their papers for review. We did not attempt to be comprehensive in our coverage of the field (in that we restricted ourselves to the conference submissions), nor did we directly invite any papers to appear without review. All of the papers you see here have been through the normal *Artificial Intelligence* review process.[1]

Here then is a collection of some of the best papers from KR'89. All are substantial revisions of their versions in the *Proceedings of the First International Conference on Principles of Knowledge Representation and Reasoning*, edited by R.J. Brachman, H.J. Levesque, and R. Reiter (Morgan Kaufmann, San Mateo, CA, 1989). Taken together, they provide a representative cross-section of current concerns, results, and methods of the field, and a good indication of research directions for the 1990s.

---

[1]We are indebted to Danny Bobrow for his encouragement of the idea and his support throughout the production of this special volume.

Artificial Intelligence 49 (1991) 5–23
Elsevier

Nonmonotonic reasoning in the framework of situation calculus

Andrew B. Baker

Department of Computer Science, Stanford University, Stanford, CA 94305, USA

Received October 1989
Revised June 1990

Abstract

Baker, A.B., Nonmonotonic reasoning in the framework of situation calculus, Artificial Intelligence 49 (1991) 5–23.

Most of the solutions proposed to the Yale shooting problem have either introduced new nonmonotonic reasoning methods (generally involving temporal priorities) or completely reformulated the domain axioms to represent causality explicitly. This paper presents a new solution based on the idea that since the abnormality predicate takes a situational argument, it is important for the meanings of the situations to be held constant across the various models being compared. This is accomplished by a simple change in circumscription policy: when *Ab* is circumscribed, *Result* (rather than *Holds*) is allowed to vary. In addition, we need an axiom ensuring that every consistent situation is included in the domain of discourse. Ordinary circumscription will then produce the intuitively correct answer. Beyond its conceptual simplicity, the solution proposed here has additional advantages over the previous approaches. Unlike the approach that uses temporal priorities, it can support reasoning backward in time as well as forward. And unlike the causal approach, it can handle ramifications in a natural manner.

1. Introduction

The formalization of reasoning about change has proven to be a surprisingly difficult problem. Standard logics are inadequate for this task because of difficulties such as the frame problem [14]; nonmonotonic reasoning seems to be necessary. Unfortunately, as demonstrated by the Yale shooting problem of Hanks and McDermott [5], the straightforward use of standard nonmonotonic logics (such as circumscription) for reasoning about action leads to counterintuitive results.

There have been a large number of solutions proposed to the shooting problem (see, e.g., [2,6,7,9,10,15,17,20]), but none of them are completely satisfactory. Some of these solutions cannot handle examples that require

0004-3702/91/$03.50 © 1991—Elsevier Science Publishers B.V.

reasoning backward in time. And others require that the domain axioms be written in a rather restrictive format. This paper presents a new approach to the shooting problem that avoids these difficulties.

In the next section, we describe the shooting problem. Section 3 surveys some of the previous solutions and their limitations. Section 4 presents our solution, albeit in a slightly simplified form; this solution is refined in Section 5. In Section 6, we consider two additional scenarios in order to compare the various approaches to nonmonotonic temporal reasoning. Concluding remarks are contained in Section 7.

This paper is a revised version of [1].

2. The shooting problem

The Yale shooting problem arises regardless of which temporal formalism is used; we will use the situation calculus [14]. A *situation* is the state of the world at a particular time. Given an *action* a and a situation s, $Result(a, s)$ denotes the new situation after action a is performed in situation s. A truth-valued *fluent* (the only kind of fluent that will concern us) is a property that may or may not hold in a given situation. If f is a fluent and s is a situation, then $Holds(f, s)$ means that the fluent f is true in situation s.

With these conventions, one might use standard first-order logic to formalize the effects of various actions, but there are some well-known problems with this monotonic approach. The *frame problem* [14], to which this paper will be limited, is that we would need to write down a great many axioms specifying those properties that are *un*changed by each action. And yet, intuitively, all of these frame axioms seem redundant; we would like to specify just the positive effects of an action, and then somehow say that nothing else changes. Part of the motivation behind the development of nonmonotonic reasoning was to formalize this notion, and thus to solve the frame problem; we will use McCarthy's *circumscription* [12,13]. If A is a formula, P is a predicate, and Z is a tuple of predicates and functions, then the circumscription of P in A with Z varied is written as $Circum(A, P, Z)$. This abbreviates a formula in second-order logic that selects those models of A in which the extension of the predicate P is minimal (in the set inclusion sense). Besides P, only those predicates and functions in Z are allowed to vary during this minimization process. For a more extensive discussion of circumscription, the reader is referred to [8].

Consider the standard default frame axiom:[1]

$$\neg Ab(f, a, s) \supset (Holds(f, Result(a, s)) \equiv Holds(f, s)). \qquad (1)$$

---

[1] Lower case letters represent variables. Unbound variables are universally quantified.

This says that the value of a fluent persists from one situation to the next unless something is abnormal. The original intention was to circumscribe *Ab* with *Holds* varied. (We will refer to this as the *standard* circumscription policy.) It was hoped that this minimization of abnormality would ensure that a fluent would persist unless a specific axiom forced this fluent to change.

Unfortunately, this approach does not work. In a sequence of events, often one can eliminate an expected abnormality at one time by introducing a totally gratuitous abnormality at another time. In this case, there will be multiple minimal models not all of which will correspond to our intuitions.

The standard example, of course, is Hanks and McDermott's Yale shooting problem [5].[2] In this problem, which we are simplifying slightly from the Hanks and McDermott version, there are two fluents, *Alive* and *Loaded*, and two actions, *Wait* and *Shoot*. The story is that if the gun is shot while it is loaded, a person (named Fred) dies:

$$Holds(Loaded, s) \supset \neg Holds(Alive, Result(Shoot, s)). \tag{2}$$

There are no axioms about *Wait*, so one would hope that the general-purpose frame axiom would ensure that *Wait* does not change anything. In the original situation, Fred is alive, and the gun is loaded:

$$Holds(Alive, S_0), \tag{3}$$

$$Holds(Loaded, S_0). \tag{4}$$

If the actions *Wait* and then *Shoot* are performed in succession, what happens?

Let Y_0 be the conjunction of axioms (1)–(4), and let $\overline{Y_0}$ be the circumscription of *Ab* in Y_0 with *Holds* varied:

$$\overline{Y_0} \equiv Circum(Y_0; Ab; Holds).$$

What does $\overline{Y_0}$ have to say about the truth value of

$$Holds(Alive, Result(Shoot, Result(Wait, S_0)))?$$

We might guess that the waiting has no effect, and thus the shooting kills Fred, but circumscription is not so cooperative. Another possibility according to circumscription is that the gun mysteriously becomes unloaded while waiting, and Fred survives. This second model contains an abnormality during the waiting that was not present in the first model, but there is no longer an abnormality during the shooting (since the gun is unloaded, Fred does not change from *Alive* to not *Alive*). So both models are minimal, and

---

[2]A similar scenario, involving the qualification problem rather than the frame problem, was discovered independently by Lifschitz and reported by McCarthy [13, p. 107].

the formalization must be altered in some way to rule out the anomalous model. [3]

3. Previous approaches

There have been a large number of solutions proposed to the shooting problem. This section discusses the two most popular groups of solutions.

3.1. Chronological minimization

One idea, proposed in various forms by Kautz [7], Lifschitz [10], and Shoham [20], is *chronological minimization* (the term is due to Shoham). This proposal claims that we should reason forward in time; that is, apply the default assumptions in temporal order. So in the shooting scenario, we should first conclude that the waiting action is not abnormal. Then, since the gun would remain loaded, we would conclude that Fred dies. Each of the above authors successfully constructs a nonmonotonic logic that captures this notion of chronological minimality. Kautz, for example, uses a modified version of circumscription in which abnormalities at earlier times are minimized at a higher priority than those at later times.

While this approach does in fact give the intuitively correct answer to the Yale shooting problem, it is nevertheless highly problematic. Its applicability seems to be limited to what Hanks and McDermott call *temporal projection* problems, or in other words, problems in which given the initial conditions, we are asked to predict what will be the case at a later time. One can also consider temporal *explanation* problems [5], i.e., problems requiring reasoning backward in time. For problems of this sort, chronological minimization generally does not work very well (see the example in Section 6.1). For this reason, chronological minimization is not a completely satisfactory solution. [4]

3.2. Causal minimization

Another approach, developed by Haugh [6] and by Lifschitz [9], is that of *causal minimization*. This method represents causality explicitly by stating that a fluent changes its value if and only if a successful action causes it to do so. The intuition here is that there is a crucial difference between the abnormality of a gun becoming unloaded while waiting, and

---

[3]The current formalization admits a third possibility: Fred might die during the waiting phase. Our solution will rule out this model also.

[4]Sandewall [19] has proposed *filter preferential entailment*, a modification of chronological minimization that avoids some of the difficulties of the ordinary version.

the abnormality of Fred dying when shot with a loaded gun: there is a *cause* for the second while the first is totally arbitrary. We will discuss the system of [9]. There, the effects of actions are represented with a predicate *Causes*(a, f, v) that indicates that if the action a is successful,[5] then the fluent f takes on the value v. With this formalism, one specifies all the known causal rules (for the current example, *Causes*(*Shoot, Alive, False*)), and then circumscribes *Causes* with *Holds* varied. Since *Causes* does not take a situational argument, there obviously cannot be a conflict in minimizing it in different situations. Therefore, the shooting problem cannot arise.

The main drawback of this proposal is that it does not allow us to write our domain axioms in unrestricted situation calculus. Instead, we must use the *Causes* predicate. This is a severe restriction on our expressive power because there is simply no way to use the *Causes* predicate to express general context-dependent effects, domain constraints, or ramifications (see Section 6.2 for a discussion of this issue). In light of this difficulty, it would be useful to solve the Yale shooting problem in the original formalism.

4. The solution

Our approach to the Yale shooting problem consists of two innovations. First of all, when we circumscribe *Ab*, instead of letting the *Holds* predicate vary, we will let the *Result* function vary. That is, we will not think of *Result*(*Wait*, S_0) as being a fixed situation, with circumscription being used to determine which fluents hold in this situation. Instead, we will assume that for each combination of fluents, there is some possible situation in which these fluents hold. Circumscription will then be used to determine which of these situations might be the result of waiting in S_0. Second, in order for this idea to succeed, we must already have every consistent situation in the domain of discourse; an axiom will be added to accomplish this.

To see why this approach makes sense, let us resist the temptation of appealing to causality or temporal priorities, and instead think about the problem in its own terms. Why is it that we prefer the model in which Fred dies to the one in which waiting unloads the gun? After all, if by making the world behave more abnormally in S_0, we could make it behave less abnormally somewhere else, this would seem to be a fair trade. The problem is that if waiting unloads the gun, then the resultant situation is really a *different* situation than it would have been, so it is not the case

---

[5]An action is successful if all of its preconditions are satisfied. Lifschitz [9] formalizes preconditions with a special *Precond* predicate; for the current paper, the only precondition would be that *Loaded* must hold for *Shoot* to succeed.

that the world behaves more normally somewhere else. In our preferred model, the abnormality was that *Alive* changed to not *Alive* when *Shoot* was performed in a situation in which the gun was loaded. In the anomalous model, the world does not behave more normally in this situation; this situation just does not come about! But the standard circumscription policy, with *Holds* varied and *Result* fixed, completely misses this subtlety. It views the *Result*(*Wait*, S_0)s in the two models as the same situation, even though different fluents hold in them.

From this perspective, the shooting problem arises from the failure to index abnormality correctly. Since the abnormality predicate *Ab* takes a situational argument, it is important for the meanings of the situations to be held constant across the various models being compared. We can accomplish this by varying *Result* instead of *Holds* during the circumscription.

First, some details need to be discussed. We will use a many-sorted language with object variables of the following sorts: for situations ($s, s_1, s_2, \ldots$), for actions ($a, a_1, a_2, \ldots$), and for fluents ($f, f_1, f_2, \ldots$). We have the situation constant, S_0, the action constants, *Wait* and *Shoot*, and the fluent constants, *Alive* and *Loaded*. Finally, we have the predicate constants *Holds*(f, s) and *Ab*(f, a, s) and the function constant *Result*(a, s) : s. Axioms (1)–(4) should be interpreted relative to these declarations.

We need a uniqueness of names axiom for actions and also a domain-closure axiom for fluents:

$$Wait \neq Shoot, \tag{5}$$

$$f = Alive \lor f = Loaded. \tag{6}$$

Now, for the important part. Suppose that for every possible combination of fluents, there is some situation in which these fluents hold. We will discuss how to achieve this in general in the next section, but for the Yale shooting problem we add the following *existence of situations* axiom:

$$\begin{aligned}
&\exists s\,(Holds(Alive, s) \land Holds(Loaded, s)) \land\\
&\exists s\,(Holds(Alive, s) \land \neg Holds(Loaded, s)) \land\\
&\exists s\,(\neg Holds(Alive, s) \land Holds(Loaded, s)) \land\\
&\exists s\,(\neg Holds(Alive, s) \land \neg Holds(Loaded, s)).
\end{aligned} \tag{7}$$

This axiom ensures that for each of the four possible fluent combinations, there will be *at least* one corresponding situation; there may in fact be more than one such situation. We could add an axiom saying that there must be exactly one such such situation (for each fluent combination); in this case, the models would be deterministic finite automata with four states. Alternatively, we could introduce the notion of time, and require that each fluent combination have a corresponding situation for each time point, and that actions always increment the time. We will not make either one of these

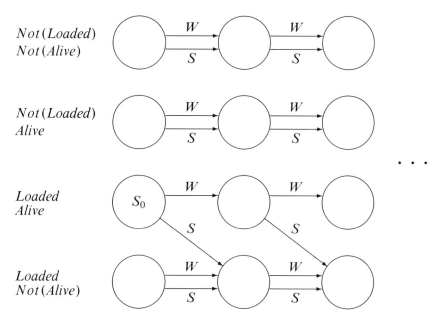

Fig. 1. A minimal model of the Yale shooting problem.

additions since neither would affect any of the results to be presented. We will, however, use the second convention in illustrating the ideas in Figs. 1 and 2.

Let Y_1 be the conjunction of axioms (1)–(7), and circumscribe *Ab* in Y_1 with *Result* varied:

$$\overline{Y_1} \equiv Circum(Y_1; Ab; Result).$$

In other words, the models of $\overline{Y_1}$ are precisely the minimal models (with respect to the above circumscription policy) of Y_1. Figures 1 and 2 are pictorial representations of two of the models of Y_1. Time flows horizontally, and each circle represents the set of situations at a given time in which the fluents to its left either hold or do not hold as indicated. The *W* arrows show the result of performing the *Wait* action, and the *S* arrows show the result of performing the *Shoot* action. Diagonal arrows represent actions that change at least one fluent, and hence are associated with at least one abnormality.

Since the *S* arrows from situations in which *Loaded* and *Alive* hold lead to situations in which *Alive* does not hold, these arrows must be diagonal. In the model of Fig. 1, these are the *only* abnormalities, and therefore this is a minimal model of Y_1 and hence a model of $\overline{Y_1}$. Figure 1 represents an intuitive model of the shooting problem. Figure 2, on the other hand, represents an unexpected model: one in which waiting in S_0 unloads the gun.

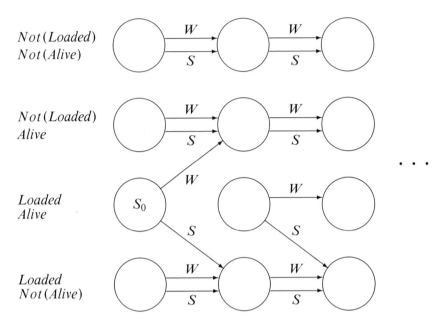

Fig. 2. A nonminimal model of the Yale shooting problem.

Note, however, that this added abnormality does not reduce the abnormality anywhere else. This model is strictly inferior to the previous one, and so it is not a model of $\overline{Y_1}$. Therefore, our technique solves the Yale shooting problem.

To state the correctness formally, we will use the following criterion:

$$[Holds(f, Result(a, s)) \equiv Holds(f, s)] \equiv$$
$$\neg[f = Alive \wedge a = Shoot \wedge$$
$$Holds(Alive, s) \wedge Holds(Loaded, s)]. \tag{8}$$

This states that the only fluent that changes its value is *Alive*, and this only happens when the *Shoot* action is performed in a situation in which the gun is loaded and Fred is alive. Along with axiom (5), (8) immediately implies that *Wait* has no effect, and this, together with the initial conditions (3)–(4), ensures that Fred dies:

$$\neg Holds(Alive, Result(Shoot, Result(Wait, S_0))).$$

Proposition 4.1. $\overline{Y_1}$ *is consistent.*

Proof. A model of $\overline{Y_1}$ can be defined in a straightforward manner. □

Proposition 4.2. $\overline{Y_1} \models (8)$.

Proof. Let M be any model of $\overline{Y_1}$. Such a model consists of the various domains: the domain of situations $|M|_s$, the domain of actions $|M|_a$, and the domain of fluents $|M|_f$; as well as interpretations for the constants:

$$M[[S_0]] \in |M|_s,$$

$$M[[Wait]] \in |M|_a, \qquad M[[Shoot]] \in |M|_a,$$

$$M[[Alive]] \in |M|_f, \qquad M[[Loaded]] \in |M|_f,$$

interpretations for the relations:

$$M[[Holds]] \subseteq |M|_f \times |M|_s,$$

$$M[[Ab]] \subseteq |M|_f \times |M|_a \times |M|_s,$$

and an interpretation for the *Result* function:

$$M[[Result]] \in (|M|_a \times |M|_s \to |M|_s).$$

We want to show that M must satisfy (8). Uniqueness of names for fluents follows from (7); this, together with the domain-closure axiom (6), ensures that without loss of generality, we can take:

$$|M|_f = \{Alive, Loaded\},$$

with *Alive* and *Loaded* interpreted as themselves. We can classify situations into four kinds with respect to which fluents hold in them, and if we let $M[[Shoot]] = Shoot$, we can classify actions into two kinds with respect to whether they are equal or not to *Shoot*. So there are eight cases that need to be considered.

Let $S_1 \in |M|_s$ be any situation in which *Alive* and *Loaded* hold:

$$\langle Alive, S_1 \rangle \in M[[Holds]],$$

$$\langle Loaded, S_1 \rangle \in M[[Holds]],$$

and let S_2 be the result of performing *Shoot* in S_1:

$$M[[Result]](Shoot, S_1) = S_2.$$

It follows from (2) that *Alive* does not hold in S_2; the only question is whether *Loaded* holds (intuitively, it should since we have not axiomatized the notion of running out of bullets). Suppose it does not. Then, from the frame axiom (1), we would have the abnormality:

$$\langle Loaded, Shoot, S_1 \rangle \in M[[Ab]]. \tag{9}$$

The existence of situations axiom (7) ensures that there is some situation S_3 in which *Loaded* holds, but *Alive* does not. But then we would be able to further minimize abnormality by making S_3 the result of the action, i.e., we could define another model M' of Y_1 that is exactly like M except that:

$$M'[[Result]](Shoot, S_1) = S_3,$$

$$M'[[Ab]] = M[[Ab]] - \langle Loaded, Shoot, S_1 \rangle.$$

This would eliminate abnormality (9) without introducing any new abnormalities (since there are only two fluents). Therefore M could not have been a minimal model of Y_1, contradicting the assumption that it was a model of $\overline{Y_1}$.

The arguments for the other seven cases are analogous. In each of these other cases, the action does not change the value of *any* of the fluents.   □

The domain-closure for fluents axiom (6) plays a crucial role in the above argument. Suppose that there were a third fluent in addition to *Alive* and *Loaded*, and that this fluent held in situations S_1 and S_2, but not in S_3. Then the above argument would fail. When we varied *Result* to go to S_3 instead of S_2, we would be introducing an additional abnormality on this new fluent. The problem is that the existence of situations axiom (7) only ensures the existence of situations corresponding to the four combinations of *Alive* and *Loaded*—not to the eight combinations of *Alive*, *Loaded*, and the mystery fluent. Axiom (6) was not included in the preliminary version of this paper [1]; Lifschitz [11] pointed out that it was necessary.

5. Existence of situations

In the last section, we violated the spirit of the nonmonotonic enterprise by adding an existence of situations axiom (7) that explicitly enumerated all possible situations. For more complicated problems, this axiom would be a bit unwieldy. In this section, we show how to write this axiom in a more general way. We present one formalization using first-order logic, and then another using second-order logic.

5.1. First-order formalization

In order to talk about combinations of fluents, we will add a new sort to the language: generalized fluents (which are a supersort of fluents), with the variables $g, g_1, g_2, \ldots$; and the functions $And(g, g):g$ and $Not(g):g$ to build up these generalized fluents. We will also alter the declaration $Holds(f,s)$ to $Holds(g,s)$ so that the first argument can be any generalized fluent. The following axioms define *And* and *Not*:

$$Holds(And(g_1, g_2), s) \equiv Holds(g_1, s) \wedge Holds(g_2, s), \tag{10}$$

$$Holds(Not(g), s) \equiv \neg Holds(g, s). \tag{11}$$

Generalized fluents will be used to reformalize the existence of situations axiom. Note that the frame axiom (1) is *not* modified to apply to all generalized fluents; it applies only to "regular" fluents (*Alive* and *Loaded*).

For our existence of situations axiom, wc would like to introduce a function $Sit(g) : s$ that maps a generalized fluent into some situation in which the fluent holds:

$$Holds(g, Sit(g)).$$

This would ensure that there is some situation such that $And(Alive, Loaded)$ holds, and one such that $And(Alive, Not(Loaded))$ holds and so on. But this would also mean that even inconsistent fluents like $And(Alive, Not(Alive))$ would be true in some situation; this contradicts (10) and (11). More generally, any domain constraint will render certain fluent combinations inconsistent (in Section 6.2, we discuss an example with the fluent *Walking* and with the constraint that one has to be alive to be walking). So instead, the existence of situations axiom will be written as a default using a new abnormality predicate $Absit(g)$:

$$\neg Absit(g) \supset Holds(g, Sit(g)). \tag{12}$$

We will circumscribe *Absit*.

Axiom (12) can be viewed as a closed-world assumption for domain constraints. We know from the other axioms that there cannot be a situation in which both *Alive* and *Not(Alive)* hold. Suppose, however, that there were also no situation in which both *Loaded* and *Not(Alive)* held. Since we are thinking of the situations as possible states of the world, this would be like saying that there is an extra domain constraint that we do not know about; axiom (12) excludes this possibility.

In order for the circumscription of *Absit* to have its intended effect, some uniqueness of names axioms will be necessary. We will use an abbreviation from [9]: UNA$[f_1, \ldots, f_n]$, where $f_1, \ldots, f_n$ are (possibly 0-ary) functions, stands for the axioms:

$$f_i(x_1, \ldots, x_k) \neq f_j(y_1, \ldots, y_l)$$

for $i < j$ where f_i has arity k and f_j has arity l, and:

$$f_i(x_1, \ldots, x_k) = f_i(y_1, \ldots, y_k) \supset (x_1 = y_1 \wedge \cdots \wedge x_k = y_k)$$

for f_i of arity $k > 0$. These axioms ensure that $f_1 \ldots, f_n$ are injections with disjoint ranges. We state that uniqueness of names applies to generalized fluents, and to our special *Sit* function:

$$\text{UNA}[Alive, Loaded, And, Not], \tag{13}$$

ALLEGHENY COLLEGE LIBRARY

UNA[*Sit*].   (14)

Let Y_2 be the conjunction of axioms (1)–(6) and (10)–(14). In addition to circumscribing *Ab* as before, we now circumscribe *Absit* with *Ab*, *Holds*, *Result*, and S_0 allowed to vary:

$$\overline{Y_2} \equiv Circum(Y_2; Absit; Ab, Holds, Result, S_0) \wedge$$
$$Circum(Y_2; Ab; Result).$$

Proposition 5.1. $\overline{Y_2}$ *is consistent.*

Proof. A model of $\overline{Y_2}$ can be defined in a straightforward manner. □

Proposition 5.2. $\overline{Y_2} \models$ (8).

Proof. Let M be any model of $\overline{Y_2}$. Consider the following four generalized fluents:

$$And(Alive, Loaded),$$
$$And(Alive, Not(Loaded)),$$
$$And(Not(Alive), Loaded),$$ (15)
$$And(Not(Alive), Not(Loaded)).$$

Axiom (13) ensures that these are all unequal, and axiom (14) ensures that the situations formed by applying *Sit* to them are also unequal. Suppose that one of these four generalized fluents were "abnormal" (with respect to *Absit*); that is, suppose for some g in (15), we had:

$$M[[g]] \in M[[Absit]].$$

This cannot happen, however, because it would violate the first circumscription: we would be able to define a model M' that is preferred to M by modifying the interpretation of *Absit* such that:

$$M'[[g]] \notin M'[[Absit]],$$

for all g in (15), and then varying *Ab*, *Holds*, *Result*, and S_0 in order to maintain consistency with the various axioms in Y_2. (These predicates and functions have to be allowed to vary during the circumscription of *Absit* for the following reason. When a generalized fluent g is not *Absit*, axioms (10)–(12) will tell us which fluents must hold in $Sit(g)$. Then, the law of change (2) might place some constraints on the *Result* function for actions performed in $Sit(g)$, and hence the frame axiom (1) might place some constraints on the *Ab* predicate. Finally, the initial conditions (3)–(4) might require that $M'[[S_0]] \neq M[[S_0]]$.)

Therefore by (12), it follows that $|M|_s$ contains situations for each of the four fluent combinations. The proposition then follows from the same argument used in the proof of Proposition 4.2. $\square$

5.2. Second-order formalization

The above approach for ensuring the existence of situations only works correctly for a finite number of fluents. If we had some fluent $Interesting(x)$, for instance, where x could range over integers, (12) would ensure the existence of a situation in which

$$And(Interesting(0), Interesting(1))$$

held, but with only finite conjunctions, it would not ensure the existence of a situation in which all integers were interesting. We can fix this by writing an existence of situations axiom in second-order logic:

$$\neg Absit_2(h) \supset (Holds(f, Sit_2(h)) \equiv h(f)) \tag{16}$$

where h is a predicate variable, with this predicate taking a fluent argument ($Absit_2$ is a predicate on fluent predicates, and Sit_2 is a function from fluent predicates to situations). The axiom states that for every non-abnormal set of fluents, there is some situation in which exactly these fluents hold.

Let Y_3 be the conjunction of (1)–(5), (16), and the following uniqueness of names axioms:

$$UNA[Alive, Loaded], \tag{17}$$

$$UNA[Sit_2]. \tag{18}$$

Note that the domain-closure axiom (6) is no longer necessary; if there are additional fluents besides *Alive* and *Load*, then (16) will apply to them as well. Note also that we no longer have any need for generalized fluents. We have:

$$\overline{Y_3} \equiv Circum(Y_3; Absit_2; Ab, Holds, Result, S_0) \wedge$$
$$Circum(Y_3; Ab; Result).$$

Since $Absit_2$ is a second-order predicate, its circumscription will be a formula in *third*-order logic; strictly speaking, this generalizes the standard definition of circumscription from [8], but this generalization is entirely straightforward.

Proposition 5.3. $\overline{Y_3}$ *is consistent.*

Proof. A model of $\overline{Y_3}$ can be defined in a straightforward manner. $\square$

Proposition 5.4. $\overline{Y_3} \models (8).$

Proof. Axiom (18) tells us that for each predicate h on fluents (i.e., for each $h \subseteq |M|_f$), $Sit_2(h)$ will be a distinct situation. Since we have no domain constraints, it must be the case that $Absit_2 = \emptyset$, (or else, by the argument used in the proof of Proposition 5.2, the first circumscription in the definition of $\overline{Y_3}$ would not be satisfied.) Therefore, for every possible combination of fluents, there is a corresponding situation. The proposition then follows by the argument that was used in the proof of Proposition 4.2. $\square$

6. Examples

In order to compare the different approaches to the Yale shooting problem, this section will discuss two additional temporal reasoning problems. Section 6.1 contains an example that requires reasoning backward in time, while Section 6.2 discusses the issue of ramifications.

6.1. The murder mystery

Consider the following temporal explanation problem, which we will call the murder mystery. In this variation on the Hanks–McDermott problem, Fred is alive in the initial situation, and after the actions *Shoot* and then *Wait* are performed in succession (the opposite of the Yale shooting order), he is dead:

$$Holds(Alive, S_0),$$

$$S_2 = Result(Wait, Result(Shoot, S_0)),$$

$$\neg Holds(Alive, S_2).$$

The system is faced with the task of determining when Fred died, and whether or not the gun was originally loaded. If we used the obvious monotonic frame axioms, we would be able to conclude that the gun was originally loaded, and that Fred died during the shooting. Unfortunately, the standard circumscription policy is unable to reach this same conclusion. It has no preference for when Fred died, and even if it were told that Fred died during the shooting, it still would not conclude that the gun was originally loaded. Surely, assuming that the gun was loaded is the only way to explain the

$$Ab(Alive, Shoot, S_0)$$

that would be entailed by Fred being shot to death, but circumscription is in the business of minimizing abnormalities—not explaining them.

Chronological minimization only makes the situation worse. It tries to delay abnormalities as long as possible, so it avoids any abnormality during the shooting phase by postponing Fred's death to the waiting phase. It therefore concludes that the gun must have been *un*loaded!

Causal minimization yields the intuitive answer since it is only by assuming that the gun was originally loaded that it can explain the death without introducing an additional causal rule.

Our method also gives the right answer, although there is a fine point that we have glossed over so far. In addition to *Result*, the situation constants S_0 and S_2 also must be allowed to vary during the circumscription of *Ab*. Since *Holds* is fixed during this circumscription, it is only by varying S_0 and S_2 that circumscription can be of any use in determining which fluents hold in these situations. In general with our approach, all situation-valued constants and functions should be allowed to vary; this did not matter for the original shooting problem since in that problem, the situation S_0 was fully specified. With this elaboration, the correctness criterion (8) is satisfied as before.

6.2. Ramifications

Often, it is impractical to list explicitly all the consequences of an action. Rather, some of these consequences will be *ramifications*; that is, they will be implied by domain constraints [4]. One of the main advantages of our method over causal minimization is that ours can handle ramifications, while causal minimization cannot.

A simple example of this limitation of causal minimization can be obtained from Hanks and McDermott's original version of the Yale shooting problem in which the gun was unloaded in the initial situation, and a *Load* action was performed before the waiting (the following example is based on one from Ginsberg [3]). Using the causal notation from [9], we assert that *Load* causes the gun to be loaded, and that *Shoot* causes Fred to be not alive (provided the appropriate preconditions are satisfied):

$$Causes(Load, Loaded, True),$$

$$Causes(Shoot, Alive, False).$$

Suppose that we now add the fluent *Walking* and a domain constraint stating that in order to be walking, one must be alive:

$$Holds(Walking, s) \supset Holds(Alive, s). \tag{19}$$

Suppose also that in addition to the usual initial conditions (3) and (4), we also know that Fred is originally walking:

$$Holds(Walking, S_0).$$

It would be nice if by minimizing *Causes* we could conclude that not only does shooting make Fred not alive; it also makes him not walking:

$$Causes(Shoot, Walking, False).   (20)$$

Unfortunately, there is another causally minimal model in which *Load* kills Fred. This model contains:

$$Causes(Load, Alive, False),   (21)$$

$$Causes(Load, Walking, False).   (22)$$

In this model, when *Load* loads the gun, it also kills Fred. Thus, there need be no situation in which the gun is loaded while Fred is walking. To see why this model is causally minimal, observe that if there were a situation in which the gun were loaded and Fred were walking, then due to the domain constraint (19), shooting Fred in this situation would force him to cease walking; and since causal minimization allows no effects without causes, (20) would have to be added (which is what we would like). In the unintended causally minimal model, however, by adding the new causal laws (21) and (22), such a situation need not occur, and thus (20) does not have to be added. Note the similarity of this difficulty to the original shooting problem: by adding spurious changes, certain states of the world never come about and thus the abnormalities that would have been associated with these states are ignored.

There have been some attempts at resolving this difficulty while remaining within the causal minimization framework, but so far none seem adequate. Lifschitz [9], for example, requires that fluents be divided into two groups, primitive and nonprimitive, with the causal laws and the frame axiom limited in application to the primitive fluents, and with the values of the nonprimitive fluents determined by their definitions in terms of the primitive fluents. This would work if we were axiomatizing *Alive* and *Dead* as we could make *Alive* a primitive fluent and *Dead* a nonprimitive fluent with the definition *Not*(*Alive*). It would not apply, however, to the current example. Neither *Walking* nor *Alive* can be defined in terms of the other, so the frame axiom must apply to both. Thus, with the causal minimization approach, we would have to explicitly assert (20). It has been argued that it will generally be intractable to precompute all the ramifications in this manner [4].[6]

The approach advocated in this paper handles ramifications correctly. Domain constraints determine which situations can exist in the model; in

---

[6]Even if this problem were solved, causal minimization has still another problem: since the *Causes* predicate does not take a situational argument, it cannot be used to formalize context-dependent effects.

the above example, there are only six types of situations that can exist: *Loaded* can be true or false, *Alive* can be true or false, and if *Alive* is true, then *Walking* can be true or false (otherwise, it must be false). The causal laws, like (2), further constrain the resultant situation of an action. So if the gun is loaded, and Fred is alive, then (2) will demand that Fred must be not alive after being shot, and the domain constraint (19) will ensure that Fred is not walking in this resulting situation. Finally, the minimization of abnormality will keep the gun loaded. The strange behavior of the causal approach cannot occur here because we require all possible situations to exist in the model.

Although the new approach can handle ramifications without introducing absurdities, it does not "solve the ramification problem". Consider a robot that is standing at location L_1, where this robot is holding an ice-cream cone. Suppose the robot now moves to location L_2. Does the ice-cream cone's absolute position persist, or does the fact that it is being held by the robot persist? (equivalent scenarios have been discussed by many authors, e.g., [4,16,18]). Based on our understanding of the domain, we would probably guess that after the robot moves, it will continue to hold the ice-cream cone. Yet, if we simply write down the domain constraint:

$$Holds(Holding(x,y),s) \land Holds(At(x,l),s) \supset$$
$$Holds(At(y,l),s),$$

then both persistence possibilities will correspond to legitimate minimal models. Clearly this is all that can be expected unless the system is supplied with additional information. If domain constraints are to be of much use for reasoning about action, we will need convenient methods for encoding this additional information that is used in resolving ambiguities. Ginsberg and Smith [4] discuss a few such methods, but more work is required.

7. Conclusion

This paper has presented a new approach to nonmonotonic temporal reasoning. The approach correctly formalizes problems requiring reasoning both forward and backward in time, and it allows for some of an action's effects to be specified indirectly using domain constraints.

It should be noted that, in a certain sense, our solution works for the same reason that causal minimization does. Causal minimization is not tempted to unload the gun because it is minimizing the extent of the *Causes* predicate rather than actual changes in the world; unloading the gun would prevent the *Causes(Shoot, Alive, False)* fact from *being used*, but it would not eliminate the fact itself. Similarly, our solution minimizes even those abnormality facts associated with situations that do not really happen. But since we stick with the standard axioms (rather than introducing a special *Causes* predicate), our approach appears to be the more robust of the two: for us, even those abnormalities that arise as ramifications can not be eliminated by the assumption of unmotivated changes.

Acknowledgement

I would like to thank Vladimir Lifschitz, Karen Myers, Arkady Rabinov, Yoav Shoham, David Smith, and especially Matthew Ginsberg for helpful comments, discussions, and encouragement. The author was supported by an AFOSR graduate fellowship.

References

[1] A.B. Baker, A simple solution to the Yale shooting problem, in: R.J. Brachman, H.J. Levesque and R. Reiter, eds., *Proceedings of the First International Conference on Principles of Knowledge Representation and Reasoning*, Toronto, Ont. (Morgan Kaufmann, San Mateo, CA, 1989) 11–20.

[2] M. Gelfond, Autoepistemic logic and formalization of common-sense reasoning, in: M. Reinfrank, ed., *Non-Monotonic Reasoning: Second International Workshop*, Lecture Notes in Computer Science **346** (Springer, Berlin, 1989) 176–186.

[3] M.L. Ginsberg, Personal communication (1988).

[4] M.L. Ginsberg and D.E. Smith, Reasoning about action I: a possible worlds approach, *Artif. Intell.* **35** (1988) 165–195.

[5] S. Hanks and D. McDermott, Nonmonotonic logics and temporal projection, *Artif. Intell.* **33** (1987) 379–412.

[6] B.A. Haugh, Simple causal minimizations for temporal persistence and projection, in: *Proceedings AAAI-87*, Seattle, WA (1987) 218–223.

[7] H.A. Kautz, The logic of persistence, in: *Proceedings AAAI-86*, Philadelphia, PA (1986) 401–405.

[8] V. Lifschitz, Computing circumscription, in: *Proceedings IJCAI-85*, Los Angeles, CA (1985) 121–127; also in: M.L. Ginsberg, ed., *Readings in Nonmonotonic Reasoning* (Morgan Kaufmann, Los Altos, CA, 1987) 167–173.

[9] V. Lifschitz, Formal theories of action, in: F.M. Brown, ed., *The Frame Problem in Artificial Intelligence: Proceedings of the 1987 Workshop*, Lawrence, KS (Morgan Kaufmann, Los Altos, CA, 1987) 35–58; also in: M.L. Ginsberg, ed., *Readings in Nonmonotonic Reasoning* (Morgan Kaufmann, Los Altos, CA, 1987) 410–432.

[10] V. Lifschitz, Pointwise circumscription, in: M.L. Ginsberg, ed., *Readings in Nonmonotonic Reasoning* (Morgan Kaufmann, Los Altos, CA, 1987) 179–193.

[11] V. Lifschitz, Personal communication (1989).

[12] J. McCarthy, Circumscription: a form of non-monotonic reasoning, *Artif. Intell.* **13** (1980) 27–39.

[13] J. McCarthy, Applications of circumscription to formalizing common-sense knowledge, *Artif. Intell.* **28** (1986) 89–116.

[14] J. McCarthy and P.J. Hayes, Some philosophical problems from the standpoint of artificial intelligence, in: B. Meltzer and D. Michie, eds., *Machine Intelligence* **4** (American Elsevier, New York, 1969) 463–502.

[15] P.H. Morris, The anomalous extension problem in default reasoning, *Artif. Intell.* **35** (1988) 383–399.

[16] K.L. Myers and D.E. Smith, The persistence of derived information, in: *Proceedings AAAI-88*, St. Paul, MN (1988) 496–500.

[17] J. Pearl, On logic and probability, *Comput. Intell.* **4** (1988) 99–103.

[18] M. Reinfrank, Multiple extensions, where is the problem?, in: F.M Brown, ed., *The Frame Problem in Artificial Intelligence: Proceedings of the 1987 Workshop*, Lawrence, KS (Morgan Kaufmann, Los Altos, CA, 1987) 291–295.

[19] E. Sandewall, Filter preferential entailment for the logic of action in almost continuous worlds, in: *Proceedings IJCAI-89*, Detroit, MI (1989) 894–899.

[20] Y. Shoham, Chronological ignorance: experiments in nonmonotonic temporal reasoning, *Artif. Intell.* **36** (1988) 279–331.

Artificial Intelligence 49 (1991) 25-60
Elsevier

The computational complexity of abduction *

Tom Bylander, Dean Allemang,
Michael C. Tanner and John R. Josephson [†]

Laboratory for Artificial Intelligence Research,
Department of Computer and Information Science,
The Ohio State University, Columbus, OH 43210, USA

Received October 1989
Revised June 1990

Abstract

Bylander, T., D. Allemang, M.C. Tanner and J.R. Josephson, The computational complexity of abduction, Artificial Intelligence 49 (1991) 25-60

The problem of abduction can be characterized as finding the best explanation of a set of data. In this paper we focus on one type of abduction in which the best explanation is the most plausible combination of hypotheses that explains all the data. We then present several computational complexity results demonstrating that this type of abduction is intractable (NP-hard) in general. In particular, choosing between incompatible hypotheses, reasoning about cancellation effects among hypotheses, and satisfying the maximum plausibility requirement are major factors leading to intractability. We also identify a tractable, but restricted, class of abduction problems.

1. Introduction

The problem of abduction can be characterized as finding the best explanation of a set of data [13]. Abduction applies to a wide variety of reasoning tasks [3]. For example, in medical diagnosis, the final diagnosis explains the signs and symptoms of the patient [24,26]. In natural language understanding, the intended interpretation of a sentence explains why the

---

*This paper is a revised and integrated version of Allemang et al. [1] and Bylander et al. [2].

[†]Dean Allemang's current address is Institut für Informatik, Universität Zürich, Winterthurerstrasse 190, CH-8057 Zürich, Switzerland. Michael C. Tanner's current address is Computer Science Department, George Mason University, Fairfax, VA 22030, USA

0004-3702/91/$ 03.50 © 1991—Elsevier Science Publishers B.V.

sentence was said [12]. In scientific theory formation, the acceptance of a hypothesis is based on how well it explains the evidence [32].

What kinds of abduction problems can be solved efficiently? To answer this question, we must formalize the problem and then consider its computational complexity. However, it is not possible to prescribe a specific complexity threshold for all abduction problems. If the problem is "small", then exponential time might be fast enough. If the problem is sufficiently large, then even $O(n^2)$ might be too slow. However, for the purposes of analysis, the traditional threshold of intractability, NP-hard, provides a rough measure of what problems are impractical [10]. Clearly, NP-hard problems will not scale up to larger, more complex domains.

Our approach is the following. First, we formally characterize abduction as a problem of finding the most plausible composite hypothesis that explains all the data. Then we consider several classes of problems of this type, the classes being differentiated by additional constraints on how hypotheses interact. We demonstrate that the time complexity of each class is polynomial (tractable) or NP-hard (intractable), relative to the complexity of computing the plausibility of hypotheses and the data explained by hypotheses.

Our results show that this type of abduction faces several obstacles. Choosing between incompatible hypotheses, reasoning about cancellation effects among hypotheses, and satisfying the maximum plausibility requirement are major factors making abduction intractable in general.

Some restricted classes of abduction problems are tractable. One kind of class is when some constraint guarantees a polynomial search space, e.g., the single-fault assumption (more generally, a limit on the size of composite hypotheses), or if all but a small number of hypotheses can be ruled out. [1] This kind of class trivializes complexity analysis because exhaustive search over the possible composite hypotheses becomes a tractable strategy.

However, we have discovered one class of abduction problems in which hypothesis assembly [13] can find the best explanation without exhaustive search. Informally, the constraints that define this class are: no incompatibility relationships, no cancellation interactions, the plausibilities of the individual hypotheses are all different from each other, and one explanation is qualitatively better than any other explanation. Unfortunately, it is intractable to determine whether the last condition holds. We consider one abduction system in which hypothesis assembly was applied, so as to examine the ramifications of these constraints in a real world situation.

The remainder of this paper is organized as follows. First, we provide a brief historical background to abduction. Then, we define our model of

---

[1] The latter constraint is not the same as "eliminating candidates" [6] or "inconsistency" [27]. If a hypothesis is insufficient to explain all the observations, the hypothesis is not ruled out because it can still be in composite hypotheses.

abduction problems and show how it applies to other theories of abduction. Next, we describe our complexity results, proofs of which are given in the appendix. Finally, we consider the relationship of these results to one abduction system.

2. Background

Peirce, who first described abductive inference [20], provided two intuitive characterizations: given an observation d and the knowledge that h causes d, it is an abduction to hypothesize that h occurred; and given a proposition q and the knowledge $p \rightarrow q$, it is an abduction to conclude p. In either case, an abduction is uncertain because something else might be the actual cause of d, or because the reasoning pattern is the classical fallacy of "affirming the consequent" and is formally invalid. Additional difficulties can exist because h might not always cause d, or because p might imply q only by default. In any case, we shall say that h *explains* d and p *explains* q, and we shall refer to h and p as *hypotheses* and d and q as *data*.

Pople pointed out the importance of abduction to AI [24], and he with Miller and Myers implemented one of the earliest abduction systems, INTERNIST-I, which performed medical diagnosis in the domain of internal medicine [16,25]. This program contained an explicit list of diseases and symptoms, explicit causal links between the diseases and the symptoms, and probabilistic information associated with the links. INTERNIST-I used a form of hill climbing—once a disease outscored its competitors by a certain threshold, it was permanently selected as part of the final diagnosis. Hypothesis assembly [13] is a generalization of this technique. Below, we describe a restricted class of problems for which hypothesis assembly can efficiently find the best explanation.

Based on similar explicit representations, Pearl [19] and Peng and Reggia [21,22] find the most probable composite hypothesis that explains all the data, a task that is known to be intractable in general [4]. Below we describe additional constraints under which this task remains intractable.

In contrast to maintaining explicit links between hypotheses and data, Davis and Hamscher's model-based diagnosis [5] determines at run-time what data need to be explained and what hypotheses can explain the data. Much of this work, such as de Kleer and Williams' [6] and Reiter's [27], place an emphasis on generating all "minimal" composite hypotheses that explain all the data. However, there can be an exponential number of such hypotheses. Current research is investigating how to focus the reasoning on the most relevant composite hypotheses [7,8,31]. However, we show below that it is intractable in general to find a composite hypothesis that explains all the data, and that even if it is easy to find explanations, generating all the relevant composite hypotheses is still intractable.

Whatever the technique or formulation, certain fundamentals of the abduction task do not change. In particular, our analysis shows how computational complexity arises from constraints on the explanatory relationship from hypotheses to data and on plausibility ordering among hypotheses. These constraints do not depend on the style of the representation or reasoning method (causal versus logical, probabilistic versus default, explicit versus model-based, ATMS or not, etc.). In other words, certain kinds of abduction problems are hard no matter what representation or reasoning method is chosen.

3. Notation, definitions, and assumptions

We use the following notational conventions and definitions. d stands for a datum, e.g., a symptom. D stands for a set of data. h stands for an individual hypothesis, e.g., a hypothesized disease. H stands for a set of individual hypotheses. H can be treated as a composite hypothesis, i.e., each $h \in H$ is hypothesized to be present, and each $h \notin H$ is hypothesized to be absent or irrelevant.

3.1. Model of abduction

An *abduction problem* is a tuple $\langle D_{all}, H_{all}, e, pl \rangle$, where:

- D_{all} is a finite set of all the data to be explained,
- H_{all} is a finite set of all the individual hypotheses,
- e is a map from subsets of H_{all} to subsets of D_{all} (H explains $e(H)$),
- pl is a map from subsets of H_{all} to a partially ordered set (H has plausibility $pl(H)$).

For the purpose of this definition and the results below, it does not matter whether $pl(H)$ is a probability, a measure of belief, a fuzzy value, a degree of fit, or a symbolic likelihood. The only requirement is that the range of pl is partially ordered.

H is *complete* if $e(H) = D_{all}$. That is, H explains all the data.

H is *parsimonious* if $\nexists H' \subset H$ ($e(H) \subseteq e(H')$). That is, no proper subset of H explains all the data that H does.

H is an *explanation* if it is complete and parsimonious. That is, H explains all the data and has no explanatorily superfluous elements. Note that an explanation exists if and only if a complete composite hypothesis exists.[2]

---

[2] Composite hypotheses that do not explain all the data can still be considered explanations, albeit partial. Nevertheless, because explaining all the data is a goal of the abduction problems we are considering, for convenience, this goal is incorporated into the definition of "explanation".

H is a *best explanation* if it is an explanation, and if there is no explanation H' such that $pl(H') > pl(H)$. That is, no other explanation is more plausible than H. It is just "*a* best" because pl might not impose a total ordering over composite hypotheses (e.g., because of probability intervals or qualitative likelihoods). Consequently, several composite hypotheses might satisfy this definition.

3.2. Relation to other work

These definitions are intended to formalize the notion of best explanation in Josephson et al. [13]. However, our definitions are not limited to that paper. We consider in detail here how Reiter's theory of diagnosis [27] and Pearl's theory of belief revision [19] can be mapped to our model of abduction.

3.2.1. Reiter's theory of diagnosis

Reiter defines a diagnosis problem as a tuple ⟨SD, COMPONENTS, OBS⟩, in which SD and OBS are finite sets of first-order sentences comprising the system description and observations, respectively; COMPONENTS is a finite set of constants; and AB is a distinguished unary predicate, interpreted as abnormal. A diagnosis is defined to be a minimal set $\Delta \subseteq$ COMPONENTS such that:

$$\text{SD} \cup \text{OBS} \cup \{\text{AB}(c) \mid c \in \Delta\} \cup \{\neg\text{AB}(c) \mid c \in \text{COMPONENTS}\backslash\Delta\}$$

is consistent. "Minimal set" means that no proper subset of Δ satisfies the same condition.

Each subset of COMPONENTS can be treated as a composite hypothesis, i.e., a conjecture that certain components are abnormal, and that all other components are normal. A diagnosis problem can then be mapped into an abduction problem as follows:

$$H_{\text{all}} = \text{COMPONENTS},$$

$$D_{\text{all}} = \text{OBS},$$

$e(H) =$ a maximal set $D \subseteq D_{\text{all}}$ such that [3]
$\quad\quad$ SD $\cup$ D $\cup$ $\{\text{AB}(h) \mid h \in H\}$ $\cup$ $\{\neg\text{AB}(h) \mid h \in H_{\text{all}}\backslash H\}$
$\quad\quad$ is consistent.

A solution for the diagnosis problem then corresponds to an explanation for the abduction problem, and vice versa. Reiter does not define any criteria for ranking diagnoses, so there is nothing to map to pl.

---

[3] There might be more than one maximal subset of observations that satisfies these conditions. If so, then $e(H)$ selects some preferred subset.

3.2.2. Pearl's theory of belief revision

A Bayesian belief network [18] is a directed acyclic graph whose nodes W are propositional variables. The probabilistic dependencies between the variables are described by specifying $P(x|s)$ for each value assignment x to a variable $X \in W$ and each value assignment s to X's parents S.[4] The intention is that

> the arcs signify the existence of direct causal influences between the linked propositions, and the strengths of the these influences are quantified by the conditional probabilities of each variable given the state of its parents. [19, p. 175]

For a particular belief revision problem [19], some subset V of the variables W is initialized with specific values. Let v be the value assignment to V. The solution to the problem is the most probable value assignment w^* to all the variables W, i.e., $P(w^*|v)$ is greater than or equal to $P(w|v)$ for any other value assignment w to the variables W. w^* is called the most probable explanation (MPE).

v can be mapped to the set of data to be explained, i.e., a value assignment x to a variable $X \in V$ is a datum. v can be explained by appropriate value assignments to the other variables $W \backslash V$. Treating value assignments of *true* as individual hypotheses, a belief revision problem can be mapped to an abduction problem as follows:

$$D_{\text{all}} = v,$$

$$H_{\text{all}} = W \backslash V,$$

$$e(H) = \text{a maximal set } D \subseteq D_{\text{all}} \text{ such that}$$
$$P(H = true \wedge H_{\text{all}} \backslash H = false|D) > 0,$$

$$pl(H) = P(H = true \wedge H_{\text{all}} \backslash H = false|e(H)).$$

The MPE corresponds to a complete composite hypothesis. If the MPE is also parsimonious, then it corresponds to the best explanation.[5] However, the MPE might assign *true* to more variables than necessary for explanatory purposes. In the context of other value assignments, $X = true$ might be more likely than $X = false$ even if $X = true$ is superfluous under the above mapping [21,22].

This lack of correspondence between the MPE and the best explanation can be rectified by creating, for each $X \in W \backslash V$, a dummy variable X' and

---

[4]For belief networks, we use a (boldface) lower case letter to stand for a (set of) value assignment(s) to a (set of) variable(s), which is denoted by a (boldface) upper case letter.

[5]One difficulty with the more "natural" mapping $pl(H) = P(H = true|v)$ is that even if the MPE is parsimonious, it might not be the best explanation.

a dummy value assignment that can be "caused" only if $X \neq X'$. With this modification, the MPE corresponds to the best explanation.

Another way of rectifying the situation is to simply ignore the parsimony constraint. With this in mind, we shall use the mapping given above.

3.2.3. Other theories of abduction

These reductions from problems in Reiter's and Pearl's theories to abduction problems provide strong evidence that our model of abduction is general enough to accommodate any theory of abduction, e.g., [6,15,21–23]. This is because our model leaves e and pl virtually unconstrained. We exploit this freedom below by defining and analyzing natural constraints on e and pl without considering the representations—logical, causal, or probabilistic—underlying the computation of e and pl. To make the analysis complete, we also show how some of these constraints can be reduced to problems in Reiter's and Pearl's theories.

3.3. Tractability assumptions

In our complexity analysis, we assume that e and pl are tractable. We also assume that e and pl can be represented reasonably, in particular, that the size of their internal representations is polynomial in $|D_{\text{all}}| + |H_{\text{all}}|$.

Clearly, the tractability of these functions is central to abduction, since it is difficult to find plausible hypotheses explaining the data if it is difficult to compute e and pl. This should not be taken to imply that the tractability of these functions can be taken for granted. For example, it can be intractable to determine explanatory coverage of a composite hypothesis [27] and to calculate the probability that an individual hypothesis is present, ignoring other hypotheses [4]. We make these assumptions to simplify our analysis of abduction problems. To reflect the complexity of these functions in our tractability results, we denote the time complexity of e and pl with respect to the size of an abduction problem as C_e and C_{pl}, respectively, e.g., nC_e indicates n calls to e.

For convenience, we assume the existence and the tractability of a function that determines which individual hypotheses can contribute to explaining a datum. Although it is not a true inverse, we refer to this function as e^{-1}, formally defined as:

$$e^{-1}(d) = \{h \mid \exists H \subset H_{\text{all}} \ (d \notin e(H) \land d \in e(H \cup \{h\}))\}.$$

Note that $h \in e^{-1}(d)$ does not imply $d \in e(h)$.

The key factors, then, that we consider in the complexity of finding a best explanation are properties of e and pl that allow or prevent tractable computation given that e, e^{-1}, and pl can be computed "easily". That is, given a particular class of abduction problems, how much of the space of composite hypotheses must be explicitly searched to find a best explanation? As demonstrated below, intractability is the usual result in classes of problems that involve significant interaction among the elements of composite hypotheses.

3.4. Simplifications

We should note that these definitions and assumptions simplify several aspects of abduction. For example, we define composite hypotheses as simple combinations of individual hypotheses. In reality, the relationships among the parts of an abductive answer and the data being explained can be much more complex, both logically and causally.

Another simplification is that *domains* are not defined. One way to do this would be to specify what data are possible (D_{poss}) and general functions for computing explanatory coverage and plausibilities based on the data (e_{gen} and pl_{gen}). Then for a specific abduction problem, the following constraints would hold: $D_{all} \subseteq D_{poss}$, $e(H) = e_{gen}(H, D_{all})$, and $pl(H) = pl_{gen}(H, D_{all})$ (cf. [1]).

The definitions of abduction problems or domains do not mention the data that do not have to explained, even though they could be important for determining e and pl. For example, the age of a patient does not have to be explained, but can influence the plausibility of a disease. We shall assume that e and pl implicitly take into account data that do not have to be explained, e.g., in the definition of domains above, these data can be an additional argument to e_{gen} and pl_{gen}.

Despite these simplifications, our analysis provides powerful insights concerning the computational complexity of abduction.

3.5. An example

We shall use the following example to facilitate our discussion:

$$H_{all} = \{h_1, h_2, h_3, h_4, h_5\},$$

$$D_{all} = \{d_1, d_2, d_3, d_4\},$$

$$e(h_1) = \{d_1\}, \qquad pl(h_1) = \text{superior},$$

$$e(h_2) = \{d_1, d_2\}, \qquad pl(h_2) = \text{excellent},$$

$$e(h_3) = \{d_2, d_3\}, \qquad pl(h_3) = \text{good},$$

$$e(h_4) = \{d_2, d_4\}, \qquad pl(h_4) = \text{fair},$$

$$e(h_5) = \{d_3, d_4\}, \qquad pl(h_5) = \text{poor}.$$

Figure 1 is a pictorial representation of the example. The values of pl should simply be interpreted as indicating relative order of plausibility. If

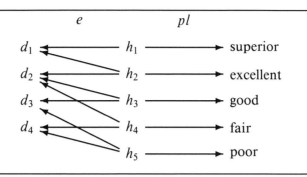

Fig. 1. Example of an abduction problem.

$e(H)$ is the union of $e(h)$ for $h \in H$, then $\{h_2, h_3, h_5\}$ is complete, but not parsimonious since h_3 is superfluous. $\{h_2, h_3\}$ is parsimonious, but not complete since it does not explain d_4. Based on the plausibility ordering criterion defined in Section 5, $\{h_1, h_3, h_4\}$ and $\{h_2, h_5\}$ would be considered the best explanations.

Using these definitions, assumptions, and example, we first discuss how properties of e affect the tractability of finding best explanations, and then consider properties of pl.

4. Complexity of finding explanations

4.1. Independent abduction problems

In the simplest problems, an individual hypothesis explains a specific set of data regardless of what other individual hypotheses are being considered. This constraint is assumed by INTERNIST-I [16], Reggia's set covering algorithm [26], Peng and Reggia's parsimonious covering theory [21,22], Pearl's belief revision theory if interactions are restricted to noisy-OR (an effect can occur only if one or more of its causes are present) [19], and Eshelman's cover-and-differentiate method [9]. The use of conflict sets [6,27] also appears to make this assumption—each conflict set corresponds to a datum to be explained, and the elements of the conflict set correspond to the hypotheses that can independently explain the datum.

Formally, an abduction problem is *independent* if:

$$\forall H \subseteq H_{\text{all}} \left(e(H) = \bigcup_{h \in H} e(h) \right).$$

That is, a composite hypothesis explains a datum if and only if one of its elements explains the datum. This constraint makes explanatory coverage equivalent to set covering [26]. Assuming independence, the explanations in our example (refer to Fig. 1) are: $\{h_1, h_3, h_4\}$, $\{h_1, h_3, h_5\}$, $\{h_1, h_4, h_5\}$, $\{h_2, h_3, h_4\}$, and $\{h_2, h_5\}$.

One way to find a best explanation would be to generate all explanations and then sort them by plausibility. However, it is well-known that there can be an exponential number of explanations. It is not surprising then that determining the number of explanations is hard.

Theorem 4.1.[6] *For the class of independent abduction problems, it is #P-complete to determine the number of explanations.*

That is, determining the number of explanations for an independent abduction problem is just as hard as determining the number of solutions to an NP-complete problem.[7]

The definition of best explanation, however, does not require that all explanations be explicitly enumerated. For example, if h is the most plausible individual hypothesis, h explains D_{all}, and $H \subset H'$ implies $pl(H) > pl(H')$, then h can be declared to be the best explanation without further search. In general, the task of finding a best explanation can be divided into two subtasks: (1) find one explanation, and (2) repeatedly find better explanations until a best one is found. In the remainder of this section then, we shall consider the complexity of generating one or more explanations. The following section discusses the complexity of finding better explanations.

For independent abduction problems, it is tractable to find an explanation. Let $n = |D_{all}| + |H_{all}|$.

Theorem 4.2. *For the class of independent abduction problems, there is an* $O(nC_e + n^2)$ *algorithm for finding an explanation, if one exists.*

Algorithm 1 performs this task within this order of complexity. Appendix A gives a detailed explanation of this algorithm, but we note several aspects of its operation here.

Algorithm 1. Finding an explanation in independent and monotonic abduction problems.

> *W stands for the working composite hypothesis.*
> *Nil is returned if no explanation exists.*

---

[6]Detailed proofs of Theorem 4.1 and other theorems are given in Appendix A.

[7]Also, it is #P-complete to determine the number of complete composite hypotheses. The definition of #P-complete comes from Valiant [33].

Determine whether an explanation exists.
If $e(H_{\text{all}}) \neq D_{\text{all}}$ then
    Return nil

Find an explanation.
$W \leftarrow H_{\text{all}}$
For each $h \in H_{\text{all}}$
    If $e(W \backslash \{h\}) = D_{\text{all}}$ then
        $W \leftarrow W \backslash \{h\}$
Return W

It is easy to check whether an explanation exists. If $\bigcup_{h \in H_{\text{all}}} e(h) \neq D_{\text{all}}$, then a union over any subset of H_{all} will not equal D_{all} either.

The loop makes one pass through the individual hypotheses. It examines each individual hypothesis in turn and removes it if no explanatory coverage is lost. Only one pass is necessary because if the result W had a superfluous element h, then h would have been superfluous for any superset of W, and thus, would have been removed by the body of the loop.

If the e^{-1} function is available (see Section 3.3 for the definition of e^{-1}), then the working hypothesis W, instead of being initialized to H_{all}, can be initialized to include only one element from $e^{-1}(d)$ for each $d \in D_{\text{all}}$. This modification has an advantage if e^{-1} is easy to compute and the working hypothesis remains "small".

4.2. Monotonic abduction problems

We now consider a more general kind of problem, in which a composite hypothesis can explain additional data that are not explained by any of its elements. For example, suppose the two inputs to an AND-gate are supposed to be 0, and so the output is supposed to be 0, but the observed output of the AND-gate is 1. If the inputs are produced by components A and B, then hypothesizing a single fault in A or B is insufficient to account for the datum, but faults in both A and B are sufficient.

This sort of interaction can also occur if two individual hypotheses have an additive interaction. For example, each of the two hypotheses can explain a small value of some measurement, but together can explain a larger measurement. In this latter case, if h only partially explains d, then $d \notin e(h)$. Note though that if adding h to a composite hypothesis can result in completely explaining d, then $h \in e^{-1}(d)$.

Formally, an abduction problem is *monotonic* [1] if:

$$\forall H, H' \subseteq H_{\text{all}} \ (H \subseteq H' \rightarrow e(H) \subseteq e(H')).$$

That is, a composite hypothesis does not "lose" any data explained by any of its subsets and might explain additional data. All independent abduction problems are monotonic, but a monotonic abduction problem is not necessarily independent. If, in Fig. 1, $\{h_2, h_3\}$ also explained d_4, then $\{h_2, h_3\}$ would also be an explanation and $\{h_2, h_3, h_4\}$ would not be. Monotonic abduction problems from the literature include Josephson's hypothesis assembly technique [1] and Pearl's belief revision theory if interactions are restricted to noisy-OR and noisy-AND [19].

Because the class of monotonic abduction problems includes the independent class, it is also hard to determine the number of explanations. In addition, we have shown that it is hard to enumerate a polynomial number of explanations.

Theorem 4.3. *For the class of monotonic abduction problems, given a set of explanations, it is NP-complete to determine whether an additional explanation exists.*

We have proven this result by a reduction from the class of independent incompatibility abduction problems, which is described below. The idea of the reduction is that the addition of an individual hypothesis to a composite hypothesis can explain the rest of the data, make nearly all the elements of the composite hypothesis superfluous, and result in a previously generated explanation. It turns out to be difficult to generate an additional explanation while avoiding this kind of interaction. Whether a similar result holds for independent abduction problems is an open question.

Although the class of monotonic problems is a superset of the class of independent problems, it is just as efficient to find an explanation. Again, let $n = |D_{\text{all}}| + |H_{\text{all}}|$.

Theorem 4.4. *For the class of monotonic abduction problems, there is an* $O(nC_e + n^2)$ *algorithm for finding an explanation, if one exists.*

Algorithm 1 performs this task within this order of complexity. Because of the monotonicity constraint, H_{all} must explain as much or more data than any other composite hypothesis. The loop in Algorithm 1 works for the same reasons as for independent abduction problems. Also, it is possible to use e^{-1} to initialize W, though one must be careful because more than one element from $e^{-1}(d)$ might be needed to explain d.

4.3. Incompatibility abduction problems

Implicit in the formal model so far is the assumption that any collection of individual hypotheses is possible. However, most domains have restrictions that invalidate this assumption. For example, a faulty digital switch cannot simultaneously be stuck-at-1 and stuck-at-0. More generally, the negation of a hypothesis can also be considered a hypothesis.

This kind of problem is neither independent nor monotonic because any composite hypothesis that contains a pair of mutually exclusive hypotheses cannot be an acceptable hypothesis, while a subset that excludes at least one hypothesis from each pair is acceptable. We call this kind of problem an *incompatibility abduction problem*.

Formally, an incompatibility abduction problem is a tuple $\langle D_{\text{all}}, H_{\text{all}}, e, pl, \mathcal{I} \rangle$, where D_{all}, H_{all}, e, and pl are the same as before and $\mathcal{I}$ is a set of two-element subsets of H_{all}, indicating pairs of hypotheses that are incompatible with each other.[8] For an incompatibility problem:

$$\forall H \subseteq H_{\text{all}} \; ((\exists I \in \mathcal{I} \; (I \subseteq H)) \rightarrow e(H) = \emptyset).$$

By this formal trick, a composite hypothesis containing incompatible hypotheses explains nothing, preventing such a composite from being complete (except for trivial cases) or a best explanation.

An *independent incompatibility abduction problem* satisfies the formula:

$$\forall H \subseteq H_{\text{all}} \; \left((\not\exists I \in \mathcal{I} \; (I \subseteq H)) \rightarrow e(H) = \bigcup_{h \in H} e(h) \right).$$

That is, except for incompatibilities, the problem is independent. In Fig. 1, if $\mathcal{I} = \{\{h_1, h_2\}, \{h_2, h_3\}, \{h_3, h_4\}, \{h_4, h_5\}\}$, then only $\{h_1, h_3, h_5\}$ and $\{h_2, h_5\}$ would be explanations.

Incompatibility abduction problems are more complex than monotonic or independent abduction problems:

Theorem 4.5. *For the class of independent incompatibility abduction problems, it is NP-complete to determine whether an explanation exists.*

We have proven this result by reduction from 3SAT [10], which is satisfiability of boolean expressions in conjunctive normal form, with no more than three literals in any conjunct. Informally, the reduction works as follows. Each 3SAT literal and its negation corresponds to an incompatible pair of hypotheses. Each conjunct of the boolean expression corresponds to a datum to be explained. Satisfying a conjunct corresponds to a hypothesis explaining a datum. Clearly then, a complete composite hypothesis exists iff the boolean expression is satisfiable. Furthermore, a complete composite hypothesis exists iff an explanation exists. Our proof shows that only $O(|H_{\text{all}}|)$ incompatible pairs are needed to give rise to intractability.

---

[8]Incompatible pairs are the most natural case, e.g., one hypothesis of the pair is the negation of the other. n mutually exclusive hypotheses can be represented as $n(n-1)/2$ incompatible pairs. Incompatible triplets (any two of the three, but not all three) and so on are conceivable, but allowing these possibilities in the formal definition do not affect the complexity results.

The underlying difficulty is that the choice between a pair of incompatible hypotheses cannot be made locally, but is dependent on the choices from all other incompatible pairs. It is interesting to note the parsimony constraint plays no role in this result. Just finding a complete composite hypothesis is hard in incompatibility abduction problems.

It follows that:

Corollary 4.6. *For the class of independent incompatibility abduction problems, it is NP-hard to find a best explanation.*

The class of incompatibility abduction problems can be reduced to both Reiter's theory of diagnosis [27] and Pearl's theory of belief revision [19].

Theorem 4.7. *For the class of diagnosis problems, relative to the complexity of determining whether a composite hypothesis is consistent with* SD $\cup$ OBS, *it is NP-complete to determine whether a diagnosis exists.*

For this theorem, a composite hypothesis is a conjecture that certain components are abnormal, and that all other components are normal.

It is easy to translate the explanatory interactions of an independent incompatibility abduction problem into first-order sentences. For example, $e^{-1}(d) = H$ can be translated to MANIFEST$(d) \rightarrow \bigvee_{h \in H}$ AB(h). $\{h, h'\} \in \mathcal{I}$ can be translated to AB$(h) \rightarrow \neg$AB(h'). It is interesting that this problem is hard even if it is easy to determine the consistency of a composite hypothesis.

Theorem 4.8. *For the class of belief revision problems, it is NP-complete to determine whether there is a value assignment $\boldsymbol{w}$ to the variables $\boldsymbol{W}$ such that $P(\boldsymbol{w}|\boldsymbol{v}) > 0$.*

This theorem directly follows from Cooper's result that it is NP-complete to determine whether $P(X = true) > 0$ for a given variable X within a belief network [4]. Also, a reduction from incompatibility abduction problems can be done as follows. Map each $h \in H_{\text{all}}$ to a "hypothesis" variable. Map each $d \in D_{\text{all}}$ to a "data" variable that can be true only if one or more of the hypothesis variables corresponding to $e^{-1}(d)$ are true (e.g., noisy-OR interaction). Map each incompatible pair into a data variable that can be true only if at most one, but not both, of the two corresponding hypothesis variables is true (e.g., NAND). Initializing all the data variables to *true* sets up the problem.

4.4. Cancellation abduction problems

Another interaction not allowed in independent or monotonic abduction problems is cancellation, i.e., when one element of a composite hypothesis "cancels" a datum that another element would otherwise explain. Cancellation can occur when one hypothesis can have a subtractive effect on another. This is common in medicine, e.g., in the domain of acid–base disorders, one disease might explain an increased blood pH, and another might explain a decreased pH, but together the result might be a normal pH [17]. Different faults in different components can result in cancellation, e.g., a stuck-at-1 input into an AND-gate might account for an output of 1, but not if the other input is stuck-at-0. Cancellation commonly occurs in the physical world. Newton's second law implies that forces can cancel each other. Cancellation in the form of feedback control is intentionally designed into devices.

Formally, we define a *cancellation abduction problem* as a tuple $\langle D_{all}, H_{all}, e, pl, e_+, e_- \rangle$. e_+ is a map from H_{all} to subsets of D_{all} indicating what data each hypothesis "produces". e_- is another map from H_{all} to subsets of D_{all} indicating what data each hypothesis "consumes". $d \in e(H)$ iff the number of hypotheses in H that produce d outnumber the hypotheses that consume d. That is:

$$d \in e(H) \leftrightarrow$$
$$|\{h \mid h \in H \land d \in e_+(h)\}| > |\{h \mid h \in H \land d \in e_-(h)\}|.$$

In Fig. 1, if we let $e_+ = e$ for individual hypotheses and if $e_-(h_1) = \{d_3\}$, $e_-(h_2) = \{d_4\}$, and $e_-(h_3) = e_-(h_4) = e_-(h_5) = \emptyset$, then the only explanations would be $\{h_1, h_3, h_5\}$ and $\{h_2, h_4, h_5\}$.

Admittedly, this is a simplified model of cancellation effects, in the sense that it captures only one kind of cancellation interaction. Nevertheless, it is sufficient to derive intractability:

Theorem 4.9. *For the class of cancellation abduction problems, it is NP-complete to determine whether an explanation exists.*

We have proven this by reduction from finding explanations in incompatibility abduction problems. Informally, the idea of the reduction is based on the following. Suppose that a datum has two potential "producers" and two potential "consumers". Now any composite hypothesis that contains both consumers cannot explain the datum. In effect, the two consumers are incompatible. Our reduction ensures that each incompatible pair in the incompatibility abduction problem is appropriately mapped to such a situation in the corresponding cancellation abduction problem. Only $O(|H_{all}|)$ "cancellations" are needed for this result, where $\sum_{h \in H_{all}} |e_-(h)|$ gives the number of cancellations.

It follows that:

Corollary 4.10. *For the class of cancellation abduction problems, it is NP-hard to find a best explanation.*

One aspect of cancellation abduction problems is more complex than incompatibility abduction problems. In an independent incompatibility abduction problem, if a complete composite hypothesis is found, then it is easy to find a parsimonious subset. However, this is not true for cancellation abduction problems.

Theorem 4.11. *For the class of cancellation abduction problems, it is coNP-complete to determine whether a complete composite hypothesis is parsimonious.*

That is, it is NP-complete to determine whether a complete composite hypothesis is not parsimonious. The idea of our reduction is the following. If a datum has three "producers" and two "consumers", we can ensure that the datum is explained by including all three producers in the composite hypothesis. However, there might be a more parsimonious composite hypothesis in which some of the producers are omitted, but finding such a composite hypothesis means that one or both consumers must be omitted as well, making them effectively incompatible.

Table 1 summarizes the results of this section. The "?" indicates that we not have yet described the complexity of finding a best explanation in independent and monotonic abduction problems.

Table 1
Computational complexity of finding explanations (P = known polynomial algorithm, NP = NP-hard).

Class of problems	Condition to achieve		
	Finding all explanations	Finding an explanation	Finding a best explanation
Independent	NP	P	?
Monotonic	NP	P	?
Incompatibility	NP	NP	NP
Cancellation	NP	NP	NP

5. Complexity of plausibility

To analyze the complexity of finding a best explanation, we need to define how to compare the plausibilities of explanations. We consider one plausibility criterion based on comparing the plausibilities of the elements of the explanations. Other plausibility criteria are considered in Bylander et al. [2], but they are less relevant to other theories of abduction.

5.1. The best-small plausibility criterion

Everything else being equal, smaller explanations are preferable to larger ones, and more plausible individual hypotheses are preferable to less plausible ones. Thus, in the absence of other information, it is reasonable to compare the plausibility of explanations based on their sizes and the relative plausibilities of their elements. When a conflict occurs, e.g., one explanation is smaller, but has less plausible elements, no ordering can be imposed without additional information.

The *best-small* plausibility criterion formally characterizes these considerations as follows:

$$pl(H) > pl(H') \quad \leftrightarrow$$
$$\exists m : H \to H' \ (m \text{ is } 1\text{-}1 \ \wedge$$
$$\forall h \in H \ (pl(h) \geq pl(m(h))) \ \wedge$$
$$(|H| = |H'| \to \exists h \in H \ (pl(h) > pl(m(h)))))).$$

That is, to be more plausible according to best-small, the elements of H need to be matched to the elements of H' so that the elements of H are at least as plausible as their matches in H'. If H and H' are the same size, then in addition some element in H must be more plausible than its match in H'. Note that if H is larger than H', then $pl(H) \not> pl(H')$. In Fig. 1, $\{h_1, h_3, h_4\}$ and $\{h_2, h_5\}$ would be the best explanations.

We have demonstrated that it is intractable to find best explanations using best-small.

Theorem 5.1. *For the class of independent abduction problems using the best-small plausibility criterion, it is NP-hard to find a best explanation.*

The simplest proof of this theorem involves a reduction from minimum cover [10]. If each individual hypothesis is given the same plausibility, then the smallest explanations (the covers with the smallest sizes) are the best explanations. A more general proof is a reduction from a special class of independent incompatibility abduction problems in which each individual hypothesis is in exactly one incompatible pair. In this reduction, each incompatible pair is mapped into two equally plausible hypotheses, at least one of which must be chosen. If the incompatibility abduction problem has any explanations, they turn out to be best explanations in the best-small problem.

We conjecture that it is possible to reduce from finding a best explanation using best-small to finding a best explanation using any "theory of belief" in which composite hypotheses that are smaller or have more plausible elements can have higher belief values. Of course, standard probability theory is an example of such a theory, as are all its main competitors. This conjecture is supported by the following theorem.

Theorem 5.2. *For the class of belief revision problems restricted to OR interactions, it is NP-hard to find the MPE.*

The restriction to OR interactions means that each effect can be true only if one or more of its parents are true. This restriction makes it easy to find a value assignment w such that $P(w|v) > 0$. Although this theorem could be demonstrated by adapting the proof for Theorem 5.1, it is useful to show that the best-small plausibility criterion has a correlate in probabilistic reasoning.

The reduction from independent abduction problems using best-small works as follows. Each $h \in H_{all}$ is mapped to a "hypothesis" variable. Each $d \in D_{all}$ is mapped to a "data" variable that is true if and only if one or more of the hypothesis variables corresponding to $e^{-1}(d)$ are true, i.e., an OR interaction. The *a priori* probabilities of the hypothesis variables being true must be between 0 and 0.5, and are ordered according to the plausibilities in the abduction problem. Initializing all the data variables to *true* sets up the problem. The MPE for this belief revision problem corresponds to a best explanation for the best-small problem. Because finding a best explanation is NP-hard, finding the MPE must be NP-hard even for belief networks that only contain OR interactions.

5.2. Ordered abduction problems

Our proofs of Theorem 5.1 depend on the fact that some individual hypotheses have similar plausibilities to other hypotheses. It turns out that finding a best explanation using best-small is tractable if the plausibilities of individual hypotheses are all different from each other and if their plausibilities are totally ordered.

Formally, an abduction problem is *ordered* if:

$$\forall h, h' \in H_{all} \ (h \neq h' \to (pl(h) < pl(h') \lor pl(h) > pl(h'))).$$

Again, let $n = |D_{all}| + |H_{all}|$.

Theorem 5.3. *For the class of ordered monotonic abduction problems using the best-small plausibility criterion, there is an* $O(nC_e + nC_{pl} + n^2)$ *algorithm for finding a best explanation.*

Algorithm 2 below performs this task within this order of complexity. It is the same as Algorithm 1 except that the loop considers the individual hypotheses from least to most plausible. The explanation that Algorithm 2 finds is a best explanation because no other explanation can have more plausible individual hypotheses; the algorithm always chooses the least plausible individual hypotheses to remove. Of course, Algorithm 2 also finds a best explanation for ordered independent abduction problems.

As with Algorithm 1, it is possible to use e^{-1} advantageously. The working hypothesis W can be initialized to include the most plausible individual hypotheses from each $e^{-1}(d)$, i.e., because of monotonic interactions, sufficient hypotheses from $e^{-1}(d)$ must be chosen so that d is explained.

Algorithm 2 is an adaptation of the hypothesis assembly algorithm described in Josephson et al. [13], and is a serial version of the parallel parsimony algorithm described in Goel [11]. In Fig. 1 assuming the independence constraint, this algorithm would find $\{h_1, h_3, h_4\}$, which is one of the two best explanations.

As in our example, there might be more than one best explanation because best-small in general imposes a partial ordering on the plausibilities of composite hypotheses. Suppose that an ordered monotonic abduction problem had only one best explanation according to best-small. Because Algorithm 2 is guaranteed to find a best explanation, then it will find the one best explanation.

Algorithm 2. Finding a best explanation in ordered independent and monotonic abduction problems using the best-small plausibility criterion.

> *W stands for the working composite hypothesis.*
> *Nil is returned if no explanation exists.*
>
> *Determine whether an explanation exists.*
> If $e(H_{\text{all}}) \neq D_{\text{all}}$ then
>   Return nil
>
> *Find a best explanation.*
> $W \leftarrow H_{\text{all}}$
> For each $h \in H_{\text{all}}$ from least to most plausible
>   If $e(W \setminus \{h\}) = D_{\text{all}}$ then
> $W \leftarrow W \setminus \{h\}$
> Return W

Corollary 5.4. *For the class of ordered monotonic abduction problems using the best-small plausibility criterion, if there is exactly one best explanation, then there is an* $O(nC_e + nC_{pl} + n^2)$ *algorithm for finding the best explanation.*

This can be informally restated as: *In a well-behaved abduction problem, if it is known that some explanation is clearly the best explanation, then it is tractable to find it.* Unfortunately, it is difficult to determine if some explanation is clearly the best explanation.

Theorem 5.5. *For the class of ordered independent abduction problems using the best-small plausibility criterion, given a best explanation, it is NP-complete to determine whether there is another best explanation.*

We have proved this by a reduction from the special class of independent incompatibility abduction problems in which each individual hypothesis is in exactly one incompatible pair. Assuming n incompatible pairs, the best-small problem is set up so that one hypothesis out of each pair must be chosen, and so that extra hypotheses plus the most plausible element of each pair is a best explanation of size $n + 2$. In our reduction, any other best-small best explanation in this reduction must be of size $n + 1$ and include an explanation for the incompatibility problem. Thus, even for ordered independent abduction problems, it is intractable to find all the best explanations, or even enumerate some number of them.

As a consequence, it does not become tractable to find the MPE for ordered abduction problems. The proof for the previous theorem can be easily adapted so that any explanation of size $n + 1$ will be more probable than any explanation of size $n + 2$.

From these theorems, we can describe what kinds of mistakes will be made by Algorithm 2. While the explanation this algorithm finds will match up qualitatively to any other explanation, there might be other "qualitatively best" explanations, which might be judged better based on more precise plausibility information.

Table 2 summarizes the results of this and the previous section.

Table 2
Computational complexity of finding best explanations using the best-small plausibility criterion (P = known polynomial algorithm, NP = NP-hard)

Class of problems	Condition to achieve	
	Finding a best explanation	Finding more than one best explanation
Ordered independent/monotonic	P	NP
Unordered independent/monotonic	NP	NP
Incompatibility	NP	NP
Cancellation	NP	NP

6. A real-world application of abduction—red blood antibody identification

6.1. Description of the domain

The RED expert system performs in the domain of blood bank antibody analysis [29]. One of the jobs done by a blood-bank technologist is to identify antibodies in a patient's serum that can react to antigens that might appear on red blood cells. This is typically done by combining, under different test conditions, samples of patient serum with samples of red blood cells known to express certain antigens. Some of these combinations might show reactions. The presence of certain antibodies in the patient serum accounts for certain reactions. The reactions are additive in the sense that if the presence of one antibody explains one reaction, and presence of another antibody explains another, then the presence of both antibodies explains both reactions. If each antibody can account for a weak result in some reaction, then the presence of both can account for a stronger result in that reaction. Also, some pairs of antibodies cannot occur together. RED's task is to decide which antibodies are present, given a certain reaction pattern. RED takes into account about 30 of the most common antibodies.

6.2. Relationship to classes of abduction problems

We now examine how this task can be categorized within the classes of abduction problems discussed in this paper.

- *Independent.* The additive nature of the reactions means that for separate reactions and compatible hypotheses, the independence constraint is met. However, since independent abduction problems do not allow for parts of data to be explained, they cannot describe additivity of reaction strengths.
- *Monotonic.* If we view a weak result for some reaction as a separate result from a strong result for the same reaction, then we can say that the phenomenon of additive reaction strengths falls into the class of monotonic abduction problems. That is, each of two antibodies alone might explain a weak reaction. Together, they would explain either a weak reaction or a strong reaction.
- *Incompatibility.* In this domain, some antibodies are incompatible with others. Also, for each antibody, RED distinguishes between two different, incompatible ways that it can react. Thus, red blood antibody identification is clearly outside of monotonic abduction problems and within the intractable class of incompatibility abduction problems. Below, we discuss why this is not usually a difficulty in this domain.
- *Cancellation.* No cancellation interactions take place in this domain.

- *Ordered.* RED rates the plausibility of the presence of an antibody on a 7-point qualitative scale. Because there are about 60 antibody subtypes, the same plausibility rating is given to several antibodies. Strictly speaking, this takes the problem out of ordered abduction problems, but we describe below why this is not usually a problem.

Incompatibility relationships and lack of plausibility ordering do not usually create difficulties in this domain for the following reasons. One is that most antibodies are usually ruled out before any composite hypotheses are considered, i.e., the evidence indicates that the antibodies cannot reasonably be part of any composite hypotheses. The more antibodies that are ruled out, the more likely that the remaining antibodies contain no or few incompatibilities, and resemble an ordered abduction problem.

Another reason is that the reaction testing is designed to discriminate between the antibodies. Thus, an antibody that is present usually explains some reaction more plausibly than any other antibody. An antibody that is not present is unlikely to have clear evidence in its favor and is usually superfluous in the context of equally or higher rated antibodies.

A final reason is that it is rare to have more than a few antibodies. Other antibodies that are rated lower than these antibodies are easily eliminated.

In rare cases, though, these reasons do not apply with the result that RED has difficulties with incompatible pairs or unordered hypotheses, or that RED selects an explanation with many antibodies whereas the preferred answer contains a smaller number of individually less plausible antibodies [28].

7. Discussion

We have discovered one restricted class of abduction problems in which it is tractable to find the best explanation. In this class, there can be no incompatibility relationships or cancellation interactions, the plausibilities of the individual hypotheses are all different from each other, and there must be exactly one best explanation according to the best-small plausibility criterion. Unfortunately, it is intractable to determine whether there is more than one best explanation in ordered abduction problems. However, it is still tractable to find one of the best-small best explanations in ordered monotonic abduction problems.

For abduction in general, however, our results are not encouraging. We believe that few domains satisfy the independent or monotonic property, i.e., they usually have incompatibility relationships and cancellation interactions. Requiring the most plausible explanation appears to guarantee intractability for abduction. It is important to note that these difficulties result from the nature of abduction problems, and not the representations or algorithms being used to solve the problem. *These problems are hard no matter what representation or algorithm is used.*

Fortunately, there are several mitigating factors that might hold for specific domains. One factor is that incompatibility relationships and cancellation interactions might be sufficiently sparse so that it is not expensive to search for explanations. However, only $O(n)$ incompatibilities or cancellations are sufficient to lead to intractability, and the maximum plausibility requirement still remains a difficulty.

Another factor, as discussed in Section 1, is that some constraint might guarantee a polynomial search space, e.g., a limit on the size of hypotheses or sufficient knowledge to rule out most individual hypotheses. For example, if rule-out knowledge can reduce the number of individual hypotheses from h to $\log h$, then the problem is tractable. It is important to note that such factors do not simply call for "more knowledge", but knowledge of the right type, e.g., *rule-out* knowledge. Additional knowledge *per se* does not reduce complexity. For example, more knowledge about incompatibilities or cancellations makes abduction harder.

The abductive reasoning of the RED expert system works because of these factors. The size of the right answer is usually small, and rule-out knowledge is able to eliminate many hypotheses. RED is able to avoid exhaustive search because the non-ruled-out hypotheses are close to an ordered monotonic abduction problem.

If there are no tractable algorithms for a class of abduction problems, then there is no choice but do abduction heuristically (unless one is willing to wait for a very long time). This poses a challenge to researchers who attempt to deal with abductive inference—provide a characterization that respects the classic criteria of good explanations (parsimony, coverage, consistency, and plausibility), but avoids the computational pitfalls that beset solutions attempting to optimize these criteria. We believe this will lead to the adoption of a more naturalistic or satisficing conceptualization of abduction [14,30], in which the final explanation is not guaranteed to be optimal, e.g., it might not explain some data. Perhaps one mark of intelligence is being able to act despite the lack of optimal solutions.

Our results show that abduction, characterized as finding the most plausible composite hypothesis that explains all the data, is generally an intractable problem. Thus, it is futile to hope for a tractable algorithm that produces optimal answers for all kinds of abduction problems. To be solved efficiently, an abduction problem must have certain features that make it tractable, and a reasoning method that takes advantage of those features. Understanding abduction, as for any portion of intelligence, requires a theory of reasoning that takes care for the practicality of computations.

Appendix A. Proofs of theorems

In this appendix, we provide a proof for each theorem in the paper. We assume that the functions e and pl are tractable with time complexities $O(C_e)$, and $O(C_{pl})$ in the size of an abduction problem, respectively (see Section 3). The reader is forewarned that many of the reduction proofs do not provide direct insight on the intuitive reasons underlying the complexity results. The proof of Theorem 4.3 is given after Theorem 4.5.

Theorem 4.1. *For the class of independent abduction problems, it is #P-complete to determine the number of explanations.*

Proof. This is in #P because each composite hypothesis $H \subseteq H_{\text{all}}$ can be generated in nondeterministic polynomial time, and it is easy to check if H is complete and parsimonious.

It is possible to reduce from determining the number of minimal vertex covers [33] to determining the number of explanations. Given a graph G with vertices V and edges E, a minimal vertex cover is a minimal subset of vertices $V' \subseteq V$ such that every edge is connected to a vertex in V'. An independent abduction problem can be constructed from G as follows:

$$D_{\text{all}} = E,$$

$$H_{\text{all}} = V,$$

$$e(H) = \{(u, v) \in E \mid u \in H \lor v \in H\},$$

$$pl(H) = \text{anything}.$$

In this construction, H is an explanation iff it corresponds to a minimal vertex cover.   □

Theorem 4.2. *For the class of independent abduction problems, there is an $O(nC_e + n^2)$ algorithm for finding an explanation, if one exists.*

Theorem 4.4. *For the class of monotonic abduction problems, there is an $O(nC_e + n^2)$ algorithm for finding an explanation, if one exists.*

Proof. For these theorems, $n = |D_{\text{all}}| + |H_{\text{all}}|$. Because the monotonic constraint is more general than the independent constraint, our discussion is oriented for Theorem 4.4. First we consider the correctness of Algorithm 1, and then consider its complexity.

The first conditional determines whether an explanation exists. Because of the monotonic constraint, H_{all} must explain as much or more than any other composite hypothesis. Hence, if H_{all} is not a complete composite hypothesis, then no composite hypothesis is complete. If H_{all} passes this test, then initializing W to H_{all} ensures that W starts off as a complete composite hypothesis.

Within the loop, W remains a complete composite hypothesis because no element is removed if it leads to explaining less than D_{all}. The fact that the result W is also parsimonious can be shown by contradiction. Suppose that $H \subset W$ and $e(H) = D_{\text{all}}$. Then, because the problem is monotonic,

$$H \subseteq H' \rightarrow e(H) = e(H') = e(W).$$

In particular, for each $h \in W \backslash H$, $e(H) = e(W \backslash \{h\}) = e(W)$. However, the loop would have removed h from W (or any superset of W) in just this case, implying that $h \notin W$, which is a contradiction. Thus, the loop produces a complete and parsimonious composite hypothesis, i.e., an explanation.

Now consider the complexity of Algorithm 1. We assume sets are represented as bit vectors. Let $k = |D_{\text{all}}|$ and $l = |H_{\text{all}}|$.

The conditional makes one call to e ($\mathrm{O}(\mathcal{C}_e)$) and checks whether its answer is equal to D_{all} ($\mathrm{O}(k)$ steps). Assigning H_{all} to W takes $\mathrm{O}(l)$ steps.

Since $|H_{\text{all}}| = l$, the loop iterates l times. The loop performs l evaluations of e ($\mathrm{O}(\mathcal{C}_e)$ each), l set comparisons ($\mathrm{O}(k)$ each), and up to l set differences of single elements ($\mathrm{O}(1)$ each). Thus the complexity of algorithm is $\mathrm{O}(l\mathcal{C}_e + kl + k + 2l)$. Since both k and l are less than n, $\mathrm{O}(n\mathcal{C}_e + n^2)$ clearly bounds the complexity of Algorithm 1.   □

Theorem 4.5. *For the class of independent incompatibility abduction problems, it is NP-complete to determine whether there is an explanation.*

Proof. We prove the NP-completeness of this problem by reducing from 3SAT [10]: given a statement in propositional calculus in conjunctive normal form, in which each term has at most three factors, find an assignment of variables that makes the statement true.

Let S be a statement in propositional calculus in 3SAT form. Let $U = \{u_1, u_2, \ldots, u_m\}$ be the variables used in S. Let n be the number of terms in S. An equivalent independent incompatibility abduction problem $\mathcal{P} = \langle D_{\text{all}}, H_{\text{all}}, e, pl, \mathcal{I} \rangle$ can be constructed by:

$$D_{\text{all}} = \{d_1, d_2, \ldots, d_n\},$$

$$H_{\text{all}} = \{h_1, h_1', h_2, h_2', \ldots, h_m, h_m'\},$$

$$e(h_i) = \{d_j \mid u_i \text{ is a factor in the } j\text{th term}\},$$

$$e(h_i') = \{d_j \mid \neg u_i \text{ is a factor in the } j\text{th term}\},$$

$$pl(H) = \text{anything},$$

$$\mathcal{I} = \{\{h_1, h_1'\}, \{h_2, h_2'\}, \ldots, \{h_m, h_m'\}\}.$$

If H is a complete composite hypothesis for $\mathcal{P}$, then S is satisfied by the following assignment.

$$u_i = \begin{cases} \text{true,} & \text{if } h_i \in H, \\ \text{false,} & \text{otherwise.} \end{cases}$$

Consider the jth term in S. Since $d_j \in e(H)$, there is some i such that either h_i or h_i' is in H and explains d_j. If $h_i \in H$ and $d_j \in e(h_i)$, then u_i is a factor in the jth term of S and by the assignment above, the term is satisfied. If $h_i' \in H$ and $d_j \in e(h_i')$, then $h_i \notin H$ and $\neg u_i$ is a factor in the jth term of S, so by the assignment above, the term is satisfied. Since j was arbitrary, it must be the case that all terms in S will be satisfied by the above assignment.

If S is satisfied by a value assignment $U' \subseteq U$ indicating:

$$u_i = \begin{cases} \text{true,} & \text{if } u \in U', \\ \text{false,} & \text{otherwise,} \end{cases}$$

then $H = \{h_i \mid u_i \in U'\} \cup \{h_i' \mid u_i \notin U'\}$ will be a complete composite hypothesis for $\mathcal{P}$.

An explanation for $\mathcal{P}$ exists if and only if a complete composite hypothesis for $\mathcal{P}$ exists. Thus, 3SAT problems reduce to independent incompatibility abduction problems. Incompatibility abduction problems are clearly in NP since it is easy to guess a composite hypothesis H and to test whether $e(H) = D_{\text{all}}$. Thus, it is NP-complete to determine whether an independent incompatibility abduction problem has an explanation.

Below, we reduce this class of problems to a number of other classes. For convenience, we shall assume that these abduction problems have the same form as the $\mathcal{P}$ constructed above: the problem is independent except for incompatibilities, each $h \in H_{\text{all}}$ is an element of exactly one $I \in \mathcal{I}$, and $|e^{-1}(d)| \leq 3$ for each $d \in D_{\text{all}}$. We refer to this special class of independent incompatibility abduction problems as *3SAT abduction problems*. □

Theorem 4.3. *For the class of monotonic abduction problems, given a set of explanations, it is NP-complete to determine whether an additional explanation exists.*

Proof. This can be reduced from 3SAT abduction problems. Let $\mathcal{P} = \langle D_{\text{all}}, H_{\text{all}}, e, pl, \mathcal{I} \rangle$ be a 3SAT abduction problem, and let $\mathcal{P}' = \langle D'_{\text{all}}, H'_{\text{all}}, e', pl' \rangle$ be a monotonic abduction problem constructed from P as follows.

$$D'_{\text{all}} = D_{\text{all}},$$

$$H'_{\text{all}} = H_{\text{all}},$$

$$e'(H) = \begin{cases} D_{\text{all}}, & \text{if } \exists I \in \mathcal{I} \ (I \subseteq H), \\ e(H), & \text{otherwise}, \end{cases}$$

$$pl'(H) = pl(H).$$

It turns out that $\mathcal{I}$ is a set of explanations for $\mathcal{P}'$. Consequently, any other explanation can only have at most one hypothesis from each pair $I \in \mathcal{I}$. Thus, it would also be a explanation for $\mathcal{P}$. □

Theorem 4.7. *For the class of diagnosis problems, relative to the complexity of determining whether a composite hypothesis is consistent with* SD $\cup$ OBS, *it is NP-complete to determine whether a diagnosis exists.*

Proof. To determine whether a solution exists for a diagnosis problem, it is sufficient to exhibit a subset of components $\Delta \subseteq$ COMPONENTS such that

$$\text{SD} \cup \text{OBS} \cup \{\text{AB}(c) \mid c \in \Delta\} \cup \{\neg\text{AB}(c) \mid c \in \text{COMPONENTS}\backslash\Delta\}$$

is consistent. Hence, diagnosis problems are in NP relative to the complexity of determining whether a composite hypothesis is consistent with SD $\cup$ OBS.

Determining whether a diagnosis exists can be reduced from finding explanations for 3SAT abduction problems. Let $\mathcal{P} = \langle D_{\text{all}}, H_{\text{all}}, e, pl, \mathcal{I}\rangle$ be a 3SAT abduction problem, and let $\mathcal{P}' = \langle\text{SD}, \text{OBS}, \text{COMPONENTS}\rangle$ be a diagnosis problem constructed from $\mathcal{P}$ as follows.

$$\begin{aligned} \text{SD} = \ &\{\text{MANIFEST}(d) \rightarrow \bigvee_{h \in e^{-1}(d)} \text{AB}(h) \mid d \in D_{\text{all}}\} \ \cup \\ &\{\text{AB}(h) \rightarrow \neg\text{AB}(h') \mid \{h, h'\} \in \mathcal{I}\}, \end{aligned}$$

$$\text{OBS} = \{\text{MANIFEST}(d) \mid d \in D_{\text{all}}\},$$

$$\text{COMPONENTS} = H_{\text{all}}.$$

An explanation for $\mathcal{P}$ exists iff there is a complete composite hypothesis H in $\mathcal{P}$, which is equivalent to whether:

$$\text{SD} \cup \text{OBS} \cup \{\text{AB}(h) \mid h \in H\} \cup \{\neg\text{AB}(h) \mid h \in H_{\text{all}}\backslash H\}$$

is consistent for $\mathcal{P}'$. Clearly, some $\text{AB}(h)$ must be true for each observation $\text{MANIFEST}(d)$. Also, $\text{AB}(h)$ and $\text{AB}(h')$ cannot be true at the same time if $\{h, h'\} \in \mathcal{I}$. □

Theorem 4.8. *For the class of belief revision problems, it is NP-complete to determine whether there is a value assignment w to the variables W such that $P(w|v) > 0$.*

Proof. Cooper [4] showed that it is NP-complete to determine whether $P(X = true) > 0$ for a given variable X. To prove the above theorem, simply let $V = \{X\}$ and $\boldsymbol{v}$ consist of $X = true$. Determining whether there is a value assignment $\boldsymbol{w}$ such that $P(\boldsymbol{w}|\boldsymbol{v}) > 0$ is equivalent to determining whether $P(X = true) > 0$.   □

Theorem 4.9. *For the class of cancellation abduction problems, it is NP-complete to determine whether an explanation exists.*

Proof. This can be shown by reduction from 3SAT abduction problems. Let $\mathcal{P} = \langle D_{\text{all}}, H_{\text{all}}, e, pl, \mathcal{I} \rangle$ be a 3SAT abduction problem. An equivalent cancellation abduction problem $\mathcal{P}' = \langle D'_{\text{all}}, H'_{\text{all}}, e', pl', e'_+, e'_- \rangle$ can be constructed by:

$$D'_{\text{all}} = D_{\text{all}} \cup \{d_I \mid I \in \mathcal{I}\}, {}^9$$

$$H'_{\text{all}} = H_{\text{all}} \cup \{h', h''\},$$

$$e'_+(h) = \begin{cases} e(h), & \text{if } h \in H_{\text{all}}, \\ \{d_I \mid I \in \mathcal{I}\}, & \text{if } h \in \{h', h''\}, \end{cases}$$

$$e'_-(h) = \begin{cases} \{d_I \mid h \in I\}, & \text{if } h \in H_{\text{all}}, \\ \emptyset & \text{if } h \in \{h', h''\}, \end{cases}$$

$$pl'(H) = pl(H).$$

Cancellation interactions are created so that each incompatible pair in $\mathcal{P}$ effectively become incompatible in $\mathcal{P}'$. For all $I \in \mathcal{I}$ and $H' \subseteq H'_{\text{all}}$, if $I \subseteq H'$, then $d_I \notin e'(H')$. Thus, no such H' can be an explanation. Hence, $\mathcal{P}'$ has a complete composite hypothesis iff $\mathcal{P}$ has a complete composite hypothesis. In particular, $H \subseteq H_{\text{all}}$ is a complete composite hypothesis for $\mathcal{P}$ if and only if $H \cup \{h', h''\}$ is a complete composite hypothesis for $\mathcal{P}'$. Consequently, $\mathcal{P}$ has an explanation if and only if $\mathcal{P}'$ has an explanation.   □

Theorem 4.11. *For the class of cancellation abduction problems, it is coNP-complete to determine whether a complete composite hypothesis is parsimonious.*

Proof. That is, it is NP-complete to determine whether a complete composite hypothesis is not parsimonious. This can be shown by reduction from 3SAT abduction problems. Let $\mathcal{P} = \langle D_{\text{all}}, H_{\text{all}}, e, pl, \mathcal{I} \rangle$ be a 3SAT abduction

---

[9]This means that D'_{all} has a datum corresponding to each $I \in \mathcal{I}$, notated as d_I.

problem, and let $\mathcal{P}' = \langle D'_{\text{all}}, H'_{\text{all}}, e', pl', e'_+, e'_- \rangle$ be a cancellation abduction problem constructed from $\mathcal{P}$ as follows:

$$H'_{\text{all}} = H_{\text{all}} \cup \{h', h'', h^*, h^{**}\},$$

$$D'_{\text{all}} = D_{\text{all}} \cup \{d_I \mid I \in \mathcal{I}\} \cup \{d_h \mid h \in H_{\text{all}}\},$$

$$e'_+(h) = \begin{cases} e(h) \cup d_h, & \text{if } h \in H_{\text{all}}, \\ \{d_I \mid I \in \mathcal{I}\}, & \text{if } h \in \{h', h''\}, \\ D_{\text{all}} \cup \{d_I \mid I \in \mathcal{I}\}, & \text{if } h = h^*, \\ \{d_h \mid h \in H_{\text{all}}\}, & \text{if } h = h^{**}, \end{cases}$$

$$e'_-(h) = \begin{cases} \{d_I \mid h \in I\}, & \text{if } h \in H_{\text{all}}, \\ \{d_h \mid h \in H_{\text{all}}\}, & \text{if } h = h^*, \\ \emptyset, & \text{if } h \in \{h', h'', h^{**}\}, \end{cases}$$

$$pl'(H) = pl(H).$$

This construction is similar to the previous one except that additional data and hypotheses are included so that H'_{all} is a complete composite hypothesis. However, any other complete composite hypothesis (which obviously must be a proper subset of H'_{all}) cannot include h^* and must satisfy cancellation interactions equivalent to $\mathcal{P}$'s incompatibilities. In particular, $H \subseteq H_{\text{all}}$ is a complete composite hypothesis for $\mathcal{P}$ if and only if $H \cup \{h', h'', h^{**}\}$ is a complete composite hypothesis for $\mathcal{P}'$. $\quad\square$

Theorem 5.1. *For the class of independent abduction problems using the best-small plausibility criterion, it is NP-hard to find a best explanation.*

Proof. This can be shown by reduction from 3SAT abduction problems. Let $\mathcal{P} = \langle D_{\text{all}}, H_{\text{all}}, e, pl, \mathcal{I} \rangle$ be a 3SAT abduction problem, and let $\mathcal{P}' = \langle D'_{\text{all}}, H'_{\text{all}}, e', pl' \rangle$ be an independent abduction problem using best-small constructed from $\mathcal{P}$ as follows:

Let f_1 be a function from $\mathcal{I}$ to H_{all}, such that $\forall I \in \mathcal{I} \ (f_1(I) \in I)$, i.e., f_1 chooses one hypothesis from each pair in $\mathcal{I}$. Let H_1 be the set of hypotheses that f_1 chooses, i.e, $H_1 = \bigcup_{I \in \mathcal{I}} \{f_1(I)\}$. Let f_2 be another function from $\mathcal{I}$ to H_{all}, such that f_2 chooses the other hypothesis from each pair in I. Now define $\mathcal{P}'$ as:

$$D'_{\text{all}} = D_{\text{all}} \cup \{d_I \mid I \in \mathcal{I}\} \cup \{d'\},$$

$$H'_{\text{all}} = H_{\text{all}} \cup \{h', h''\},$$

$$e'(h) = \begin{cases} e(h) \cup \{d_I \mid h \in I\}, & \text{if } h \in H_{\text{all}}, \\ \{d'\} \cup D_{\text{all}} \backslash e(H_1), & \text{if } h = h', \\ \{d'\}, & \text{if } h = h'', \end{cases}$$

$$\forall I \in \mathcal{I} \ (pl'(f_1(I)) = pl'(f_2(I))),$$

$$\forall h \in H_{\text{all}} \ (pl'(h) < pl'(h') < pl'(h'')).$$

The remaining orderings of pl' do not matter. Let $n = |\mathcal{I}|$. Note that one hypothesis out of each $I \in \mathcal{I}$ must be chosen to explain all the d_I. Either h' or h'' must be chosen to explain d'. Hence, explanations must be of size $n + 1$ or larger. Now $H = H_1 \cup \{h'\}$ is an explanation of size $n + 1$, where $n = |\mathcal{I}|$. Because h' makes h'' superfluous, any other explanation of greater size must include more than n elements of H_{all}. According to best-small, this would match h' of H against a lower ranking hypothesis, so H must be better than any larger explanation. No other explanation can be smaller, so to get a better explanation according to best-small, h'' must be chosen, and only one hypothesis out of each $I \in \mathcal{I}$ can be accepted so that they explain D_{all}, i.e., a solution to the 3SAT abduction problem $\mathcal{P}$. Such an explanation would be a best explanation and also show that H is not a best explanation. Hence, finding the best explanation would solve the 3SAT abduction problem. Thus, finding a best explanation for independent abduction problems using the best-small plausibility criterion is NP-hard. □

Theorem 5.2. *For the class of belief revision problems restricted to OR inter-actions, it is NP-hard to find the most probable explanation.*

Proof. We reduce from finding a best explanation in independent abduction problems using the best-small plausibility criterion. Let $\mathcal{P} = \langle D_{\text{all}}, H_{\text{all}}, e, pl \rangle$ be an independent abduction problem where pl satisfies the best-small plausibility criterion. A belief revision problem $\mathcal{P}'$ that preserves the orderings among complete composite hypotheses determined by pl, but might create additional orderings, is:

$$\boldsymbol{W} = \{X_d \mid d \in D_{\text{all}}\} \cup \{X_h \mid h \in H_{\text{all}}\},$$

$$\boldsymbol{V} = \{X_d \mid d \in D_{\text{all}}\},$$

$$\boldsymbol{S}_d = \{X_h \mid d \in e(h)\},$$

$$\boldsymbol{S}_h = \emptyset,$$

$$\boldsymbol{v} = \{X = true \mid X \in V\},$$

$$\forall \boldsymbol{s}_d \ ((\boldsymbol{s}_d \rightarrow \exists X_h \ (d \in e(h) \wedge X_h = true)) \rightarrow \\ P(X_d = true | \boldsymbol{s}_d) = 1),$$

$$\forall \boldsymbol{s}_d \ ((\boldsymbol{s}_d \rightarrow \forall X_h \ (d \in e(h) \rightarrow X_h = false)) \rightarrow \\ P(X_d = true | \boldsymbol{s}_d) = 0),$$

$$\forall X_h \ (0 < P(X_h = true) < 0.5),$$

$$\forall X_h, X_{h'}\ (pl(h) < pl(h') \rightarrow P(X_h = true) < P(X_{h'} = true)),$$

$$\forall X_h, X_{h'}\ (pl(h) = pl(h') \rightarrow P(X_h = true) = P(X_{h'} = true)).$$

Note that $P(X_d = true) = 1$ iff there is some h such that $d \in e(h)$ and $P(X_h = true) = 1$. The network thus consists solely of OR interactions. As a consequence, the conditional probabilities can be concisely represented. This ensures that the size of $\mathcal{P}'$ is polynomial in the size of $\mathcal{P}$.

For convenience, we use $P(H|D)$ to denote the probability that X_h is *true* for $h \in H$ and X_h is *false* for $h \in H_{\mathrm{all}} \setminus H$, given that X_d is *true* for $d \in D$ and X_d is *false* for $d \in D_{\mathrm{all}} \setminus D$. If a value assignment $\boldsymbol{w}$ to all the variables $\boldsymbol{W}$ assigns *true* to all X_d and to only X_h such that $h \in H$, it is easy to verify that $P(\boldsymbol{w}|\boldsymbol{v}) = P(H|D_{\mathrm{all}})$.

If H is a complete composite hypothesis for the abduction problem $\mathcal{P}$, then H can be compared to other complete composite hypotheses in the belief revision problem $\mathcal{P}'$ using the expression:

$$\prod_{h \in H} P(h) \prod_{h \in H_{\mathrm{all}} \setminus H} (1 - P(h)),$$

where $P(h)$ denotes $P(X_h = true)$. By Bayes' theorem:

$$P(H|D_{\mathrm{all}}) = \frac{P(H)P(D_{\mathrm{all}}|H)}{P(D_{\mathrm{all}})}.$$

Because of the way the conditional probabilities are set up, H implies D_{all}, so $P(D_{\mathrm{all}}|H) = 1$. Because $P(D_{\mathrm{all}})$ will always be in the denominator, it is sufficient to compare $P(H)$ with $P(H')$ if H' is another complete composite hypotheses. $P(H)$ is calculated by the expression given above. Obviously $P(H|D_{\mathrm{all}}) > 0$ if H is a complete composite hypothesis.

If H is not a complete composite hypothesis, then $P(D_{\mathrm{all}}|H) = 0$, and so $P(H|D_{\mathrm{all}}) = 0$. [10]

Suppose H^* is the composite hypothesis that corresponds to the MPE $\boldsymbol{w}^*$ for the belief revision problem. To show that H^* is a best explanation, we need to show that H^* is complete, H^* is parsimonious, and that no other explanation H is better than H^* based on the best-small plausibility criterion. From the above discussion, it should be clear that H^* is complete.

Now if H^* were not parsimonious, then some $h \in H^*$ is superfluous, i.e., $H^* \setminus \{h\}$ is complete. However, because $1 - P(h) > P(h)$, it would follow that $P(H^* \setminus \{h\}) > P(H^*)$, which contradicts the fact that H^* corresponds to the MPE. Thus, it must be the case that H^* is parsimonious. Since H^* is also complete, H^* is an explanation.

---

[10]Or undefined if no complete composite hypothesis exists, in which case, no explanation or MPE exists.

Finally, suppose that another explanation H is better than H^* according to the best-small plausibility criterion. Then there exists a 1–1 function m from H to H^* that satisfies the following conditions: for each $h \in H$, $P(h) \geq P(m(h))$; and either H is smaller than H^*, or there exists an $h \in H$ such that $P(h) > P(m(h))$.

Using the function m, a 1–1 function m' from H_{all} to H_{all} can be constructed as follows:

$$m'(h) = \begin{cases} m(h), & \text{if } h \in H, \\ m^{-n}(h), & \text{if } h \in H^* \backslash H \wedge m^{-n}(h) \in H \wedge \\ & \quad m^{-(n+1)}(h) \text{ does not exist,} \\ h, & \text{otherwise.} \end{cases}$$

The domain of m is mapped into the range of m. Whatever is in m's range, but not in m's domain, is inversely mapped into elements in m's domain, but not in m's range. Everything left over is neither in m's range nor domain, and is mapped to itself.

Because of the best-small constraint, the following can be shown for m':

$$\begin{aligned} P(h) &\geq P(m'(h)), & &\text{if } h \in H, \\ 1 - P(h) &> P(m'(h)), & &\text{if } h \in H^* \backslash H \wedge \exists h' \in H \\ & & & \quad (m(h') = h), \\ 1 - P(h) &= 1 - P(m'(h)), & &\text{otherwise.} \end{aligned}$$

Since this mapping matches the factors of $P(H)$ to those of $P(H^*)$, it shows that $P(H) \geq P(H^*)$. Furthermore, best-small guarantees that either $P(h) > P(m(h))$ for some $h \in H$ or that H is smaller, implying there is some $h \notin H$ such that $1 - P(h) > P(m'(h))$. Thus, $P(H) > P(H^*)$.

However, this contradicts the fact that H^* is the MPE. Thus, it must be the case that the MPE for the belief revision problem $\mathcal{P}'$ corresponds to a best explanation for the abduction problem $\mathcal{P}$. Because finding a best explanation is NP-hard, it is also the case that finding the MPE is NP-hard, even if the belief network is restricted to OR interactions. □

Theorem 5.3. *For the class of ordered monotonic abduction problems using the best-small plausibility criterion, there is an* $O(nC_e + nC_{pl} + n^2)$ *algorithm for finding a best explanation.*

Proof. Again, $n = |D_{\text{all}}| + |H_{\text{all}}|$. Algorithm 2 is different from Algorithm 1 in only one way: instead of iterating over elements of H_{all} in an arbitrary order in the loop, a specific order is imposed. Thus, by similar arguments as for Theorem 4.4, Algorithm 2 will also find an explanation, if one exists. The change to the loop will result in the addition of at most $O(|H_{\text{all}}|)$ evaluations of pl and $O(|H_{\text{all}}| \log |H_{\text{all}}|)$ steps to sort H_{all} based on pl. Clearly then, the complexity of Algorithm 2 conforms to the order of complexity in the theorem. We now show that the explanation it finds will be a best explanation.

Let W be the explanation it returns. Suppose that, according to the best-small plausibility criterion, there is a better explanation H. Then $|H| \leq |W|$ and there must be a match m of H's elements to W's elements, such that H's elements are just as or more plausible than W's. The matching hypotheses from H to W cannot all have the same plausibility—that would imply that $H \subset W$ because the abduction problem is ordered. However, because W is parsimonious, no proper subset of W can be complete. Thus, at least one element of H must be more plausible than its match in W.

Suppose that the least plausible element $h_1 \in H$ is more plausible than the least plausible element $w_1 \in W$. This implies that all elements of H are more plausible than w_1. Because H is an explanation, that would imply that w_1 is superfluous in the context of higher-rated hypotheses, and that the loop in Algorithm 2 would have removed w_1 from the working hypothesis, implying that $w_1 \notin W$, a contradiction. It must be the case then, that $w_1 \in H$, otherwise H would not match up with W.

Suppose that the m least plausible elements of H are exactly the same as those of W. Call this set W_m. Further suppose that H and W differ on their $(m + 1)$st least plausible elements. Let h_{m+1} and w_{m+1} be these elements, respectively. Consider the hypotheses $W' \subset H_{\text{all}}$ that are more plausible than w_{m+1}. Now by the time that w_{m+1} is considered for removal in the loop, the working hypothesis must be $W_m \cup \{w_{m+1}\} \cup W'$. Since w_{m+1} was not found to be superfluous, it must be the case that $W_m \cup W'$ is not complete. Thus, the $(m + 1)$st least plausible element of H cannot be an element of W'. Because $h_{m+1} \neq w_{m+1}$, h_{m+1} must be less plausible than w_{m+1}, which contradicts the supposition that H is a better explanation than W.

Hence, by mathematical induction, no H can be a better explanation than W according to the best-small plausibility criterion. Therefore, for ordered monotonic abduction problems, Algorithm 2 tractably finds a best explanation. □

Theorem 5.5. *For the class of ordered independent abduction problems using the best-small plausibility criterion, given a best explanation, it is NP-complete to determine whether an additional best explanation exists.*

Proof. This reduction is similar to that of Theorem 5.1. Let $\mathcal{P} = \langle D_{\text{all}}, H_{\text{all}}, e, pl, \mathcal{I} \rangle$ be a 3SAT abduction problem, and let $\mathcal{P}' = \langle D'_{\text{all}}, H'_{\text{all}}, e', pl' \rangle$ be an ordered independent abduction problem constructed from $\mathcal{P}$ as follows:

Let f_1 be a function from $\mathcal{I}$ to H_{all}, such that f_1 chooses one hypothesis from each pair in $\mathcal{I}$. Let H_1 be the set of hypotheses that f_1 chooses. Let f_2 be a function from $\mathcal{I}$ to H_{all} that chooses the other hypothesis from each pair in $\mathcal{I}$. Now define $\mathcal{P}'$ as:

$$D'_{\text{all}} = D_{\text{all}} \cup \{d_I \mid I \in \mathcal{I}\} \cup \{d', d''\},$$

$$H'_{\text{all}} = H_{\text{all}} \cup \{h', h'', h^*\},$$

$$e'(h) = \begin{cases} e(h) \cup \{d_I \mid h \in I\}, & \text{if } h \in H_{\text{all}}, \\ \{d'\} \cup D_{\text{all}} \backslash e(H_1), & \text{if } h = h', \\ \{d''\}, & \text{if } h = h'', \\ \{d', d''\}, & \text{if } h = h^*, \end{cases}$$

$$\forall I \in \mathcal{I} \ (pl'(f_1(I)) > pl'(f_2(I))),$$

$$\forall h \in H_{\text{all}} \ (pl'(h) < pl'(h^*) < pl'(h'') < pl'(h')).$$

The remaining orderings for pl' do not matter. Now $H = H_1 \cup \{h', h''\}$ is a best explanation of size $n + 2$, where $n = |\mathcal{I}|$. Because one hypothesis out of each pair in $\mathcal{I}$ (a total of n hypotheses) is needed to explain $\{d_I \mid I \in \mathcal{I}\}$, and because H includes the more plausible hypothesis of each pair and the two most plausible hypotheses overall, no other explanation of size $n + 2$ or greater can be as good as H. Hence, to construct another best explanation, h' and h'' must be excluded, h^* must be included, and only one hypothesis out of each pair in $\mathcal{I}$ can be accepted, i.e., a solution to the 3SAT abduction problem $\mathcal{P}$. Thus, another best explanation for $\mathcal{P}'$ exists only if $\mathcal{P}$ has an explanation. $\square$

Acknowledgement

Thanks to B. Chandrasekaran, Ashok Goel, Jack Smith, and Jon Sticklen for their comments on the numerous versions of this paper. The referees have also made a substantial contribution. Any remaining errors are our responsibility, of course. This research has been supported in part by the National Library of Medicine, grant LM-04298; the National Heart, Lung and Blood Institute, NIH Grant 1 R01 HL 38776-01; the National Science Foundation through a graduate fellowship; the Defense Advanced Research Projects Agency, RADC contract F30602-85-C-0010; the Air Force Office of Scientific Research, contract F49620-89-C-0110; and the National Science Foundation, grant IRI-8902142.

References

[1] D. Allemang, M.C. Tanner, T. Bylander and J.R. Josephson, On the computational complexity of hypothesis assembly, in: *Proceedings IJCAI-87*, Milan, Italy (1987) 1112–1117.

[2] T. Bylander, D. Allemang, M.C. Tanner and J.R. Josephson, Some results concerning the computational complexity of abduction, in: *Proceedings First International Conference on Principles of Knowledge Representation and Reasoning*, Toronto, Ont. (1989) 44–54.

[3] E. Charniak and D. McDermott, *Introduction to Artificial Intelligence* (Addison-Wesley, Reading, MA, 1985).

[4] G. Cooper, The computational complexity of probablistic inference using Bayesian belief networks, *Artif. Intell.* **42** (1990) 393–405.

[5] R. Davis and W. Hamscher, Model-based reasoning: troubleshooting, in: H.E. Shrobe, ed., *Exploring Artificial Intelligence* (Morgan Kaufmann, San Mateo, CA, 1988) 297–346.

[6] J. de Kleer and B.C. Williams, Diagnosing multiple faults, *Artif. Intell.* **32** (1987) 97–130.

[7] J. de Kleer and B.C. Williams, Diagnosis with behavioral modes, in: *Proceedings IJCAI-89*, Detroit, MI (1989) 1324–1330.

[8] D. Dvorak and B. Kuipers, Model-based monitoring of dynamic systems, in: *Proceedings IJCAI-89*, Detroit, MI (1989) 1238–1243.

[9] L. Eshelman, MOLE: a knowledge-acquisition tool for cover-and-differentiate systems, in: S. Marcus, ed., *Automating Knowledge Acquisition for Expert Systems* (Kluwer, Boston, MA, 1988) 37–80.

[10] M.R. Garey and D.S. Johnson, *Computers and Intractability* (Freeman, New York, 1979).

[11] A. Goel, P. Sadayappan and J.R. Josephson, Concurrent synthesis of composite explanatory hypotheses, in: *Proceedings Seventeenth International Conference on Parallel Processing*, St. Charles, IL (1988) 156–160.

[12] J.R. Hobbs, M. Stickel, P. Martin and D. Edwards, Interpretation as abduction, in: *Proceedings 26th Annual Meeting of the Association for Computational Linguistics*, Buffalo, NY (1988) 95–103.

[13] J.R. Josephson, B. Chandrasekaran, J.W. Smith and M.C. Tanner, A mechanism for forming composite explanatory hypotheses, *IEEE Trans. Syst. Man Cybern.* **17** (3) (1987) 445–454.

[14] J.R. Josephson and A. Goel, Practical abduction, Tech. Report, Laboratory for AI Research, Department of Computer and Information Science, Ohio State University, Columbus, OH (1990).

[15] H.J. Levesque, A knowledge-level account of abduction, in: *Proceedings IJCAI-89*, Detroit, MI (1989) 1061–1067.

[16] R.A. Miller, J.E. Pople and J.D. Myers, INTERNIST-I: an experimental computer-based diagnostic consultant for general internal medicine, *New England J. Med.* **307** (1982) 468–476.

[17] R.S. Patil, P. Szolovits and W.B. Schwartz, Modeling knowledge of the patient in acid-base and electrolyte disorders, in: P. Szolovits, ed., *Artificial Intelligence in Medicine* (Westview Press, Boulder, CO, 1982) 191–226.

[18] J. Pearl, Fusion, propagation, and structuring in belief networks, *Artif. Intell.* **29** (1986) 241–288.

[19] J. Pearl, Distributed revision of composite beliefs, *Artif. Intell.* **33** (1987) 173–215.

[20] C.S. Peirce, Abduction and induction, in: J. Buchler, ed., *Philosophical Writings of Peirce* (Dover, New York, 1955) Chapter 11, 150–156..

[21] Y. Peng and J.A. Reggia, A probabilistic causal model for diagnostic problem solving, *IEEE Trans. Syst. Man Cybern.* **17** (1987) 146–162.

[22] Y. Peng and J.A. Reggia, A probabilistic causal model for diagnostic problem solving II, *IEEE Trans. Syst. Man Cybern.* **17** (1987) 395–406.

[23] D. Poole, Explanation and prediction: an architecture for default and abductive reasoning, *Comput. Intell.* **5** (1989) 97–110.

[24] H.E. Pople, On the mechanization of abductive logic, in: *Proceedings IJCAI-73*, Stanford, CA (1973) 147–152.

[25] H.E. Pople, The formation of composite hypotheses in diagnostic problem solving: an exercise in synthetic reasoning, in: *Proceedings IJCAI-77*, Cambridge, MA (1977)

1030–1037.

[26] J.A. Reggia, D.S. Nau and P. Wang, Diagnostic expert systems based on a set covering model, *Int. J. Man-Mach. Stud.* **19** (1983) 437–460.

[27] R. Reiter, A theory of diagnosis from first principles, *Artif. Intell.* **32** (1987) 57–95.

[28] J.W. Smith, J.R. Josephson, M.C. Tanner, J.R. Svirbely and P. Strohm, Problem solving in red cell antibody identification: RED's performance on 20 cases, Tech. Report, LAIR, Department of Computer and Information Science, Ohio State University, Columbus, OH (1986).

[29] J.W. Smith, J.R. Svirbely, C.A. Evans, P. Strohm, J.R. Josephson and M.C. Tanner, RED: a red-cell antibody identification expert module, *J. Med. Syst.* **9** (3) (1985) 121–138.

[30] J. Sticklen, Distributed abduction, in: R. Huber, C. Kulikowski, J.M. Krivine and J.M. David, eds., *Artificial Intelligence in Scientific Computation: Towards Second Generation Systems* (Baltzer, Basel, Switzerland, 1989).

[31] P. Struss and O. Dressler, "Physical negation": integrating fault models into the general diagnostic engine, in: *Proceedings IJCAI-89*, Detroit, MI (1989) 1318–1323.

[32] P. Thagard, *Computational Philosophy of Science* (MIT Press, Cambridge, MA, 1988).

[33] L.G. Valiant, The complexity of enumeration and reliability problems, *SIAM J. Comput.* **8** (1979) 410–421.

Artificial Intelligence 49 (1991) 61–95
Elsevier

Temporal constraint networks*

Rina Dechter**

Computer Science Department, Technion—Israel Institute of Technology, Haifa 32000, Israel

Itay Meiri and Judea Pearl

Cognitive Systems Laboratory, Computer Science Department, University of California, Los Angeles, CA 90024, USA

Received November 1989
Revised July 1990

Abstract

Dechter, R., I. Meiri and J. Pearl, Temporal constraint networks, Artificial Intelligence 49 (1991) 61–95.

This paper extends network-based methods of constraint satisfaction to include continuous variables, thus providing a framework for processing temporal constraints. In this framework, called temporal constraint satisfaction problem (TCSP), variables represent time points and temporal information is represented by a set of unary and binary constraints, each specifying a set of permitted intervals. The unique feature of this framework lies in permitting the processing of metric information, namely, assessments of time differences between events. We present algorithms for performing the following reasoning tasks: finding all feasible times that a given event can occur, finding all possible relationships between two given events, and generating one or more scenarios consistent with the information provided.

We distinguish between simple temporal problems (STPs) and general temporal problems, the former admitting at most one interval constraint on any pair of time points. We show that the STP, which subsumes the major part of Vilain and Kautz's point algebra, can be solved in polynomial time. For general TCSPs, we present a decomposition scheme that performs the three reasoning tasks considered, and introduce a variety of techniques for improving its efficiency. We also study the applicability of path consistency algorithms as preprocessing of temporal problems, demonstrate their termination and bound their complexities.

*This work was supported in part by the National Science Foundation, Grant #IRI 8815522, and by the Air Force Office of Scientific Research, AFOSR 90 0136.
**Present address: Information and Computer Science Department, University of California, Irvine, CA, USA.

0004-3702/91/$03.50 © 1991 — Elsevier Science Publishers B.V.

1. Introduction

Problems involving temporal constraints arise in various areas of computer science such as scheduling, program verification, and parallel computation. Research in common-sense reasoning [22, 41], natural language understanding [3, 24], and planning [34], has identified new types of temporal reasoning problems, specific to AI applications. Several formalisms for expressing and reasoning about temporal knowledge have been proposed, most notably, Allen's interval algebra [2], Vilain and Kautz's point algebra [49], linear inequalities (Malik and Binford [33], Valdés-Pérez [46]), and Dean and McDermott's time map [13]. Each of these representation schemes is supported by a specialized constraint-directed reasoning algorithm. At the same time, extensive research has been carried out over the past years on problems involving general constraints (Montanari [36], Mackworth [31], Gaschnig [21], Freuder [19, 20], Haralick and Elliott [23], Nudel [37], Dechter and Pearl [16]), yet much of this work has not been extended to problems involving temporal constraints.

This paper presents a unified approach to temporal reasoning based on constraint-network formalism. Using this formalism, we were able to develop:

(1) a formal basis for relating various algorithmic schemes, permitting the analysis of their complexity and range of applicability;
(2) an economical representation, called a *minimal network*, which encodes all temporal relations between a pair of event points, including absolute bounds on their time difference;
(3) an efficient scheme of generating specific temporal scenarios, consistent with the given constraints.

We envision a temporal reasoning system to consist of a temporal knowledge base, a routine to check its consistency, a query answering mechanism and an inference mechanism capable of discovering new information. The primitive entities in the knowledge base are *propositions* with which we normally associate temporal intervals, e.g., "I was driving a car" or "the book was lying on the table"; each interval representing the time period during which the corresponding proposition holds. The temporal information might be relative (e.g., "P_1 occurred before P_2"), or metric (e.g., "P_1 had started at least 3 hours before P_2 was terminated"). To express less specific information, disjunctive sentences may also be needed (e.g., "you can come in before or after lunch hour"); a subclass of such sentences will be addressed in this paper. We also allow references to absolute time (such as 4:00 p.m.), and to the duration of propositions (e.g., "P lasted at least two hours"). Given temporal information of this kind, we want to derive answers to queries such as: is it possible that proposition P holds at time t? what are the possible times at which proposition P holds? what are the possible temporal relationships between two propositions P_1 and P_2?

There have been several suggestions of how to represent temporal information. If propositions stand for events, and each proposition P_i is associated with an interval $I_i = [a_i, b_i]$, then information about the timing of events can be expressed by means of constraints on the intervals or their associated beginning and ending points. Allen [2] defined temporal knowledge to consist of constraints on the 13 possible relationships that can exist between any pair of intervals. Since finding all the feasible relationships between a given pair of intervals is intractable, Vilain and Kautz [49] suggested that the information be expressed by means of constraints on the beginning and ending point of each interval. This approach gives rise to a polynomial time algorithm, but can handle only a limited class of problems. Recently, Ladkin and Maddux [27] have proposed an algebraic approach to problems similar to those posed by Allen and Vilain and Kautz.

One of the requirements of our system is the ability to deal with metric information. Since both Allen's interval algebra and Vilain and Kautz's point algebra do not offer a convenient mechanism for dealing with such information, we take a different approach. We consider time points as the variables we wish to constrain—where a time point may be a beginning or an ending point of some event, as well as a neutral point of time such as 4:00 p.m. Malik and Binford [33] and Valdés-Pérez [46] suggested constraining the *temporal distance* between time points. Namely, if X_i and X_j are two time points, a constraint on their temporal distance would be of the form $X_j - X_i \leq c$, which gives rise to a set of linear inequalities on the X_i's. Such constraints, however, are insufficient; we must allow disjunctive sentences. Consider the following example:

Example 1.1. John goes to work either by car (30–40 minutes), or by bus (at least 60 minutes). Fred goes to work either by car (20–30 minutes), or in a carpool (40–50 minutes). Today John left home between 7:10 and 7:20, and Fred arrived at work between 8:00 and 8:10. We also know that John arrived at work about 10–20 minutes after Fred left home. We wish to answer queries such as: "Is the information in the story consistent?", "Is it possible that John took the bus, and Fred used the carpool?", "What are the possible times at which Fred left home?", and so on.

Let P_1 be the proposition "John was going to work", and P_2 the proposition "Fred was going to work". P_1 and P_2 are associated with intervals $[X_1, X_2]$ and $[X_3, X_4]$, respectively, where X_1 represents the time John left home while X_4 represents the time Fred arrived at work. Several temporal constraints are given in the story. From the fact that it takes John either 30–40 minutes or more than 60 minutes to get to work, the temporal distance between X_1 and X_2 is constrained by

$$30 \leqslant X_2 - X_1 \leqslant 40 \quad \text{or} \quad X_2 - X_1 \geqslant 60 \,. \tag{1.1}$$

Similar constraints apply to $X_4 - X_3$ and $X_2 - X_3$. Choosing $X_0 = 7{:}00$ a.m., the fact that John left home between 7:10 and 7:20 imposes the constraint

$$10 \leqslant X_1 - X_0 \leqslant 20 \,. \tag{1.2}$$

The constraint on $X_4 - X_0$ assumes a similar form.

This paper introduces a framework based on constraint-network formalism for representing and processing such problems. Within this framework several solution methods are established. Section 2 presents the temporal constraint satisfaction problem (TCSP). Section 3 deals with a restricted, simpler TCSP (called STP), solvable in polynomial time. Sections 4–6 offer some techniques for solving the general TCSP: decomposition into several STPs, approximation schemes, and network-based approaches. Section 7 relates the TCSP model to other temporal reasoning models, while Section 8 provides a summary and concluding remarks.

2. The TCSP model

The definitions needed for describing a temporal constraint satisfaction problem follow closely those developed for the general CSP [36]. A *temporal constraint satisfaction problem* (*TCSP*) involves a set of variables, $X_1, \ldots, X_n$, having continuous domains; each variable represents a time point. Each constraint is represented by a set of intervals[1]:

$$\{I_1, \ldots, I_n\} = \{[a_1, b_1], \ldots, [a_n, b_n]\} \,. \tag{2.1}$$

A unary constraint, T_i, restricts the domain of variable X_i to the given set of intervals; namely, it represents the disjunction

$$(a_1 \leqslant X_i \leqslant b_1) \vee \cdots \vee (a_n \leqslant X_i \leqslant b_n) \,. \tag{2.2}$$

A binary constraint, T_{ij}, constrains the permissible values for the distance $X_j - X_i$; it represents the disjunction

$$(a_1 \leqslant X_j - X_i \leqslant b_1) \vee \cdots \vee (a_n \leqslant X_j - X_i \leqslant b_n) \,. \tag{2.3}$$

We assume that constraints are always given in a *canonical form* where all intervals are pairwise disjoint.

A *network of binary constraints* (a *binary TCSP*) consists of a set of variables, $X_1, \ldots, X_n$, and a set of unary and binary constraints. Such a

[1] For simplicity we assume closed intervals; however, the same treatment applies to open and semi-open intervals.

network can be represented by a *directed constraint graph*, where nodes represent variables and an edge $i \rightarrow j$ indicates that a constraint T_{ij} is specified; it is labeled by the interval set. Each input constraint, T_{ij}, implies an equivalent constraint T_{ji}; however, only one of them will usually be shown in the constraint graph. A special time point, X_0, is introduced to represent the "beginning of the world". All times are relative to X_0, thus we may treat each unary constraint T_i as a binary constraint T_{0i} (having the same interval representation). For simplicity we assume $X_0 = 0$. The constraint graph of Example 1.1 is given in Fig. 1.

A tuple $X = (x_1, \ldots, x_n)$ is called a *solution* if the assignment $\{X_1 = x_1, \ldots, X_n = x_n\}$ satisfies all the constraints. A value v is a *feasible value* for variable X_i, if there exists a solution in which $X_i = v$. The set of all feasible values of a variable is called the *minimal domain*. The network is *consistent* if at least one solution exists.

We define the following binary operations on constraints: union, intersection and composition, respecting their usual set-theoretic definitions.

Definition 2.1. Let $T = \{I_1, \ldots, I_l\}$ and $S = \{J_1, \ldots, J_m\}$ be constraints, i.e., sets of intervals of a real variable t (t corresponds to $X_j - X_i$ in case of binary constraints).

(1) The *union* of T and S, denoted by $T \cup S$, admits only values that are allowed by either one of them, namely,

$$T \cup S = \{I_1, \ldots, I_l, J_1, \ldots, J_m\} \,. \tag{2.4}$$

(2) The *intersection* of T and S, denoted by $T \oplus S$, admits only values that are allowed by both of them, namely,

$$T \oplus S = \{K_1, \ldots, K_n\} \,, \tag{2.5}$$

where $K_k = I_i \cap J_j$ for some i and j. Note that $n \le l + m$.

(3) The *composition* of T and S, denoted by $T \otimes S$, admits only values r for which there exist $t \in T$ and $s \in S$, such that $t + s = r$, namely,

$$T \otimes S = \{K_1, \ldots, K_n\} \,, \tag{2.6}$$

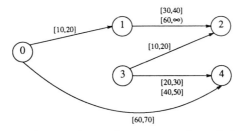

Fig. 1. A constraint graph representing Example 1.1.

where $K_k = [a + c, b + d]$ for some $I_i = [a, b]$ and $J_j = [c, d]$. Note that $n \leqslant l \times m$.

A pictorial illustration of the intersection and composition operations is given in Fig. 2. Note that for some of these operations the resulting interval representation is not in canonical form. For instance, the composition operation results in four intervals; however, due to overlap, only three of them appear in the canonical form. These three operations parallel the usual operations of union, intersection and composition in general constraint networks [36]. In particular, when T and S represent binary constraints on the differences $X_j - X_i$ and $X_k - X_j$, respectively, $T \otimes S$ admits only pairs of values (x_i, x_k) for which there exists a value x_j, such that (x_i, x_j) is permitted by T and (x_j, x_k) is permitted by S.

These operations are extended to operations on networks in the usual way. Given networks T and S, on the same set of variables, we define

$$(T \cup S)_{ij} = T_{ij} \cup S_{ij} \tag{2.7}$$

$$(T \oplus S)_{ij} = T_{ij} \oplus S_{ij} \, , \tag{2.8}$$

where i and j range over all pairs of variables.

A partial order among constraints can be defined as follows. A binary constraint T is *tighter* than S, denoted by $T \subseteq S$, if every pair of values allowed by T is also allowed by S; namely, for every interval $I \in T$ there exists an

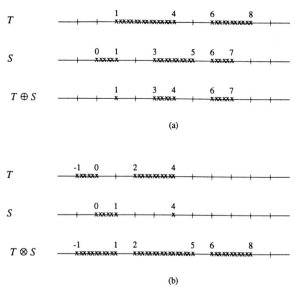

Fig. 2. Operations on constraints: (a) intersection, (b) composition.

interval $J \in S$ such that $I \subseteq J$. The tightest constraint is the *empty constraint*, $\emptyset$ (if the network contains an empty constraint, then it is trivially inconsistent). The most relaxed constraint is the *universal constraint*, $(-\infty, \infty)$. Edges corresponding to universal constraints are usually omitted from the constraint graph.

A partial order among binary constraint networks having the same set of variables can be defined as follows. A network T is tighter than network S, denoted $T \subseteq S$, if the partial order $\subseteq$ is satisfied for all the corresponding constraints; namely, for all pairs i, j, $T_{ij} \subseteq S_{ij}$. Two networks are *equivalent* if they represent the same solution set. A network may have many equivalent representations; in particular, there is one equivalent network which is minimal with respect to $\subseteq$, called the *minimal network* (note that the minimal network is unique because equivalent networks are closed under intersection). The arc constraints specified by the minimal network are called the *minimal constraints*.

A network is *decomposable*[2] [36], if every locally consistent assignment[3] to any set of variables, S, can be extended to a solution. The importance of decomposability lies in facilitating the construction of a solution by a *backtrack-free search* [20].

Given a constraint network, the first interesting problem is to determine its consistency. If the network is consistent we may wish to find some specific solutions, each representing a possible scenario, or to answer queries concerning the set of all solutions. The interesting queries are:

(1) "What are the possible times at which X_i could occur?" (asking for the minimal domain of X_i).
(2) "What are all the possible relationships between X_i and X_j?" (asking for the minimal constraint between X_i and X_j).

Computing the full minimal network would provide answers to all such queries. The rest of the paper presents several techniques for solving these tasks.

3. The simple temporal problem (STP)

A TCSP in which all constraints specify a single interval is called a *simple temporal problem* (*STP*). In such a network, each edge, $i \rightarrow j$, is labeled by an interval, $[a_{ij}, b_{ij}]$, which represents the constraint

$$a_{ij} \leqslant X_j - X_i \leqslant b_{ij} . \tag{3.1}$$

Alternatively, the constraint can be expressed as a pair of inequalities:

---

[2] In [36] decomposability is defined for minimal networks only.
[3] An assignment of values to a set of variables, S, is *locally consistent*, if it satisfies the constraints applicable to S; namely, those involving only variables in S (including the unary constraints).

$$X_j - X_i \leq b_{ij} \,, \tag{3.2}$$

$$X_i - X_j \leq -a_{ij} \,. \tag{3.3}$$

Thus, solving an STP amounts to solving a set of linear inequalities on the X_i's.

The problem of solving a system of linear inequalities is well known in the operations research literature. It can be solved by the (exponential) simplex method [10] or Khachiyan's algorithm [25], which is rather complicated in practice. Fortunately, the special class of linear inequalities characterizing the STP admits a simpler solution; the inequalities are given a convenient graph representation, to which a shortest paths algorithm can be applied [6, 29, 30, 42]. In the AI literature, a similar data structure, called a *time map*, was introduced by Dean and McDermott [13] to facilitate planning, but was not formulated mathematically.

Formally, we associate an STP with a directed edge-weighted graph, $G_d = (V, E_d)$, called a *distance graph* (to be distinguished from the constraint graph). It has the same node set as G, and each edge, $i \rightarrow j$, is labeled by a weight a_{ij}, representing the linear inequality $X_j - X_i \leq a_{ij}$. In Example 1.1, if we assume that John used a car and Fred used a carpool, we get an STP having

$$T_{12} = \{[30, 40]\} \quad \text{and} \quad T_{34} = \{[40, 50]\} \,, \tag{3.4}$$

and a distance graph as depicted in Fig. 3.

Each path from i to j in G_d, $i_0 = i, i_1, \ldots, i_k = j$, induces the following constraint on the distance $X_j - X_i$:

$$X_j - X_i \leq \sum_{j=1}^{k} a_{i_{j-1}, i_j} \,. \tag{3.5}$$

If there is more than one path from i to j, then it can be easily verified that the intersection of all the induced path constraints yields

$$X_j - X_i \leq d_{ij} \,, \tag{3.6}$$

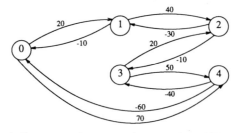

Fig. 3. A distance graph representing a portion of Example 1.1.

where d_{ij} is the length of the shortest path from i to j. Based on this observation, the following condition for consistency of an STP can be established:

Theorem 3.1 (Shostak [42], Liao and Wong [30], Leiserson and Saxe [29]). *A given STP, T, is consistent if and only if its distance graph, G_d, has no negative cycles.*

Proof. Suppose there is a negative cycle, C, consisting of nodes $i_1, \ldots, i_k = i_1$. Summing the inequalities along C yields $X_{i_1} - X_{i_1} < 0$, which cannot be satisfied. Conversely, if there is no negative cycle in G_d, then the shortest path between each pair of nodes is well-defined. For any pair of nodes, i and j, the shortest paths satisfy $d_{0j} \leq d_{0i} + a_{ij}$; thus

$$d_{0j} - d_{0i} \leq a_{ij} . \tag{3.7}$$

Hence, the tuple $(d_{01}, \ldots, d_{0n})$ is a solution of the given STP. $\square$

Corollary 3.2. *Let G_d be the distance graph of a consistent STP. Two consistent scenarios are given by*:

$$S_1 = (d_{01}, \ldots, d_{0n}) , \tag{3.8}$$

$$S_2 = (-d_{10}, \ldots, -d_{n0}) , \tag{3.9}$$

which assign to each variable its latest and earliest possible time, respectively.

Proof. The proof of Theorem 3.1 shows that S_1 is a solution. To show that S_2 is a solution, note that for all i and j, $d_{i0} \leq a_{ij} + d_{j0}$, or

$$(-d_{j0}) - (-d_{i0}) \leq a_{ij} , \tag{3.10}$$

yielding S_2 as a solution. $\square$

From the above discussion it follows that a given STP can be effectively specified by a complete directed graph, called *d-graph*, where each edge, $i \rightarrow j$, is labeled by the shortest path length, d_{ij}, in G_d; it corresponds to a more explicit representation of our STP (see (3.5) and (3.6)).

Theorem 3.3 (Decomposability). *Any consistent STP is decomposable relative to the constraints in its d-graph.*

Proof. It suffices to show that any instantiation of a subset S of k variables

$(1 \leq k < n)$ that satisfies all the shortest path constraints applicable to S, is extensible to any other variable. This will be shown by induction on $|S| = k$.

For $k = 1$, S consists of a single variable, X_i, instantiated to x_i. We will show that for any other variable, X_j, we can find an assignment $X_j = v$ which satisfies the shortest path constraints between them. The value v must satisfy

$$-d_{ji} \leq v - x_i \leq d_{ij} . \tag{3.11}$$

Since all cycles in the distance graph are nonnegative, we have $d_{ji} + d_{ij} \geq 0$ and, hence, there exists a value v satisfying (3.11).

Assume that the theorem holds for $|S| = k - 1$; we must show that it holds for $|S| = k$. Without loss of generality, let $S = \{X_1, \ldots, X_k\}$, and let $\{X_i = x_i \mid 1 \leq i \leq k\}$ be an assignment that satisfies the shortest path constraints among the variables in S. Let $X_{k+1} \not\in S$. We need to find a value $X_{k+1} = v$ which satisfies the shortest path constraints between X_{k+1} and all variables in S. In other words, v must satisfy

$$v - x_i \leq d_{i,k+1} , \tag{3.12}$$

$$x_i - v \leq d_{k+1,i} , \tag{3.13}$$

for $i = 1, \ldots, k$, or

$$v \leq \min\{x_i + d_{i,k+1} \mid 1 \leq i \leq k\} , \tag{3.14}$$

$$v \geq \max\{x_i - d_{k+1,i} \mid 1 \leq i \leq k\} . \tag{3.15}$$

Suppose the minimum is attained at i_0, and the maximum at j_0. Thus, v must satisfy

$$x_{j_0} - d_{k+1,j_0} \leq v \leq x_{i_0} + d_{i_0,k+1} . \tag{3.16}$$

Since x_{i_0} and x_{j_0} satisfy the constraint between them, we have

$$x_{j_0} - x_{i_0} \leq d_{i_0,j_0} . \tag{3.17}$$

This, together with $d_{i_0,j_0} \leq d_{i_0,k+1} + d_{k+1,j_0}$, yields

$$x_{j_0} - d_{k+1,j_0} \leq x_{i_0} + d_{i_0,k+1} . \tag{3.18}$$

Therefore, there exists a value v which satisfies the condition of (3.16). $\square$

The importance of Theorem 3.3 lies in providing an efficient algorithm for assembling a solution to a given STP; we simply assign to each variable any value that satisfies the d-graph constraints relative to previous assignments (starting with $X_0 = 0$). Decomposability guarantees that such a value can always be found, regardless of the order of assignment. A second by-product of decomposability is that the domains characterized by the d-graph are minimal.

Corollary 3.4. *Let G_d be the distance graph of a consistent STP. The set of feasible values for variable X_i is $[-d_{i0}, d_{0i}]$.*

Proof. According to Theorem 3.3, the assignment $X_0 = 0$ can be extended by assigning any value v satisfying $v \in [-d_{i0}, d_{0i}]$ to X_i. This assignment, in turn, can be extended to a full solution. Thus, v is a feasible value. $\square$

We have noted that the d-graph represents a tighter, yet equivalent network of the original STP. From Theorem 3.3 we can now conclude that this new network is the minimal network.

Corollary 3.5. *Given a consistent STP, T, the equivalent STP, M, defined by*

$$\forall i, j, \quad M_{ij} = \{[-d_{ji}, d_{ij}]\}, \tag{3.19}$$

is the minimal network representation of T.

Proof. See Appendix A. $\square$

Illustration. Consider the distance graph of Fig. 3. Since there are no negative cycles, the corresponding STP is consistent. The shortest path distances, d_{ij}, are shown in Table 1. The minimal domains are $10 \le X_1 \le 20$, $40 \le X_2 \le 50$, $20 \le X_3 \le 30$ and $60 \le X_4 \le 70$. In particular, one special solution is the tuple $(d_{01}, \ldots, d_{04})$, namely, the assignment

$$\{X_1 = 20, X_2 = 50, X_3 = 30, X_4 = 70\}, \tag{3.20}$$

which selects for each variable its latest possible time. According to this

Table 1
Lengths of shortest paths in the distance graph of Fig. 3.

	0	1	2	3	4
0	0	20	50	30	70
1	−10	0	40	20	60
2	−40	−30	0	−10	30
3	−20	−10	20	0	50
4	−60	−50	−20	−40	0

Table 2
The minimal network corresponding to Fig. 3.

	0	1	2	3	4
0	[0]	[10, 20]	[40, 50]	[20, 30]	[60, 70]
1	[−20, −10]	[0]	[30, 40]	[10, 20]	[50, 60]
2	[−50, −40]	[−40, −30]	[0]	[−20, −10]	[20, 30]
3	[−30, −20]	[−20, −10]	[10, 20]	[0]	[40, 50]
4	[−70, −60]	[−60, −50]	[−30, −20]	[−50, −40]	[0]

solution, John left home at 7:10 and arrived at work at 7:50, while Fred left home at 7:30 and arrived at work at 8:10. The minimal network is given in Table 2. Notice that the minimal network is symmetric in the sense that if $T_{ij} = \{[a, b]\}$, then $T_{ji} = \{[−b, −a]\}$. An alternative scenario, in which John used a bus and Fred used a carpool (i.e., $T_{12} = \{[60, \infty)\}$ and $T_{34} = \{[40, 50]\}$), results in a negative cycle and is therefore inconsistent.

The d-graph of an STP can be constructed by applying *Floyd–Warshall*'s all-pairs-shortest-paths algorithm [38] to the distance graph (see Fig. 4). The algorithm runs in time $O(n^3)$, and detects negative cycles simply be examining the sign of the diagonal elements d_{ii}. It constitutes, therefore, a polynomial time algorithm for determining the consistency of an STP, and for computing both the minimal domains and the minimal network. Once the d-graph is available, assembling a solution requires only $O(n^2)$ time, because each successive assignment needs to be checked against previous assignments and is guaranteed to remain unaltered. Thus, finding a solution can be achieved in $O(n^3)$ time.

All-pairs-shortest-paths algorithm
1. for $i := 1$ to n do $d_{ii} \leftarrow 0$;
2. for $i, j := 1$ to n do $d_{ij} \leftarrow a_{ij}$;
3. for $k := 1$ to n do
4.   for $i, j := 1$ to n do
5. $d_{ij} \leftarrow \min\{d_{ij}, d_{ik} + d_{kj}\}$;

Fig. 4. Floyd–Warshall's algorithm.

4. The general TCSP

Having solved the STP, we now return to the general problem in which edges may be labeled by several intervals. Davis [12] showed that determining consistency for a general TCSP is NP-hard.

Theorem 4.1 (Davis [12]).
  (i) *Deciding consistency for a TCSP is NP-hard.*
  (ii) *Deciding consistency for a TCSP with no more than two intervals per edge is NP-hard.*

Proof. (i) Reduction from 3-coloring. Let $G = (V, E)$ be a graph to be colored. We construct a TCSP, T, in the following way. For each node, V_i, we introduce a variable, X_i, and a unary constraint on X_i,

$$X_i \in \{[1], [2], [3]\} , \tag{4.1}$$

where [1], [2] and [3] stand for the three admissible colors. With each edge $(i, j) \in E$ we associate a binary constraint

$$X_j - X_i \in \{[-2], [-1], [1], [2]\} . \tag{4.2}$$

Equation (4.2) restricts X_i and X_j to have different colors. Hence, T is consistent if and only if G is 3-colorable.

  (ii) Again, reduction from 3-coloring. We construct a TCSP, T, as follows. For each node, V_i, we introduce two variables, X'_i and X''_i, having domains

$$X'_i \in \{[1], [2, 3]\} , \tag{4.3}$$

$$X''_i \in \{[1, 2], [3]\} , \tag{4.4}$$

and restrict X'_i and X''_i to be equal:

$$X'_i = X''_i . \tag{4.5}$$

This forces X'_i and X''_i to assume integer values as in (4.1). To restrict the colors of nodes V_i and V_j to be different, the following binary constraints are introduced:

$$X'_j - X'_i \in \{[-2], [-1, 2]\} , \tag{4.6}$$

$$X''_j - X'_i \in \{[-2, -1], [1, 2]\} , \tag{4.7}$$

$$X'_j - X''_i \in \{[-2, 1], [2]\} . \tag{4.8}$$

T is consistent if and only if the graph is 3-colorable. □

A straightforward way of solving the general TCSP is to decompose it into several STPs, solve each one of them, and then combine the results. Given a binary TCSP, T, we define a *labeling* of T as a selection of one interval from each constraint. Each labeling defines an STP graph whose edges are labeled by the selected intervals. We can solve any of the TCSP tasks by considering all its STPs. Specifically, the original network is consistent iff there is a labeling whose associated STP is consistent. Any solution of T is also a solution of one of its STPs and vice versa. Also, the minimal network of T can be computed from the minimal networks associated with its individual STPs, as stated in the following theorem:

Theorem 4.2. *The minimal network, M, of a given TCSP, T, satisfies $M = \bigcup_l M_l$, where M_l is the minimal network of the STP defined by labeling l, and the union is over all the possible labelings.*

Proof. We first note that the solution set of T is identical to the union of the solution sets of its labelings. Hence, $\bigcup M_l$ is equivalent to T. M is by definition the tightest of all networks equivalent to T, and therefore $M \subseteq \bigcup M_l$. Now suppose that M is strictly tighter than $\bigcup M_l$. Then, there exist a pair of variables, i and j, a labeling, s, and a value, d, such that $d \in (M_s)_{ij}$ but $d \notin M_{ij}$. Let x and y be values of the variables i and j, respectively, such that $y - x = d$. According to the minimality of M_s, this partial assignment can be extended to a solution of s, which is also a solution of T; hence $d \in M_{ij}$, yielding a contradiction. Therefore, $\bigcup M_l \subseteq M$. □

Illustration. The minimal network of Example 1.1 is shown in Table 3. In this case, only 3 of the 4 possible labelings contribute to the minimal network.

The complexity of solving a general TCSP by generating all the labelings and solving them independently is $O(n^3 k^e)$, where k is the maximum number of intervals labeling an edge, and e is the number of edges.

Table 3
The minimal network of Example 1.1.

	0	1	2	3	4
0	[0]	[10, 20]	[40, 60] [70]	[20, 50]	[60, 70]
1	[−20, −10]	[0]	[30, 40] [60]	[10, 30] [40]	[40, 60]
2	[−70] [−60, −40]	[−60] [−40, −30]	[0]	[−20, −10]	[0, 30]
3	[−50, −20]	[−40] [−30, −10]	[10, 20]	[0]	[20, 30] [40, 50]
4	[−70, −60]	[−60, −40]	[−30, 0]	[−50, −40] [−30, −20]	[0]

This brute-force enumeration process can be pruned significantly by running a backtracking search on a meta-CSP whose variables are the TCSP's edges, and the domains are the possible intervals. Backtrack assigns an interval to an edge, as long as the condition of Theorem 3.1 is satisfied and, if no such assignment is possible, it backtracks.

Formally, let T be a given TCSP, and let $G = (V, E)$ be its associated constraint graph. Let $\mathrm{CSP}(T)$ be a discrete CSP with variables $X_1, \ldots, X_m$, where $m = |E|$, and variable X_i corresponds to edge $e_i \in E$. The domain of X_i consists of the intervals $I_1, \ldots, I_k$ that label e_i in G. The constraints are not given explicitly (as a list of allowed or disallowed combinations), instead, any assignment, $\{X_{i_1} = I_{i_1}, \ldots, X_{i_s} = I_{i_s}\}$, is consistent, if and only if the corresponding STP is consistent. Clearly, each solution of $\mathrm{CSP}(T)$ corresponds to a consistent labeling of G and, thus, any algorithm that finds all the solutions of $\mathrm{CSP}(T)$ can be used to solve T. A backtrack algorithm that computes the minimal network of a TCSP is shown in Fig. 5. It is defined by two recursive procedures: **Forward** and **Go-back**. The first extends a current partial assignment if possible, and the second handles dead-end situations. The procedures maintain a list of candidate intervals, C_i, for each variable X_i.

Forward$(I_1, \ldots, I_i)$
1. if $i = m$ then
2. $M \leftarrow M \cup \mathrm{Solve\text{-}STP}(I_1, \ldots, I_m)$, and
3.   Go-Back$(I_1, \ldots, I_m)$;
4. $C_{i+1} \leftarrow \emptyset$;
5. for every I_j in D_{i+1} do
6.   if Consistent-STP$(I_1, \ldots, I_i, I_j)$ then
7. $C_{i+1} \leftarrow C_{i+1} \cup \{I_j\}$;
8. If $C_{i+1} \neq \emptyset$ then
9. $I_{i+1} \leftarrow$ first element in C_{i+1}, and
10.   remove I_{i+1} from C_{i+1}, and
11.   Forward$(I_1, \ldots, I_i, I_{i+1})$
12. else
13.   Go-Back$(I_1, \ldots, I_i)$;

Go-back$(I_1, \ldots, I_i)$
1. if $i = 0$ then exit
2. if $C_i \neq \emptyset$ then
3. $I_i \leftarrow$ first element in C_i, and
4.   remove I_i from C_i, and
5.   Forward$(I_1, \ldots, I_i)$
6. else
7.   Go-back$(I_1, \ldots, I_{i-1})$;

Fig. 5. A backtrack algorithm.

Backtrack is initiated by calling "Forward" with $i = 0$, namely, the instantiated list is empty. The procedure "Solve-STP($I_1, \ldots, I_m$)" returns the
minimal network of the STP defined by $\{I_1, \ldots, I_m\}$. The procedure "Consis-
tent-STP($I_1, \ldots, I_i, I_j$)" determines if the partial STP defined by
$\{I_1, \ldots, I_i, I_j\}$ is consistent; it can be done either by using an all-pairs-
shortest-paths algorithm, or by an improved algorithm to be described in
Section 5. At the beginning of the algorithm, $M = \emptyset$ and, upon termination, M
contains the minimal network (if $M = \emptyset$, then the network is inconsistent). If
our task is to find a single solution, then once we find a consistent labeling we
may construct a solution using the technique described in the previous section.

Although the worst-case complexity of this approach is also $O(n^3 k^e)$, it
enables us to utilize enhancement techniques which, in practice, prove to
substantially reduce the complexity of backtrack below its worst-case value.
Such techniques include backjumping [21], variable ordering [15, 20, 40], value
ordering [16, 23] and learning schemes [14]. Moreover, with some investment
of storage space, the work done on any partial instantiation can be utilized
toward its extension (without redoing the problem afresh), and this reduces the
time complexity to $O(n^2 k^e)$.

In the following sections we will present alternative approaches for solving
the general TCSP. In particular, Section 5 discusses path consistency algorithms
that can be used either as an approximation, or as a preprocessing step before
applying backtracking. Section 6 shows how the topology of the constraint
graph can be exploited to yield more efficient algorithms.

5. Path consistency algorithms

Imposing local consistency among subsets of variables may serve as a
preprocessing step to improve backtrack. Local consistency algorithms, especially path consistency, might also serve as a good approximation scheme which
often yields the minimal network. In this section we study the applicability of
path consistency and its weaker version, directional path consistency, in the
TCSP framework.

Floyd–Warshall's algorithm, used for solving the STP, can be considered a
relaxation algorithm—in every step of the process the label of an edge is
updated by an amount that depends only on the current labels of adjacent
edges. In fact, there is a rich family of similar algorithms [1, 7, 28, 39, 43, 44],
all based on the same principle. Montanari [36] was the first to use such an
algorithm, called *path consistency*, in the context of constraint satisfaction
problems. This was further explored and analyzed by Mackworth [31], and
Mackworth and Freuder [32].

Pursuing its traditional role [31, 36], path consistency in the context of a
TCSP is defined as follows:

Definition 5.1. A path through nodes $i_0, i_1, \ldots, i_m$ is *path consistent* iff for any pair of values, v_0 and v_m, such that $v_m - v_0 \in T_{i_0 i_m}$, there exists a sequence of values, $v_1, \ldots, v_{m-1}$, such that $v_1 - v_0 \in T_{i_0 i_1}$, $v_2 - v_1 \in T_{i_1 i_2}, \ldots,$ and $v_m - v_{m-1} \in T_{i_{m-1} i_m}$. A *network* is path consistent iff every path is consistent.

Using the operations $\oplus$ and $\otimes$ (denoting intersection and composition), Montanari's path consistency algorithm (equivalent to Mackworth's [31] PC-1) is shown in Fig. 6. The algorithm imposes local consistency among triplets of variables until a fixed point is reached, or until some constraint becomes empty indicating an inconsistent network. Clearly, the algorithm computes a network which is equivalent to the original one. For discrete-domain CSPs, Montanari showed that the algorithm terminates and that the resulting network is indeed path consistent. In our case, due to the continuous domains of TCSPs, one cannot guarantee that the algorithm terminates. It is clear, however, that running the algorithm indefinitely will result in a limit network. Each step of the algorithm yields a tighter network, and since the network is bounded below by the minimal network, a limit point is assured. Moreover, analysis shows that for all practical purposes PC-1 terminates in a finite number of steps. This will be shown in two parts; first for STPs, then for general TCSPs.

Comparing Figs. 4 and 6, PC-1 is seen to be a generalization of the all-pairs-shortest-paths algorithm. When applied to an STP, the relaxation step that updates T_{ij} amounts to two local operations of updating the shortest path length, d_{ij}, in Floyd–Warshall's algorithm. Therefore:

Theorem 5.2. *Applying PC-1 to an STP network is identical to applying Floyd–Warshall's algorithm to its distance graph.*

An immediate corollary of this theorem is that PC-1 terminates and produces a path consistent network. See also [11, 31, 36] for additional relationships between shortest paths algorithms and path consistency.

Regarding general TCSPs, two questions must be addressed; first, does PC-1 terminate and compute a path consistent network and, second, is the resulting

---

Algorithm PC-1
1. repeat
2. $S \leftarrow T$;
3.   for $k := 1$ to n do
4.   for $i, j := 1$ to n do
5. $T_{ij} \leftarrow T_{ij} \oplus T_{ik} \otimes T_{kj}$, and
6.   if $T_{ij} = \emptyset$ then exit (the network is inconsistent);
7. until $S = T$;

Fig. 6. A path consistency algorithm.

network minimal. We will next show that the answer to the first question is affirmative while the answer to the second is negative.

It is simple to show that PC-1 terminates for *integral* TCSPs, where the extreme points of all intervals are integers. This is so because each intersection operation at Step 5 must tighten a constraint by an integral amount. For nonintegral TCSPs, the same argument holds if the extreme points are rational numbers (these will be called *rational* TCSPs); we simply multiply all quantities by the greatest common divisor of the extreme points. This was shown more formally by Ladkin [26]. Thus, since all practical problems are expressible by rational numbers, PC-1 can be regarded as terminating. Once termination has been ascertained, the path consistency of the resulting network can be established by straightforward application of Montanari's proof [36]; the continuous nature of temporal domains plays no role. Summarizing, we have:

Theorem 5.3. *Algorithm PC-1 computes a path consistent network.*

Now that we have established that PC-1 terminates and computes a path consistent network, the question arises whether the resulting network is minimal. Montanari showed that when the constraints obey the distributivity property (i.e., that composition distributes over intersection), any path consistent network is both minimal and decomposable. Moreover, in such a case only one application of the main loop (Steps 1–7) is sufficient for reaching the fixed point. When constraints are defined by one interval (the STP case), the distributivity property holds and indeed, for this case, the path consistent network is minimal (Corollary 3.5), decomposable (Theorem 3.3), and requires only one iteration (see Floyd–Warshall's algorithm). Unfortunately, distributivity does not hold for the multi-interval TCSP, as can be seen in the following example:

Example 5.4. Consider the network shown in Fig. 7 where, for convenience, both directions of each edge are explicitly given. There are two paths from node 1 to node 3, representing the constraints $T_{13} = \{[25, 50]\}$ and $S_{13} = \{[0, 30], [40, 50]\}$ (the latter is obtained by composing T_{12} with T_{23}). Perform-

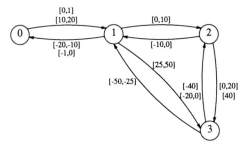

Fig. 7. A nondistributive network.

ing intersection first, and then composition, we get

$$T_{01} \otimes (T_{13} \oplus S_{13}) = \{[0, 1], [10, 20]\} \otimes \{[25, 30], [40, 50]\}$$
$$= \{[25, 31], [35, 70]\} . \tag{5.1}$$

Performing composition first, and then intersection, results in

$$(T_{01} \otimes T_{13}) \oplus (T_{01} \otimes S_{13}) = \{[0, 31], [40, 51], [10, 50], [50, 70]\}$$
$$\oplus \{[25, 51], [35, 70]\}$$
$$= \{[25, 70]\} . \tag{5.2}$$

Clearly, distributivity does not hold. Indeed, if we apply path consistency to this network then after one iteration we have $T_{03} = \{[25, 70]\}$, whereas in the minimal network (shown in Table 4), $M_{03} = \{[25, 31], [35, 70]\}$. Interestingly, another application of the main loop does result in a fixed point which is also the minimal network (see Section 6).

In general CSPs it is well known that path consistency may not converge to the minimal network. The next example (tailored after Montanari [36]) will demonstrate that this phenomenon persists also in temporal problems; path consistency does not even detect inconsistency.

Example 5.5. Consider the 3-coloring problem on K_4, the complete graph of four nodes. The problem is obviously inconsistent and at the same time path consistent—every set of three nodes can be 3-colored. Translating this problem into TCSP notation, as in the proof of Theorem 4.1, yields the desired example. The problem consists of four variables, $X_1, \ldots, X_4$, each having a domain $\{[1], [2], [3]\}$, connected by six binary constraints

$$X_j - X_i \in \{[-2], [-1], [1], [2]\} , \tag{5.3}$$

Table 4
The minimal network of Example 5.4.

	0	1	2	3
0	[0]	[0, 1] [10, 20]	[0, 30]	[25, 31] [35, 70]
1	[−20, −10] [−1, 0]	[0]	[0, 10]	[25, 30] [40, 50]
2	[−30, 0]	[−10, 0]	[0]	[15, 20] [40]
3	[−70, −35] [−31, −25]	[−50, −40] [−30, −25]	[−40] [−20, −15]	[0]

for $i, j = 1, \ldots, 4$, $i \neq j$. The resulting network is already path consistent, yet PC-1 will fail to detect its inconsistency.

A more efficient path consistency algorithm is the temporal equivalent of Mackworth's PC-2 [31], shown in Fig. 8. The function REVISE$((i, k, j))$ updates T_{ij} by considering the length-2 path from i to j through k,

$$T_{ij} \leftarrow T_{ij} \oplus T_{ik} \otimes T_{kj} , \tag{5.4}$$

and returns true if T_{ij} has been modified. The function RELATED-PATHS$((i, k, j))$ returns the set of length-2 paths that need to be considered if T_{ij} is changed. The details of RELATED-PATHS are given in [31].

For discrete CSPs, path consistency can be achieved in time polynomial in n, the number of variables, and k, the maximum domain size [32]. We will now show that the temporal mirror of PC-2 achieves path consistency in $O(n^3 R^3)$, where R is the maximum *range* of any constraint (expressed in terms of the coarsest possible time units).

Definition 5.6. Let $T_{ij} = \{[a_1, b_1], \ldots, [a_n, b_n]\}$. The *range* of T_{ij} is $b_n - a_1$. The range of a TCSP is the maximum range over all constraints.

Theorem 5.7. *Temporal path consistency can be achieved in* $O(n^3 R)$ *relaxation steps and* $O(n^3 R^3)$ *arithmetic operations, where R is the range of the TCSP expressed in the coarsest possible time units.*

Proof. The worst-case running time of PC-2 occurs when every constraint interval is decreased by only one time unit each time it is tightened by REVISE. In this case, if R is the maximum constraint range, each constraint might be updated $O(R)$ times. Also, in the worst case, when a constraint is modified $O(n)$ paths are added to Q (see [31]). Thus, if we use the number of relaxation steps (calls to REVISE) as the complexity measure, then, since there are $O(n^2)$ constraints, the total complexity of PC-2 is $O(n^3 R)$. A more realistic measure would be the number of arithmetic operations. Each relaxation operation, $A \oplus B \otimes C$, where l, m and n are the number of intervals in A, B and C,

---

Algorithm PC-2
1. $Q \leftarrow \{(i, k, j) \mid (i < j) \text{ and } (k \neq i, j)\}$;
2. while Q is not empty do
3.   select and delete a path (i, k, j) from Q, and
4.   if REVISE$((i, k, j))$ then $Q \leftarrow Q \cup$ RELATED-PATHS$((i, k, j))$;

Fig. 8. PC-2—a more efficient path consistency algorithm.

respectively, involves $O(l + m \times n)$ arithmetic operations. Thus, since each relaxation step may involve as many as $O(R^2)$ operations, the total time is $O(n^3 R^3)$. □

For comparison to chronological backtracking, note that R must be at least as large as k (the number of intervals per constraint). However, $O(k^e)$ may reflect a lower complexity than $O(R^3)$, in case the edges are labeled by a few intervals.

Although path consistency algorithms are not guaranteed to compute the minimal network, they often provide a practical alternative and a complementary approach to the decomposition scheme. Moreover, they are readily amenable to parallel and distributed computation. In preliminary experiments on small random problems (each consisting of 5–7 variables), PC-1 always found the minimal network.[4] On the basis of these experiments, it appears that path consistency will substantially reduce the amount of work done by backtracking. To fully assess the benefits of the path consistency scheme, full-scale experimental studies should be undertaken.

Some problems may benefit from a weaker version of path consistency, called *directional path consistency* [16], that can be enforced more efficiently.

Definition 5.8 [16]. Let d be an ordering on the variables, and let X_i precede X_j in d iff $i < j$. A constraint graph, G, is *directional path consistent* with respect to d, if for every pair of values, v_i and v_j, such that $v_j - v_i \in T_{ij}$, and for every $k > i, j$, there exists a value v_k such that $v_k - v_i \in T_{ik}$ and $v_j - v_k \in T_{kj}$.

Given a TCSP, T, its associated constraint graph, $G = (V, E)$, and an ordering, d, directional path consistency can be achieved by algorithm DPC, shown in Fig. 9, which is the temporal counterpart of that given in [16].

DPC is similar to PC-1, but unlike the latter, it is a single pass algorithm. Note also that in Step 4, the set of edges E is increased dynamically by the relaxation operation of Step 3. The network defined by the final set of edges is called the *induced graph*.

Algorithm DPC
1. for $k := n$ down to 1 by -1 do
2.   for all $i, j < k$ such that $(i, k), (j, k) \in E$ do
3. $T_{ij} \leftarrow T_{ij} \oplus T_{ik} \otimes T_{kj}$, and
4. $E \leftarrow E \cup (i, j)$, and
5.   if $T_{ij} = \emptyset$ then exit (the network is inconsistent);

Fig. 9. DPC—an algorithm enforcing directional path consistency.

[4] Yaara Levi and Margalit Pinkas, personal communication.

If one of the constraints becomes empty (at Step 5), then the original network must have been inconsistent. However, as in the case of nontemporal CSPs, we are not guaranteed that the algorithm will always detect an inconsistency if one exists. Next we show that such a guarantee can be assured for STPs.

Definition 5.9. Let T be a TCSP. A cycle $i_0, \ldots, i_k = i_0$ is called *valid* if and only if

$$0 \in T_{i_0,i_1} \otimes \cdots \otimes T_{i_{k-1},i_k} . \tag{5.5}$$

Lemma 5.10. *A given STP, T, is consistent if and only if all the cycles in its constraint graph are valid.*

Proof. See Appendix B. $\square$

Theorem 5.11. *Given an STP, T, algorithm DPC halts at Step 5 if and only if the network is inconsistent.*

Proof. The *only if* part is trivial; we will show the *if* part. Suppose the network is inconsistent; then, according to Lemma 5.10, there exists an invalid cycle C. Let the nodes of C be the set $\{i_1, \ldots, i_k\}$, and order it along d, namely, i_j will be processed after i_k whenever $j < k$. We next prove the following lemma.

Lemma 5.12. *For all j, $0 \le j \le k - 3$, when node i_{k-j} is about to be processed (Step 1), there exists an invalid cycle C_j, consisting of nodes $\{i_1, \ldots, i_{k-j}\}$.*

Proof. By induction on j. The lemma holds for $j = 0$ because the cycle $C_0 = C$ was assumed to be invalid in the original network, and DPC can only render constraints tighter. Thus, C_0 must remain invalid when node i_k is processed.

   Assume the lemma holds for $j - 1$, $j > 0$. By the induction hypothesis, when node i_{k-j+1} was about to be processed, there was an invalid cycle C_{k-j+1} consisting of nodes $\{i_1, \ldots, i_{k-j+1}\}$. Let s and r be the neighbors of i_{k-j+1} in C_{k-j+1}, and let P_{rs} be the path from r to s in C_{k-j+1}. When node i_{k-j+1} is processed, the constraint T_{sr} is tightened, and the newly created cycle is

$$C_{k-j} = (s, r) \cup P_{rs} . \tag{5.6}$$

The constraint along C_{k-j} is tighter than the constraint along C_{k-j+1}, and thus C_{k-j} is invalid. Between the time that i_{k-j+1} is processed until the time i_{k-j} is processed, DPC further tightens the constraints along C_{k-j}. Thus, the cycle remains invalid while i_{k-j} is being processed. $\square$

   According to Lemma 5.12, when node i_3 is about to be processed, there exists an invalid cycle C_3, consisting of nodes i_1, i_2 and i_3. Let $T_{i_1,i_3} = \{[a, b]\}$, $T_{i_3,i_2} = \{[c, d]\}$ and $T_{i_2,i_1} = \{[e, f]\}$. At Step 3 the constraint T_{i_1,i_2} is updated such that

$$T_{i_1,i_2} = \{[\max(-f, a + c), \min(-e, b + d)]\} \,. \tag{5.7}$$

Since C_3 is invalid, $0 \not\in [a + c + e, b + d + f]$. If $a + c + e > 0$, then $a + c > -e$, and $T_{i_1,i_2} = \emptyset$. Otherwise, $b + d + f < 0$, or $b + d < -f$, and thus $T_{i_1,i_2} = \emptyset$. Hence, at Step 5 the algorithm must halt. □

It is well known that for general CSPs, directional path consistency can be achieved more efficiently than full path consistency [16]; instead of $O(n^3)$, DPC runs in $O(nW^*(d)^2)$ time, where $W^*(d)$ is the maximum number of parents that a node possesses in the induced graph. To assess the savings in the context of temporal problems, recall that each relaxation step involves $O(R^2)$ arithmetic operations, thus yielding a worst-case bound of $O(nW^*(d)^2R^2)$ operations. Another upper bound emerges from the fact that with every node processed the number of intervals recorded may increase by a factor not greater than k, thus giving a total of at most $O(k^n)$ intervals and arithmetic operations in any relaxation step. Hence, the upper bound is $O(nW^*(d)^2k^n)$.

For STPs, each relaxation step involves a constant number of arithmetic operations, and thus consistency for STPs can be determined in $O(nW^*(d)^2)$, in contrast with $O(n^3)$ needed for full path consistency. $W^*(d)$ could be substantially lower than n, and can be found in time $O(|V| + |E|)$ prior to the actual processing [5, 9, 45].

Note that directional path consistency is generally speaking weaker than full path consistency and, hence, might lead to a higher number of dead ends for backtrack. However, the use of directional path consistency yields more dramatic savings if it is embedded within backtracking as the consistency checking routine, "Consistent-STP" (Fig. 5). Instead of checking consistency by the $O(n^3)$ Floyd–Warshall algorithm, we can reduce the search effort of backtrack by a factor of roughly $(n/W^*(d))^2$ using DPC. In the next section we characterize a class of problems that gain fuller benefit from the efficiency of directional path consistency.

6. Network-based algorithms

So far we have presented techniques for processing networks of a general structure. The topology of the constraint graph did not play any role in the choice of the solution technique. However, considering the topological features of the constraint network may guide us, as they do in nontemporal CSPs, in selecting efficient solution methods, having lower worst-case complexity than naive backtracking.

We first consider the task of finding a single solution to TCSPs. The infinite domains associated with temporal problems prevent us from searching exhaustively through the space of possible scenarios. Instead, we must seek ways of constructing a solution in a guided manner. If the network is decomposable (such as in the case of STPs), a solution can be assembled incrementally, without backtracking, under any ordering we choose. If the network is not decomposable, the feasibility of achieving a backtrack-free solution relies on the topology of the constraint graph. Freuder [20] and Dechter and Pearl [16] have identified sufficient conditions for a network to yield a backtrack-free solution, invoking the notion of higher-order consistency. To demonstrate, we will focus on a class of networks that admit a particularly efficient method when applied to temporal problems. This class is called *series–parallel networks*, and is equivalent to the *regular width-2* networks of [16].

Definition 6.1. A network is said to be *series–parallel* with respect to a pair of nodes, i and j, if it can be reduced to the edge (i, j) by repeated application of the following *reduction* operation: select a node of degree 2 or less, remove it from the network, and connect its neighbors (unless they are connected already). If the network is series–parallel with respect to *any* pair of nodes, it is called a series–parallel network.

Testing whether a network is series–parallel requires $O(|V|)$ time and, as a by-product, the testing algorithm produces an ordering d for which $W^*(d) = 2$, that corresponds to an admissible sequence of reduction operations [4, 50]. It can be shown [16] that enforcing directional path consistency, in an ordering opposite to d, renders such networks backtrack-free, and computes the minimal constraint between the first two nodes in d. If the network is inconsistent, some constraint will become empty, otherwise, a consistent solution can be constructed in a backtrack-free fashion. Since $W^*(d) = 2$, DPC runs in $O(nK)$ time, where K is the maximum number of intervals labeling any edge in the induced graph. The solution construction phase requires an additional $O(nK)$ arithmetic operations.

Montanari [36] showed that full path consistency computes the minimal constraint on every pair of nodes, relative to which the network is series–parallel. In this respect, running full path consistency can be viewed as running DPC along several orderings in parallel, giving any pair of nodes a chance of being the first.

Illustration. Consider the network of Example 1.1. The network is obviously series–parallel, admitting any sequence of reduction operations. Applying DPC in the ordering $d = (0, 1, 2, 3, 4)$ results in the network shown in Fig. 10.

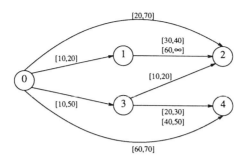

Fig. 10. A directional path consistent network of Example 1.1.

Since no constraint becomes empty, the network is consistent, and a solution can be constructed backtrack-free along *d*. Moreover, since the network is series–parallel with respect to any pair of nodes, full path consistency computes the full minimal network (see Section 5).

A generalization of directional path consistency, called *adaptive consistency* [16, 17], can render any network backtrack-free by recording higher-order constraints on the neighbors of the nodes processed. This method, although it exhibits a low worst-case complexity in general CSPs, turns out to be ineffective in temporal problems, primarily due to difficulties in storing and processing higher-order interval constraints.

Another approach which exploits the structure of the constraint graph, involves decomposition into *nonseparable components*. We shall show that this can facilitate finding both a consistent solution and the minimal network.

Definition 6.2 (Even [18]). A connected graph $G = (V, E)$ is said to have a *separation vertex* v (sometimes also called an *articulation* point) if there exist vertices a and b, $a \neq v$ and $b \neq v$, such that all the paths connecting a and b pass through v. In this case we also say that v separates a from b. A graph which has a separation vertex is called *separable*, and one which has none is called *nonseparable*. Let $V' \subseteq V$. The induced subgraph $G' = (V', E')$ is called a *nonseparable component* if G' is nonseparable and if for every larger V'', $V' \subset V'' \subseteq V$, the induced subgraph $G'' = (V'', E'')$ is separable.

Definition 6.3 (Even [18]). Let $C_1, \ldots, C_m$ be the nonseparable components of the connected graph $G = (V, E)$, and let $s_1, \ldots, s_p$ be its separating vertices. The *superstructure* of G, $\bar{G} = (\bar{V}, \bar{E})$, is defined as follows:

$$\bar{V} = \{s_1, \ldots, s_p\} \cup \{C_1, \ldots, C_m\}, \tag{6.1}$$

$$\bar{E} = \{(s_i, C_j) \mid s_i \text{ is a vertex of } C_j \text{ in } G\}. \tag{6.2}$$

It is well known that the superstructure is a tree. The nonseparable components and their superstructure can be found in time $O(|E|)$ (see [18]).

Definition 6.4. Let $G = (V, E)$ be a constraint graph of a TCSP, T, and let $C = (V', E')$ be a nonseparable component of G. The *minimal network of component C*, M_C, is the minimal network of the TCSP defined by C.

Theorem 6.5. *Let M be the minimal network of a consistent TCSP, T, and let M_C be the minimal network of a nonseparable component, $C = (V', E')$, in the constraint graph, $G = (V, E)$, of T. Then, for all $i, j \in V'$, $M_{ij} = (M_C)_{ij}$.*

Proof. Clearly, $M_{ij} \subseteq (M_C)_{ij}$. To prove $(M_C)_{ij} \subseteq M_{ij}$, we show that every value in $(M_C)_{ij}$ also appears in M_{ij}. Let $v \in (M_C)_{ij}$. There exists a labeling, L_1, of C, having minimal network M_{L_1}, in which $v \in (M_{L_1})_{ij}$. Since T is consistent, the TCSP defined by $G - C = (V, E - E')$ is also consistent, and thus there exists a consistent labeling, L_2, of $G - C$. Consider the labeling L whose restrictions to C and $G - C$ are L_1 and L_2, respectively. Let T_L be the STP corresponding to L. T_L is consistent; otherwise, according to Lemma 5.10 it contains an invalid cycle. This cycle must be entirely contained in either C or $G - C$, contradicting the consistency of either L_1 or L_2. Let M_L be the minimal network of T_L. The distance graph of T_L shows that $(M_L)_{ij} = (M_{L_1})_{ij}$, because the shortest paths lengths within C are not affected by the edges of $G - C$. Hence, $v \in (M_L)_{ij}$, thus $v \in M_{ij}$. $\square$

Theorem 6.5 suggests an efficient algorithm for determining consistency and computing the minimal network of a general network. We first find the nonseparable components, $C_1, \ldots, C_m$, and then solve each one of them independently. If all the components are found to be consistent, then the entire network is consistent, and the minimal networks of the individual components coincide with the overall minimal network. If we use backtracking to solve each of the components, then the worst time complexity of this method is $O(nr^3k^c)$, where r and c denote the largest number of nodes and the largest number of edges in any component, respectively; and k, as before, denotes the maximum number of intervals labeling any edge in the graph. When the topology of any component admits a special, more efficient algorithm, it can be applied directly to that component without affecting the solution of the rest of the problem.

We still must find the minimal constraints on pairs that reside in two different components. This will be determined by Theorem 6.6, after demonstrating how a solution can be constructed to a given TCSP T. We start by finding a solution to the nonseparable component C_0 that contains node 0. All the separation vertices that are connected to C_0 in the superstructure, $\bar{G}$, are instantiated. Then we choose an instantiated separation vertex i, and find a solution to any nonseparable component C_i that is connected to i in $\bar{G}$, and whose vertices have not been instantiated yet. We continue in this fashion until all the variables are instantiated. Since $\bar{G}$ is a tree, we are guaranteed that once a partial solution of some component has been established, it does not need to be revised.

Theorem 6.6. *Let $G = (V, E)$ be the constraint graph of a given TCSP. Let i and j be two nodes that reside in different nonseparable components of G, namely, $i \in C_i$ and $j \in C_j$. Let P be the unique path*

$$P: \quad C_i = C_{i_1}, i_1, C_{i_2}, i_2, \ldots, i_k, C_{i_{k+1}} = C_j , \tag{6.3}$$

that connects C_i and C_j in the superstructure of G. Then,

$$M_{ij} = M_{i,i_1} \otimes M_{i_1,i_2} \cdots \otimes M_{i_{k-1},i_k} \otimes M_{i_k,j} . \tag{6.4}$$

Proof. It suffices to show that

$$M_{i,i_1} \otimes M_{i_1,i_2} \cdots \otimes M_{i_{k-1},i_k} \otimes M_{i_k,j} \subseteq M_{ij} . \tag{6.5}$$

Let

$$v \in M_{i,i_1} \otimes M_{i_1,i_2} \cdots \otimes M_{i_{k-1},i_k} \otimes M_{i_k,j} . \tag{6.6}$$

By definition of the composition operation, there exist values $v_0, \ldots, v_k$, such that $v_0 \in M_{i,i_1}$, $v_j \in M_{i_j,i_{j+1}}$ for $j = 1, \ldots, k-1$, $v_k \in M_{i_k,j}$, and

$$\sum_{j=0}^{k} v_j = v . \tag{6.7}$$

By the minimality of the individual minimal networks, we can construct a solution $X = (x_1, \ldots, x_n)$, that satisfies

$$x_{i_1} - x_i = v_0 , \tag{6.8}$$

$$x_{i_{j+1}} - x_{i_j} = v_j , \tag{6.9}$$

for $j = 1, \ldots, k-1$, and

$$x_j - x_{i_k} = v_k . \tag{6.10}$$

Hence,

$$x_j - x_i = v , \tag{6.11}$$

and thus $v \in M_{ij}$. $\square$

The cost of computing a minimal constraint, M_{ij}, using the above method, is $O(k^{cd})$; where c is the size of the largest component that resides along the path connecting C_i and C_j, and d is the length of that path. An alternative upper bound is given by $O(k^e)$. Thus, a full recovery of the minimal network costs $O[n^2 k^{\min(cn,e)}]$.

Illustration. Consider the network of Example 5.4 (Fig. 7). There are two nonseparable components: $C_1 = \{0, 1\}$ and $C_2 = \{1, 2, 3\}$. Component C_1 is a tree and thus already minimal. To compute the minimal network of C_2, we can either apply path consistency (note that C_2 is series–parallel with respect to any pair of nodes) or solve separately the two possible labelings. If M is the minimal network then, by Theorem 6.5:

$$M_{01} = Z_{01}, \qquad M_{12} = Z_{12}, \qquad M_{13} = Z_{13}, \qquad M_{23} = Z_{23}, \qquad (6.12)$$

where Z_{ij} are constraints taken from the minimal networks of the components. The rest of the network can be computed using (6.4):

$$M_{02} = M_{01} \otimes M_{12}, \tag{6.13}$$

$$M_{03} = M_{01} \otimes M_{13}. \tag{6.14}$$

Recall that in this example path consistency does compute the minimal network (see Section 5). This phenomenon can be explained by Theorems 6.5 and 6.6. We already noted that path consistency computes the minimal networks of both components. We now show that in general, this should suffice for computing the minimal constraints on edges that go across components. When path consistency terminates, the computed constraints, T_{ij}, satisfy:

$$T_{02} \subseteq T_{01} \otimes T_{12} \tag{6.15}$$

and

$$T_{03} \subseteq T_{01} \otimes T_{13}. \tag{6.16}$$

Together with (6.12)–(6.14), we get

$$T_{02} \subseteq M_{02}, \tag{6.17}$$

$$T_{03} \subseteq M_{03}. \tag{6.18}$$

Since M is minimal, $T_{02} = M_{02}$ and $T_{03} = M_{03}$; namely, path consistency computes the full minimal network.

Finally, we note that another network-based approach for solving general CSPs, the *cycle-cutset method* [14], cannot be employed beneficially in temporal problems. The reason is that the backtracking used in the solution of TCSPs instantiates arcs, rather than variables, and many such instantiations are needed to decompose the original network.

7. Relations to other formalisms

In this section we relate the TCSP model to two other models of temporal reasoning—Allen's interval algebra and Vilain and Kautz's point algebra. We show how the constraints in these representation schemes can be encoded within the TCSP model. To facilitate such encoding, we allow the interval representation of our constraints to include open and semi-open intervals, with the obvious effect on the definitions of the union and intersection operations. Similarly, an interval that results from a composition operation may be open on one side or on both sides, depending on the operands. For example,

$$\{[1,2],(6,8)\} \otimes \{[0,3),(12,15]\}$$
$$= \{[1,5),(6,11),(13,17],(18,23)\} . \tag{7.1}$$

It is easy to verify that all our theorems still hold with this extended provision.

Any constraint network in Vilain and Kautz's point algebra [49] is a special case of a TCSP, lacking metric information. It can be viewed as a CSP involving a set of variables, $X_1, \ldots, X_n$, and binary constraints of the form $X_i R X_j$, where

$$R \in \{<, \leq, >, \geq, =, \neq\} . \tag{7.2}$$

The translation into TCSP is straightforward. Constraints of the form $X_j < X_i$ and $X_j \leq X_i$ are expressed by the interval representations $T_{ij} = \{(-\infty, 0)\}$ and $T_{ij} = \{(-\infty, 0]\}$, respectively. The constraint $X_i = X_j$ translates into $T_{ij} = \{[0]\}$. The only relation that needs to be represented by a disjunction is $X_i \neq X_j$, translated into $T_{ij} = \{(-\infty, 0), (0, \infty)\}$.

Vilain and Kautz have addressed the tasks of determining consistency and computing the minimal network for problems expressed in the point algebra. They suggested the use of path consistency for computing the minimal network, which turned out to be insufficient [47]. Van Beek [47] addressed a subset of the point algebra, called PA, which excludes $\neq$. He showed that constraint networks in PA may be solved in time $O(n^3)$ by applying path consistency. This follows immediately from the TCSP representation, since every constraint network in PA is equivalent to an STP with edges labeled by intervals from

$$\{(-\infty, 0), (-\infty, 0], [0], [0, \infty), (0, \infty)\} .\tag{7.3}$$

Thus, when the constraints are taken from (7.3), path consistency for TCSP coincides with path consistency for PA. Moreover, algorithms devised for solving STPs' tasks reduce to equivalent, often simpler algorithms for solving the same tasks in PA. For example, directional path consistency can determine consistency in PA in $O(nW^*(d)^2)$ operations, which amounts to linear time when $W^*(d)$ is bounded.

The full point algebra, including the inequality constraint $\neq$, translates into TCSPs with disjunctions, for which our general methods can be applied, and the special structure of the constraints exploited. In [47] it is shown that enforcing 4-consistency suffices for computing the minimal network in the point algebra. This result takes special advantage of the nonmetric nature of the relations in (7.2). More recently, it has been found that path consistency is sufficient for determining consistency in the full point algebra [35]. This establishes an $O(n^3)$ complexity for general networks in Vilain and Kautz's point algebra.[5] A more efficient method has been reported recently by Van Beek [48], requiring $O(n^2)$ time (see also [35]).

In contrast, Allen's interval algebra [2] cannot be translated into binary TCSPs. It can be viewed as a CSP involving a set of variables, $X_1, \ldots, X_n$, whose domains are pairs of time points, representing the beginning and ending times of temporal events. The allowed relationships between pairs of variables are taken from the set

$$\{before, meets, overlaps, during, starts, finishes\} ,\tag{7.4}$$

their inverses, and the equality relation—a total of 13 relations. The translation into TCSP introduces nonbinary constraints. For example, the constraint

$$A \ (before \lor after) \ B ,\tag{7.5}$$

where intervals A and B are given by $A = [X_1, X_2]$ and $B = [X_3, X_4]$, cannot be encoded by a binary TCSP constraint [49]; it requires the 4-ary constraint

$$(X_2 < X_3) \lor (X_4 < X_1) .\tag{7.6}$$

Problems involving higher-order constraints can be expressed as disjunctions of STPs, and solutions can be assembled by taking the union of the individual STP solutions. Although the number of such subproblems may be large, advantage can be taken of the simple procedures available for solving each

[5] We have recently learned that this had also been established by Ladkin and Maddux, The algebra of constraint satisfaction problems and temporal reasoning, Tech. Rept., Kestrel Institute, Palo Alto, CA (1988).

STP. It seems likely, however, that unless metric constraints are specified, the representation suggested in [2] can be handled more conveniently.

8. Summary and conclusions

This paper provides a formal framework for dealing with temporal constraints, encouraging the transference of algorithms and theoretical results developed for general constraint satisfaction problems. We distinguish between simple temporal problems (STPs) and general temporal problems, the former admitting at most one interval constraint on any pair of time points. We show that the STP can be solved in polynomial time, using the well-known Floyd–Warshall's all-pairs-shortest-paths algorithm. For general TCSPs, we present a decomposition scheme that provides answers to the reasoning tasks considered, but its computational efficiency, in the worst case, might be limited. The decomposition scheme might be improved by traditional constraint satisfaction techniques, such as backjumping, learning, various ordering schemes and preprocessing techniques. We studied the applicability of path consistency algorithms as preprocessing of temporal problems, demonstrated their termination and bounded their complexity; they seem to offer a practical compromise in very complex problems. In particular, the more efficient directional path consistency was shown to retain the essential properties of full path consistency in determining consistency for STPs and in enhancing backtrack search of general TCSPs. Among the specialized network-based algorithms, only the one employing decomposition into nonseparable components was found applicable to TCSPs. It offers a method for computing the minimal network in time exponential in the largest nonseparable component.

We see the main application of our framework to be in temporal reasoning tasks involving metric information, namely, expressions involving absolute time differences (e.g. "John came home an hour after Mary"). In this respect, the expressiveness of our language supercedes that of Allen's interval algebra. However, it can be considered weaker than the interval algebra, being limited to problems involving constraints on pairs of time points. Our framework subsumes Vilain and Kautz's point algebra as a special case, and provides an arsenal of techniques and intuitions for solving problems in this domain. The natural extension of this work is to explore TCSPs with higher-order expressions (e.g., "John drives to work at least 30 minutes more than Fred does"; $X_2 - X_1 + 30 \leqslant X_4 - X_3$), with the aim of exploiting the unique algebraic features provided by the linearity and continuity of temporal constraints. An extension of this work, integrating our quantitative analysis with the qualitative framework of Allen's algebra can be found in a recent article.[6]

---

[6] I. Meiri, Combining qualitative and quantitative constraints in temporal reasoning, in: *Proceedings AAAI-91*, Anaheim CA (1991).

Appendix A. Proof of Corollary 3.5

Corollary 3.5. *Given a consistent STP, T, the equivalent STP, M, defined by*

$$\forall i,j, \quad M_{ij} = \{[-d_{ji}, d_{ij}]\}, \tag{A.1}$$

is the minimal network representation of T.

Proof. We will show that M is the minimal network by showing that it cannot be tightened any more; in other words, starting with the assignment $X_0 = 0$, for any $d \in [-d_{ji}, d_{ij}]$ there exists a solution $X = (x_0, \ldots, x_n)$ in which $x_j - x_i = d$.
  Case 1.

$$d \leq d_{0j} - d_{0i}. \tag{A.2}$$

According to Corollary 3.4, $X_i = d_{0i}$ is a feasible value. Clearly,

$$d_{0i} + d \geq d_{0i} - d_{ji}, \tag{A.3}$$

and since

$$d_{ji} \leq d_{j0} + d_{0i}, \tag{A.4}$$

we get

$$d_{0i} + d \geq -d_{j0}. \tag{A.5}$$

Together with (A.2) we have

$$-d_{j0} \leq d_{0i} + d \leq d_{0j}. \tag{A.6}$$

Therefore, the assignment $X_j = d_{0i} + d$ satisfies the unary domain constraints on variable X_j, and

$$\{X_0 = 0, X_i = d_{0i}, X_j = d_{0i} + d\} \tag{A.7}$$

satisfies the constraints applicable to $\{X_0, X_i, X_j\}$. By Theorem 3.3 this partial assignment can be extended to a solution.
  Case 2.

$$d \geq d_{0j} - d_{0i}. \tag{A.8}$$

According to Corollary 3.4, $X_j = d_{0j}$ is a feasible value. Clearly,

$$d_{0j} - d \geq d_{0j} - d_{ij}, \tag{A.9}$$

and since

$$d_{ij} \leq d_{i0} + d_{0j} \,, \tag{A.10}$$

we get

$$d_{0j} - d \geq -d_{i0} \,. \tag{A.11}$$

Together with (A.8) we have

$$-d_{i0} \leq d_{0j} - d \leq d_{0i} \,. \tag{A.12}$$

Therefore, the assignment $X_i = d_{0j} - d$ satisfies the unary domain constraints on variable X_i, and

$$\{X_0 = 0, \, X_i = d_{0j} - d, \, X_j = d_{0j}\} \tag{A.13}$$

satisfies the constraints applicable to $\{X_0, X_i, X_j\}$. By Theorem 3.3, this partial assignment can be extended to a solution.   □

Appendix B. Proof of Lemma 5.10

Lemma 5.10. *A given STP, T, is consistent if and only if all the cycles in its constraint graph are valid.*

Proof. If the network is consistent, then all the cycles are valid, since if there was an invalid cycle $C, i_0, \ldots, i_k = i_0$, then the path constraint along C would yield

$$X_{i_0} - X_{i_0} \neq 0 \,, \tag{B.1}$$

reflecting inconsistency.

Conversely, assume that all the cycles are valid. We will show that the network is consistent. According to Theorem 3.1 we only need to show that there is no negative cycle in the corresponding distance graph. Suppose there was such a negative cycle, C, consisting of nodes $i_0, \ldots, i_k = i_0$, and edge weights $a_{0,1}, a_{1,2}, \ldots, a_{k-1,k} = a_{k-1,0}$. Since C is negative, we have

$$\sum_{j=1}^{k} a_{i_{j-1}, i_j} < 0 \,. \tag{B.2}$$

Moreover, from (3.1)–(3.3) we obtain

$$-a_{i_j, i_{j-1}} \leq a_{i_{j-1}, i_j} \tag{B.3}$$

for $j = 1, \ldots, k$. Thus, combining (B.2) and (B.3) yields

$$0 \notin \left[\sum_{j=1}^{k} -a_{i_j, i_{j-1}}, \sum_{j=1}^{k} a_{i_{j-1}, i_j} \right]. \tag{B.4}$$

At the same time, applying the composition along C gives

$$T_{i_0, i_1} \otimes \cdots \otimes T_{i_{k-1}, i_k} = \left[\sum_{j=1}^{k} -a_{i_j, i_{j-1}}, \sum_{j=1}^{k} a_{i_{j-1}, i_j} \right], \tag{B.5}$$

thus rendering C invalid—a contradiction. $\square$

References

[1] A.V. Aho, J.E. Hopcroft and J.D. Ullman, *The Design and Analysis of Computer Algorithms* (Addison-Wesley, Reading, MA, 1974).
[2] J.F. Allen, Maintaining knowledge about temporal intervals, *Commun. ACM* **26** (11) (1983) 832–843.
[3] J.F. Allen, Towards a general theory of action and time, *Artif. Intell.* **23** (2) (1984) 123–154.
[4] S. Arnborg, Efficient algorithms for combinatorial problems on graphs with bounded decomposability—a survey, *BIT* **25** (1985) 2–23.
[5] S. Arnborg, D.G. Corneil and A. Proskurowski, Complexity of finding embeddings in a *k*-tree, *SIAM J. Algebraic Discrete Methods* **8** (2) (1987) 177–184.
[6] B. Aspvall and Y. Shiloach, A polynomial time algorithm for solving systems of linear inequalities with two variables per inequality, *SIAM J. Comput.* **9** (4) (1980) 827–845.
[7] R.C. Backhouse and B.A. Carré, Regular algebra applied to path-finding problems, *J. Inst. Math. Appl.* **15** (1975) 161–186.
[8] C.E. Bell and A. Tate, Use of a longest path algorithm to manage temporal information and restrict search in an automated planner, Working Paper Series No. 85-34, Artificial Intelligence Applications Institute, University of Edinburgh, Scotland (1985).
[9] U. Bertelé and F. Brioschi, *Nonserial Dynamic Programming* (Academic Press, New York, 1972).
[10] G.B. Dantzig, *Linear Programming and Extensions* (Princeton University Press, Princeton, NJ, 1962).
[11] E. Davis, Constraint propagation with interval labels, *Artif. Intell.* **32** (3) (1987) 281–331.
[12] E. Davis, Private communication (1989).
[13] T.L. Dean and D.V. McDermott, Temporal data base management, *Artif. Intell.* **32** (1987) 1–55.
[14] R. Dechter, Enhancement schemes for constraint processing: backjumping, learning, and cutset decomposition, *Artif. Intell.* **41** (3) (1990) 273–312.
[15] R. Dechter and I. Meiri, Experimental evaluation of preprocessing techniques in constraint satisfaction problems, in: *Proceedings IJCAI-89*, Detroit, MI (1989) 271–277.
[16] R. Dechter and J. Pearl, Network-based heuristics for constraint satisfaction problems, *Artif. Intell.* **34** (1) (1987) 1–38.
[17] R. Dechter and J. Pearl, Tree clustering for constraint networks, *Artif. Intell.* **38** (3) (1989) 353–366.
[18] S. Even, *Graph Algorithms* (Computer Science Press, Rockville, MD, 1979).
[19] E.C. Freuder, Synthesizing constraint expressions, *Commun. ACM* **21** (11) (1978) 958–965.
[20] E.C. Freuder, A sufficient condition of backtrack-free search, *J. ACM* **29** (1) (1982) 24–32.
[21] J. Gaschnig, Performance measurement and analysis of certain search algorithms, Tech. Rept. CMU-CS-79-124, Carnegie-Mellon University, Pittsburgh, PA (1979).
[22] S. Hanks and D.V. McDermott, Default reasoning, nonmonotonic logics, and the frame problem, in: *Proceedings AAAI-86*, Philadelphia, PA (1986) 328–333.

[23] R.M. Haralick and G.L. Elliott, Increasing tree search efficiency for constraint satisfaction problems, *Artif. Intell.* **14** (1980) 263–313.

[24] K. Kahn and G.A. Gorry, Mechanizing temporal knowledge, *Artif. Intell.* **9** (1977) 87–108.

[25] L.G. Khachiyan, A polynomial algorithm in linear programming, *Soviet Math. Dokl.* **20** (1979) 191–194.

[26] P.B. Ladkin, Metric constraint satisfaction with intervals, Tech. Rept. TR-89-038, International Computer Science Institute, Berkeley, CA (1989).

[27] P.B. Ladkin and R.D. Maddux, On binary constraint networks, Tech. Rept., Kestrel Institute, Palo Alto, CA (1989).

[28] D.J. Lehmann, Algebraic structures for transitive closure, *Theor. Comput. Sci.* **4** (1977) 59–76.

[29] C.E. Leiserson and J.B. Saxe, A mixed-integer linear programming problem which is efficiently solvable, in: *Proceedings 21st Annual Allerton Conference on Communications, Control, and Computing* (1983) 204–213.

[30] Y.Z. Liao and C.K. Wong, An algorithm to compact a VLSI symbolic layout with mixed constraints, *IEEE Trans. Computer-Aided Design of Integrated Circuits and Systems* **2** (2) (1983) 62–69.

[31] A.K. Mackworth, Consistency in networks of relations, *Artif. Intell.* **8** (1) (1977) 99–118.

[32] A.K. Mackworth and E.C. Freuder, The complexity of some polynomial network consistency algorithms for constraint satisfaction problems, *Artif. Intell.* **25** (1) (1985) 65–74.

[33] J. Malik and T.O. Binford, Reasoning in time and space, in: *Proceedings IJCAI-83*, Karlsruhe, FRG (1983) 343–345.

[34] D.V. McDermott, A temporal logic for reasoning about processes and plans, *Cogn. Sci.* **6** (1982) 101–155.

[35] I. Meiri, Faster constraint satisfaction algorithms for temporal reasoning, Tech. Rept. R-151, UCLA Cognitive Systems Laboratory, Los Angeles, CA (1990).

[36] U. Montanari, Networks of constraints: fundamental properties and applications to picture processing, *Inf. Sci.* **7** (1974) 95–132.

[37] B. Nudel, Consistent-labeling problems and their algorithms: expected-complexities and theory-based heuristics, *Artif. Intell.* **21** (1983) 135–178.

[38] C.H. Papadimitriou and K. Steiglitz, *Combinatorial Optimization: Algorithms and Complexity* (Prentice-Hall, Englewood Cliffs, NJ, 1982).

[39] D.S. Parker, Partial order programming, Tech. Rept. CSD-870067, UCLA, Los Angeles, CA (1987).

[40] P.W. Purdom, Search rearrangement backtracking and polynomial average time, *Artif. Intell.* **21** (1983) 117–133.

[41] Y. Shoham, *Reasoning about Change: Time and Causation from the Standpoint of Artificial Intelligence* (MIT Press, Cambridge, MA, 1988).

[42] R. Shostak, Deciding linear inequalities by computing loop residues, *J. ACM* **28** (4) (1981) 769–779.

[43] R.E. Tarjan, A unified approach to path problems, *J. ACM* **28** (3) (1981) 577–593.

[44] R.E. Tarjan, Fast algorithms for solving path problems, *J. ACM* **28** (3) (1981) 594–614.

[45] R.E. Tarjan and M. Yannakakis, Simple linear-time algorithms to test chordality of graphs, test acyclicity of hypergraphs and selectively reduce acyclic hypergraphs, *SIAM J. Comput.* **13** (3) (1984) 566–579.

[46] R.E. Valdés-Pérez, Spatio-temporal reasoning and linear inequalities, Artificial Intelligence Laboratory, AIM-875, MIT, Cambridge, MA (1986).

[47] P. Van Beek, Approximation algorithms for temporal reasoning, in: *Proceedings IJCAI-89*, Detroit, MI (1989) 1291–1296.

[48] P. Van Beek, Reasoning about qualitative temporal information, in: *Proceedings AAAI-90*, Boston, MA (1990) 728–734.

[49] M. Vilain and H. Kautz, Constraint propagation algorithms for temporal reasoning, in: *Proceedings AAAI-86*, Philadelphia, PA (1986) 377–382.

[50] J.A. Wald and C.J. Colbourn, Steiner trees, partial 2-trees, and minimum IFI networks, *Networks* **13** (1983) 159–167.

Artificial Intelligence 49 (1991) 97–128
Elsevier

Impediments to universal preference-based default theories *

Jon Doyle

Laboratory for Computer Science, Massachusetts Institute of Technology,
545 Technology Square, Cambridge, MA 02139, USA

Michael P. Wellman

Wright Laboratory AI Office, WL/AAA-1, Wright-Patterson AFB, OH 45433, USA

Received November 1989
Revised September 1990

Abstract

Doyle, J. and M.P. Wellman, Impediments to universal preference-based default theories, Artificial Intelligence 49 (1991) 97–128.

Research on nonmonotonic and default reasoning has identified several important criteria for preferring alternative default inferences. The theories of reasoning based on each of these criteria may uniformly be viewed as theories of rational inference, in which the reasoner selects maximally preferred states of belief. Though researchers have noted some cases of apparent conflict between the preferences supported by different theories, it has been hoped that these special theories of reasoning may be combined into a universal logic of nonmonotonic reasoning. We show that the different categories of preferences conflict more than has been realized, and adapt formal results from social choice theory to prove that every universal theory of default reasoning will violate at least one reasonable principle of rational reasoning. Our results can be interpreted as demonstrating that, within the preferential framework, we cannot expect much improvement on the rigid lexicographic priority mechanisms that have been proposed for conflict resolution.

1. Introduction

The proliferation of formalisms for nonmonotonic inference [16] attests to a diverse set of methods for reasoning by default. These include circum-

---

*This paper is a revision and expansion of [12]. Authors listed alphabetically.

0004-3702/91/$ 03.50 © 1991—Elsevier Science Publishers B.V.

scriptive inference [29,31,35], which draws those conclusions valid in all minimal models of a set of axioms; autoepistemic inference [39,42] and default logic [49], which permit rules of inference to refer to unprovable statements as well as provable ones; specificity-based taxonomic inference [60], which makes assumptions based on the most specific of the relevant prototypes; and chronologically ignorant inference [56], which draws conclusions based on the shortest or simplest possible histories of events. In addition to these generic patterns, there are often domain-dependent reasons for adopting default policies in particular problem situations. Unfortunately, none of these theories of default reasoning constitutes a comprehensive universal theory that indicates which assumptions are appropriate in every circumstance, all things considered.[1] All the known generic inferential patterns cover only some of the considerations relevant to drawing the best overall conclusions, and individual default rules concern only specific propositions. This proliferation of formalisms is unsatisfying in the absence of an explanation for why it exists. Our purpose in this paper is to investigate the natural question of whether there is some deeper or more comprehensive theory which combines or unifies all patterns (those known and those awaiting discovery) of nonmonotonic inference.

Toward this end, some theories have been proposed as unifications or partial unifications of some of these ways of making assumptions [13,25,31,32,56]. At the same time, doubts about the existence of complete unifications have also been expressed because the different theories of nonmonotonic inference may indicate conflicting conclusions when the underlying default rules conflict. Early indications of difficulty appeared with Hanks and McDermott's [19] so-called "Yale shooting problem". Subsequently, Touretzky et al. [61] argued that the gross differences between competing theories of inheritance stem from disparate underlying intuitions about how to make assumptions. As they put it, the differing theories reflect a "clash of intuitions". Recently, Poole [47] displayed another fundamental clash among intuitive properties of default inference.

Unification in the face of these conflicts is possible only if we can divide responsibility among the different methods so that each theory of particular cases provides the right criterion of correctness for inferential problems appearing in its domain. Making this division requires identification of the various conflicts and the sets of cases in which they arise. But it is not feasible to detect all potential conflicts in advance, and there are simply too many to resolve manually. Instead we must seek some way of detecting and

---

[1] Indeed, none even constitutes a universal representational formalism which can express the mechanisms or principles of all the known (and the undiscovered) theories of default reasoning. Whether there is a universal representational formalism is an interesting question, but not one that will be addressed in this paper.

resolving them automatically as they arise in reasoning. Of course, we do not wish conflicts to be resolved in arbitrary ways, so our question becomes whether there is a universal theory that automatically combines all particular correctness criteria in a rational manner.

The answer is no: *any universal theory of default inference based on combining correctness criteria must sometimes produce irrational conclusions* (with respect to a very weak standard of rationality) unless one criterion is a comprehensive theory by itself. Put differently, the only way to guarantee rational conclusions is to rationally resolve the problematic conflicts in advance and then use this resolution as the universal theory. Since prior manual resolution seems infeasible (even if we make the rather dubious assumption that people can resolve every specific conflict correctly), some degree of irrationality seems inevitable, whether because of an imperfect automatic conflict resolution method or a manually constructed theory that does not resolve all conflicts. To support this conclusion, we use Shoham's formalism [4,56] to translate questions about nonmonotonic inference into the context of rational decision making. This translation allows us to adapt Arrow's [1,2] celebrated results about the impossibility of universal social choice rules to the case of nonmonotonic inference. We also draw on the literature of social choice to consider some possible ways around these results.

2. Preferential theories of default reasoning

The initial theories of default, circumscriptive, autoepistemic, chronologically ignorant, and specificity-based taxonomic inference had very different appearances. Despite their diversity, Shoham [56] has shown how to cast a number of these theories in similar form, as sound inference with respect to models maximal in some partial order. In the more general form of his construction [4], a nonmonotonic logic is characterized by a partial preorder (that is, a reflexive and transitive relation) $\sqsubseteq$ over a set $\mathcal{M}$ of *interpretations*, which, depending on the base logical language $\mathcal{L}$, represent truth assignments, models, Kripke structures, or similar objects. We write $\sqsubset$ to mean the strict part of $\sqsubseteq$, so that $M \sqsubset M'$ iff $M \sqsubseteq M'$ but $M' \not\sqsubseteq M$, and write $\sim$ to mean the reflexive part of $\sqsubseteq$, so that $M \sim M'$ iff $M \sqsubseteq M'$ and $M' \sqsubseteq M$. The meaning of a nonmonotonic theory in these logics is then obtained by modifying the usual notions of satisfaction and entailment to take the model ordering into account. A model M $\sqsubseteq$-*satisfies* a formula P, written $M \models_{\sqsubseteq} P$, iff $M \models P$ and there is no model M' such that $M' \models P$ and $M \sqsubset M'$. A formula P $\sqsubseteq$-*entails* a formula Q, written $P \models_{\sqsubseteq} Q$, iff $M \models Q$ whenever $M \models_{\sqsubseteq} P$. Substitution of these variants for the usual satisfaction and entailment concepts yields a complete description of the nonmonotonic logic $\mathcal{L}_\sqsubseteq$.

Shoham illustrates the construction by providing orders corresponding to circumscription [29], the minimal knowledge logic of Halpern and Moses [18], his own chronological ignorance [56], and a few others. In circumscription, for example, models are ranked by minimality according to subset relations among extensions of specific predicates designated as abnormalities. That is, $M_1 \sqsubseteq M_2$ if the extension of the circumscribed predicate P in M_1 contains its extension in M_2 and the two interpretations agree on all other functions and predicates. To capture chronological ignorance, models are ordered according to amount known about histories. These and other theories thus have the same formal structure, differing from each other only in how they order different models.

More generally, the theory may be formulated so that maximization is based on arguments or other epistemic notions as well as truth or belief. For example, Touretzky's [60] theory of inheritance with exceptions compares alternative resolutions by means of an "inferential distance" ordering based on paths or arguments for conclusions, in addition to the conclusions themselves. Such criteria may be captured in a simple variant of Shoham's framework in which the notion of satisfaction in a model is replaced by satisfaction in a mental state, where mental states may include information (e.g., paths or arguments) in addition to the beliefs of the reasoner. In this framework, a nonmonotonic logic is characterized by a preorder $\sqsubseteq$ over a set Σ of possible mental states and a "satisfaction" relation $\models$ between states and sentences such that P is a belief in S iff $S \models P$. We then modify the earlier definition of $\sqsubseteq$-satisfaction to say that S $\sqsubseteq$-satisfies P, written $S \models_\sqsubseteq P$ iff $S \models P$ and there is no state $S' \in \Sigma$ such that $S' \models P$, and $S \sqsubset S'$. We redefine $\sqsubseteq$-entailment accordingly, with $P \models_\sqsubseteq Q$ meaning that $S \models Q$ whenever S $\sqsubseteq$-satisfies P. We observe without proof that all of our results apply equally well to orders over entire mental states as long as all epistemic states are consistent, that is, as long as either $S \not\models P$ or $S \not\models \neg P$ for every state S and proposition P.[2]

One natural interpretation of inference in the preferential framework is as *rational* selection of maximally preferred states of belief, or of those conclusions that hold in all maximally preferred states. Shoham's terminology is in accordance with this interpretation, as he calls $\sqsubseteq$ a *preference* order,

[2]For an illustration of this point, see the treatment of rational belief revision presented in [10]. Belief revision and default reasoning are closely related, as belief revision concerns how beliefs change nonmonotonically with increasing time, while default reasoning concerns how conclusions change nonmonotonically with increasing knowledge.

Table 1
Pascal's utility assessments of the possible consequences of his decision
about belief in God.

	God exists	doesn't
Believe	$+\infty$	$-\varepsilon$
Doubt	$-\infty$	$+\varepsilon$

and the corresponding logical notions *preferential* satisfaction and entailment. [3] In fact, this view of nonmonotonic inference is more than just an
interpretation: it provides a justification for the formal structures of the
various nonmonotonic logics. The original theories provided precise formal
concepts, but motivated explanations of why these concepts were interesting
appeared only later, when Doyle [6,9], Shoham [55], and others [26,28]
justified default rules by an appeal to decision-theoretic rationality, saying that an agent should adopt a default conclusion or default rule if the
expected inferential utility of holding it exceeds that of not holding it.
Default rules and other assumption-making mechanisms are ordinarily not
presented in terms of rational choice, and their mechanizations usually
involve no decision-theoretic calculations. But they are used when the information needed in deliberation about actions and their consequences may be
guessed with reasonable accuracy and when mistaken guesses do not lead to
serious consequences. In such cases, guessing avoids the costs of acquiring
and analyzing the needed information, and so represents a rational response
to computational problems involving incomplete information. [4]

In fact, the notion of rationally adopted beliefs is quite an old idea,
traceable at least back to the seventeenth century in the form of "Pascal's
wager". Pascal [45] framed his problem of belief in God in the following
way: he can either believe or doubt the existence of God, and God may or
may not exist. If God exists and Pascal believes, he gains eternal salvation,
but if he doubts he suffers eternal damnation. If God does not exist, belief
may lead Pascal to forgo a few possible pleasures during his life that doubt
would permit him to enjoy. We summarize Pascal's evaluations in the decision matrix shown in Table 1, where ε represents the finite amount of
pleasure enjoyed or foregone due to belief during his life. Of course, these
same quantities modify the first column as well, but finite modifications to
infinite quantities are negligible. Since Pascal did not judge God's existence

---

[3]In the earlier version of this paper [12], we criticized Shoham's definition of $\sqsubset$ in [56]
as opposite in sense to the usual notion of preference. That criticism was wrong, based on a
misreading of Shoham's definition. Sorry.

[4]See [11] for more discussion of the roles of decision-theoretic and economic notions of
rationality in artificial intelligence.

impossible, the expected utility of belief is $+\infty$, dominating the expected utility of doubt, $-\infty$. This convinced Pascal that doubt was not a viable alternative for him. Rational assumptions also play a large role in William James' [22] theory of the "will to believe". James argued that cases of rational belief are ubiquitous in mundane reasoning, an assessment corroborated by the pervasiveness of default reasoning in artificial intelligence.

3. Resolving conflicting preferences about defaults

Each of the existing formalisms for nonmonotonic reasoning is either the direct expression of a single criterion for preference among competing interpretations, such as taxonomic specificity, or a means to specify a class of preference criteria, such as default rules (see Section 4.3). Since each can be viewed as a special theory of rational inference, many have hoped or expected that with careful analysis one could combine the choices made by the different theories of nonmonotonic reasoning into a single rational choice, yielding in effect a universal theory of default reasoning. Unfortunately, the potential for conflict among these criteria impedes integration attempts.

3.1. Examples of conflicts

The famous "Yale shooting problem" of Hanks and McDermott [19] illustrates that basic nonmonotonic logics are too weak to arbitrate conflicts among abnormality minimization of different properties. Initially, in their example, a gun is loaded and Fred is alive. After an interval of waiting, the gun is fired at Fred. Fred's survival is a problem for default reasoning because loaded guns normally stay loaded during waits, and living people normally remain alive after actions. Which violation is more abnormal? In this view, the normality of loadedness after waiting and life after shooting are two conflicting criteria. Defenders of nonmonotonic logics have responded by proposing a third criterion—such as chronological minimization [56] or some causality theory [30]—to resolve the issue. However, as Hanks and McDermott point out, in some contexts other criteria (perhaps even chronological *max*imization for diagnostic reasoning) may be compelling, leading to further unresolvable conflicts. It seems a good bet that enterprising researchers will always be able to generate problems that fall through the cracks of fixed configurations of criteria.

In fact, numerous examples suggest that conflicts are unavoidable. The most widely-known conflicts occur in inference from the most specific prototypes, where multiple dimensions of specificity within a taxonomic lattice can result in conflicting preferences between conclusions. An example is the famous "Nixon diamond" (so called because of the shape of its diagram when written as an inheritance network; perhaps also because it is so hard): Republicans are typically not pacifists, Quakers are typically pacifists, and Nixon is a Republican Quaker. The question is, is Nixon a pacifist or not? Since neither default is more specific than the other, one cannot tell simply from the information given in the taxonomic lattice. Moreover, though one might resolve the question of Nixon's pacifism empirically, such a resolution need not generalize to correctly resolve all formally similar but substantively dissimilar conflicts among other taxonomic defaults.

Conflicts are also possible between pairs of more global preference criteria. For example, ordering assumptions according to their statistical predictivity can conflict with specificity orders. A case in point is Loui's [34] "Mets victory problem", which asks for the probability that the Mets will win today. Statistics are available for three conditions: the game is at home, Dwight Gooden pitches, and Keith Hernandez plays. All three hold for today's game. The difficulty is that the most specific reference class of events, that in which all three conditions hold, may contain so few games that the resulting prediction is much less reliable than a prediction made from one of the more general reference classes in which only one or two of these conditions holds. This problem is a very practical concern for actuaries, who must estimate probabilities for various classifications of events. In their terminology, the *credibility* of a sample of events conflicts with its specificity. As Longley-Cook puts it, when they try to slice the cake too many ways at once they are "left with a useless collection of crumbs" [33].

Similarly, conflicts may occur within reasoners that have multiple informants or refer to multiple authorities to obtain their information. For instance, Milton Friedman presents arguments for free trade, while Lester Thurow presents arguments for controlled trade. These arguments seem individually coherent, but are mutually contradictory. Which conclusion should one believe? Most practical artificial intelligence systems are designed to incorporate all the available knowledge about the relevant subjects by combining expertise from multiple sources. In the simplest approach, one might encode each expert's knowledge as a separate set of rules in the system, or as justifications for a subset of the rules which name the expert proffering them. In this case, as Thomason [59] points out, conflicts between experts become conflicts within the expert system. Of course, the system designer can instead try to reconcile these conflicts at design time, but this may not always be feasible if some conflicts are too subtle to detect, or if the experts themselves knowingly hold mutually irreconcilable opinions. Thus if the system must perform in isolation from the original experts, one must expect it will sometimes have to deal with conflicts as they arise. For instance, many adults have had the experience of having to administer medications to themselves or to their children while on vacation, only to find that several medications have been prescribed by different doctors or for different symptoms, with each medication contra-indicating the others.

Yet another class of conflicts arises when criteria of social, ethical, or moral acceptability of conclusions rule out the conclusions indicated by statistical criteria. To use Levesque's [28] example, it may be statistically compelling but socially unacceptable to conclude that a given computer scientist is male. Or for a more consequential conflict, consider "redlining", the practice of not lending money to anyone in neighborhoods deemed to be bad credit risks. Redlining may be justified on statistical grounds, but is often prohibited because it may impede economic recovery of the neighborhood and discriminate against ethnic or racial groups.

These examples suggest that conflicts between preferential criteria among beliefs are unavoidable. While one might view this situation as a reflection of the limits of current epistemology, perhaps a better view is that these conflicts reflect the more general problem of irreconcilable conflicts among values examined by Van Frassen [63].

3.2. Skeptical and credulous conflict resolution

Any comprehensive mechanism for nonmonotonic reasoning must embody some way of handling the conflicts that arise among the different patterns of inference. Some theories provide explicit criteria for resolving unproblematic conflicts. Inheritance theories, for example, resolve conflicts between more specific and less specific information in favor of the former. But as noted above, this rule does not help when neither conflicting preference is more specific than the other. There are two major approaches taken to resolve such problematic conflicts: to choose to satisfy one preference instead of another, and to refuse to satisfy any of the conflicting preferences. Each of the different theories proposed for nonmonotonic reasoning takes one of these approaches. For example, nonmonotonic logic, autoepistemic logic, default logic, and "credulous" inheritance [61] describe how a single set of axioms and rules may yield several different, often incompatible sets of conclusions closed under inference. In these theories, problematic conflicts between specific defaults are resolved in every possible way, with each different set of conclusions representing a maximal consistent set of preferences. In contrast, Shoham's logics, circumscription, closed-world reasoning [48], Pollock's defeasible inference [46], and so-called "skeptical" inheritance [21,57] resemble ordinary logic in that they describe how a set of axioms or rules yields a single set of conclusions closed under inference. These theories handle conflicts either by failing to draw any conclusions involving dissonant problematic preferences or by drawing every conclusion from them (explicit inconsistency).

Both approaches have their defenders. Pollock [46], for example, advocates skepticism in the face of problematic conflicts on the grounds that

Table 2
Consequences of actions for the decision
faced by the hungry donkey.

Action	Result
Eat nearby hay	Live
Eat distant apples	Live
Refuse to decide	Starve

belief should be based on epistemically defensible positions. But neither skepticism nor credulity is always rational. The agent cannot always rationally choose to remain skeptical about questions very important to its prosperity, whether the skepticism stems from too much information (conflicting preferences) or from too little information (incomplete beliefs). In either case, it may be better to adopt a stance on some issue and risk error than to take no stance at all and risk paralysis. Nor can the agent always rationally choose to be credulous, particularly in situations involving serious consequences of error.

For example, the following elaboration of the classical example of Buridan's ass presents a case where skepticism fails as a rational inference policy. A hungry donkey has to choose whether to eat a nearby bale of hay or a more distant bucket of apples. The donkey prefers nearby food to distant fodder, but also prefers apples to hay. If the skeptical approach is followed, the donkey should refrain from choosing to eat either the hay or the apples. But this is irrational, since eating keeps the donkey alive while not eating makes the donkey starve (see Table 2). Correspondingly, credulity is not necessarily rational for a parent who finds two children fighting, each of whom claims the other started the fight. Because the need for skepticism and credulity may vary with circumstances, we seek a language for expressing when to be skeptical and when to be credulous.

4. Social choice and nonmonotonic logics

Any acceptable universal theory of default reasoning must provide a rationale for its treatment of conflicts, whether credulous, skeptical, or sometimes one or the other. It should also be potentially mechanizable. As noted earlier, placing responsibility for resolving potential conflicts on the human designer is infeasible because for large sets of criteria it is difficult to anticipate all of the potential conflicts and all of the varying circumstances that may influence how the conflicts should be resolved. Furthermore, introduction of new criteria may necessitate completely restructuring the global preference order. A more satisfactory solution would exploit the concept of *modularity* to base conflict resolution mechanisms on general rules of combination that could be applied either manually or automatically as the need arises, so that the same solution still suffices when new criteria are discovered. As is widely recognized, modular design is critical to the successful construction of complex structures, and large commonsense knowledge bases certainly count as such.

4.1. Aggregation policies

To investigate this approach formally, we say that an *aggregation policy* is a function that specifies the global preorder corresponding to any given set of individual preorders. Let the set I index the set of preference orders that are to be combined, so that if $i \in I$, $\sqsubseteq_i$ denotes the preference order corresponding to the ith pattern of inference to be included in the unified logic.[5] The multicriteria nonmonotonic logic problem is then to aggregate the set of preorders $\{\sqsubseteq_i \mid i \in I\}$ into a global preference preorder $\sqsubseteq$.

In this framework, the preferences based on a single criterion, such as predicate minimization, specificity, or chronological ignorance, might be represented by an individual order $\sqsubseteq_i$. Alternatively, individual orders might represent more narrow criteria corresponding to the separate predicates to minimize, the respective dimensions of specificity, or individual default rules (as in Section 4.3). In any case, each $\sqsubseteq_i$ reflects a distinct attribute, encoding the local preferences over interpretations according to its dictates. Modularity or generality of the aggregation method may be ensured by including a large number of vacuous preference orders (trivial preorders such that $M \sqsubseteq_i M'$ if and only if $M = M'$) to be replaced by more substantive orders as new criteria are discovered.

For example, one simple aggregation function is unanimous decision: $M_1 \sqsubseteq M_2$ iff $M_1 \sqsubseteq_i M_2$ for all $\sqsubseteq_i$ that rank the two. This policy, of course, is extremely skeptical as it fails to resolve any conflicts whatsoever.

Another aggregation function comes from applying a voting scheme, for example, majority rule among the criteria: $M_1 \sqsubseteq M_2$ iff

$$|\{i \in I \mid M_1 \sqsubseteq_i M_2\}| \geq |\{i \in I \mid M_2 \sqsubseteq_i M_1\}|.$$

Technically, however, simple majority rule is not a legal aggregation policy because the resulting global order $\sqsubseteq$ is not guaranteed to be transitive when there are more than two models to be ranked. (The intransitivity of majority rule is also known as "Condorcet's voting paradox", after the eighteenth century social scientist who discovered it [50].)

---

[5]Use of an ordered index set (e.g., $I = \{0, \ldots, n\}$) does not generally reflect any prioritization of these criteria. See Section 4.5 for a discussion of mechanisms where the ordering is significant.

Other aggregation functions organize the criteria in a hierarchy and delegate authority to each criterion according to its place in the hierarchy. We discuss this class of priority-based mechanisms extensively in Section 4.5.

An alternate formalization would be to take the aggregation policy to be a function from individual orders to a set of globally maximal elements, rather than to a global preference order. This would allow for voting schemes that selected a winning candidate without necessarily producing a ranking among the also-rans. Adopting this framework, although slightly more flexible in some respects, would not significantly affect the results of our analysis. We return to this point in Section 5.3.

This formalization covers the result of preference aggregation but abstracts from the process by which aggregation occurs. In particular, it does not seek to characterize processes (such as some forms of negotiation, persuasion, or intimidation) in which the preference orders themselves may change during aggregation. The preference aggregation framework merely describes the functional relationship between individual preferences at the start and group decisions at the end of some unspecified aggregation process.

The group decision-making analogy can be taken quite literally. The problem of designing aggregation policies has been studied extensively in economics, under the heading *social choice theory*. In the language of social choice theory, the ranked interpretations $M_1, M_2, \ldots$ are *candidates*, the $\sqsubseteq_i$ are *individual orders*, and the global order is the *social ranking*. The aggregation policy itself is called a *social choice function*. The main result of social choice theory is a startling theorem due to Arrow [1] that establishes the impossibility of social choice functions possessing several specific desirable and apparently reasonable properties. In Sections 4.3 and 4.4, we show that slightly modified versions of this result apply to preferential nonmonotonic logics, with important implications for the potential construction of universal default formalisms. We first discuss the hypotheses underlying these results.

4.2. Aggregation principles

The principled design of an aggregation policy for multicriteria preferences begins with a consideration of properties we think a reasonable policy should exhibit. The properties we propose are analogs of Arrow's desiderata for social choice. We first present the proposed properties, and then discuss their desirability. [6]

(1) *Collective rationality.* The global preorder $\sqsubseteq$ is a function of the individual orders $\sqsubseteq_i$, which are unrestricted, possibly partial, preorders.

---

[6]Consult sources on social choice theory [2,50] for somewhat more rigorous versions of these desiderata, though for the case of total preorders.

That is, if Π denotes the set of all preorders over $\mathcal{M}$, an aggregation
policy for criteria indexed by I is a function from Π^I to Π.

(2) *Pareto principle (unanimity)*. If $M_1 \sqsubset_i M_2$ for some $i \in I$ and for
no $j \in I$ does $M_2 \sqsubset_j M_1$, then $M_1 \sqsubset M_2$. In other words, the global
order agrees with uncontested strict preferences.

(3) *Independence of irrelevant alternatives (IIA)*. The relation of M_1 and
M_2 according to the global order depends only on how the individual
orders rank those two candidates. That is, the global order restricted
to a subset of candidates is equivalent to an aggregation of the
individual orders restricted to that subset.

(4) *Nondictatorship (noncomprehensive criteria)*. There is no $i \in I$ such
that for every M_1 and M_2, $M_1 \sqsubseteq M_2$ whenever $M_1 \sqsubseteq_i M_2$, regardless
of the $\sqsubseteq_j$ for $j \neq i$. That is, there is no "dictator" whose preferences
automatically determine the group's, independent of the other individual orderings. This principle reflects our presumption that each
criterion provides only one consideration of limited scope, that no
criterion is itself the universal theory.

(5) *Conflict resolution*. If $M_1 \sqsubseteq_i M_2$ for some i, then $M_1 \sqsubseteq M_2$ or
$M_2 \sqsubseteq M_1$. That is, if two candidates are comparable in an individual
order, then they are comparable in the global order. [7]

Technically, these desiderata are a bit more general than Arrow's, as his
framework requires the preferences to be total rather than partial preorders.
That is, while social choice theory uses total orders in which, for each x and
y, either $x \sqsubset y$, $y \sqsubset x$, or $x \sim y$, preferential nonmonotonic logic allows
the additional possibility that x and y are unrelated. Our divergence from
Arrow's problem is most apparent in the conflict resolution principle, which
for Arrow is implicit in the requirement that the global order be total.

Collective rationality is just a statement of the aggregation framework
in preferential nonmonotonic logics. It stipulates that aggregation policies
define general methods for combining multiple preference criteria that yield
answers no matter what preferential criteria are employed. In particular, it
ensures modularity of the aggregation method by requiring that aggregation
succeeds even when vacuous criteria are replaced by nontrivial new criteria.

The Pareto principle is clearly a desirable property of aggregation functions; reversing an uncontested preference would be difficult to justify.

IIA has been perhaps the most controversial condition among social choice
theorists. In the logical context, however, it corresponds closely to the
expected property of model preference that if M is maximal among a set
of models, it is maximal in any subset including M. Adding an axiom

---

[7] This weakens slightly the conflict resolution condition stated in our earlier paper [12],
which required the global order to provide strict resolutions whenever one of the criteria
expressed a strict preference. Such strictness is not necessary.

that rules out only nonmaximal models of P should have no effect on the preferential entailments of P. For example, suppose $M \sqsubset_1 M' \sqsubset_1 M''$ and $M \sqsubset_2 M'' \sqsubset_2 M'$. If these are the only two criteria and the aggregate order makes M' the maximum element of $\{M', M''\}$, then IIA and the Pareto principle require that the aggregate order also makes M' the maximum element of $\{M, M', M''\}$.

Moreover, the independence condition is necessary in a precise sense for the existence of a satisfactory semantics of individual preference criteria. An aggregation function violating IIA cannot be "strategy proof" [15]; that is, it will be susceptible to strategic voting, in which an individual might best realize its own preferences by misrepresenting them to the aggregation procedure. For example, faced with a bully who "aggregates" his preferences with those of his victims by doing the opposite of what the victim wants, Br'er Rabbit professes a great aversion to being thrown into the briar patch even though that is what he actually desires. In such cases of strategic voting, the preferential interpretation of individual criteria does not reflect their true impact on the global order. Indeed, because of consequences such as these, no one has proposed default theories violating IIA. On the other hand, computational mechanisms implementing nonmonotonic reasoning commonly violate this property by employing rules in which preferences depend on the set of explicitly represented alternatives rather than on the (perhaps hard to compute) set of implicitly represented alternatives. One may view some processes of human negotiation (especially advertising) similarly, as cases in which the negotiation does not merely seek to determine the relevant existing preferences, but instead seeks to change preferences through repetition and association of different alternatives.

The condition ruling out dictators has two independent justifications, corresponding to its descriptive and normative readings. In the first of these, the condition simply states the problem faced by theorists of nonmonotonic reasoning at this time: namely, that all known (and foreseeable) preference criteria to be aggregated provide at best only single considerations to be weighed in making assumptions, and that each of them is prone to override in the face of enough opposition by other criteria. In this descriptive reading, the condition merely rules out the trivial solution to the aggregation problem; it says we cannot simply assume we possess some universal criterion that we in actuality lack. The second justification for the condition is that the existence of a sovereign authority undermines the decentralized representation of preferences motivating aggregation by obviating the need for combination of criteria. It is easy to see why decentralization is a normative ideal in the social choice context, but in the case of reasoning, the normative justification is less obvious. One can justify decentralization in terms of good programming practice, reflecting the limits of human theorists and designers to fully analyze complex structures. Alternatively, decentralization might be justified as reflecting the limitations of scope exhibited by humans and other sources of available information. But there is no objection in principle to monolithic solutions when the problem can be understood fully. In such cases, decentralization must be judged pragmatically. We defer discussion of the practical consequences of dictatorship to Section 4.5.

The conflict resolution condition rules out complete skepticism about conflicting preferences by mandating that the global order commit to some relationship, even if only indifference, whenever the individual orders express a preference. That is, it permits the global order to be skeptical about conflicting strict preferences between two alternatives only by explicitly considering them to be equally desirable. This does not rule out skepticism about conclusions, however, since in preferential nonmonotonic logics the conclusions drawn from equally preferable interpretations are just those conclusions holding in each of the interpretations. For example, if the order is indifferent between interpretations in which Nixon is pacifist and interpretations in which Nixon is not pacifist, then neither pacifism nor nonpacifism will be conclusions of the logic. (Credulity may be achieved simply by linearly ordering the incompatible interpretations so that, for example, all interpretations in which Nixon is pacifist are preferred to those in which Nixon is not pacifist.)

That skepticism about preferences is no panacea becomes apparent when we consider languages that permit explicit expression of preferences about skepticism about belief. The preferential framework applies directly to modal logics of belief, and in such a language we might express a preference for skepticism about a proposition P (as we exhibit in Section 4.3), that is, a preference to believe neither P nor $\neg P$. This preference for skepticism could conflict with a preference for credulity (believing P or $\neg P$) or for a particular stance on P (e.g., believing P). We cannot decide to be skeptical about whether to be skeptical about P, since each of P and $\neg P$ must either be a belief or not. Since there is no recourse to higher-level skepticism about belief, conflict resolution at this level is a requirement, not merely an axiom.

As noted earlier, the conflict resolution principle is relevant only when the aggregate order may be partial. Our first theorem concerns the special case in which all orders are total, for which it states that the desirable and apparently reasonable properties enumerated above are not simultaneously satisfiable by any aggregation policy for preferences expressed by total preorders. (We return to the case of partial preorders in Section 4.4.)

Theorem 4.1 (Arrow). *If the set of possible interpretations includes more than two models, no aggregation policy mapping total individual preorders to a total global preorder satisfies the properties* (1)–(4) *above.*

Proof. With the restriction to total preorders, this is exactly Arrow's theorem applied to choices among models. For a proof of the original result see Arrow [2], Roberts [50, Chapter 7], or any book on social choice theory.   □

There is no problem finding good aggregation policies for choices among only two alternatives. But for the case of default reasoning there are always many possible candidates to choose from (for example, all possible models); hereafter we take it for granted that there are at least three.

4.3. Default rules

Arrow's theorem as expressed above need not rule out good aggregation policies for nonmonotonic reasoning, as the preferences occurring in this context may be of a special form which permits satisfactory aggregation. To investigate whether this is the case, let us consider aggregating a set of default rules in the sense of Reiter [49]. A default rule $P : Q_1, \ldots, Q_n/R$ specifies that R should be concluded if P is believed and $\neg Q_k$ is not believed, for each k, $1 \leq k \leq n$.[8]

In order to express preferences about when to be skeptical and when to commit to belief, we require models which describe belief states as well as the contents of beliefs. For this purpose, we employ Moore's models for autoepistemic logic [41].[9] As Konolige [25] shows, default theories correspond naturally to autoepistemic theories in which each default is rewritten in the form $LP \wedge \neg L\neg Q_1 \wedge \cdots \wedge \neg L\neg Q_n \supset R$, where we read LP as "P is believed" and $\neg LP$ as "P is not believed". Each Moore model M is a pair $M = (K, V)$ of an ordinary valuation V and a Kripke structure K. A Kripke structure contains a set of possible worlds and an "accessibility" relation on these worlds. The truth of a formula is evaluated with respect to each world, and a formula of the form LP is true in a world W just in case P is true in every world accessible from W. In Moore's semantics, each K is required to be a complete structure for the modal logic S5, that is, an equivalence relation in which every possible world is accessible from every possible world. Moore proves that such models are in exact correspondence with stable autoepistemic theories, that is, deductively closed sets of sentences which contain LP whenever they contain P and contain $\neg LP$ otherwise.

With such interpretations, we may express default rules as preferences in a natural way. Let us first introduce a bit of helpful notation. If p and q are mutually inconsistent sentences, then they are satisfied by disjoint sets

---

[8]Actually, Reiter wrote defaults as $P : MQ_1, \ldots, MQ_n/R$, but we omit the M markers.

[9]One can also formalize these preferences using "situations" to describe belief states, as in Levesque's logic of explicit belief [27], or use the belief states directly, as discussed in Section 2.

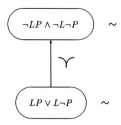

Fig. 1. The order expressing preference for skepticism about P.

of models, and we write $p \prec q$ (q preferred to p) to mean that $M \sqsubset M'$ iff $M \models p$ and $M' \models q$, and that $M \sim M'$ for all models M, M' of p and all models M, M' of q. In other words, the models of p (respectively q) are all equally preferable (the agent is indifferent among them), but all models of q are preferred to all models of p.

We may then express a preference for skepticism about P by

$$LP \vee L\neg P \prec \neg LP \wedge \neg L\neg P,$$

which says that believing neither P nor its negation is preferred to believing either, and depict this relationship as in Fig. 1. A preference for credulity about P is expressed by the opposite order.

Similarly, a default rule $P : Q_1, \ldots, Q_n / R$ may be expressed by the preferences $\sigma \prec \sigma' \prec \sigma''$ (read transitively), where

$$\sigma = LP \wedge \neg L\neg Q_1 \wedge \cdots \wedge \neg L\neg Q_n \wedge \neg LR,$$

$$\sigma' = LP \wedge (L\neg Q_1 \vee \cdots \vee L\neg Q_n),$$

and

$$\sigma'' = \neg LP \vee (LP \wedge \neg L\neg Q_1 \wedge \cdots \wedge \neg L\neg Q_n \wedge LR).$$

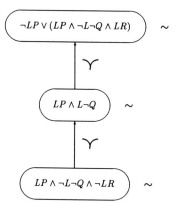

Fig. 2. The total preorder expressed by the default rule $P : Q/R$.

That is, if P is believed, the default rule $P : Q_1, \ldots, Q_n/R$ prefers believing R to believing any $\neg Q_k$, and prefers believing either R or some $\neg Q_k$ to believing none of these. As all models satisfy one of σ, σ', or σ'', it never happens that two of them are incomparable. Thus these preferences induce a total preorder (shown in Fig. 2): any two models are related by $\sim$ or $\sqsubset$, and hence by $\sqsubseteq$.

While there may be other motivated ways of interpreting default rules as preference orders over states of belief (see, for example, [13,20,56]), the interpretation above seems a natural one, and is corroborated by previous results of Doyle [6,7] which showed that the extensions of default theories are Pareto-optimal choices, that is, correspond to maximal consistent sets of default-rule preferences. [10]

We now improve on Theorem 4.1 by showing that restricting the individual orderings to those arising from default rules is not sufficient to forestall the impossibility theorem.

Theorem 4.2. *No policy for aggregating every set of default rules into a total global preorder satisfies the properties (2)–(4) above.*

Proof. Since Theorem 4.1 applies whenever the class of possible individual orders contains every possible ordering of at least three alternatives (even if the usual case involves aggregating only a subset of these), it suffices to show that each pattern of preferences among three alternatives can be expressed by some default rule. Any three alternatives will do, as the set of candidate models can be arbitrarily constrained to these by nondefeasible axioms. In fact, we show that even normal defaults (those of the form $P : R/R$) can express all patterns among the alternatives chosen.

Let $R_1, \ldots, R_6$ be six logically independent propositions, and $: R_k/R_k$ defaults for $1 \leq k \leq 6$. Each default $: R_k/R_k$ expresses the preferences

$$\phi_k \prec \phi'_k \prec \phi''_k,$$

where

$$\phi_k = \neg L \neg R_k \wedge \neg L R_k,$$

$$\phi'_k = L \neg R_k,$$

$$\phi''_k = \neg L \neg R_k \wedge L R_k.$$

---

[10]Not all Pareto-optimal choices are extensions, however, which is one of the points of divergence of preferential nonmonotonic logics from default logic. For example, while our preferential interpretations of default rules express preferences satisfied by default logic, the nonmonotonic logic that results from considering *all* maximally preferred models can yield contrapositive conclusions not reached by default logic. (That is, $\neg Q$ will be a maximally preferred conclusion from axioms P, $\neg R$, and the sole default rule $P : Q/R$.)

Table 3
Six default rules which result in all possible preference orders over $\sigma_1, \sigma_2, \sigma_3$.

Default	Preferences
$: R_1/R_1$	$\sigma_1 \prec \sigma_2 \prec \sigma_3$
$: R_2/R_2$	$\sigma_1 \prec \sigma_3 \prec \sigma_2$
$: R_3/R_3$	$\sigma_2 \prec \sigma_3 \prec \sigma_1$
$: R_4/R_4$	$\sigma_2 \prec \sigma_1 \prec \sigma_3$
$: R_5/R_5$	$\sigma_3 \prec \sigma_2 \prec \sigma_1$
$: R_6/R_6$	$\sigma_3 \prec \sigma_1 \prec \sigma_2$

Consider now three sets of models constructed by conjoining all permutations of the individual default conditions:

$$\sigma_1 = \phi_1 \wedge \phi_2 \wedge \phi_3'' \wedge \phi_4' \wedge \phi_5'' \wedge \phi_6',$$

$$\sigma_2 = \phi_1' \wedge \phi_2'' \wedge \phi_3 \wedge \phi_4 \wedge \phi_5' \wedge \phi_6'',$$

$$\sigma_3 = \phi_1'' \wedge \phi_2' \wedge \phi_3' \wedge \phi_4'' \wedge \phi_5 \wedge \phi_6.$$

As Table 3 indicates, the six defaults express every strict preference order among elements from these three sets of models. Thus, the individual preferences for these elements are effectively unrestricted by the form of default rules. Because these elements could constitute the entire candidate set (given, for instance, a nondefeasible axiom of the form $\sigma_1 \vee \sigma_2 \vee \sigma_3$), Theorem 4.1 applies directly.   □

4.4. A general impossibility theorem

The special case of default rules by itself does much damage to hopes for a unified theory of nonmonotonic reasoning since a general theory should cover at least these. But one might still escape this limitation by dropping the restriction that the preorders be total. The following theorem shows that the impossibility result recurs if we require global orders to be as complete as the individual orders.

Theorem 4.3. *No aggregation policy satisfies the properties* (1)–(5) *above.*

Proof (Sketch). The only difference between the multicriteria aggregation problem considered here and the classic social choice setup is that the individual and global orders can be partial whereas individual and social rankings are taken to be total. Partiality is constrained, however, by the conflict resolution condition's restriction that the global order be at least as complete as the constituent orders. An examination of Arrow's proof of Theorem 4.1 [2] reveals that it does not depend on totality of the individual orders, and presumes totality of the global orders only for cases where an individual expresses a preference. The validity of this presumption is enforced by our conflict resolution condition; hence the result generalizes to our situation. □

The conflict resolution principle is an extreme condition in that it rules out all skepticism about conflicting preferences. However, the negative implications of Theorem 4.3 do not hinge on this extremity. Dictatorial consequences are inevitable to whatever extent conflicts are resolved. The following corollary expresses this formally.

Corollary 4.4. *Suppose an aggregation policy satisfies properties* (1)–(3). *Then for any subset of candidates for which conflict resolution is satisfied, there exists a dictator whose preferences among this subset are adopted globally regardless of the preferences of the other criteria.*

Proof. By the independence of irrelevant alternatives, the global preference for a subset of candidates depends only on individual preferences among that subset. Therefore, the projection of the aggregation function onto this restricted domain must obey identical properties. Since conflict resolution is satisfied by hypothesis, Theorem 4.3 entails the impossibility of nondictatorship. □

Corollary 4.4 highlights the central tradeoff between skepticism and appeal to central authority in the design of preference aggregation schemes. The conflict resolution strategies admitted by the dictatorship condition form a class we call *lexicographic priority mechanisms*. Because this is the only kind of conflict resolution consistent with the other conditions, it is worth exploring the nature of these strategies in some detail.

4.5. Lexicographic priority mechanisms

In a "dictatorial" conflict resolution strategy, there exists a criterion which always gets its way regardless of what other criteria oppose it. In schemes where the dictator necessarily expresses a preference over all candidates (as in the usual social choice framework), this leads to very uninteresting choice mechanisms. Where the criteria may be expressed by partial preorders, a dictatorial aggregation policy may be slightly more complicated. In this case, there is a secondary dictator deciding conflicts among the candidates for which this criterion expresses no preference. This cascade of dictators continues until all conflicts are resolved.

As an example, we exhibit the preference aggregation function corresponding to the *stratified logic* scheme of Brown and Shoham [4]. Modifying their notation slightly, the problem is to determine the global order $\sqsubseteq$ from an ordered set of individual orders $\sqsubseteq_i$, $0 \leq i \leq n$. According to their definition, $M \sqsubseteq M'$ iff $M \sqsubseteq_j M'$ for some $j \leq n$ and $M \sim_i M'$ for all $i < j$. In other words, criterion 1 serves as dictator: the global preference order $\sqsubseteq$ is equivalent to $\sqsubseteq_1$ except where the latter is indifferent. In that case, $\sqsubseteq_2$ decides, regardless of the $\sqsubseteq_i$ for $i > 2$, unless it too is indifferent. Each underling criterion comes into play only when all of its superiors express indifference.

Choice rules of this form are called *lexicographic* because they resemble the method for ordering words alphabetically: compare the first letters; if tied compare the second, and so on. The implication of Corollary 4.4 is that every conflict resolution method satisfying collective rationality, unanimity, and IIA is necessarily equivalent to a lexicographic priority mechanism for some fixed sequence of criteria.

Note, however, that in stratified logics the dictator reigns even over unrelatedness; that is, if M and M' are not related by $\sqsubseteq_1$, they are not related by $\sqsubseteq$. According to the definition of Section 4.2, dictators are authoritative over indifference but not unrelatedness. In fact, overruling an explicit preference with unrelatedness sometimes violates the Pareto principle and always violates the conflict resolution principle. Thus, despite their lexicographic flavor, stratified logics do not satisfy our aggregation principles.

In McCarthy's prioritized circumscription [36], minimizing the abnormality of each predicate is a distinct preference criterion, and the global minimization is based on a lexicographic decision procedure using a predefined order on the predicates. Grosof [17] generalizes this to arbitrary partial preorders on arbitrary model-preference criteria, but the prioritization resolves conflicts only to the extent that the orders are *stratified* in the lexicographic sense illustrated above.

An example of lexicographic choice in everyday societal decision making is the judicial hierarchy of courts. The supreme court is the dictator, and in general the outcome of a dispute is decided by the highest court that addresses the case. Because each case is heard only along an ancestral line of courts, conflicts never arise among jurisdictions that are not strictly ordered by authority. As long as this constraint is satisfied, any order-preserving linearization of the structure will yield the same result under lexicographic choice as the original hierarchy.

Konolige's hierarchic autoepistemic theories [24] work much the same way for nonmonotonic reasoning. A fixed hierarchy is established initially to decide which criterion will be authoritative in case of conflict. Although the ordering of sub-theories is partial, conflicts are resolved only among theories that are linearly ordered in the hierarchy.

The main problem with lexicographic choice methods is that they are too rigid in how they combine criteria of limited expertise. Once assigned a position in the sequence, a criterion cannot be overridden by those below it, even by unanimous opposition. Thus, any criterion that is not absolute must be placed below those that potentially outweigh it, with the consequence that these other criteria *always* hold sway when in conflict with the original. If different criteria should properly be authoritative in varying situations, no lexicographic priority mechanism will be adequate for the conflict resolution task. For example, there exists no lexicographic method implementing majority rule for three criteria choosing among two candidates.

Another way of expressing this inflexibility of lexicographic orderings is to observe that they do not specify very many implicit preferences. We distinguish here the explicitly specified preferences from those implicitly determined by the aggregation function. Lexicographic choice determines relatively few implicit preferences, namely those defined by the transitive closure of the explicitly specified pairwise priorities. In contrast, more flexible aggregation rules like majority voting specify few (if any) explicit preferences beyond the individual preferences, but determine large numbers of implicit preferences. Since explicit preferences must be specified in advance, the designer of a lexicographic default reasoning system must essentially anticipate all potential conflicts in the process of specifying the criteria and their priorities. This means that if a new preference criterion is discovered, it cannot be considered an incremental addition to the set of criteria. Instead, it must be fit into the existing ordering, perhaps by replacement of the existing criteria by new versions that incorporate the new considerations, or by invention of further "higher-level" criteria to resolve conflicts arising within the expanded set. This certainly goes against the spirit of modular preference aggregation, in which the general combination rule accommodates new criteria without the need to explicitly reconsider or revise existing preference criteria.

Though fixed lexicographic orderings are too inflexible to capture all desirable choice rules, one can always find a lexicographic rule to achieve a particular outcome by adding a new criterion that dictates over the existing set. This, in fact, is the way many have proposed to resolve the Yale shooting problem and other conflicts: by expanding the set of criteria to include such factors as causality or chronological minimality. But while we may expect manual "patching" to be a useful way of incrementally improving any aggregation method, it seems imprudent to rely on it as the sole mechanism for resolving conflicts. As argued earlier, resolving all conflicts manually in advance is simply not feasible. Even if the effort is spread out over time, there are simply too many conflicts potentially requiring resolution. Worse still, the new special-purpose criteria may conflict with existing criteria in unanticipated ways; these conflicts will be hidden from view and so never explicitly considered because the new criteria are installed in a dictatorial position. Finally, there are no grounds to assume that we will always be able to find a simple criterion suitable for selection as the next dictator, nor does it seem reasonable to suppose that external (specifically, human) resolvers will be available at the time an important conflict happens to arise to make the necessary decisions, or that they will be able to make these decisions as quickly as needed. [11] Instead, prudence dictates that some mechanism be in place for resolving conflicts automatically between the time they are discovered and the time (if ever) the "right" resolution is found. Any conflict may indicate the need to seek out new principles or preferences. But sole reliance on timely human discovery of effective new criteria seems as unjustified as reliance on some *deus ex machina*.

4.6. Petty dictators

The existence of dictators might not be so distasteful if the identity of the dictator could vary depending on the candidates being ranked. For example, the path through a hierarchy or the structure of the hierarchy itself might depend on the choice involved. Conceptually, each dictator would wield authority only over some designated subdomain. This arrangement, however, does not satisfy the definition of "dictator", and therefore the theorems above indicate its incompatibility with the other aggregation principles listed in Section 4.2. Nevertheless, Corollary 4.4 suggests that by satisfying conflict resolution only partially we might limit the scope of dictatorships to specialized choice contexts.

The concept of limited realms of absolute authority has sometimes been called *liberalism* in social choice theory, by analogy to the idea that an individual's preferences should be the sole factor in choice among matters pertaining peculiarly to that individual (such as whether one sleeps on one's back or on one's stomach). Remarkably, the notion of liberalism is inconsistent with even the Pareto principle, as shown by Sen [53]. To see this, suppose that $\sqsubseteq_i$ is authoritative with respect to M_1 over M_2, and that $\sqsubseteq_j$ is authoritative about M_3 over M_4. In addition, suppose all criteria (including $\sqsubseteq_i$ and $\sqsubseteq_j$) prefer M_2 over M_3 and M_4 over M_1. There is no global order consistent with unanimous preference as well as the individual authorities, even though the subdomains of dictatorship are disjoint.

5. Paths toward possibility results

The impact of the impossibility result is proportional to the judged importance of conforming to the premise conditions, as well as the degree to

[11]McDermott [37] rhetorically asks whether Lifschitz will always be there to bail us out when existing inference mechanisms prove inadequate.

which they need to be relaxed in order to achieve "possibility". For social choice, Theorem 4.1 has had great force due to the apparent reasonableness of the conditions and its demonstrated robustness despite countless mathematician-years spent laboriously tweaking axioms. For nonmonotonic logics, the reasonability of the desiderata is more in question, and further scrutiny is needed to determine the robustness of our results.

Paralleling the investigations made in social choice, one can identify three primary options for dealing with impossibility. The first and most direct way out is to restrict or expand the specification of preferences and the basic construction of nonmonotonic logics from them. The second approach attempts to find compromises among the conflicting desiderata, and to analyze the tradeoffs involved in different compromises. A third option is to investigate modifications of the output required of preference aggregation policies, requiring only that aggregation indicate maximal models, not full orders. We discuss these paths toward possibility in turn.

5.1. Modifying the expressiveness of preferences

The impossibility result is fundamentally a statement about the relation between the expressive power of a preferential nonmonotonic logic and the difficulty of combining multiple criteria. To accept the aggregation principles and yet avoid the implications of Theorem 4.3, the language for representing preferences needs to be more or less expressive than the framework presented above.

For example, the impossibility result can be circumvented by expanding the language of preferences to include some expression of intensity of preference.[12] More specifically, the ordinal expressiveness of the individual preferences $\sqsubseteq_i$ can be strengthened in two ways. The first is to allow *intercriteria comparisons*, permitting statements of the form "criterion i likes M_1 more than criterion j likes M_2". A circumscriptive example would be a comparison of the degrees of abnormality of two predicates in different situations, perhaps by counting their abnormal instances. The second enhancement introduces *intracriteria intensities*, where i's degree of preference for M_1 over M_2 can be compared to its preferences for M_3 over M_4. For example, the degree of chronological minimization might be measured by the temporal distance between events. Taken alone, intercriteria comparison only opens the door a crack, leading to aggregation policies that are almost-but-not-quite dictatorial (in a precise sense described, for example, by Roberts [51]). And incorporating only intracriterial intensity comparisons does not help at all. Together, however, the

---

[12]Strictly speaking, this only circumvents the theorem if the intensity information is *mandatory*.

two measures induce a fully cardinal description of preferences (that is, a numeric measure of degree of preference), which leads immediately to satisfactory aggregation functions of the sort recommended by multi-attribute utility theory [23]. In this case, each criterion may be represented by a real-valued function over interpretations and a global utility function may be constructed by a weighted combination of these. Numeric comparison of utility values then defines the global preference order.

Although it solves the preference aggregation problem, we suspect that designers of nonmonotonic logics will not be eager to require in effect that numeric utility measures be assigned to every interpretation. Numeric representations are typically avoided because they are excessively precise and present an intolerable specification burden on the source of default assertions. To make this approach palatable, one would have to find some qualitative (direct) expression of the available preference information (going beyond purely ordinal comparisons) from which the numerical measures could be automatically constructed. Unfortunately, this global comparative information is just what seems to be lacking in our intuition in many cases, as indicated in Section 3. Nevertheless, it may be possible to learn pragmatically useful numerical measures through experience.

Similarly, limiting the expressive power of preferences by restricting the form of the individual partial preorders that are handled by the aggregation policy can lead to acceptable policies operating over the smaller domain. Theorem 4.3 declares the impossibility of a completely general aggregation policy but does not rule out satisfactory aggregation in special cases. Social choice theorists have explored this route in depth, but the special cases they consider (such as single-peakedness, a condition that the candidates be orderable according to one global dimension) do not appear to be viable for the multicriteria preference problem. On the other hand, one might discover aggregable special cases particularly well-suited for nonmonotonic reasoning, whether or not they make sense in the original social choice context. Theorem 4.2 demonstrates that the particular case of normal default rules is not special enough to avoid the difficulties of aggregation; other candidates, however, have yet to be investigated.

5.2. Modifying the aggregation principles

If we insist on maintaining the ordinality of constituent preferences and the universality of the aggregation policy, we must consider which of the desiderata may be abandoned or relaxed.

At the extreme, we could simply give up on global rationality, permitting

⊑ to be intransitive or inconsistent. The effect of intransitivity would be to make more models maximal as compared with those maximal under the transitive closure of the relation, and thus make the nonmonotonic consequences of a theory less complete. Rychlik [52] proposes such an intransitive scheme, and motivates it with an example where chronological ignorance loses force over long durations. However, it is our view that this situation and similar ones are better modeled by recognizing competing preference criteria (e.g., decay of persistence) rather than weakening the underlying concept of preference. Transitivity appears to be a minimal requirement for the interpretation of ⊑ as a "preference relation" in the spirit of rational choice. If it is necessary to abandon transitivity (and ideal rationality of choice along with it), we need not make a virtue of it. Instead, we might abandon transitivity on the simple pragmatic grounds that it is too costly or impossible to enforce in computationally convenient conflict resolution schemes (such as majority rule or random choice).

The effect of inconsistency depends on whether one uses the strict or non-strict order in defining nonmonotonic entailment. The resulting conclusions will be either inconsistent (models exist, but none are maximal) or skeptical (the relevant models are indifferent), respectively.

Similarly, any of the other aggregation principles may be relaxed.

- We could choose to live with a bit of dependence on irrelevant alternatives. This would mean that the preferential semantics imperfectly describe the effects of individual orders, as criteria might better achieve their objectives by misrepresenting their preferences.
- We could accept skepticism in some cases in which credulity would be better.
- We could accept the rule of imperfect dictators which correctly resolve many conflicts but which wrongly resolve others.

Intelligent compromise on these principles requires a much better understanding of the tradeoffs we face. One task here is to obtain a deeper analysis of the sources of impossibility. If we can characterize a subclass of preference profiles that fully account for the pessimistic conclusions of Theorem 4.3, we can limit our desiderata violations to that class. This step is simply a less drastic version of the suggestion above that we restrict the expressive power of the language to exclude the problematic cases. For example, while we argued above that skepticism as a response to all conflicts is irrational, it would be less objectionable to suspend commitment when the conflict is further classified as one of the particularly difficult instances.

To justify this approximation approach, however, we need some way of judging the expected utility of different aggregation procedures when the costs and consequences of inferences are taken into account. This means estimating the likelihoods with which different conflicts appear and the risks and benefits that different forms of irrationality entail in each of these cases. For example, information about the reasoning process in which the conflicts arise might be used to determine the cases in which suspending judgment is rational because determining the proper resolution would take too long, or in which errors would occur infrequently enough to ignore. Or alternatively, this information might make it possible to compare the expected utility of imperfect dictators (based on the expected probability and consequences of their errors) with the expected effort of revising the dictatorial priorities in a way that improves their performance. In the context of voting, Tullock [62] argues that systems such as majority decision will produce satisfactory, approximately rational results given large enough numbers of voters. Although the conditions and assumptions underlying his conclusions are not clearly applicable to the default reasoning case, investigations of this sort suggest that regularities in preference structures may mitigate the undesirable consequences of the impossibility results.

5.3. Modifying the output of aggregation

Approaches that modify the expressiveness of preferences can be viewed as variations on the *input* of aggregation policies. In a dual manner, we can attempt to escape the impossibility result by modifying the *output* produced by the aggregation process. Social choice theorists have investigated one variation in which maximal elements are selected directly without constructing the entire global preference order. Formally, the aggregation returns a *choice function* mapping candidate sets to subsets of maximal elements. This particular modification seems appropriate for nonmonotonic logic because the concepts of preferential satisfaction and entailment distinguish only between maximal and nonmaximal elements of the preference order.

However, this apparent weakening of the aggregation framework does not offer much improvement in the prospects for obtaining satisfactory aggregation functions. Sen [54] points out that proofs of the various impossibility results typically apply directly to the case of choice of maximal elements. The key observation is that the choice function induces a relation R (roughly speaking, $M_1 \, R \, M_2$ means "M_1 is chosen over M_2 in the context of some candidate set") that fulfills the role of the global preference order $\sqsubseteq$ in derivations of the original theorems.

6. Applications to mental societies

Reasoning has been viewed in social terms in artificial intelligence by several authors. The most prominent example is Minsky [40], who explicitly models thinking as the aggregate activity of many small mental agents. In the context of nonmonotonic reasoning, Borgida and Imilienski [3] appeal to committee decision-making as a metaphor for default inference, and Doyle [5,7,8] presents nonmonotonic reasoning from a group decision-theoretic perspective. Related views of thinking can be found in economics, philosophy, and psychology [43,44,58,59].

The central tenet of Minsky's *Society of Mind* [40] is the rejection of the single-self viewpoint in favor of a mind made up of many, largely autonomous, agencies. If this idea is to be taken seriously, then analyses of behavior which take as primitive such single-self concepts as beliefs, preferences, and goals should be regarded with some degree of skepticism. More precisely, the presumption of consistency among these objects must be carefully scrutinized. Social choice theory is well-suited for this kind of study because it aims to characterize global properties of aggregate behavior without requiring mechanistic descriptions of the individual components.

It appears at first glance that the impossibility results discussed above should also explain inconsistencies in belief and preferences for minds—even under the most optimistic hypothesis about the rationality of its component agencies. Representing the individual preferences by $\sqsubseteq_i$ and taking the global, single-self preferences to be the output of the aggregation function, the impossibility theorems apply directly.

Indeed, the results have immediate consequences for the society-of-mind model proposed by Doyle [6]. This is not surprising, as the agents in this model correspond to a form of default rule that can be interpreted preferentially as described in Section 4.3. Theorem 4.2 implies that either IIA is violated in constructing the admissible extensions or the set of agents contains a dictator.

Unfortunately, few of the other society-of-mind theories are concrete enough to be analyzed in this fashion.[13] For the more general framework, we need to ask the obvious questions about whether mental agencies can have some way of circumventing the conditions. To some extent, the case against consistent preferences in a mental society shares a common basis with the arguments we offer against universal default theories. However, differences in the domain (mental agencies versus preferential criteria) lead to important conceptual distinctions in our interpretation of the results.

The case against dictatorship is, if anything, stronger in the mental society context, as decentralization is an explicit and fundamental attribute of these theories. Even if not absolute, dictatorial individuals represent an uncomfortable concentration of power that is more characteristic of bureaucratic structures than societies of autonomous agents.

---

[13]Fagin and Halpern's logic of local reasoning [14] might be one of these few.

The dictum against cardinal representations of intensity of preference, however, is more difficult to defend for mental agents, especially since several architectures for reasoning involve numeric representations for degrees of belief or other states (for example, neural networks). Without a theory of the ultimate source of preferences, it is hard to justify specific constraints on their form. Finally, the universality standard we imposed on preferential default theories may not apply as forcefully to mind societies. Mental societies may manage to function satisfactorily despite an inability to incorporate or obey particular preference criteria.

These trap doors prevent us from offering any sweeping conclusions about the possibility of globally rational agents built from societies of autonomous individuals. For analyzing specific society-of-mind architectures, however, the tools of social choice theory are likely to prove quite useful.

7. Conclusions

We proved in Section 4 that any universal theory of default inference based on combining noncomprehensive preference criteria must sometimes produce irrational conclusions, or alternatively, the only way to guarantee rational conclusions is to manually resolve all conflicts in advance. Our argument may be summarized as follows:

(1) It is natural to formalize nonmonotonic logics as theories of preferential or rational inference. From this viewpoint, defaults express preferences about what to believe (or more generally, about what states of mind to inhabit), and the theories of different nonmonotonic inferences embody different criteria about how to identify the most preferred conclusions.

(2) Unfortunately, these theories are very incomplete. Individual defaults only concern specific propositions, and all known theoretical inferential criteria cover only some of the considerations relevant to choosing conclusions rationally.

(3) These theories are also somewhat incompatible. Individual defaults may express conflicting preferences, and different criteria may indicate conflicting conclusions.

(4) It is not feasible to resolve these conflicts in advance. Therefore, any universal theory must rely on some method that takes the available set of preference criteria and combines them into a global criterion.

(5) If conflicts are to be resolved rationally, the preferences resulting from the resolution must agree with the original criteria when those criteria agree and must result in the same ordering for pairs of alternatives independent of what other alternatives are under consideration.

(6) But we prove, with respect to this weak sense of rationality, that there are no rational methods for aggregating criteria represented by preference orders unless the resulting order is simply one of the criteria being aggregated. Therefore, the only way to achieve rationality is to impose a priority ranking on the criteria, and to revise the ranking whenever new conflicts become important.

More fundamentally, resolving even simple conflicts requires empirical information about which resolution is best (or is of maximal expected utility to the reasoner). While designers might try to supply artificial reasoners with some of this information, most of it must be left unsaid as too hard to foresee or too voluminous to state explicitly. One cannot expect a purely theoretical combination method to possess this empirical information, so a purely theoretical solution to conflicting defaults seems unlikely (cf. [38]).

Of course, our results apply only to the case in which none of the available criteria is a comprehensive universal theory by itself, and would be irrelevant if someone were to discover a good comprehensive theory. But at present, all criteria are clearly limited in scope, and our strong expectation is that all theories discovered in the future will be similarly limited.

The impossibility results presented above expose previously unarticulated difficulties in the quest toward universal default mechanisms. We do not believe that these results constitute an indictment of the preferential framework. Instead, translating questions about nonmonotonic reasoning into the language of rational inference and social choice provides a rational justification for the nondeductive structure of some nonmonotonic logics and yields valuable insights into their design. Moreover, the problem is not attributable to the use of logical or mathematical formalisms for describing or mechanizing reasoning, nor is it due to limitations on the computational resources available for carrying out reasoning. Instead, our results delimit the nature of feasible forms of rationality for an agent that integrates preferences from multiple sources, independent of its representational structure, computational power, or extent of knowledge.

To address the problems posed by our results, we must continue to investigate special theories of reasoning and the conditions under which each of these is to be preferred or to be avoided. We expect that further analysis from the social choice perspective will suggest promising approaches, both because it provides the vocabulary for expressing concepts related to aggregation policies, and because it allows artificial intelligence studies to draw on a large literature of detailed investigations of social choice questions.

Acknowledgement

We thank Daniel Bobrow, Ruy Cardoso, Gerald de Jong, David Etherington, Benjamin Grosof, Ronald Loui, Joseph Schatz, Yoav Shoham, Mark
Stefik, and Peter Szolovits for valuable discussions and probing questions.
The comments of the anonymous referees helped identify some minor errors
and suggested clarifications of several issues. Jon Doyle's work on this paper
was supported by National Institutes of Health Grant No. R01 LM04493
from the National Library of Medicine.

References

[1] K.J. Arrow, *Social Choice and Individual Values* (Yale University Press, New Haven, CT, 2nd ed., 1963).
[2] K.J. Arrow, Values and collective decision-making, in: P. Laslett and W.G. Runciman, eds., *Philosophy, Politics and Society (third series)* (Basil Blackwell, Oxford, 1967) 215–232.
[3] A. Borgida and T. Imilienski, Decision making in committees—a framework for dealing with inconsistency and non-monotonicity, in: *Proceedings Workshop on Non-Monotonic Reasoning*, New Paltz, NY (1984) 21–32.
[4] A.L. Brown Jr and Y. Shoham, New results on semantical nonmonotonic reasoning, in: M. Reinfrank, J. de Kleer, M.L. Ginsberg et al. eds., *Non-Monotonic Reasoning* (Springer, New York, 1989) 19–26.
[5] J. Doyle, A society of mind: multiple perspectives, reasoned assumptions, and virtual copies, in: *Proceedings IJCAI-83*, Karlsruhe, FRG (1983) 309–314.
[6] J. Doyle, Some theories of reasoned assumptions: an essay in rational psychology, Tech. Report 83-125, Department of Computer Science, Carnegie-Mellon University, Pittsburgh, PA (1983).
[7] J. Doyle, Reasoned assumptions and Pareto optimality, in: *Proceedings IJCAI-85*, Los Angeles, CA (1985) 87–90.
[8] J. Doyle, Artificial intelligence and rational self-government, Tech. Report CS-88-124, Department of Computer Science, Carnegie-Mellon University, Pittsburgh, PA (1988).
[9] J. Doyle, Constructive belief and rational representation, *Comput. Intell.* 5 (1989) 1–11.
[10] J. Doyle, Rational belief revision, Presented at the Third International Workshop on Nonmonotonic Reasoning, Stanford, CA (1990).
[11] J. Doyle, Rationality and its roles in reasoning (extended abstract), in: *Proceedings AAAI-90*, Boston, MA (1990) 1093–1100.
[12] J. Doyle and M.P. Wellman, Impediments to universal preference-based default theories, in: R.J. Brachman, H.J. Levesque and R. Reiter, eds., *Proceedings of the First International Conference on Principles of Knowledge Representation and Reasoning*, Toronto, Ont. (Morgan Kaufmann, San Mateo, CA, 1989) 94–102.
[13] D.W. Etherington, *Reasoning with Incomplete Information* (Pitman, London, 1988).
[14] R. Fagin and J.Y. Halpern, Belief, awareness, and limited reasoning: preliminary report, in: *Proceedings IJCAI-85*, Los Angeles, CA (1985) 491–501.
[15] A. Gibbard, Manipulation of voting schemes: a general result, *Econometrica* 41 (1973) 587–601.
[16] M.L. Ginsberg, ed., *Readings in Nonmonotonic Reasoning* (Morgan Kaufmann, Los Altos, CA, 1987).
[17] B.N. Grosof, Generalizing prioritization, Manuscript (February 1990).
[18] J.Y. Halpern and Y. Moses, Towards a theory of knowledge and ignorance: preliminary

report, in: *Proceedings Workshop on Non-Monotonic Reasoning*, New Paltz, NY (1984) 125–143.

[19] S. Hanks and D. McDermott, Nonmonotonic logic and temporal projection, *Artif. Intell.* **33** (1987) 379–412.

[20] J.F. Horty and R.H. Thomason, Deontic foundations for nonmonotonic reasoning, Presented at the Third International Workshop on Nonmonotonic Reasoning, Stanford, CA (1990).

[21] J.F. Horty, R.H. Thomason and D.S. Touretzky, A skeptical theory of inheritance in nonmonotonic semantic networks, *Artif. Intell.* **42** (1990) 311–348.

[22] W. James, *The Will to Believe and Other Essays in Popular Philosophy* (Longmans, Green, and Co., New York, 1897).

[23] R.L. Keeney and H. Raiffa, *Decisions with Multiple Objectives: Preferences and Value Tradeoffs* (Wiley, New York, 1976).

[24] K. Konolige, Hierarchic autoepistemic theories for nonmonotonic reasoning, in: *Proceedings AAAI-88*, St. Paul, MN (1988) 439–443.

[25] K. Konolige, On the relation between default and autoepistemic logic, *Artif. Intell.* **35** (1988) 343–382; see also Errata, *Artif. Intell.* **41** (1989/90) 115.

[26] C.P. Langlotz and E.H. Shortliffe, Logical and decision-theoretic methods for planning under uncertainty, *AI Mag.* **10** (1989) 39–47.

[27] H.J. Levesque, A logic of implicit and explicit belief, in: *Proceedings AAAI-84*, Austin, TX (1984) 198–202.

[28] H.J. Levesque, Making believers out of computers, *Artif. Intell.* **30** (1986) 81–108.

[29] V. Lifschitz, Pointwise circumscription: preliminary report, in: *Proceedings AAAI-86*, Philadelphia, PA (1986) 406–410.

[30] V. Lifschitz, Formal theories of action, in: F.M. Brown, ed., *The Frame Problem in Artificial Intelligence: Proceedings of the 1987 Workshop* (Morgan Kaufmann, Los Altos, CA, 1987) 35–57.

[31] V. Lifschitz, Between circumscription and autoepistemic logic, in: R.J. Brachman, H.J. Levesque and R. Reiter, eds., *Proceedings of the First International Conference on Principles of Knowledge Representation and Reasoning*, Toronto, Ont. (Morgan Kaufmann, San Mateo, CA, 1989) 235–244.

[32] F. Lin and Y. Shoham, Argument systems: a uniform basis for nonmonotonic reasoning, in: R.J. Brachman, H.J. Levesque and R. Reiter, eds., *Proceedings of the First International Conference on Principles of Knowledge Representation and Reasoning*, Toronto, Ont. (Morgan Kaufmann, San Mateo, CA, 1989) 245–255.

[33] L.H. Longley-Cook, An introduction to credibility theory, *Proc. Casualty Actuarial Soc.* **49** (1962) 194.

[34] R.P. Loui, Computing reference classes, in: J.F. Lemmer and L.N. Kanal, eds., *Uncertainty in Artificial Intelligence* 2 (North-Holland, Amsterdam, 1988) 273–289.

[35] J. McCarthy, Circumscription—a form of non-monotonic reasoning, *Artif. Intell.* **13** (1980) 27–38.

[36] J. McCarthy, Applications of circumscription to formalizing common-sense knowledge, *Artif. Intell.* **28** (1986) 89–116.

[37] D. McDermott, AI, logic, and the frame problem, in: F.M. Brown, ed., *The Frame Problem in Artificial Intelligence: Proceedings of the 1987 Workshop* (Morgan Kaufmann, Los Altos, CA, 1987) 105–118.

[38] D. McDermott, A critique of pure reason, *Comput. Intell.* **3** (1987) 151–160.

[39] D. McDermott and J. Doyle, Non-monotonic logic—I, *Artif. Intell.* **13** (1980) 41–72.

[40] M. Minsky, *The Society of Mind* (Simon and Schuster, New York, 1986).

[41] R.C. Moore, Possible world semantics for autoepistemic logic, in: *Proceedings Workshop on Non-Monotonic Reasoning*, New Paltz, NY (1984) 21–32.

[42] R.C. Moore, Semantical considerations on nonmonotonic logic, *Artif. Intell.* **25** (1985) 75–94.

[43] R.A. Mundell, *Man and Economics* (McGraw-Hill, New York, 1968).

[44] M. Nowakowska, *Language of Motivation and Language of Actions* (Mouton & Co., The Hague, 1973).

[45] B. Pascal, *Pensées sur la religion et sur quelques autres sujets* (Harvill, London, 1962); Translated by M. Turnell, originally published 1662.

[46] J.L. Pollock, Defeasible reasoning, *Cogn. Sci.* **11** (1987) 481–518.

[47] D. Poole, What the lottery paradox tells us about default reasoning, in: R.J. Brachman, H.J. Levesque and R. Reiter, eds., *Proceedings of the First International Conference on Principles of Knowledge Representation and Reasoning*, Toronto, Ont. (Morgan Kaufmann, San Mateo, CA, 1989) 333–340.

[48] R. Reiter, On closed world data bases, in: H. Gallaire and J. Minker, eds., *Logic and Data Bases* (Plenum, New York, 1978) 55–76.

[49] R. Reiter, A logic for default reasoning, *Artif. Intell.* **13** (1980) 81–132.

[50] F.S. Roberts, *Discrete Mathematical Models* (Prentice-Hall, Englewood Cliffs, NJ, 1976).

[51] K.W.S. Roberts, Possibility theorems with interpersonally comparable welfare levels, *Rev. Econ. Stud.* **47** (1980) 409–420.

[52] P. Rychlik, The generalized theory of model preference (preliminary report), in: *Proceedings AAAI-90*, Boston, MA (1990) 615–620.

[53] A. Sen, The impossibility of a Paretian liberal, *J. Political Econ.* **78** (1970) 152–157.

[54] A. Sen, Social choice theory: a re-examination, *Econometrica* **45** (1977) 53–89.

[55] Y. Shoham, Nonmonotonic logics: meaning and utility, in: *Proceedings IJCAI-87*, Milan, Italy (1987) 388–393.

[56] Y. Shoham, *Reasoning about Change: Time and Causation from the Standpoint of Artificial Intelligence* (MIT Press, Cambridge, MA, 1988).

[57] L.A. Stein, Skeptical inheritance: computing the intersection of credulous extensions, in: *Proceedings IJCAI-89*, Detroit, MI (1989) 1153–1158.

[58] R.J. Sternberg, Intelligence is mental self-government, in: R.J. Sternberg and D.K. Detterman, eds., *What is Intelligence? Contemporary Viewpoints on its Nature and Definition* (Ablex, Norwood, NJ, 1986) 141–148.

[59] R.H. Thomason, The context-sensitivity of belief and desire, in: M.P. Georgeff and A.L. Lansky, eds., *Reasoning about Actions and Plans: Proceedings of the 1986 Workshop* (Morgan Kaufmann, Los Altos, CA, 1986) 341–360.

[60] D.S. Touretzky, *The Mathematics of Inheritance Systems* (Morgan Kaufmann, Los Altos, CA, 1986).

[61] D.S. Touretzky, J.F. Horty and R.H. Thomason, A clash of intuitions: the current state of nonmonotonic multiple inheritance systems, in: *Proceedings IJCAI-87*, Milan, Italy (1987) 476–482.

[62] G. Tullock, The general irrelevance of the general impossibility theorem, *Q. J. Econ.* **81** (1967) 256–270.

[63] B.C. Van Frassen, Values and the heart's command, *J. Philos.* **LXX** (1973) 5–19.

Artificial Intelligence 49 (1991) 129–159
Elsevier

Embedding decision-analytic control in a learning architecture

Oren Etzioni

Department of Computer Science and Engineering, FR-35, University of Washington, Seattle, WA 98195, USA

Received October 1989
Revised September 1990

Abstract

Etzioni, O., Embedding decision-analytic control in a learning environment, Artificial Intelligence 49 (1991) 129–159.

An autonomous agent's control problem is often formulated as the attempt to minimize the expected cost of accomplishing a goal. This paper presents a three-dimensional view of the control problem that is substantially more realistic. The agent's control policy is assessed along three dimensions: deliberation cost, execution cost, and goal value. The agent must choose which goal to attend to as well as which action to take. Our control policy seeks to maximize satisfaction by trading execution cost and goal value while keeping deliberation cost low. The agent's control decisions are guided by the MU heuristic—*choose the alternative whose marginal expected utility is maximal.* Thus, when necessary, the agent will prefer easily-achieved goals to attractive but difficult-to-attain alternatives. The MU heuristic is embedded in an architecture with record-keeping and learning capabilities. The architecture offers its control module expected utility and expected cost estimates that are gradually refined as the agent accumulates experience. A programmer is not required to supply that knowledge, and the estimates are provided without recourse to distributional assumptions.

1. Introduction and motivation

In a paper dating back to 1975, Simon and Kadane defined the problem of satisficing search. Satisficing search seeks to minimize *expected* search effort while treating goal nodes as interchangeable. A resource-bounded autonomous agent requires a substantially more realistic view of the world. First, the agent must trade the value of the sought goal against the expected cost of reaching the goal [36]. Second, the agent has to curtail its deliberation time, otherwise little time will be left to act.

0004-3702/91/$03.50 © 1991—Elsevier Science Publishers B.V.

This paper proposes a decision-theoretic formulation of the agent's control problem. To achieve satisfactory performance the agent has to trade deliberation cost, execution cost, and goal value. The formulation is thus called "three-dimensional". We show that finding an optimal solution to the control problem is NP-hard, which suggests that the deliberation cost of acting optimally can be prohibitive. A heuristic, inspired by Simon and Kadane's paper, is suggested and proven close to optimal in two special cases. The heuristic trades execution cost and goal value while keeping deliberation cost low.

The heuristic, and other decision-theoretic approaches, presuppose that the agent possesses extensive knowledge about its world in the form of cost, probability and utility estimates. Below, we argue that embedding a decision-theoretic control mechanism within an architecture with record-keeping and learning capabilities is a plausible approach to accumulating the requisite knowledge.

1.1. A critique of simple satisficing search

Simon and Kadane introduce their approach with the fanciful example of searching for a treasure chest. Chests may be buried in any of a number of excavation sites. The agent's problem is to find a treasure chest as quickly as possible. Given expected cost and probability of success figures for the excavation of each site, Simon and Kadane derive a search strategy for the agent that provably minimizes the expected cost of the search. They proceed to generalize the strategy to the case where ordering constraints hold between different excavation operations. While mathematically pleasing, Simon and Kadane's formulation makes several important simplifications. It is the burden of this paper to remove some of these simplifications while retaining Simon and Kadane's original insight that minimizing expected search effort is an important component of the control problem.

Simon and Kadane presuppose that probability of success and expected cost figures are available for each potential search action. In practice, such figures must be computed. Section 3.2 describes a mechanism that enables an agent to estimate these figures based on its problem-solving experiences. Although Simon and Kadane do not report on a complexity analysis of their procedure for computing an optimal search strategy, the procedure analyzes every node in the search graph. Consequently, the procedure's complexity is at least linear in the size of the graph. The search graphs in typical AI problems (e.g., chess) are sufficiently large that the computational cost of such a procedure is prohibitive. This paper proposes a tractable procedure for control.

Satisficing search does not distinguish between goals, nor does it distinguish between methods for achieving a given goal. But even the simple treasure chest example warrants such distinctions. The value of the treasures in different chests may vary, and distinct excavation procedures may yield varying portions of the treasures. A more powerful search control mechanism would not blindly seek to minimize search effort. Instead, the mechanism would trade search effort and treasure value in an attempt to maximize the expected utility of the search subject to the agent's resource constraints.

Satisficing search aims to achieve a single goal. An agent often has multiple goals, however. For example, there may be several islands with different treasures buried on each. The agent may wish to carry off as many treasures as it can before an impending native attack. The degree of the agent's satisfaction is the sum of the values of the treasures it is able to abscond with. We refer to multiple goals of this sort as *value-additive*. Value-additive goals are distinct from conjunctive subgoals in that failing to achieve one goal does not impinge on trying to achieve the rest. Value-additive goals are distinct from disjunctive subgoals in that the agent wishes to achieve more than one of them. This paper focuses on value-additive goals.

1.2. Preview of the paper

The control problem for a resource-bounded autonomous agent is essentially an economic problem—the problem of utilizing resources to maximize satisfaction. It is not surprising, therefore, that the central notions underlying our approach to the problem, opportunity cost and marginal utility, are both borrowed from economic theory [32]. Our approach heeds Doyle's dictum that AI look to other disciplines for ideas and analytical tools [7].

When the utilization of a resource (such as time or money) for some action *A* means that another action cannot be performed, *A* is said to have an opportunity cost. Attending graduate school, for example, has the opportunity cost of not being able to earn a higher salary in industry. If several actions contend for the same resource, then the opportunity cost of choosing one of them is the maximum of the utilities of the others. The opportunity cost of time is at the crux of a time-bounded agent's control problem. Taking one course of action means that time may not be available to take another, and deliberating about which action to perform robs the agent of time that could have been used to act. Opportunity cost is defined precisely in Section 2.3.

The degree to which an agent desires a goal can be represented by a utility measure over world states. A state in which a goal is achieved has a higher utility than one in which it is not. In the treasure chest example, a simple utility measure is the value of the treasures the agent has amassed at any given point in time. A utility measure can also model partial goal satisfaction. The utility of achieving a goal with a given method is a function of the goal's worth and the degree to which the method satisfies the goal.

Given a utility function, marginal utility may be defined as the derivative of the utility function with respect to a cost variable (time in this case). We employ marginal utility as a choice criterion between the options available to an agent. Picking the option whose marginal utility is greatest maximizes the ratio of utility to execution cost. Thus, an easy-to-obtain but small treasure chest may be preferred to one that is valuable but difficult-to-reach. Maximizing marginal utility enables the agent to trade goal utility for search effort.

The balance of the paper is as follows: The next section formulates precisely the control problem introduced above. Section 3 outlines our solution to the problem, emphasizing the importance of learning capabilities in Section 3.3. Section 4 analyzes the solution in two special cases that have proven amenable to precise theoretical treatment. A discussion of related work and the conclusion follow. The conclusion calls for the integration of decision-analytic and machine learning approaches to the control problem.

2. The control problem

2.1. Formulating the control problem

This section formulates the agent's control problem in decision-theoretic terms: an optimal control policy is one whose expected utility is maximal. It is important to note that optimality is defined relative to the agent's world model. Modifying that model by making new distinctions will change what is optimal. We return to this point in Section 3.3.

Although our formulation is substantially more realistic than Simon and Kadane's, it still focuses on certain aspects of the problem at the expense of others. Rather than aiming for complete generality, our strategy has been to make incremental progress by addressing the critique in Section 1.1. We have noted the points at which simplifications were made.

More specifically, the aspects we have chosen to highlight are the following:

- the opportunity cost of time,
- the relationship between symbolic goals and utility functions,
- the sequencing of multiple methods and goals,
- tradeoffs between goal value, execution cost, and probability of success,
- the knowledge required for decision-analytic control,
- the impact of approximate knowledge on the agent's decision quality.

Aspects of the problem we have not studied include:

- complex interactions between methods and goals,
- construction of plans from primitive actions,
- reactive execution,

- sophisticated deliberative policies.

2.2. Basic definitions

Below we present the definitions used to formulate the control problem. We begin by introducing some notation which is used to define goal value and method utility.

- S: the set of world states, s denotes an element of S;
- G: the agent's goal set, g denotes an element of G;
- m: a method m is a sequence of actions aimed at achieving a goal;
- $m(s)$: the unique state that results from executing m in s;
- $t(s)$: the time in state s, two states s_1 and s_2 are distinct if $t(s_1) \neq t(s_2)$;
- $i(g)$: the intrinsic value of g;
- $d(s, g)$: the degree, from 0 to 1, to which g is satisfied in s.

The value of a goal g in a state s, $v(s, g)$, is an arbitrary function F of the current time in s, and g's intrinsic value multiplied by the degree to which g is satisfied in s.

$$v(s, g) = F(i(g)d(s, g), t(s)).$$

The function F models the dependence of goal value on time. For example, when achieving g after some time t is worthless, $F(x, y) = 0$ for all y greater than t and for all x.

The function v is defined for both single goals and sets of goals. The value of a goal set, $v(s, G)$, is the sum of the values of the individual goals. Since value is invariably defined relative to the agent's goal set, we drop G from v's argument list. Thus, $v(s) \equiv v(s, G)$.

$$v(s) = \sum_{g \in G} v(s, g).$$

The goal set is assumed to be value-additive (Section 1.1). This is a strong assumption. It implies that the values of the individual goals are mutually independent. Classical planning research has been concerned with conjunctive goals.[1] The assumption implicit in that body of work is that the planning problem is solved only if each and every goal is achieved. In our model, the value of achieving each goal is independent of the status of other goals. See [14] for further analysis of the relationship between goals and utility functions.

Let $U(s, m)$ denote the utility of executing m in s. The utility of a method is its "added value",

$$U(s, m) = v(m(s)) - v(s).$$

---

[1] See [4] for a historical overview.

The time to execute a method m in s, $T(s,m)$, is defined analogously.

$$T(s,m) = t(m(s)) - t(s).$$

Our excavation example can be modeled as follows. The treasures sought by the agent constitute its value-additive goal set. Different excavation procedures correspond to the different methods. The proportion of the treasure retrieved by each excavation procedure is the degree to which its goal is satisfied. The time of the impending native attack forms a deadline. Before the deadline, the value of each treasure is its worth in dollars. A treasure is worthless if found after the deadline.

We assume that a method is deterministic. That is, $m(s)$ is always the same for any given state s. The agent does not know $m(s)$ for the current world state, however. The agent could execute m to find out, but it has many methods it could potentially execute and limited time. Consequently, the agent relies on *expected values* for the utility and cost of each method, estimated before execution, in making its control decisions.

What are expected values? The states encountered by the agent, initially, can be viewed as randomly drawn from some probability distribution π_0. Since the utility U and time cost T are functions of m and s, they are random variables. Thus, we can define the expected values of U and T. The expected utility of m, $EU(m)$, is the sum over all states of the probability that the agent will encounter the state multiplied by the utility of executing m in that state.

$$EU(m) = \sum_{s \in S} \pi_0(s) U(s,m).$$

The expected time cost of m, $ET(m)$, is defined analogously. The state s is not an argument to EU and ET because the expectation is over the distribution of possible states.

2.3. Opportunity cost

We now move from individual methods to method sequences. Let σ be a method sequence of length k. Thus, $\sigma = (m_1..m_k)$. The agent executes the method sequence σ as follows: it moves through the methods in order, checking whether each method's goal is achievable in the current state. If so, the agent executes the method. If the goal cannot be achieved, the agent moves to the next method on the list. A goal cannot be achieved if it has already been satisfied (even partially), or if a previous method has rendered the goal unachievable. For example, if the previous excavation procedure used dynamite at the treasure's site, then either some of the treasure has been retrieved or the treasure was inadvertently destroyed. Either way, the agent ought to move to another goal.

We assume that each method can be executed from any state. Considerably more sophisticated models of execution are possible. However, the current model suffices for the analysis carried out in this paper.

Executing σ in state s leads to the state $\sigma(s)$. The definition of $U(s, \sigma)$ is analogous to the definition of $U(s, m)$.

$$U(s, \sigma) = v(\sigma(s)) - v(s).$$

Likewise, the definitions of $T(\sigma)$, $EU(\sigma)$, and $ET(\sigma)$ mirror the corresponding definitions for a single method.

Let $\sigma^*(s)$ be an optimal method sequence in s. An optimal method sequence is one whose expected utility is maximal. Let $\gamma(s, m)$ denote the opportunity cost of choosing the method m in s. $\gamma(s, m)$ is the maximal utility achievable by a method sequence that does not start with m.

$$\gamma(s, m) = \max_{m' \in M-m} U(s, m'\sigma^*).$$

The *net* utility $N(s, m)$ of m at s is its opportunity cost subtracted from the utility of an optimal method sequence that starts with m.

$$N(s, m) = U(s, m\sigma^*) - \gamma(s, m).$$

The net utility of m is nonnegative exactly when m is optimal.

We denote the expected opportunity cost of m by $E\gamma(m)$, and the expected net utility of m by $EN(m)$.

2.4. Constructing method sequences

The three-dimensional control problem (Fig. 1) can be solved by computing the expected net utility of each method.

Theorem 2.1. *Repeatedly choosing a method whose expected net utility is maximal yields an optimal method sequence.*[2]

Given:

- a set of value-additive goals G,
- a set of methods M_g for each goal $g \in G$,
- for all methods m, $ET(m)$ and $EU(m)$.

Determine: A method sequence whose expected utility is maximal.

Fig. 1. The three-dimensional control problem.

[2]Proofs of the results are in the appendix.

There are several problems with the algorithm implicit in Theorem 2.1. Executing a method modifies the probability distribution over states. Thus, the expected net utility of a method depends on the methods executed before it. As a result, the number of distinct expectations necessary for computing the expected net utility of a method grows exponentially with the number of methods executed before it. The algorithm requires massive amounts of information that the agent is unlikely to possess. Our heuristic control procedure, presented in Section 3.1, is only able to circumvent this problem by making strong independence assumptions.

Aside from demanding an excessive amount of knowledge from the agent, the algorithm is also computationally intractable. In fact, the three-dimensional control problem is NP-hard in the number of goals in the agent's goal set G (denoted by $|G|$).

Theorem 2.2. *The three-dimensional control problem is NP-hard.*

Designing agents that rely on $|G|$ remaining small, thereby circumventing this hardness result, seems ill-advised. The performance of such agents can deteriorate rapidly as $|G|$ increases. Relying on a control procedure whose expected behavior is reasonable, but is prohibitively slow in the worst case, is also questionable. Such a procedure can fail in an emergency, with dire consequences. To be robust, an agent's core control routine has to be fast [37]. The agent may choose to deliberate in certain cases but, to guarantee its survival, a snap-decision to act should be possible at any time. To guarantee the ability to act quickly, we have chosen a control procedure whose running time increases slowly with the number of options available to the agent. [3]

2.5. Discussion

The three-dimensional control problem is defined in Fig. 1. The agent is given a set of goals and methods for achieving them. Its task is to derive a method sequence whose expected utility is optimal based on expected utility and expected cost figures for the individual methods. An agent tackling the problem must have a means of deriving or estimating these figures. Thus, the control problem gives rise to a learning problem which is addressed in Section 3.

The problem formulation makes a number of important simplifications. First, the control problem is defined for an off-line control mechanism. No analysis is provided of how to dynamically modify the flow of control

[3] The *flexible computation* [19] or *anytime* algorithm [6] approaches provide an attractive alternative means of providing this guarantee.

at execution time. Second, the only resource we consider is time. Third, we have not modeled the cost of switching between different goals and the cost of recovering from failed methods. Fourth, we have not considered methods whose outcomes, for a given state, are stochastic. Fifth, we have not analyzed complex relationships between goals. We believe that the problem formulation can be elaborated to model these considerations. Finally, we do not model the synthesis of methods from primitive actions. We agree with Hanks [15] that this process is better handled by symbolic planning techniques.

The three-dimensional view of control is not explicitly represented in Fig. 1. However, the presence of multiple methods for satisfying (to varying degrees) multiple goals implies a range of possible execution cost and goal utility tradeoffs. Since utility can vary with time, the cost of deliberation can be modeled as well. Thus, all three dimensions are implicit in the formulation of the control problem.

The architecture, described below, addresses both the intractability and the knowledge demands of decision-theoretic control. Sampling techniques are used to estimate the relevant knowledge, and a greedy control heuristic circumvents the computational difficulty inherent in the three-dimensional control problem. We refer to our approach as *decision-analytic* (rather than decision-theoretic) to underscore its heuristic nature.

3. The agent's architecture

The previous section formulated the control problem in general terms. This section proposes a solution. The section opens by describing the agent's control cycle. Although the problem formulation allows a wide range of deliberative strategies, our agent utilizes a greedy control heuristic. Thus, our solution to the three-dimensional control problem does not treat all three dimensions equally. Goal value and execution cost are traded while keeping deliberation cost low. See [5,11,20,30] for discussions of more sophisticated deliberative strategies.

We do not assume that the agent is given adequate expected utility and expected cost estimates for its methods. The reminder of the section explains how the agent acquires and refines these estimates over time.

3.1. The agent's control cycle

A description of the agent's control cycle appears in Fig. 2. In a nutshell, the agent chooses methods in a best-first fashion where the "best" method is the one whose estimated *marginal expected utility* is maximal.

Marginal utility (per unit cost) is the derivative of the utility function with respect to the cost variable (time in our case). Since method execution

(1) For each method (of each goal):

    (a) Estimate the expected utility U and expected cost T of the method using the procedure in Fig. 4.

    (b) Form the method's key: U/T.

(2) Sort the methods on their keys in decreasing order.

(3) Execute the methods in succession, skipping methods whose goal is already achieved.

Fig. 2. The agent's control cycle.

cannot be interrupted in our model, the marginal utility of a method can be thought of as the method's average utility per unit time. Average utility is computed by dividing a method's utility by its execution time. Maximizing marginal expected utility is a greedy control heuristic. The agent picks the method that is expected to maximize the "return" for its time investment. We refer to this heuristic as the MU heuristic. A heuristic is used because the control problem is computationally intractable (Theorem 2.2).

Employing the MU heuristic enables the agent to trade goal value for reduced execution cost. Thus, when necessary, the agent will prefer easily-achieved goals to attractive but difficult-to-attain alternatives. For example, the agent will prefer a treasure worth one thousand dollars, which can be found in five minutes, to a treasure worth three thousand dollars which requires one hour to excavate. However, the agent will prefer a sixty thousand dollar treasure, which requires an hour to excavate, to the five-minute treasure above.

Although the control cycle in Fig. 2 does not mention deliberation, the agent is not necessarily committed to acting immediately. It may be possible to apply the control cycle to decide between deliberating and acting based on the marginal expected utilities of both options. Then, the routine could be used again to choose between deliberative procedures or between different courses of action. The details of this idea have not been worked out. Clearly, however, this extension to the basic control mechanism would necessitate estimating the utility of deliberative procedures. This topic is not addressed here, but see [30] for an elegant treatment of this problem.

3.2. Keeping records

Initially, the agent executes its methods in a default order. After the execution of each method, the agent records how long the execution took, and the utility obtained from the execution. If the method is an excavation procedure, for example, a clock is consulted before the procedure begins and after it terminates to determine its time cost. The utility of the excavation is determined by evaluating the result. The result may be a pile of gravel (with utility 0) an unmolested treasure chest (with utility equal to the value of the chest), or a portion of the buried treasure (with utility corresponding to the portion's value).

Thus, each method execution yields a datum on the method's utility and time cost which the agent records for future reference. The record has four components: a description of the state prior to method execution, the name of the method executed, the time consumed by the method, and the utility derived. Note that keeping the record requires minimal computational effort on the agent's part. In contrast, computing the net utility of a method would require attempting to compute the optimal method sequence at each point—an intractable task.

The states encountered by the agent can be viewed as randomly drawn from a population. The records collected by the agent are a sample from that population. Decision-analytic control requires expected or *mean* utility and time consumption figures for each method. The agent can estimate these figures by computing *sample means*. The estimation of expectations by sample means is a simple and well-understood statistical procedure. Furthermore, as shown in Section 4.1, the distance of a sample mean from the true mean is likely to decrease rapidly as the sample size increases.

Several researchers (e.g., Natarajan [27] and Wefald and Russell [38]) have suggested using statistical inference to estimate the figures required by decision-analytic control. In Section 4 we build on their suggestions by using distribution-free statistics to quantify the accuracy and reliability of the estimates. We are able to show that the quality of the control mechanism's decisions is a well-behaved function of the accuracy and reliability of these estimates.

3.3. Making new distinctions

While statistical sampling is a powerful tool, it does not guarantee that the agent's performance will be satisfactory. Surprisingly, even precise knowledge of the expected utility and cost of the various methods does not guarantee good performance. The agent's performance depends critically on the set of distinctions it is able to make.

Consider, for example, an agent which has two methods, A and B, at its disposal. Suppose that method A only succeeds in states of type A and that the probability of states of type A is 0.55. Similarly, method B only succeeds in states of type B, and the probability of states of type B is 0.45. If the utility of success is 1 and the utility of failure is 0, then the expected utility of method A is 0.55 and the expected utility of method B is 0.45. If the agent has time to execute exactly one of the two methods then choosing method A is clearly better because, on average, method A will have a higher utility than method B. However, always choosing method A can still result in relatively poor performance. An agent that chooses method A in states of type A, and method B in states of type B would achieve a utility of 1 in every case—a significant improvement.

What basis does the agent have for alternating between A and B? If the agent draws distinctions between different types of states, then it can choose method A in states of one type, and method B in states of another. For example, suppose that the two methods are "digging with a shovel" and "using dynamite". Suppose further that the agent distinguishes between states on the basis of the kind of rock at the excavation site. Then, digging would have higher expected utility for limestone, but not for granite.

More formally, the agent wishes to compare $U(s, A)$ and $U(s, B)$ where s is the current state. When $U(s, A)$ and $U(s, B)$ are not known, decision theory dictates consulting $EU(A)$ and $EU(B)$, and choosing the method whose expected utility is maximal. On average, this procedure is optimal. For any given state s, however, the method chosen may be the wrong one. Suppose $EU(A) > EU(B)$, but $U(s, B) > U(s, A)$ for the current state s. Then, making the "optimal" choice results in a loss of $U(s, B) - U(s, A)$. In some cases, *making "optimal" choices can actually result in poor performance.*

Making distinctions can reduce the average loss due to "misleading expectations" by enabling the agent to choose one method in some cases and a different method in others. Suppose that the agent divides the states encountered into states where some condition c is true, and states where c is false. Let E^c denote expectation over the states where c is true, and let $E^{\bar{c}}$ denote expectation over the states where c is false. Suppose further that the expected utility of B is greater than that of A when taken over the states in which c holds. That is, $E^c U(B) > E^c U(A)$. Since $EU(A) > EU(B)$ and $E^c U(B) > E^c U(A)$, it follows that $E^{\bar{c}} U(A) > E^{\bar{c}} U(B)$.

Making the distinction enables the agent to choose method B in the states where c is true. The expected utility gained by making the distinction, $EG(c)$, is the probability that c holds, $p(c)$, multiplied by the difference between $E^c U(B)$ and $E^c U(A)$.[4]

$$EG(c) = p(c)[E^c U(B) - E^c U(A)].$$

The reasoning is as follows. Drawing the distinction is only useful if it changes the agent's action choice in a way that increases the agent's expected

---

[4]Note the similarity, modulo notation, of our formula to Russell and Wefald's statement of the value of computation in their equation 7 [30, p. 404]. The connection is not surprising if you consider that drawing a distinction is a "computational action" in Russell and Wefald's sense.

utility. This only occurs in the states where c is true. The agent would have chosen A in those states, but it is more profitable to choose B. The profit is the expected difference between the two method choices. See [2] for a detailed analysis of drawing distinctions in the context of a somewhat different model.

In general, the quality of decisions based on expectations depends on the variance of the populations involved. If a population's variance is zero, for example, its mean will provide perfectly accurate estimates, and lead to perfect decisions. If the variance of the population is high, on the other hand, the mean will be a poor estimator of individual values in the population. Thus, the agent's goal in making distinctions is to reduce the variance of the populations it is tracking. A formal analysis of these considerations is provided in [9].

3.4. Memory organization

Section 3.3 demonstrated the utility of partitioning the set of world states into classes by making distinctions. This section considers how to index these classes, so that the agent can quickly find reliable estimates for the figures it needs. The indexing mechanism we describe has been referred to as a discrimination net [12], a decision tree [28], and a classification tree [3]. We refer to it as a classification tree. Such trees have been used to store classes of states for a search engine (e.g., [33]). Our contribution is to suggest that classification trees are useful for indexing sample means which, in turn, satisfy the knowledge demands made by decision-analytic control.

What is a classification tree? Each internal node in a classification tree (including the root) contains a test. Each edge from a parent node to a child node corresponds to one possible outcome of the test at the parent. A leaf node contains objects in the classification tree's domain that passed all the tests on the unique path from the root to the leaf. An object is propagated through the tree to the appropriate leaf as follows. The test at the current node (initially, the root) is applied to the object. Based on the test's outcome the object is moved to the appropriate child node, and the procedure recurs until the object reaches a leaf.

The agent uses classification trees to organize its sample of records. The ideal estimate is drawn from a large sample whose variance is low. Different distinctions may yield low-variance samples for different methods, or even for the cost and utility of the same method. Consequently, a separate classification tree is maintained for each figure to be estimated. Since the agent requires two estimates per method (utility and cost), it will keep $2k$ classification trees for k methods.

We use a simple example to illustrate the classification tree's operation. The agent's tests are expressions in the language used to describe states.

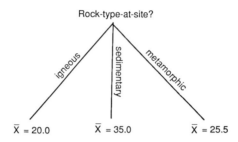

Fig. 3. The expected utility of digging.

The objects are the agent's records. The state in each record is a list of attribute-value pairs. The classification tree's tests are simply attribute names.[5] The different possible values for the attribute are the possible outcomes of the test. Only a small number of values is allowed for each attribute. For example, the agent may separate its excavations based on the type of rock in which the treasure is buried. Thus, the attribute tested might be *rock-type-at-site* and its possible values could be *igneous, sedimentary, and metamorphic*.

Initially, the tree consists of a single node and the entire sample is kept at that node. Once the sample variance exceeds a threshold, the sample is split using one of the attributes.[6] As a result, the tree is expanded as more and more records are propagated through it. A snapshot of a hypothetical classification tree for estimating the expected utility of the method "digging with a shovel" appears in Fig. 3. The algorithm for retrieving estimated costs and utilities appears in Fig. 4. The algorithm takes a minimal sample-size threshold as input. The threshold provides a lower bound on the reliability of conclusions drawn from the sample. The algorithm returns the sample mean from the most specific class whose sample size exceeds the threshold, and which contains s. The most specific class is used to provide estimates based on closely related states.[7]

As described thus far, the agent's indexing scheme is space intensive. Every record collected by the agent is retained. If the agent's space limitations are exceeded, however, the agent can discard records at low-variance leaf nodes and merely retain the sample mean, variance, and size at the nodes.

---

[5]More expressive languages for both state description and tests are possible. We use attribute-value pairs to facilitate the exposition. It should be noted, however, that many of the inductive algorithms for constructing classification trees rely on the simplicity of this language [28].

[6]Various criteria for choosing the splitting attribute have been suggested in the classification tree literature [28]. We pick the attribute that minimizes the sum of the sample variances after the split. This appears to be a relatively unimportant design choice [24].

[7]See [31, p. 29] for a discussion which motivates this design choice.

(1) Let $n_{\delta,\varepsilon}$ denote the minimal sample-size threshold.
(2) Find the relevant classification tree.
(3) Propagate s through the tree to a leaf node l.
(4) Let $P = (r, ..., l)$ denote the path from the root r to the leaf l.
(5) Traverse P in reverse order until the first node f whose sample size is at least $n_{\delta,\varepsilon}$ is reached.
(6) Return the sample mean associated with node f.

Fig. 4. The algorithm for retrieving estimated costs and utilities.

4. Analysis

What guarantees can we make on the performance of an agent using the MU heuristic? In two special cases described below we demonstrate that the heuristic is either close to optimal (in the single method case, Section 4.2), or optimal (in the single goal case, Section 4.3). Furthermore, the heuristic's divergence from optimality is shown to decrease linearly with the inaccuracy of the estimates used. Hoeffding's inequality, introduced in Section 4.1, demonstrates that the accuracy and reliability of the agent estimates increases quickly as the agent accumulates experience. Finally, Section 4.4 shows that the heuristic will always choose a *dominant* method over inferior alternatives. Thus, if one option appears better than another in every regard, the MU heuristic will choose that option. Section 4.5 discusses the stringent assumptions made in the analysis, and possible approaches to weakening them.

4.1. Distribution-free mean estimation

This section introduces the distribution-free statistical theory used to analyze the quality of the agent's estimates in Sections 4.2 and 4.3. The central observation is that the distance of a sample mean, $\bar{X}$, from the population mean, μ, is a rapidly decreasing function of the sample's size. Hoeffding's inequality [18] makes this observation precise. The inequality provides us with a lower bound on the probability that $\bar{X}$ is within ε of the true mean *without making distributional assumptions.* The inequality does presuppose a fixed (but arbitrary) probability distribution in which the range of the random variable is bounded. Hence, applying the inequality to the agent's records amounts to assuming that method application does not change the expected utility and cost of subsequent methods.

Let X be an independent random variable such that $a < X < b$; $\bar{X}$ is the mean of a random sample of X; n is the sample size. Hoeffding's inequality is the following.

$$p(|\bar{X} - \mu| \leq \varepsilon) \geq 1 - 2e^{-2n\varepsilon^2/(b-a)^2}.$$

Note that when the product $n\varepsilon^2$ approaches 0, the inequality no longer provides a useful bound on the probability that $\bar{X}$ is close to μ.

Models used in previous work (e.g., [2,23,30,35]) have made strong distributional assumptions. For example, Russell and Wefald as well as Lee and Mahajan assume a normal distribution, and Smith assumes a uniform distribution. Our approach is unique in employing distribution-free statistical theory. In fairness, when distributional assumptions are empirically validated (e.g., [23]) they facilitate more efficient sampling. However, since the statistical inference required is merely the estimation of expected values, an inference for which adequate distribution-free theory exists, it seems more parsimonious to dispense with distributional assumptions in the general case.

Hoeffding's inequality enables us to compute the minimal sample size $n_{\delta,\varepsilon}$ required to bound the reliability and accuracy of an estimated mean by $1 - \delta$ and ε respectively. As the following definition demonstrates, the minimal sample size scales logarithmically with the desired reliability and quadratically with the desired accuracy.[8]

$$n_{\delta,\varepsilon} = \frac{(b-a)^2}{2\varepsilon^2} \ln\left(\frac{2}{\delta}\right).$$

If the value of $n_{\delta,\varepsilon}$ is substituted for n in Hoeffding's inequality, the resultant inequality is $p(|\bar{X} - \mu| \leq \varepsilon) \geq 1 - \delta$. Therefore, given values for any pair out of the triple ε, δ, and $n_{\delta,\varepsilon}$, the value of the third parameter may be computed via Hoeffding's inequality.

The analysis in Section 4 makes use of this observation to determine the accuracy of its estimates given samples and desired reliability levels. The accuracy and reliability guarantees are derived for the proximity of $\bar{X}$ to μ. The control procedure in Section 3.1 uses $\bar{X}$ to estimate utility or cost for a given method execution. Note that although the average or expected error of such an estimate is bounded, the error in any particular instance is not.

4.2. *The multiple goals, single method case*

Given a set of value-additive goals, a single method for achieving each goal whose success is guaranteed, and a deadline, the agent's (specialized) control problem is isomorphic to the knapsack problem. We can define the optimization version of the knapsack problem as follows:

---

[8]Results obtained by [17] in a concept learning application suggest that this bound can be improved upon.

Instance: A finite set I, for each $i \in I$ there is a weight $w(i) \in \mathbf{Z}^+$, a value $v(i) \in \mathbf{Z}^+$, and a positive integer "weight capacity" B. $\forall i \in I, w(i) \leq B$.

Question: What is the subset $I' \subseteq I$ such that $\sum_{i \in I'} v(i)$ is as large as possible, subject to the constraint $\sum_{i \in I'} w(i) \leq B$?

In the control case the items correspond to methods. The value of an item may be interpreted as the utility of achieving a goal with a given method; the utility of executing a method after the deadline is 0 in this case. The weight of an item becomes the time required to execute the method, and the weight capacity of the knapsack is a deadline. The knapsack problem is known to be NP-hard. It follows that the multiple goals, single method control problem is NP-hard.

Theorem 4.1. *The multiple goals, single method control problem is NP-hard.*

Thus, we expect that an agent facing a large number of independent goals and a deadline will not be able to tractably determine its optimal course of action.

Powerful approximation algorithms exist for the knapsack problem. Garey and Johnson [13, p. 135] remark that it is not difficult to show that the following approximation algorithm comes within a factor of two of optimal:[9]

Step 1. Pick the item in I whose value is maximal and call it *max*.

Step 2. Sort the items $i \in I$ in decreasing order on their value-density $v(i)/w(i)$.

Step 3. Starting with I' empty, proceed sequentially through I, each time adding the next $i \in I$ to I' whenever the sum of the weights of the items already in I' does not exceed $B - w(i)$.

Step 4. Compare the combined value of the elements in I' with $v(max)$ and take the better of the two.

Essentially, the algorithm sorts the items on their value-density and places them in the knapsack in that order. This scheme is equivalent to Step 2 in our control cycle (Fig. 2). Marginal utility corresponds to value-density. We use the term marginal utility to underscore the connection between our approach and economic theory.

Two steps must be taken before Garey and Johnson's guarantee on the performance of their algorithm can be mapped to our single method case. First, since the actual value and weight figures are not known for our items (the methods), Garey and Johnson's guarantee must be shown to hold for

---

[9]Many approximation algorithms exist for the knapsack problem (e.g., [21]). We chose this particular algorithm to demonstrate the efficacy of the MU heuristic.

expected value and weight figures (Theorem 4.2). Second, since we can only estimate the expected value and weight figures, the divergence from optimality ought to be a well-behaved function of the quality of the estimates (Theorem 4.3).

Let σ^h be the packing produced by the value-density algorithm run on expected value and weight figures, and let σ^* be the packing of the knapsack whose expected value is maximal. Define the value of a sequence, $v(\sigma)$, to be the sum of the values of the elements of σ.

Theorem 4.2. *Given the expected value and weight of each item, $2Ev(\sigma^h) - Ev(\sigma^*) \geq 0$.*

The value-density algorithm's packing is within a factor of two of optimal. This theorem does not suffice because we only have estimates of the expected utility and time cost for the methods. The statistical theory presented in Section 4.1 demonstrates that we can bound the divergence of our estimates from the true expected value by using sufficiently large samples. However, is the divergence of the value-density algorithm from optimality a well-behaved function of the estimates' accuracy? The answer is yes.

Let $\bar{v}$ and $\bar{w}$ stand for the expected weight and expected value estimates whose inaccuracy is bounded by ε with probability at least $1-\delta$ as guaranteed by Hoeffding's inequality. Let k be the number of items in the set I. Suppose that for any set of items $I' \subseteq I$ we have $\bar{w}(I') \leq B$ if and only if $Ew(I') \leq B$. That is, no item is excluded from a packing due to the inaccuracy in the estimation of its weight. In practice, we can enforce this assumption by introducing a leniency of εk in the deadline. Given $\bar{v}$ and $\bar{w}$ for each item, the divergence of the packing produced by the value-density algorithm from the optimal one is linear in $1/\varepsilon$ with probability that is linear in $1/\delta$.

Theorem 4.3. *Given $\bar{v}$ and $\bar{w}$, $2Ev(\sigma^h) - Ev(\sigma^*) + 3\varepsilon k \geq 0$ with probability at least $1 - 3k\delta$.*

Thus, the MU heuristic proves to have satisfactory and well-understood performance.

4.3. The single goal, multiple methods case

Consider the case where the agent attends to a single goal, but pays a constant cost c for every time unit spent on that goal. For example, the agent may be seeking a single treasure but consuming valuable fuel at the cost of c dollars per second. Let $P(m)$ denote the probability that executing a method m renders the goal unachievable by subsequent methods. We assume that this probability, the expected utility, and the expected cost of each method

Given:

- A goal g.
- A constant cost c per time unit.
- A set of methods M for achieving the goal g.
- For each method $m \in M$:

  An expected time cost $ET(m)$.
  An expected utility $EU(m)$.
  A probability $P(m)$.

Determine: A method sequence whose expected utility is maximal.

Fig. 5. The single goal control problem.

are independent of the order in which the methods are executed. As usual, the agent seeks to maximize the expected utility of its actions.

In this case, the utility of executing m, in a state s, decreases at a constant rate c with $T(s, m)$. We can derive this observation from the definition of method utility.

$$U(s, m) = v(m(s)) - v(s)$$
$$= i(g)d(m(s), g) - ct(m(s)) - v(s).$$

Since the goal is not satisfied in state s, $v(s) = 0 - ct(s)$. Therefore,

$$U(s, m) = i(g)d(m(s), g) - ct(m(s)) + ct(s)$$
$$= i(g)d(m(s), g) - cT(s, m).$$

The expected utility of a method is defined as follows.

$$EU(m) = i(g)Ed(m, g) - cET(m).$$

The agent does not execute methods whose expected utility is negative. We assume that all such methods have been removed from the method set M.

Let $\sigma = (m_1 .. m_k)$ stand for an ordering of M. The agent seeks to find a σ whose expected utility is maximal.

$$EU(\sigma) = \sum_{m_i \in \sigma} EU(m_i) \prod_{j=1}^{i-1} (1 - P(m_j)).$$

A precise statement of the single goal control problem appears in Fig. 5.

Naively, the optimal method ordering can be found by computing the expected utility for all possible method orderings, but for k methods this takes $O(k!)$ time. Theorem 4.4 suggests an equivalent $O(k \log k)$ procedure.

Theorem 4.4. *Sorting M on $EU(m)/P(m)$ in decreasing order results in an optimal method sequence.*

Many previous formulations of the control problem (e.g., [2,34,35]) have focused on minimizing the expected time for achieving the goal given a set of equal-utility methods with binary outcomes (either success or failure) and varying costs. In these formulations, a method's failure does not interfere with subsequent methods. Thus, $P(m)$ can be interpreted as m's probability of success. Such formulations are easily accommodated within our framework by making some additional simplifying assumptions—namely, setting c to 1 and assuming that $U(m)$ is identical for all methods m in M.

Under these assumptions the key on which the methods are sorted, $EU(m)/P(m)$, reduces to:

$$[P(m)U(m) - ET(m)]/P(m).$$

Since $U(m)$ is the same for each method, subtracting $U(m)$ from each key does not affect the result of sorting the methods. Thus, the key simplifies to $-ET(m)/P(m)$ or equivalently $P(m)/ET(m)$, which is a result obtained by [2,34,35] and others. Under the stated assumptions, sorting methods on this key is equivalent to sorting the methods on their marginal expected utility. Thus, *employing the MU heuristic leads to optimal behavior in this special case.*

In practice, we do not know $ET(m)$ and $P(m)$ for each method, but these parameters can be estimated from samples as discussed in Section 4.1. Let $\bar{P}(m)$ and $\bar{T}(m)$ be estimates of $P(m)$ and $ET(m)$ that, by Hoeffding's inequality, are within ε or α of the truth with probability at least $1 - \delta$. That is,

$$p(|\bar{P}(m) - P(m)| \leq \varepsilon) \geq 1 - \delta$$

and

$$p(|\bar{T}(m) - ET(m)| \leq \alpha) \geq 1 - \delta.$$

The inequality implies that the accuracy of the estimates is likely to increase rapidly as the agent accumulates experience.

Define σ^h to be the method ordering produced by sorting the methods on $\bar{P}(m)/\bar{T}(m)$, and let σ^* be the optimal method ordering. Define the time cost of a sequence, $T(\sigma)$, to be the sum of the time costs of the elements of σ.

Theorem 4.5. $ET(\sigma^h) - ET(\sigma^*)$ *is linear in* $1/\varepsilon$ *and* $1/\alpha$ *with probability linear in* $1/\delta$. [10]

That is, the expected cost of the method ordering produced by sorting on the estimates provided diverges from the optimal expected cost by an amount that decreases linearly with the inaccuracy of the estimates, with probability that grows linearly with the reliability of the estimates.

4.4. The dominant method case

The previous subsections covered two special cases: the multiple goals, single method case, and the single goal, multiple methods case. This section offers a weaker but more general guarantee on the behavior of the MU heuristic.

A method is said to *dominate* another method for achieving a given goal if, according to the agent's beliefs, the dominating method is no worse along any dimension, and better along at least one. For example, if method A has lower expected cost and higher expected utility than method B, then method A dominates method B. If we consider $>, <, =$ as three possible qualitative relationships between two methods along a given dimension, then we may observe five distinct (up to symmetry) qualitative relationships between methods compared on their cost and utility.

Of the five, three represent dominance relations (in one remaining case the methods are interchangeable and the other case represents a tradeoff). Thus, it is important to guarantee that a control heuristic exploits dominance relations. As Wellman [39, p. xvi] puts it, "the ability to separate tradeoffs from obvious choices defines a lower bound on competence for decision-making agents".

If one method dominates another, the MU heuristic will choose the dominating method. The reasoning is as follows. Suppose method A dominates method B. By definition $EU(A) \geq EU(B)$, $ET(A) \leq ET(B)$, and method A is strictly superior to B along one of these dimensions. Therefore, $EU(A)/ET(A) > EU(B)/ET(B)$. Thus, the marginal expected utility of method A is greater than the marginal expected utility of method B, and the dominating method will be chosen by the MU heuristic. Again, this observation assumes method independence.

4.5. Discussion

The analysis in this section has relied on strong independence assumptions, simple models of the relationship between utility and time, and restrictions either on the number of methods available to the agent or the number of goals

---

[10] A similar result was obtained by Barnett [2].

under consideration. Our independence assumptions, although common (cf. [2,30,35]), need to be weakened. Further analysis allowing weak (e.g., binary or tree-structured) dependence relations is likely to be fruitful.

It should be noted that the rapid convergence of sample means to true means is very robust. Hence, even when the probability distribution over states changes gradually due to the agent's actions or to changes in the world, sample means (with more recent observations weighted more heavily, perhaps) are still likely to provide useful estimates of the figures necessary for decision-analytic control.

Our approach can be divided into three parts: problem formulation (Section 2), agent architecture (Section 3), and analysis (Section 4). Although our problem formulation is quite general and the architecture is quite flexible, numerous commitments and assumptions were required to carry out the analysis in this section. It is plausible, therefore, that our agent will operate successfully even when the stringent assumptions made in the analysis are violated.

5. Concluding remarks

5.1. Previous work and future prospects

The fundamental appeal of decision-theoretic control is perceived by some as the promise of designing agents that will make provably optimal control choices by considering the expected utility of different courses of action or computation. A rational reconstruction of work in the field leads us to question this goal and suggest another.

Simon and Kadane [34] and Sproull [36] were among the first to apply decision-theoretic ideas within AI. Neither research effort addressed how the knowledge demanded by decision-theoretic control could be acquired. The work of Abramson and Korf [1], Lee and Mahajan [23], Natarajan [27], Rendell [29], and Wefald and Russell [38] suggested that an agent can *estimate* the probabilities, costs, and utilities that are grist for the decision-theoretic mill by sampling its own experience.

It is natural to inquire whether relying on estimates allows decision theory to maintain its potent optimality guarantees. Most previous work has not addressed this question.[11] Theorems 4.3 and 4.5 guarantee that the MU heuristic converges to optimal (or close to optimal) performance as the agent accumulates experience, but only under stringent assumptions.

A second difficulty associated with decision-theoretic control is its computational intractability. The paramount obstacle here is the intractability

---

[11]See [2] for an exception.

of computing or even estimating opportunity cost, the utility of foregone alternatives. Previous work has assumed this problem out of existence. In contrast, the MU heuristic recognizes that normative decision-theoretic control is intractable, and circumvents computing opportunity costs by relying on marginal expected utilities.

A third difficulty associated with decision-theoretic control is the choice of an appropriate policy for deliberation. Deliberation has an opportunity cost that must be accounted for in any realistic agent architecture. The MU heuristic implies that deliberation is warranted only when its marginal expected utility exceeds the marginal expected utility of acting. The problem of computing the utility of deliberation is not addressed here, but see [30].

Given the formidable challenges listed above, it seems reasonable to question whether decision theory can deliver on its promise of provably optimal agents (cf. [15]). We believe that although optimality results (like our own) may be attainable in narrowly circumscribed contexts, general optimality results are not forthcoming. Decision theory can, however, serve a more modest goal. The theory provides a framework and a vocabulary in which to formulate and analyze control problems (cf. [8,16]). These are useful, independent of optimality results, in choosing dominating courses of action [39], making tradeoffs [5], and overcoming uncertainty. In our view, the virtue of applying decision theory to agent control is the theory's descriptive power, not its guarantee of optimality.

5.2. Machine learning and decision-analytic control

Section 3.3 demonstrated that acquiring a partition of world states into low-variance classes is essential for satisfactory performance. Consider, for example, the problem of choosing moves in a chess game. There is no single "optimal chess move" that is appropriate in all chess positions in which it is legal. Rather, the 10^{40} or so chess positions have to be partitioned into classes for which good moves can be determined. Previous work on decision-analytic control has not adequately addressed the problem of learning to partition the set of world states into low-variance classes.

In contrast, research on learning problem solvers (LPSs) [22,25,26] has skirted many of the issues addressed by decision-analytic control. The learning work focuses on acquiring preference rules that map classes of states to fixed control choices. For example, a preference rule might dictate digging with a shovel whenever the rock at the excavation site is limestone. Instead of associating utility and cost estimates with each method, LPSs acquire rigid preferences. As a result, current LPSs are not able to trade goal value for execution cost, or rationally choose between plans with differing risks and rewards. Yet these are precisely the strengths of decision-analytic control.

It follows that combining learning capabilities with decision-analytic control is useful. The architecture outlined in Section 3 is a plausible basis for such a combination. Instead of acquiring rigid preference rules, learning methods (either inductive or analytic) can aim to partition the state-space into low-variance classes. As argued earlier, this partitioning capability is necessary for the success of decision-analytic control. Furthermore, the scheme has the following advantages over currently existing LPSs:

- By utilizing its indexing mechanism, the agent can exploit approximate information in the form of estimated utilities and costs to guide *any* of its control decisions. Thus, even when the agent does not know what the best action is, it can quickly make an educated guess. In contrast, a LPS offers no guidance whatsoever on choices not covered by previously acquired preference rules. See [10] for a more detailed discussion of this issue.
- Estimating the variance of existing classes serves to focus the learning process on the classes that need to be refined.
- The problems of learning to choose between multiple goals, and methods with different risk and rewards, is reduced to a set of well-understood concept-learning and parameter estimation problems.

In short, work on learning problem solvers is complementary to work on decision-analytic control. Embedding decision-analytic control in an architecture with learning capabilities will be a boon to both.

Appendix A

Some of the following proofs use the addition rule of the probability calculus. The rule is reviewed below for the reader's convenience.

$$P(A \vee B) \leq P(A) + P(B).$$

Theorem 2.1. *Repeatedly choosing a method whose expected net utility is maximal yields an optimal method sequence.*

Proof. (By contradiction.) Let σ^h be the method sequence constructed by repeatedly choosing the method whose expected opportunity cost is minimal. Suppose that σ^h is suboptimal. There is, therefore an optimal sequence σ^* that is identical to σ^h up to a given method choice, and diverges from σ^h at that point. Let m^h be the method chosen in σ^h at that point, and let m^* be the alternative chosen in σ^*. All expectations are taken over the same probability distribution.

Let $EU(m'\sigma^*)$ be the expected opportunity cost of m^*. We know the following by definition:

$$EN(m^*) = EU(m^*\sigma^*) - EU(m'\sigma^*),$$
$$EN(m^h) = EU(m^h\sigma^*) - EU(m^*\sigma^*).$$

Since m^* is optimal we know that:

$$EU(m^*\sigma^*) > EU(m^h\sigma^*),$$
$$EU(m^*\sigma^*) > EU(m'\sigma^*).$$

Therefore,

$$EN(m^*) > EN(m^h).$$

This yields a contradiction, because σ^h was constructed by choosing the method whose expected net utility is maximal. Therefore, the assumption that σ^h is suboptimal is false, and the theorem holds. □

Theorem 2.2. *The three-dimensional control problem is NP-hard.*

Proof. We use the *restriction* technique [13, p 63.]. Namely, we show that a subset of the instances of the three-dimensional control problem defines a problem that is NP-hard. *A fortiori*, the general control problem is NP-hard.

Theorem 4.1 states that the multiple goals, single method (MGSM) control problem introduced in Section 4.2 is NP-hard. The MGSM control problem is a restricted version of the three-dimensional control problem in which only a single method is available to achieve each goal. Since the MGSM control problem is NP-hard, the three-dimensional control problem is NP-hard *a fortiori*. □

Theorem 4.1. *The multiple goals, single method control problem is NP-hard.*

Proof. By reduction of the knapsack problem. □

Theorem 4.2. *Given the expected value and weight of each item, $2Ev(\sigma^h) - Ev(\sigma^*) \geq 0$.*

Proof. Recall that the density d of an item i is the ratio of its value and weight. The value (weight) of a sequence is the sum of the values (weights) of its elements. The density of a method sequence σ is the ratio of its value and weight.

$$d(\sigma) = v(\sigma)/w(\sigma).$$

Two lemmas are proved to facilitate the proof's exposition.

Lemma A.1. *If $\forall I_1 \in \sigma_1$ and $\forall I_2 \in \sigma_2$ we have that $d(I_1) \geq d(I_2)$, then $d(\sigma_1) \geq d(\sigma_2)$.*

Proof. By induction on the lengths of σ_1 and σ_2. □

Suppose that the item values and weights given to the algorithm are fixed values rather than expectations.

Lemma A.2. $2v(\sigma^h) - v(\sigma^*) \geq 0.$

Proof. Recall that *max* is the element in I whose value is maximal. Let $\sigma = \sigma_1...\sigma_k$ be the set of items placed in the knapsack by the algorithm traversing the sorted set I. σ^h is set to σ if $v(\sigma) > v(max)$, and set to *max* otherwise.

Let $\sigma_{1/2}$ stand for the first n items in σ such that $w(\sigma_1..\sigma_{n-1}) < \frac{1}{2}B$ and $w(\sigma_1..\sigma_n) \geq \frac{1}{2}B$.

There are two cases to consider:

Case 1. Suppose $\forall i \in \sigma^*, w(i) \leq \frac{1}{2}B$. Then, $\forall j \in \sigma_{1/2}$ and $\forall i \in \sigma^*$ we know that either $d(i) \leq d(j)$ or $i \in \sigma_{1/2}$. To see this fact, consider an arbitrary pair i, j such that i does not belong to $\sigma_{1/2}$. Consider the point at which the algorithm placed j into $\sigma_{1/2}$. If $d(i) > d(j)$ then the algorithm would have added i to $\sigma_{1/2}$, unless i would not fit in the knapsack. But $w(i) \leq \frac{1}{2}B$ by assumption, and $w(a_1..a_{k-1}) < \frac{1}{2}B$ by definition of $\sigma_{1/2}$. So at any point i would fit. The fact that i was not added to $\sigma_{1/2}$ implies that $d(i) \leq d(j)$.

Therefore, by Lemma A.1,

$$d(\sigma_{1/2}) \geq d(\sigma^*).$$

Since $2w(\sigma_{1/2}) \geq w(\sigma^*)$ by definition, it follows that $2v(\sigma_{1/2}) \geq v(\sigma^*)$. Since $v(\sigma^h) \geq v(\sigma_{1/2})$, the lemma holds in this case.

Case 2. Suppose $\sigma^* = p \cup S$ and $w(p) > \frac{1}{2}B$. Then, $\forall i \in S, w(i) < \frac{1}{2}B$. Now there are two possibilities.

   (a) $v(p) \geq v(S)$. Then, $v(max) \geq v(p)$ means that $2v(max) \geq v(\sigma^*)$.
   (b) $v(S) > v(p)$. But $w(S) \leq B - w(p)$. Therefore, $w(\sigma) > w(S)$ (if $w(\sigma) \leq w(S)$ you could at least add p to σ). Since $\forall i \in S$ we know that $w(i) \leq \frac{1}{2}B$ and $S \subset \sigma^*$, the argument given in case 1 applies to S. Therefore, $d(\sigma_{1/2}) \geq d(S)$. But $w(S) < \frac{1}{2}B < w(\sigma_{1/2})$, therefore $v(\sigma_{1/2}) \geq v(S)$. Since $v(S) > v(p)$ in this possibility, it follows that $2v(\sigma_{1/2}) > v(S) + v(p) = v(\sigma^*)$.

So both possibilities imply that $2v(\sigma^h) > v(\sigma^*)$.

Cases 1 and 2 are mutually exclusive and exhaustive. Therefore the lemma holds. □

The theorem follows from Lemma A.2 and the fact that the expectation of a sum is equal to the sum of the expectations of the individual summands. □

Theorem 4.3. *Given $\bar{v}$ and $\bar{w}$, $2Ev(\sigma^h) - Ev(\sigma^*) + 3\varepsilon k \geq 0$ with probability at least $1 - 3k\delta$.*

Proof. Recall that we are assuming that for any set of items $\sigma \subseteq I$ we have $\bar{w}(\sigma) \leq B$ if and only if $Ew(\sigma) \leq B$. We refer to this assumption as the leniency assumption.

By the definition of $\bar{v}$ and the addition rule, we know that for every set of items σ, $v(\sigma) \geq \bar{v}(\sigma) - k\varepsilon$ with probability at least $1 - k\delta$. From this observation and the leniency assumption it follows that $v(\sigma^*) \leq \bar{v}(\sigma^*) + k\varepsilon$ with probability at least $1 - k\delta$, and that $2v(\sigma^h) \geq 2\bar{v}(\sigma^h) - 2k\varepsilon$ with probability at least $1 - 2k\delta$. Therefore, with probability at least $1 - 3k\delta$, we have the following:

$$v(\sigma^*) - 2v(\sigma^h) \leq \bar{v}(\sigma^*) + k\varepsilon - 2\bar{v}(\sigma^h) + 2k\varepsilon.$$

By Theorem 4.2 we know that $\bar{v}(\sigma^*) - 2\bar{v}(\sigma^h) \leq 0$. It follows that $v(\sigma^*) - 2v(\sigma^h) \leq 3k\varepsilon$ with probability at least $1 - 3k\delta$, and the theorem holds. □

Theorem 4.4. *Sorting M on $EU(m)/P(m)$ in decreasing order results in an optimal method ordering.*

Proof. Our proof mirrors the proof given by Simon and Kadane for the special case of minimizing expected cost.

Let A and D denote possibly empty method sequences. When A is empty, $EU(A) = 0$. Let $\sigma = (\sigma_1..\sigma_k)$. Define $F(\sigma)$ to be the probability that the goal can still be achieved after σ is executed.

$$F(\sigma) = \prod_{i=1}^{k}(1 - P(\sigma_i)).$$

Let $F(\sigma) = 1$ when σ is empty.

Consider the effect of reordering the methods b and c on the expected net utility of the method sequence $AbcD$.

$$EU(AbcD) - EU(AcbD)$$
$$= EU(A) + F(A)EU(bcD) - EU(A) - F(A)EU(cbD).$$

The right-hand side simplifies to

$$F(A)[EU(bc) + F(bc)EU(D) - EU(cb) - F(cb)EU(D)].$$

By the commutativity of multiplication $F(bc) = F(cb)$. Therefore the right-hand side is

$$F(A)[EU(bc) - EU(cb)]$$
$$= F(A)[EU(b) + (1 - P(b))EU(c)$$
$$- EU(c) - (1 - P(c))EU(b)]$$
$$= F(A)[EU(b)P(c) - EU(c)P(b)].$$

Note that $EU(b)P(c) - EU(c)P(b)$ is positive exactly when $EU(b)/P(b) > EU(c)/P(c)$. Therefore, sorting the methods in decreasing order on $EU(m)/P(m)$ results in a method ordering that maximizes the expected net utility of the method sequence. $\square$

Theorem 4.5. $ET(\sigma^h) - ET(\sigma^*)$ *is linear in* $1/\varepsilon$ *and* $1/\alpha$ *with probability linear in* $1/\delta$.

Proof. Recall that the method ordering produced by sorting the methods on $\bar{T}(m)/\bar{P}(m)$ is σ^h, and the optimal ordering is σ^*. The proof proceeds as follows. First, we consider method sequences of length 2, and then we generalize the analysis to sequences of arbitrary length.

Let $\sigma^h = (xy)$. By the definition of σ^h:

$$\bar{P}(x)/\bar{T}(x) \geq \bar{P}(y)/\bar{T}(y), \tag{A.1}$$

where $\bar{P}(m)$ is within ε of $P(m)$ with probability at least $1 - \delta$, and $\bar{T}(m)$ is within α of $ET(m)$ with probability at least $1 - \delta$. It follows that:

$$(P(x) + \varepsilon)/(ET(x) - \alpha) \geq (P(y) - \varepsilon)/(ET(y) + \alpha)$$

with probability at least $1 - 4\delta$. The probability bound is derived by the following argument. Four events have to occur for the inequality to hold. Namely, the four estimates have to be within ε (or α) of the true value. If any of the events does not occur, the inequality may not hold. The probability of one of the events *not* occurring is bounded above by δ. The probability of any of the four events not occurring is bounded above by 4δ by the addition rule. Thus, the probability that the inequality holds is bounded below by $1 - 4\delta$.

Multiplying out and canceling terms, we get:

$$P(x)ET(y) + \alpha P(x) + \varepsilon ET(y)$$
$$\geq P(y)ET(x) - \alpha P(y) - \varepsilon ET(x).$$

Multiplying by -1, adding $ET(x) + ET(y)$ to both sides, and simplifying, we get:

$$ET(xy) - ET(yx) \leq \alpha P(x) + \varepsilon ET(y) + \alpha P(y) + \varepsilon ET(x). \tag{A.2}$$

Note that if the sequence xy is not optimal then the sequence yx is. Therefore, the right-hand side of inequality A.2 bounds the expected suboptimality of σ^h for method sequences of length two. Since the bound is linear in ε and α, it follows that the theorem holds for method sequences of length two.

We now generalize the proof to a method sequence of length k. Any reordering of σ^h can be expressed as a series of k^2 swaps of adjacent methods. The swaps can be executed so that inequality A.1 holds before each swap. Therefore, the gain from each swap is bounded by the right-hand side of inequality A.2. The gain from any reordering of the methods is bounded by $k^2[\alpha P(x) + \varepsilon ET(y) + \alpha P(y) + \varepsilon ET(x)]$ which is still linear in ε and α. All this holds so long as each of the estimates is indeed inside its predicted interval. Since $2k$ estimates are used, by the addition rule, the cumulative probability of the bound is at least $1 - 2k\delta$ which is linear in $1/\delta$. $\square$

Acknowledgement

This paper describes research done primarily at Carnegie Mellon University's School of Computer Science. The conceptual framework presented above was developed through numerous illuminating discussions with Tom Mitchell. My thinking was also influenced by Steve Hanks, Stuart Russell, and Eric Wefald. Jonathan Amsterdam, Ruth Douglas, Danny Sleator, Doug Tygar, and Raúl Valdés-Pérez contributed to the formal aspects of this paper. Jim Blythe, Mark Boddy, Murray Campbell, Rich Caruana, Tom Dean, Steve Hanks, Haym Hirsh, Craig Knoblock, Sven Koenig, Tom Mitchell, Prasad Tadepalli, and the anonymous reviewers provided helpful comments on previous drafts.

This research was sponsored by the Avionics Lab, Wright Research and Development Center, Aeronautical Systems Division (AFSC), U.S. Air Force, Wright-Patterson AFB, OH 45433-6543 under Contract F33615-90-C-1465, Arpa Order No. 7597. The author was supported by an AT&T Bell Labs Ph.D. Scholarship.

The views and conclusions contained in this document are those of the author and should not be interpreted as representing the official policies, either expressed or implied, of the U.S. government.

References

[1] B. Abramson and R.E. Korf, A model of two-player evaluation functions, in: *Proceedings AAAI-87*, Seattle, WA (1987) 90–94.

[2] J.A. Barnett, How much is control knowledge worth? a primitive example, *Artif. Intell.* **22** (1984) 77–89.

[3] L. Breiman, *Classification and Regression Trees* (Wadsworth, Belmont, CA, 1984).

[4] D. Chapman, Planning for conjunctive goals, *Artif. Intell.* **32** (1987) 333–378.

[5] T. Dean, Decision-theoretic control of inference for time-critical applications, Brown University, Providence, RI (1990).

[6] T. Dean and M. Boddy, An analysis of time-dependent planning, in: *Proceedings AAAI-88*, St. Paul, MN (1988) 49–54.

[7] J. Doyle, Big problems for artificial intelligence, *AI Mag.* **9** (1988) 19–22.

[8] J. Doyle, Rationality and its roles in reasoning (extended abstract), in: *Proceedings AAAI-90*, Boston, MA (1990) 1093–1100.

[9] O. Etzioni, Hypothesis filtering: a practical approach to reliable learning, in: *Proceedings Fifth International Conference on Machine Learning*, Ann Arbor, MI (1988) 416–429.

[10] O. Etzioni and T.M. Mitchell, A comparative analysis of chunking and decision-analytic control, in: *Working Notes of the AAAI Spring Symposium on AI and Limited Rationality*, Menlo Park, CA (1989) 40–45.

[11] M.R. Fehling, D. Einav, and J.S. Breese, Adaptive planning and search, in: *Proceedings AAAI Spring Symposium on AI and Limited Rationality*, Menlo Park, CA (1989) 46–54.

[12] E.A. Feigenbaum and H.A. Simon, Performance of a reading task by an elementary perceiving and memorizing program, *Behav. Sci.* **8** (1963).

[13] M.R. Garey and D.S. Johnson, *Computers and Intractability: A Guide to the Theory of NP-completeness* (Freeman, New York, 1979).

[14] P. Haddawy and S. Hanks, Issues in decision-theoretic planning: symbolic goals and numeric utilities, University of Illinois at Urbana-Champaign, IL (1990).

[15] S. Hanks, Controlling inference in planning systems: who, what, when, why, and how, Tech. Report 90-04-01, University of Washington, Seattle, WA (1990).

[16] O. Hansson and A. Mayer, Probabilistic heuristic estimates, *Ann. Math. Artif. Intell.* **2** (1990) 209–220.

[17] D. Haussler, Quantifying inductive bias: AI learning algorithms and Valiant's learning framework, *Artif. Intell.* **36** (1988) 177–222.

[18] W. Hoeffding, Probability inequalities for sums of bounded random variables, *J. Am. Stat. Assoc.* **58** (1963) 301.

[19] E.J. Horvitz, Reasoning about beliefs and actions under computational resource constraints, in: *Proceedings 1987 Workshop on Uncertainty in Artificial Intelligence*, Seattle, WA (1987).

[20] E.J. Horvitz, G.F. Cooper and D.E. Heckerman, Reflection and action under scarce resources: theoretical principles and empirical study, in: *Proceedings IJCAI-89*, Detroit, MI (1989) 1121–1127.

[21] O.H. Ibarra and C.E. Kim, Fast approximation algorithms for the knapsack and sum of the subset problems, *J. ACM* **23** (1975) 463–368.

[22] J.E. Laird, P.S. Rosenbloom and A.Newell, Chunking in Soar: the anatomy of a general learning mechanism, *Mach. Learn.* **1** (1986) 11–46.

[23] K.F. Lee and S. Mahajan, A pattern classification approach to evaluation function learning, *Artif. Intell.* **36** (1988) 1–26.

[24] J. Mingers, An empirical comparison of selection measures for decision-tree induction, *Mach. Learn.* **3** (1989) 319–342.

[25] S. Minton, J.G. Carbonell, C.A. Knoblock, D.R. Kuokka, O. Etzioni, and Y. Gil, Explanation-based learning: a problem-solving perspective, *Artif. Intell.* **40** (1989) 63–118; also: Tech. Report CMU-CS-89-103, Carnegie Mellon University, Pittsburgh, PA (1989).

[26] T.M. Mitchell, J.Allen, P. Chalasani, J. Cheng, O. Etzioni, M. Ringuette and J.C. Schlimmer, Theo: a framework for self-improving systems, in: K. VanLehn, ed., *Architectures for Intelligence* (Erlbaum, Hillsdale, NJ, 1990).

[27] K.S. Natarajan, Adaptive search: an approach to optimize search effort for problem solving, Tech. Report 12228, IBM Thomas Watson Research Center, Yorktown Heights,

NY (1988).

[28] J.R. Quinlan, Induction of decision trees, *Mach. Learn.* **1** (1986) 81–106.

[29] L. Rendell, A new basis for state-space learning systems and a successful implementation, *Artif. Intell.* **20** (1983) 369–392.

[30] S. Russell and E. Wefald, Principles of metareasoning, in: *Proceedings First International Conference on Principles of Knowledge Representation and Reasoning*, Toronto, Ont. (1989) 400–411.

[31] W.C. Salmon, *Scientific Explanation and the Causal Structure of the World* (Princeton University Press, Princeton, NJ, 1984).

[32] P.A. Samuelson, *Economics* (McGraw-Hill, New York, 10th ed., 1976).

[33] J.C. Schlimmer, Refining representations to improve problem solving quality, in: *Proceedings Sixth International Workshop on Machine Learning*, Ithaca, NY (1989) 457–460.

[34] H.A. Simon and J.B. Kadane, Optimal problem-solving search: all-or-none solutions, *Artif. Intell.* **6** (1975) 235–247.

[35] D.E. Smith, Controlling backward inference, *Artif. Intell.* **39** (1989) 145–208.

[36] R.F. Sproull, Strategy construction using a synthesis of heuristic and decision-theoretic methods, Tech. Report CSL-77-2, Xerox PARC, Palo Alto, CA (1977).

[37] M. Tambe, A. Newell and P. Rosenbloom, The problem of expensive chunks and its solution by restricting expressiveness, *Mach. Learn.* **5** (1990) 299–348.

[38] E. Wefald and S. Russell, Adaptive learning of decision-theoretic search control knowledge, in: *Proceedings Sixth International Workshop on Machine Learning*, Ithaca, NY (1989) 408–411.

[39] M. Wellman, Formulation of tradeoffs in planning under uncertainty, Ph.D. Thesis, Tech. Report MIT/LCS/TR-427, MIT, Cambridge, MA (1988).

Artificial Intelligence 49 (1991) 161–198
Elsevier

The substitutional framework for sorted deduction: fundamental results on hybrid reasoning

Alan M. Frisch

*Department of Computer Science and Beckman Institute, University of Illinois,
405 North Mathews Avenue, Urbana, IL 61801, USA*

Received November 1989
Revised September 1990

Abstract

Frisch, A.M., The substitutional framework for sorted deduction: fundamental results on hybrid reasoning, Artificial Intelligence 49 (1991) 161–198.

Researchers in artificial intelligence have recently been taking great interest in hybrid representations, among them sorted logics—logics that link a traditional logical representation to a taxonomic (or sort) representation such as those prevalent in semantic networks. This paper introduces a general framework—the substitutional framework—for integrating logical deduction and sortal deduction to form a deductive system for sorted logic. This paper also presents results that provide the theoretical underpinnings of the framework. A distinguishing characteristic of a deductive system that is structured according to the substitutional framework is that the sort subsystem is invoked only when the logic subsystem performs unification, and thus sort information is used only in determining what substitutions to make for variables. Unlike every other known approach to sorted deduction, the substitutional framework provides for a *systematic* transformation of unsorted deductive systems into sorted ones.

1. Introduction

Recently, researchers in artificial intelligence have been taking great interest in hybrid representations—representation systems that consist of two or more integrated subsystems, each of which may employ distinct representation languages and inference systems. Included among such systems are:

- sorted logics (e.g. [11,26,38]), which integrate logical languages and languages for sort information,

0004-3702/91/$ 03.50 © 1991—Elsevier Science Publishers B.V.

- a deductive database system that incorporates special mechanisms for sort information [28,29],
- systems that combine assertional information and terminological information (e.g. KRYPTON [6] and KL-TWO [36]),
- systems that combine a weak logic with a taxonomic representation (e.g. [15,27]),
- logic programming systems that integrate Horn clause reasoning with inheritance (e.g. LOGIN [1] and HORNE [19]) or with more general forms of constraints (e.g. RHET [3] and constraint logic programming systems [7,22,35]), and
- logics with built-in theories (e.g. theory resolution [33]).

Researchers often cite two advantages of using hybrid representations. They point out that, instead of expressing all information in a single general-purpose representation language, it is often easier to express different kinds of information in representation languages specialized to each. Secondly, they claim that the use of specialized representations enables them to use specialized, and hence more efficient, methods of reasoning.

One particular form of hybrid representation that has been receiving a good deal of attention is sorted logic. Sorted logics can be seen as hybrid representations that link a traditional logical representation to a taxonomic representation such as those prevalent in semantic networks. The taxonomic component, which I shall call a sort module, contains information about relationships among various categories, or *sorts*. The logic component uses as its representation language a standard first-order predicate calculus that is augmented with sorted variables—variables that are restricted to taking on values that are in a specified sort.

In axiomatizing a domain, many researchers—both in mathematics (e.g. Feferman [14]) and in artificial intelligence (e.g. Hayes [20,21], McDermott [25], and Allen [2])—have long preferred sorted logics to unsorted ones. The sorted logics are more natural because one usually wants to make a general claim about every individual in a certain class rather than every individual in the entire universe. However, only recently have researchers begun to explore the possibility of using the sorted logics in automated deductive systems. Some extremely powerful deductive systems for sorted logic have been built and, in several test cases, have demonstrated dramatic superiority over unsorted systems. Among these demonstrations are solutions to two puzzle-like deduction problems—Schubert's Steamroller problem[1] [9,37] and Lewis Carroll's Salt and Mustard problem [12]—and work on a deductive parsing problem [16] and a deductive database problem [5].

[1]A comparison of solutions to Schubert's Steamroller problem has been compiled by Stickel [34].

Constructing a hybrid reasoning system involves more than just building a multitude of components, each with its specialized representation language and specialized deductive methods. The various deductive systems must be integrated in a manner that enables the knowledge represented and deduced by one component to be available for other components to use. Even if each component is a complete deductive system, the entire system may be incomplete if the components are not integrated in a proper manner. Designers of existing hybrid systems have addressed these problems, but, by and large, this has been done one system at a time. Little effort has been made on addressing these problems for a class of hybrid reasoning systems.[2]

A common way for two deductive components to interact is for one component to use some special form of unification that invokes the second deductive system as a subroutine. In some, though not all, systems this is the only use made of the information stored in the second component.

There are a number of sorted logics whose deductive systems are prime examples of this architecture. Sorts commonly enter a sorted logic in two ways: variables can be restricted to range over the elements of a specified sort, and predicates and functions can be restricted to take arguments of specified sorts. When performing unification in a sorted logic these restrictions can be used to eliminate certain substitutions from consideration. To do this the unification algorithm calls upon a second deductive mechanism, the sort module, to decide whether certain sentences are consequences of the information that it has stored. For example, the sort module may store the information that Clyde is in the sort of elephants and that everything in the sort of elephants is in the sort of mammals. During unification the sort module may be asked to deduce that Clyde is in the sort of mammals.

Suppose that we are given an unsorted logical language with ordinary variables and a deductive system that operates on that language by using unification to handle variables. Now suppose that we extend the unsorted language to a sorted language and wish to extend the unsorted deductive system to operate on the sorted language. Furthermore, suppose we wish to do this repeatedly for many languages and deductive systems. Must we initiate a large research project to work on each deductive system individually or is there a set of principles and a systematic way to generate these new systems?

In all previous work, each system for sorted deduction and its completeness proof is produced from scratch. No general principles or methods have been available to do this systematically. For example, the recent theses of Cohn

---

[2]Stickel's [33] work on theory resolution and Jaffar and Lassez's [22] work on constraint logic programming are the best examples of efforts in this direction. Stickel's results show how a broad range of theories can be built into resolution. Jaffar and Lassez's results show how a range of constraint processing mechanisms can be built into Horn clause logic programming.

[8,11] and Walther [38] present sorted logics and develop resolution-based deductive systems for them. Neither of these deductive systems is generated systematically from a deductive system for unsorted logics. Consequently, each of these theses is forced to conclude by raising an open question: how can other unsorted deductive systems be extended to deal with a sorted logic?

This paper introduces a framework for integrating logical deduction and sortal deduction to form deductive systems for logics with sorted variables. In a deductive system constructed according to this framework the sort module is invoked *only* when the logic module performs unification. Because the sort information is used only when making substitutions, this framework is called the *substitutional framework.*

The substitutional framework provides not only an architecture for sorted deduction, but also a method for systematically transforming unsorted deduction systems into sorted ones. As we shall see, these transformations are applicable to all deductive systems that handle quantified variables schematically by using unification. Furthermore, the framework provides a method for systematically transforming a completeness proof for an unsorted system into one for the corresponding sorted system.

Besides expanding and improving upon the presentation of a previous paper [17], this paper addresses some additional issues, most notably inadmissible formulas—formulas containing expressions that may denote the empty sort—and normal form transformations. Furthermore, this paper generalizes the previous results to accommodate a richer sorted language. The language to which the previous results apply includes variables restricted by sort symbols, whereas the language to which the present results apply additionally includes variables restricted by arbitrary Boolean combinations of sort symbols.

The remainder of this paper is organized as follows. Section 2 discusses the substitutional architecture in more detail, giving examples of substitutional and nonsubstitutional hybrid reasoners. After Section 3 presents the syntax and semantics of a first-order language with sorted variables, Section 4 gives an overview of the substitutional framework. Section 5 presents some fundamental definitions and theorems on which the substitutional framework rests. In particular, that section addresses the problems associated with inadmissible formulas, generalizes the notions of substitutions and unifiers to account for sorted variables, and generalizes the Herbrand Theorem accordingly. Using resolution as an example, Section 6 illustrates how ordinary deduction systems and their completeness proofs can be transformed into sorted deduction systems and their completeness proofs. In order to focus on the main ideas of the substitutional framework, discussion of certain issues peripheral to these ideas has been relegated to the appendices. The first appendix discusses the computation of sorted unifiers and the second presents normal form transformations for the sorted language.

2. The substitutional architecture

The distinguishing characteristic of a substitutional reasoner is that it consists of a primary reasoner that invokes an embedded special-purpose reasoner only to perform certain prescribed inferences during unification. Information flows only from the embedded reasoner to the primary reasoner. Another way to look at the architecture is to view a substitutional reasoner as a primary reasoner that uses a unification algorithm that is extended to perform certain built-in inferences.

The language that the primary reasoner uses, and that the extended unification algorithm must operate on, contains *restricted variables*. Unlike ordinary variables that range over the entire domain, restricted variables have information associated with them that specifies a subset of the domain over which they are to range. In sorted logics the restrictions are always monadic—that is, each restriction limits the range of only a single variable. For example, the variable x may be restricted to take on a value from the set of mammals. Though the scope of this paper is limited to monadic restrictions, the framework can be extended to handle higher-degree restrictions that specify dependencies among the values that two or more variables can take. For example, the variables x and y may be constrained so that x takes on a value that is greater than the value of y.

The substitutional architecture has been one of the most common and most successful architectures for hybrid reasoning, being used in a wide range of reasoners including logic programming systems [4,19], general-purpose resolution systems [32,38], a deductive database system [28,29], a parser for logic grammars [16], and a knowledge retriever [15]. In spite of their popularity, it was not until 1986 [15] that anyone raised the possibility that all of these systems could be explained with a common set of principles. This is the first piece of work to examine these principles in a general setting. It should be pointed out, however, that the above-mentioned deductive systems of Walther and of Schmidt-Schauß have special provisions for handling equalities, an issue that is not addressed in this paper.

All of the substitutional systems referred to in the last paragraph allow only monadic restrictions. Several more-recent efforts have developed substitutional logic programming systems that use higher-degree restrictions, usually called constraints. RHET [3] is a logic programming system that has a fairly sophisticated sort system, as does its ancestor HORNE [4,19], but also incorporates some simple mechanisms for handling constraints. Constraint logic programming (CLP) [22] provides a broad framework for generalizing Horn clause logic programming to incorporate higher-degree restrictions in a substitutional architecture. A number of CLP systems have been built, including CLP($\mathcal{R}$) [23] and CHIP [35].

The CLP framework as it currently stands and the substitutional framework as presented here are each more general than the other along different dimensions. The substitutional framework is more general in that it can handle a wide range of deductive systems, whereas the CLP framework has been developed only for SLD resolution as used in logic programming. On the other hand, CLP is more general in that it can handle arbitrary restrictions, whereas this paper only considers monadic restrictions. My current research is aimed at developing a single framework that subsumes both the CLP and substitutional frameworks.

The basic idea of reasoning about taxonomic information during unification dates back to Reiter's [28] work on deductive databases. The results reported in the present paper greatly generalize his results. To begin with, Reiter's results pertain to a language that is much weaker than that employed here. His language, which can best be described as "database logic", has no existential quantifiers or function symbols other than 0-arity ones. Thus the only terms that occur in the language are constants and variables, and therefore much of the difficulty of sorted unification is avoided. Furthermore, Reiter only considered integrating sorted unification into a particular deductive system, O-resolution. He proved the completeness of sorted O-resolution, but because the proof is an argument about the syntactic form of O-deductions, there is no apparent way in which it generalizes to other forms of deduction.

Reiter also observed that there are certain cases in which sorted O-resolution is incomplete and he identified an extremely strict condition *sufficient* for its completeness. Though he pointed out that this condition is not necessary for completeness, he did not identify a necessary condition. The present paper identifies a condition that is both necessary and sufficient for completeness, not just for sorted O-resolution, but for any form of sorted deduction that falls into the substitutional framework. This result thus identifies the limitations inherent in building taxonomic reasoning into unification.

A clearer view of what substitutional reasoners are can be obtained by considering some nonsubstitutional reasoners. To begin with, not all systems based on sorted logic are substitutional. Cohn's [11] LLAMA system is a complex sorted resolution system consisting of numerous reasoning components integrated by a variety of methods. LLAMA reasons about sorts during unification but, because the logic is sufficiently rich, the system's architecture must go beyond the substitutional framework in order to obtain completeness. Consequently, during unification the LLAMA sort module can pass back literals to the primary reasoner, which then get included as additional disjuncts in the resolvent clause. Such literals are called prosthetic literals and are discussed at length in a paper by Cohn [12]. Thus, unlike ordinary resolution and the sorted resolution presented later in this paper, a literal can appear in a resolvent even though it is not an instance of a literal in one of its parents. Thus some sort information enters the representation used by the primary reasoner, something that does not happen in a substitutional reasoner.

Like the substitutional framework, theory resolution [33] is not a particular system, but rather an architecture and framework for constructing hybrid systems. The comparison between these two frameworks is particularly interesting because each provides a method for embedding special-purpose reasoners into the resolution rule of inference. The essence of resolution comprises two fundamental ideas; one forms the foundation of theory resolution and the other forms the foundation of substitutional reasoning. The first idea is that at the ground (variable-free) level resolution looks for local evidence of unsatisfiability. The local evidence comes in the form of a pair of clauses, one containing a literal and the other containing its complement. Theory resolution generalizes this idea; instead of merely looking for a pair of literals that are unsatisfiable by themselves, it looks for a set of literals that are unsatisfiable when taken in conjunction with a given background theory. Thus, the theory resolution rule of inference applies to a set of clauses containing a set of literals that, together with the background theory, are unsatisfiable.

The second fundamental idea in resolution is that a clause with variables is treated as schematic for the set of all its ground instances. In resolving two clauses with variables, resolution behaves as if it were resolving all of the ground instances of the two clauses together. This simulation of ground resolution is precisely what unification achieves. The result is that every derivation involving clauses with variables is schematic for one or more ground derivations. The substitutional framework extends this paradigm for handling variables by allowing constraints to be placed on expressions to restrict the set of ground instances for which they are schematic. Whether or not a particular ground expression satisfies the constraints depends on a background theory. This is handled by building into unification certain constraint satisfaction procedures that invoke the embedded reasoner to ascertain certain logical consequences of the background theory.

Thus the substitutional framework extends resolution by replacing the simple notion of an instance of an expression with one that takes a background theory into account, whereas theory resolution replaces the simple notion of unsatisfiability with one that takes a background theory into account. The two essential components of resolution are orthogonal, and hence so are the two proposed extensions. The two extensions could be combined in a single system and a theoretical understanding of the resulting system could be obtained straightforwardly from our current theoretical understanding of each.

The basic ideas embodied in theory resolution and in the substitutional framework are applicable outside of the resolution setting. The substitutional framework could be used to extend any reasoner that treats variables schematically by using unification. Theory resolution could be used to extend any inference rule that operates by recognizing unsatisfiable formulas. Furthermore, one could imagine extending relations other than unsatisfiability—subsumption, for example—to be relative to a background theory.

3. The sorted language

This section introduces a language called Sorted First-Order Predicate Calculus (SFOPC) that extends the ordinary First-Order Predicate Calculus (FOPC) by introducing sort symbols and variables that are restricted to range over specified sorts. There is little about this extension that is particular to FOPC; any first-order language containing standard quantified variables can be extended in the same manner. In this paper SFOPC is used for illustrative purposes. Indeed, all the ideas, definitions and theorems presented here in terms of SFOPC were originally developed for a three-valued logic [15].

SFOPC is written with a lexicon that contains the usual function and predicate symbols. In addition, the SFOPC lexicon contains a countable set of sort symbols. Typographically, sort symbols are written entirely in small capitals as such: MAMMAL. Semantically, a sort symbol, like a monadic predicate, denotes a subset of the domain, called a sort.

The key syntactic feature of SFOPC is its use of *restricted variables*, variables that are restricted to range over specified subsets of the domain. A restricted variable is a pair, $x{:}\tau$, where x is a variable name and τ is a *restriction*. A restriction is either atomic, in which case it is a sort symbol, or it is molecular, in which case it is composed of atomic restrictions and the connectives $\wedge$, $\vee$, $\neg$, and $\rightarrow$. For example, $x{:}\text{DOG}$ and $y{:}\text{MAMMAL} \wedge \neg\text{DOG}$ are restricted variables. A molecular restriction, like an atomic restriction, denotes a subset of the domain.

An SFOPC representation has certain properties that depend on the set of restrictions that it uses. To obtain certain properties one may wish to limit the restrictions used in a representation. For example, sorted languages often limit themselves to atomic restrictions. Henceforth $\mathcal{R}$ shall name the set of (not necessarily atomic) restrictions that are used in constructing an SFOPC representation. In essence, SFOPC is a class of languages parameterized by $\mathcal{R}$.

We shall require that only a finite number of sort symbols occur in $\mathcal{R}$. This imposes no limitations that affect the ultimate goal of performing deduction on a finite representation, but the restriction is useful in proving a lemma, called the Ascending Chain Lemma, in Section 5. This assumption does not imply that $\mathcal{R}$ is finite since an infinite set of boolean expressions can be built from a finite set of sort symbols.

SFOPC consists of two disjoint sublanguages that share the same lexicon. The first sublanguage is for expressing general information and the second sublanguage, which is used in the sort module, is for representing information about the relationships among sorts. The sentences of the first sublanguage are called "$\mathcal{R}$-sentences" whereas those of the second are called "S-sentences".

$\mathcal{R}$-sentences are similar to ordinary FOPC sentences except that they may contain variables restricted by expressions in $\mathcal{R}$. An example of an $\mathcal{R}$-sentence is the sentence shown in (1), which has a single restriction, DOG.

$$\forall x\text{:DOG } Drink(x\text{:DOG}, beer) \vee Eat(x\text{:DOG}, meat). \tag{1}$$

To avoid confusion I never write a formula containing two distinct variables that have the same variable name. That is, no formula contains variables $x\text{:}\tau$ and $x\text{:}\tau'$ where τ and τ' are distinct. This enables use of the following shorthand. If a formula has multiple occurrences of the same variable then the restriction often is written only on the first occurrence. For example, (1) can be abbreviated as (2).

$$\forall x\text{:DOG } Drink(x, beer) \vee Eat(x, meat). \tag{2}$$

For clarity, variables are sometimes written in angle brackets, such as $\langle x\text{:DOG} \vee \text{CAT}\rangle$. τ and ω are used as meta-linguistic symbols that always stand for a restriction. Henceforth, the term "variable" refers generally to either an ordinary variable or a restricted variable.

Semantically, a restricted variable ranges only over the subset of the domain denoted by its restriction. Formally this is captured by the following semantic rules for *restricted quantifiers* (quantifiers with restricted variables). In these semantic rules $[[\psi]]^{M,e}$ is the semantic value assigned to an expression or symbol ψ by a model M and an assignment to variables e, and $e[d/x]$ is the assignment to variables that is identical to e with the possible exception that x is assigned d. (Recall that $[[\tau]]^{M,e}$ is a subset of the domain.)

$$[[\forall x\text{:}\tau\, \phi]]^{M,e} = \begin{cases} \text{True,} & \text{if for every } d \in [[\tau]]^{M,e}, \\ & \quad [[\phi]]^{M,e[d/x]} = \text{True,} \\ \text{False,} & \text{otherwise.} \end{cases}$$

$$[[\exists x\text{:}\tau\, \phi]]^{M,e} = \begin{cases} \text{True,} & \text{if for some } d \in [[\tau]]^{M,e}, \\ & \quad [[\phi]]^{M,e[d/x]} = \text{True,} \\ \text{False,} & \text{otherwise.} \end{cases}$$

Notice that if τ is a restriction that denotes the entire domain in some model M, then $[[\forall x{:}\tau\ \phi]]^{M,e} = [[\forall x\ \phi]]^{M,e}$ and $[[\exists x{:}\tau\ \phi]]^{M,e} = [[\exists x\ \phi]]^{M,e}$. Consequently, unrestricted variables are often treated as restricted variables implicitly restricted to the "universal" sort. Also notice that if τ denotes the empty set in some model, then that model assigns True to $\forall x{:}\tau\ \phi$ and False to $\exists x{:}\tau\ \phi$, regardless of the denotation of ϕ. The subset of the domain denoted by a restriction is determined in the obvious manner:

$$[[\tau \vee \omega]]^{M,e} = \{d \mid d \in [[\tau]]^{M,e} \text{ or } d \in [[\omega]]^{M,e}\},$$

$$[[\neg\tau]]^{M,e} = \{d \mid d \notin [[\tau]]^{M,e}\},$$

$$[[\tau \wedge \omega]]^{M,e} = \{d \mid d \in [[\tau]]^{M,e} \text{ and } d \in [[\omega]]^{M,e}\},$$

$$[[\tau \rightarrow \omega]]^{M,e} = \{d \mid d \notin [[\tau]]^{M,e} \text{ or } d \in [[\omega]]^{M,e}\}.$$

Though sorted logics typically stipulate that sorts are nonempty, SFOPC imposes no such requirement. Restrictions that are not known to be satisfied by any individual do present difficulties, which are addressed later in this paper. However, merely requiring sorts to be nonempty does not force the denotations of restrictions to be nonempty—DOG $\wedge$ ¬DOG would still denote the empty set—so this requirement is not adopted and the difficulties are dealt with in other ways.

Whereas $\mathcal{R}$-sentences employ restricted variables, the role of S-sentences is to express relationships among the sorts and the sortal behavior of the functions. S-sentences are constructed like ordinary sentences of FOPC except that they contain no ordinary predicate symbols; in their place are sort symbols acting as monadic predicate symbols. Hence, every atomic S-formula is of the form $\tau(t)$, where τ is a sort symbol and t is an ordinary term. In the obvious way I use the terms *S-formula* and *S-literal*. Here are examples of S-sentences:

DOG$(fido) \wedge$ DOG$(mother(fido))$.

$\forall x$ DOG$(x) \rightarrow$ MAMMAL(x).

$\forall x, y$ ODD$(x) \wedge$ EVEN$(y) \rightarrow$ ODD$(sum(x,y))$.

S-formulas are assigned truth values as one would expect: an atomic formula $S(t)$ is assigned True if the domain element denoted by t is a member of the set denoted by S, and a molecular S-formula is assigned a value in the usual Tarskian manner.

A representation consisting of a set of SFOPC sentences can be partitioned into a set of $\mathcal{R}$-sentences and a set of S-sentences. The S-sentences are stored in the sort module, and, according to the substitutional framework, only get called into play when the reasoning engine operating on the $\mathcal{R}$-sentences performs unification. The set of S-sentences stored in the sort module will be referred to as a *sort theory*.

SFOPC is no more expressive than FOPC; each sentence of SFOPC is logically equivalent to one (of about the same length) of FOPC. Clearly the addition of sort symbols does not make the language more expressive since they behave semantically like monadic predicate symbols. Nor does the addition of restricted variables enhance the expressiveness of the language. To see this, observe that any formula containing restricted quantifiers can be rewritten to a logically equivalent one without restricted quantifiers on the basis of two logical equivalences: [3]

$$\forall x{:}\tau\ \psi \equiv \forall x\ \tau(x) \to \psi',$$

$$\exists x{:}\tau\ \psi \equiv \exists x\ \tau(x) \land \psi',$$

where ψ' is the result of substituting x for all free occurrences of $x{:}\tau$ in ψ, and $\tau(x)$ is the result of replacing every sort symbol ω in τ with $\omega(x)$. The formula that results from removing all restricted quantifiers from a formula ϕ by this rewriting process is called the *normalization* of ϕ and is denoted by ϕ^{N}. So, for example, (4) is the normalization of (3) and the two sentences are logically equivalent.

$$\forall x{:}\mathrm{MAN}\ \exists\langle y{:}\mathrm{BLONDE} \land \mathrm{WOMAN}\rangle\ Loves(x,y). \tag{3}$$

$$\forall x\ Man(x) \to (\exists y\ Blonde(y) \land Woman(y) \land Loves(x,y)). \tag{4}$$

Finally, if Φ is a set of formulas, then $\Phi^{\mathrm{N}} = \{\phi^{\mathrm{N}} \mid \phi \in \Phi\}$.

Though SFOPC only adds syntactic sugar to FOPC, traditional sorted logics truly differ from FOPC. Instead of having a sort theory, traditional sorted logics have a *sort structure*, which is an ordering on the sort symbols. The sort structure is not represented in the logical language but is used in the meta-linguistic specification of the syntax and semantics of the language. In dealing with these sorted logics one can speak of the sort of a term. Strictly speaking, this cannot be done in SFOPC; only elements of the domain have sorts. The denotations of terms and of sorts can vary from model to model and hence a term can denote objects of different sorts in different models. Though there are ways of translating sentences of a traditional sorted logic to FOPC—and hence to SFOPC—not everything is captured by the translation. Further discussion of traditional sorted logics and their relationship to SFOPC is beyond the scope of this paper. However, the interested reader is referred to a paper by Cohn [13] that overviews the dimensions along which traditional sorted logics vary and to another paper

---

[3]Two formulas or sets of formulas, ψ and ϕ, are logically equivalent (written $\psi \equiv \phi$) if, and only if, they are satisfied by precisely the same models.

by the same author [10] that discusses the mapping of traditional sorted logics to classical logic.

To simplify the exposition of the remainder of the paper we consider only sentences in Skolem Normal Form (SNF), that is, sentences that are free of existential quantifiers and whose universal quantifiers are in prenex position (i.e., at the beginning of the sentence). Hence, "quantifier" always means universal quantifier and a quantified sentence is always a universally quantified sentence in prenex form. This assumption is common in work on deduction and does not result in a loss of generality since any set of FOPC sentences can be mechanically transformed to SNF without affecting its satisfiability or unsatisfiability. Appendix B shows how any set of SFOPC sentences can be transformed to SNF in a similar manner.

4. The substitutional framework

Since the introduction of resolution in 1965, nearly every automated deductive system has handled universally quantified variables by using a unification algorithm. The method is ubiquitous, being used in theorem provers, rewrite systems, parsers, logic-programming systems, logic databases, question-answering systems, and planners. [4] By paralleling this general approach to deduction with ordinary variables, the substitutional framework for deduction with restricted variables achieves the same degree of generality.

The gist of this approach is that a quantified sentence is treated as a schema standing for the set of its ground instances. The justification for this is found in Herbrand's Theorem, which states that a set of quantified sentences is satisfiable if, and only if, the set containing every ground instance of every one of the sentences is satisfiable.

A deductive system that operates on ground sentences can be made to operate on quantified sentences by replacing tests for equality between expressions with tests for unifiability between them. Sometimes this is all that needs to be done, though sometimes additional mechanisms must be incorporated. In either case, the idea is that deductions on quantified sentences are themselves schematic for deductions on ground sentences. A schematic deduction is said to *lift* each deduction that is an instance of it.

Given a deductive system based on unification we would like to show that it does indeed treat quantified sentences as schemas. This usually takes the form of a *lifting theorem* for the deductive system stating that every

---

[4]The substitutional framework applies to all of these systems. Collectively, they are referred to as "deductive systems".

deduction that can be made from the ground instances of a set of sentences can be made schematically from the sentences themselves.

The substitutional approach to handling restricted quantifiers is built upon the notion of *well-sorted substitution* in the same way that the method for handling ordinary quantifiers is built upon the notion of substitution. The well-sortedness of a substitution is relative to a sort theory; to simplify terminology a substitution that is well sorted with respect to sort theory Σ is called a Σ-*substitution*. Intuitively, a Σ-substitution is a substitution that respects the restrictions attached to the variables it replaces. Thus, an algorithm for performing Σ-unification must query the sort module in order to obtain certain information about Σ. The sort module must deduce an answer to the query from the sort theory. The computational complexity of responding to these queries, and hence the complexity of Σ-unification, depends upon the structure of Σ.

It is a simple matter to extend an unsorted deductive system $\mathcal{D}$ to a sorted deductive system, $\mathcal{D}_S$, that operates on the new, sorted language. One need only replace the unification algorithm of $\mathcal{D}$ with a sorted unification algorithm. Notice that the resulting system, $\mathcal{D}_S$, uses the sort module in only one place—in its computation of unifiers. Thus, the interface between the original deductive methods of $\mathcal{D}$ and the newly-incorporated deductive methods of the sort module is extremely simple. Furthermore, integrating the two kinds of deductive methods does not involve restructuring $\mathcal{D}$. So, for example, if $\mathcal{D}$ is based on a set of proof rules, no new rules need be added to obtain the corresponding proof system for the sorted language. In contrast, when extending a resolution proof system to deal with sorted logic, Cohn [8] was forced to formulate and incorporate additional proof rules; the expressiveness of his logic makes it impossible to build a complete deductive system by modifying only the unification component of a standard resolution system.

$\mathcal{D}_S$ treats quantified sentences as sentence schemas in much the same way that $\mathcal{D}$ does. The only difference is that a sentence with restricted variables does not stand for the set of all its ground instances, but only for its well-sorted ground instances. This treatment of restricted quantifiers is justified by the *Sorted Herbrand Theorem*. This theorem states that, under certain circumstances, a sort theory Σ and a set S of $\mathcal{R}$-sentences are jointly satisfiable if, and only if, the set of all Σ-ground instances of S is satisfiable. In saying that S and Σ can be replaced by the Σ-ground instances of S, the Sorted Herbrand Theorem justifies using Σ only in computing Σ-unifiers. Notice that Σ must be used in generating the correct instances of S, but once they are obtained Σ is irrelevant because ground instances have no variables and hence no sort symbols.

To show that $\mathcal{D}_S$ correctly treats schemas with restricted variables, one must prove the *Lifting Theorem* for $\mathcal{D}_S$. This theorem asserts that every deduction that can be made from the Σ-ground instances of a set of sorted sentences can be made schematically from the sentences themselves. In general, lifting theorems for unsorted deduction systems hold because of certain properties of substitutions and unifiers. Because Σ-substitutions and Σ-unifiers also have these properties, as is shown in Section 5.2, the lifting theorems for the corresponding sorted deduction systems hold. On the basis of this observation, a proof of the lifting theorem for $\mathcal{D}$ can be transformed simply and systematically to a proof of the Lifting Theorem for $\mathcal{D}_S$. Section 6 illustrates this by systematically transforming the proof of the Lifting Theorem for Resolution to one for sorted resolution.

5. Fundamental definitions and results

5.1. Admissibility

This section considers the complications that may arise from having restrictions that can denote the empty set. Let us first introduce some terminology to aid the discussion.

Definition 5.1 (*Admissible*). A restriction τ is Σ-*satisfiable* if $\Sigma \models \tau(t)$ for some ground term t; otherwise τ is Σ-unsatisfiable. Any syntactic object—such as a variable, expression, set of expressions, or derivation—is said to be Σ-*admissible* if it contains no Σ-unsatisfiable restrictions. A term t Σ-*satisfies* τ if $\Sigma \models \overline{\forall}\, \tau(t)$. [5]

For cleanliness, the "Σ" is often omitted from these terms.

Whereas every admissible expression, including every expression of FOPC, has ground instances, we shall see that inadmissible expressions have none. Consequently, an inadmissible derivation is *not* schematic for any ground derivations. Since completeness requires that every ground proof is lifted by some schematic proof, inadmissible schematic proofs can be eliminated without affecting completeness.

Ordinarily, if ϕ is a formula containing no free occurrences of x then $\forall x\, \phi$ and ϕ are logically equivalent. However, this is not the case in SFOPC when x has an unsatisfiable restriction. For example, $\forall \langle x{:}\text{CAT} \wedge \neg\text{CAT} \rangle\, P \wedge \neg P$ is a valid sentence, but $P \wedge \neg P$ is unsatisfiable. Thus, a quantifier cannot be considered vacuous unless the variable that it quantifies is admissible.

Avoiding the elimination of nonvacuous quantifiers requires some subtlety. For instance, one must be careful not to resolve $\forall x{:}\text{CAT}\ Meows(x)$ and

---

[5] Here, and in general, an expression of the form $\overline{\forall}\phi$ denotes the universal closure of ϕ—that is, the formula $\forall x_1 \ldots x_n\, \phi$ where $x_1, \ldots, x_n$ are the freely-occurring variables of ϕ.

$\forall x{:}\neg\text{CAT}\ \neg Meows(x)$ to form $\square$, the empty clause, which is unsatisfiable. The correct resolvent is $\forall\langle x{:}\text{CAT} \wedge \neg\text{CAT}\rangle\ \square$, which is a valid sentence.

Traditional sorted logics avoid these difficulties by excluding inadmissible expressions from the language. This is accomplished by allowing only atomic restrictions in the language and stipulating that every sort symbol denotes a nonempty set.

There is no way to exclude inadmissible sentences from SFOPC, unless the grammar of $\mathcal{R}$-sentences is severely restricted or made dependent on the content of the sort theory. The alternative, which is adopted here, is to allow inadmissible sentences in the language but design the inference system so that no derivation contains inadmissible sentences. This is accomplished by designing the inference rules to *preserve admissibility*, that is, to derive only admissible formulas from admissible formulas. If the formulas input to such a deduction system are admissible, then only admissible formulas will ever be derived. In a substitutional reasoner new restrictions are introduced only by the application of substitutions, and hence this is the only place where inadmissibility can arise. Thus we can ensure that the inference rules preserve admissibility by considering only substitutions that map admissible expressions to admissible expressions. Accordingly, our definition of well-sorted substitutions requires that they preserve admissibility.

5.2. Well-sorted substitutions and unifiers

Roughly speaking, a substitution is well sorted relative to a sort theory if it respects the restrictions attached to the variables it replaces and if it preserves admissibility. More precisely:

Definition 5.2 (*Well-sorted substitution*). A substitution θ is well sorted relative to a sort theory Σ if, and only if, for every variable $x{:}\tau$
- $\langle x{:}\tau\rangle\theta$ Σ-satisfies τ, and
- if $x{:}\tau$ is Σ-admissible then so is $\langle x{:}\tau\rangle\theta$.

Two special cases of this definition are worth noting. If θ is well sorted relative to Σ and maps $x{:}\tau$ to a ground term t, then it must be that $\Sigma \models \tau(t)$. In other words, Σ must entail that the object denoted by t is in the set denoted by τ. If θ maps $x{:}\tau$ to a variable $y{:}\omega$ then it must be that $\Sigma \models \forall y{:}\omega\ \tau(y)$. That is, Σ must entail that ω is a subset of τ.

Expression e' is said to be a *well-sorted instance* of e relative to Σ if $e' = e\theta$, for some substitution θ that is well sorted relative to Σ. In the obvious way, I speak of well-sorted ground instances of an expression and write $e_{\Sigma_{gr}}$ to denote the set of all well-sorted instances of e that are ground. Observe that every well-sorted instance of an inadmissible expression is inadmissible. Thus, since all ground expressions are admissible, inadmissible expressions have no well-sorted ground instances. On the other hand, every admissible expression has at least one well-sorted ground instance. Thus it follows that an expression has a well-sorted ground instance if, and only if, the expression is admissible. Finally notice that well-sorted substitutions are defined so as to preserve admissibility; every well-sorted instance of an admissible expression is itself admissible.

Substitutions, well-sorted or not, are functions and therefore can be composed. If θ and σ are substitutions then their composition, $\theta \cdot \sigma$, is $\lambda e.\sigma(\theta(e))$. In other words, $\theta \cdot \sigma$ is such that $e(\theta \cdot \sigma) = (e\theta)\sigma$.

Because they are substitutions, well-sorted substitutions enjoy all the properties possessed by substitutions in general. So, for example, since the composition of substitutions is associative, so is the composition of well-sorted substitutions. For other reasons the set of all well-sorted substitutions has many properties possessed by the set of all ordinary substitutions. For example, the set of well-sorted unifiers contains the identity substitution and is closed under composition.

Lemma 5.3 (Identity Lemma). *The identity substitution, ε, is well sorted relative to any sort theory.*

Proof. ε maps every variable $x{:}\tau$ to itself and any sort theory entails $\forall x{:}\tau\, \tau(x)$ since $\forall x{:}\tau\, \tau(x)$ is a valid sentence. Clearly ε preserves admissibility. □

Lemma 5.4 (Composition Lemma). *If σ and θ are well-sorted substitutions relative to Σ, then so is $\theta \cdot \sigma$.*

Proof. I assume θ and σ are Σ-well sorted, and show that for any variable $x{:}\tau$, $x(\theta \cdot \sigma)$ Σ-satisfies τ and that $\theta \cdot \sigma$ preserves admissibility.

- For any variable $x{:}\tau$, $x(\theta \cdot \sigma)$ Σ-satisfies τ: Let $\phi[y_1{:}\omega_1,\ldots,y_n{:}\omega_n]$ be $x{:}\tau\theta$, where $y_1{:}\omega_1,\ldots,y_n{:}\omega_n$ are the free variables of the term. (Subsequently, an expression of the form $\psi[t_1,\ldots,t_n]$ shall refer to the expression that results from replacing all free occurrences of $y_i{:}\omega_i$ in ϕ by t_i, for $1 \le i \le n$.) Since θ is Σ-well sorted, Σ entails

$$\overline{\forall}\tau(\phi[y_1{:}\omega_1,\ldots,y_n{:}\omega_n])$$

which normalized is

$$\overline{\forall}\omega_1(y_1) \wedge \cdots \wedge \omega_n(y_n) \to \tau(\phi[y_1,\ldots,y_n]). \tag{5}$$

For $1 \le i \le n$ let ψ_i be $\langle y_i{:}\omega_i\rangle\sigma$. Since σ is Σ-well sorted, Σ entails

$$\overline{\forall}\omega_1(\psi_1) \wedge \cdots \wedge \omega_n(\psi_n). \tag{6}$$

By combining (6) and (5) with modus ponens we can conclude that Σ entails

$$\overline{\forall}\tau(\phi[\psi_1,\ldots,\psi_n])$$

which is

$$\overline{\forall}\tau(\langle x{:}\tau\rangle\theta\sigma).$$

In other words, $x(\theta\cdot\sigma)$ Σ-satisfies τ.

• $\theta\cdot\sigma$ preserves admissibility: Since $x{:}\tau$ is admissible and θ and σ preserve admissibility, we have that $(\langle x{:}\tau\rangle\theta)\sigma = \langle x{:}\tau\rangle\theta\cdot\sigma$ is admissible. Thus $\theta\cdot\sigma$ preserves admissibility. □

The usual notions of what it means for a substitution to be a unifier can be adapted to well-sorted substitutions as follows:

Definition 5.5 (*Well-sorted unifier*). Let E be a set of expressions and θ be a substitution. θ is a *well-sorted unifier* of E relative to Σ (also called a Σ-unifier) if it is a unifier of E and is well sorted relative to Σ.

A difficulty arises if one tries to adapt, in the obvious manner, the standard generality ordering for substitutions. The difficulty arises because it is sometimes impossible to find a unifier of two sorted expressions that does not introduce new variables. For instance, every unifier of $x{:}\mathrm{A}$ and $y{:}\mathrm{B}$ relative to the sort theory $\{\forall x\, \mathrm{C}(x) \rightarrow \mathrm{A}(x), \forall x\, \mathrm{C}(x) \rightarrow \mathrm{B}(x)\}$ is of the form $\{z{:}\mathrm{C}/x{:}\mathrm{A}, z{:}\mathrm{C}/y{:}\mathrm{B}\}$, where z is a newly introduced variable. For every way of choosing a new variable to introduce, there is a different unifier and, with the usual notion of generality, none is more general than any other. It should be clear that we would like to say that these substitutions are equally general, that it does not matter how the newly-introduced variable is chosen, provided that conflicting names are avoided.

Therefore, generality shall be defined to be insensitive to how newly-introduced variables are chosen. This is accomplished by dividing the set of variables into two disjoint categories, the *variables of concern*, henceforth denoted by $\mathcal{V}$, and the *parameters*. Henceforth, all references to expressions should be taken to refer to expressions containing no parameters, unless otherwise stated. All variables shall be taken to be variables of concern unless written with an overscore as such: $\bar{x}{:}\tau$. Generality is defined to be sensitive only to the variables of concern.

Definition 5.6 (*Restricting the domain of a substitution*). $\theta|_V$ is the substitution such that

$$x(\theta|_V) = \begin{cases} x\theta, & \text{if } x \in V, \\ x, & \text{if } x \notin V. \end{cases}$$

Definition 5.7 (*Σ-more general*). Let θ_1 and θ_2 be substitutions that are well sorted relative to Σ. θ_1 is *Σ-more general* than θ_2 (written $\theta_1 \geq_\Sigma \theta_2$) if, and only if, $(\theta_1 \cdot \sigma)|_V = \theta_2|_V$ for some substitution σ that is well sorted relative to Σ. Two substitutions that are Σ-more general than each other are said to be *Σ-variants*.

The reader can now verify that $\{\bar{z}{:}C/x{:}A, \bar{z}{:}C/y{:}B\}$ is equally as general as any other substitution that differs only by introducing a parameter other than $\bar{z}$, and that it is strictly more general than any that introduces a variable of concern instead of $\bar{z}$.

When new variables are introduced during a deduction it is important that they do not accidentally coincide with certain other variables in the proof. This can be accomplished by exploiting the definition of generality. After each deduction step simply expand the set V to contain all variables that occur in newly-derived formulas. If the deduction rules only use unifiers that are as general as possible, it is assured that all introduced variables are parameters (at that point) and therefore do not coincide with any other variables in the proof.

The set of all unsorted unifiers of a set of expressions contains substitutions that are more general than every other unifier in the set. These so-called most general unifiers are important because any one of them can serve as a representative for the entire set. On the other hand, the set of all Σ-unifiers of a set of expressions may not contain a Σ-most general element. It will, however, contain *maximally-general Σ-unifiers*, Σ-unifiers for which no others are strictly Σ-more general. Here is an example:

Example 5.8 (*Σ-unifiers*). Let

$$\Sigma = \{\text{ODD}(one),$$
$$\forall x, y \; \text{ODD}(x) \wedge \text{ODD}(y) \rightarrow \text{EVEN}(sum(x,y)),$$
$$\forall x, y \; \text{EVEN}(x) \wedge \text{EVEN}(y) \rightarrow \text{EVEN}(sum(x,y))\},$$

$$E = \{z{:}\text{EVEN}, sum(v,w)\},$$

$$\theta_1 = \{sum(\bar{x}{:}\text{EVEN}, \bar{y}{:}\text{EVEN})/z, \bar{x}{:}\text{EVEN}/v, \bar{y}{:}\text{EVEN}/w\},$$

$$\theta_2 = \{sum(\bar{x}{:}\text{ODD}, \bar{y}{:}\text{ODD})/z, \bar{x}{:}\text{ODD}/v, \bar{y}{:}\text{ODD}/w\}.$$

Then θ_1 and θ_2 are each maximally-general Σ-unifiers of E and neither θ_1 nor θ_2 is Σ-more general than the other.

Indeed, a finite set of expressions may have an infinite number of maximally-general Σ-unifiers, none of which are Σ-more general than any others. For instance:

Example 5.9 (*Σ-unifiers*). Let

$$\Sigma = \{\forall x \ \mathrm{T}(i(x)) \rightarrow \mathrm{T}(i(s(x))), \ \mathrm{T}(i(a))\},$$

$$E = \{z{:}\mathrm{T}, \ i(s(y))\}.$$

Then

$$\{\{a/y, \ i(s(a))/z{:}\mathrm{T}\}, \ \{s(a)/y, \ i(s(s(a)))/z{:}\mathrm{T}\}, \ldots\}$$

is an infinite set of maximally-general Σ-unifiers of E and none of these is Σ-more general than any of the others.

In performing unsorted deduction there is no need to consider all unifiers of two expressions; it suffices to consider only a most general unifier. A most general unifier forms a basis from which all other unifiers can be generated by composing it with other substitutions. A similar basis can be formed for the set of Σ-unifiers of two sorted expressions. As the preceding examples illustrate, it may be necessary to form the basis from a set of unifiers rather than a single unifier. Since the basis should be as small as possible, it should not contain two substitutions such that one is more general than the other. The basis we speak of is called a *Σ-complete set of incomparable unifiers* (or ΣCIU) and is defined as follows.

Definition 5.10 (*Σ-complete set of incomparable unifiers*). Let E be a set of expressions and let Θ be a set of substitutions that are well sorted relative to Σ. Then Θ is a *Σ-complete set of incomparable unifiers* (or ΣCIU) of E if, and only if:
  (1) Θ is correct; if $\theta \in \Theta$ and $\theta \geq_\Sigma \theta'$ then θ' is a Σ-unifier of E;
  (2) Θ is complete; if θ' is a Σ-unifier of E then for some $\theta \in \Theta, \theta \geq_\Sigma \theta'$;
  (3) the members of Θ are incomparable; Θ does not contain two distinct substitutions such that one is Σ-more general than the other.

An important property is that every set of admissible expressions is guaranteed to have a ΣCIU. This property follows directly from the following lemma. Here we will say that a quasi-ordering (one that is reflexive and transitive, but not necessarily anti-symmetric) contains an infinite strictly-ascending chain if there exists an infinite sequence of elements each of which is strictly greater than all previous ones.

Lemma 5.11 (Ascending Chain Lemma). *Given any sort theory, Σ, the set of admissible expressions ordered by Σ-generality contains no infinite strictly-ascending chain.*

Proof. The lemma follows from two observations:

- It is well known that the set of unsorted expressions ordered by generality contains no infinite strictly-ascending chain. Hence, neither does the set of sorted expressions ordered by ordinary (unsorted) generality.
- Since the set of sort symbols that occurs in $\mathcal{R}$ is finite (recall this requirement from Section 3), $\mathcal{R}$ contains only a finite number of restrictions that are not logically equivalent to each other. Hence, the set of sorted variables ordered by Σ-generality contains no infinite strictly-ascending chain.   □

If a set E of admissible expressions has no unifier, then its ΣCIU is the empty set. If E is unifiable, then it follows from the Ascending Chain Lemma that for any unifier θ of E there is a maximally-general Σ-unifier of E that is Σ-more general than θ. Consequently, a ΣCIU of E can always be constructed out of maximally-general Σ-unifiers.[6]

Theorem 5.12 (ΣCIU Existence Theorem). *Every set of admissible expressions has a ΣCIU, for any sort theory Σ.*

Indeed, as the following theorem shows, every ΣCIU is constructed out of maximally-general Σ-unifiers in just this way.

Theorem 5.13 (ΣCIU Structure Theorem). *Let Θ be a ΣCIU of a set of admissible expressions E and let θ be a substitution. Then Θ contains a Σ-variant of θ if, and only if, θ is a maximally-general Σ-unifier of E.*

Proof.
($\Rightarrow$) Suppose Θ contains θ', a variant of θ. By incomparability, Θ contains no substitution Σ-greater than θ' and, by completeness, no Σ-substitution strictly Σ-more general than θ' unifies E. Thus θ', and accordingly θ, is a maximally-general Σ-unifier of E.

---

[6]If the number of sort symbols occurring in $\mathcal{R}$ were not restricted, then the Ascending Chain Lemma would not hold. Nevertheless, I conjecture that E would still have a ΣCIU provided that only a finite number of sort symbols occur in E and Σ. This latter restriction is weaker than the former; the former limits the number of sort symbols that can occur in the unifiers, but the latter does not. I conjecture that even though Σ-unifiers can introduce sort symbols not occurring in E or Σ, maximally-general Σ-unifiers never do so.

($\Leftarrow$) If θ is a maximally-general Σ-unifier of E, then by the correctness condition Θ contains some Σ-unifier $\theta' \geq_\Sigma \theta$. Since θ is a maximally-general Σ-unifier, θ' is not strictly Σ-more general than θ. Hence, θ and θ' must be Σ-variants. □

There is no effective procedure for finding a ΣCIU of two arbitrary admissible expressions relative to an arbitrary sort theory since the ΣCIU may be infinite. No algorithm can even determine whether an arbitrary substitution is well-sorted since it would have to decide logical consequences of the sort theory.[7] However, ΣCIUs can be computed for sort theories that are restricted in certain ways. Space precludes an extensive discussion of sorted unification and algorithms for computing it. However, since sorted unification is at the very heart of substitutional reasoning, Appendix A is devoted to presenting a particular restriction on the form of a sort theory, the monomorphic tree restriction, and giving an algorithm that computes a ΣCIU of any two expressions provided that Σ meets the restriction. It should be noted that the ability to enumerate the set of proofs in a substitutional system requires only the enumerability of ΣCIUs, not their computability.

Several researchers, most notably Walther [39] and Schmidt-Schauß [31,32], have studied sorted unification. Such studies typically consider sorted unification with respect to a sort signature, rather than a sort theory. The present theory formulation appears to generalize the signature formulations, so results obtained in a signature formulation can be translated to the theory formulation. Rather than discuss the signature formulations, present the known results, and translate them to the theory formulation, Appendix A merely presents some simple results for the theory formulation. The results reformulate, rather than improve, previous results. In ongoing research, Frisch and Cohn [18] have developed a *universal* sorted unification algorithm, which can operate with an arbitrary sort theory, and are now attempting to show that it subsumes all known algorithms for sorted unification.[8]

5.3. The Sorted Herbrand Theorem

The Sorted Herbrand Theorem relates the satisfiability of a set of SFOPC clauses to the satisfiability of their well-sorted ground instances, provided that the sort theory corresponds—in a sense to be made clear—with some model. In particular, the correspondence must hold over the so-called *in-*

---

[7]Sort theories are *not* necessarily in monadic FOPC since they may contain function symbols of arbitrary arity.

[8]The alert reader will notice the reference to an algorithm for an undecidable problem. Given an oracle for deciding certain consequences of the sort theory, this "algorithm" can enumerate a ΣCIU of any two sorted expressions.

stances of $\mathcal{R}$—the set of all ground formulas of the form $\tau(t)$, where τ is a restriction in $\mathcal{R}$ and t is a ground term.

Definition 5.14 (*$\mathcal{R}$-correspondence*). A model M and a sort theory Σ $\mathcal{R}$-correspond if, and only if, M is a model of Σ and Σ entails every instance of $\mathcal{R}$ that is satisfied by M.

Observe that if a model and sort theory $\mathcal{R}$-correspond then the instances of $\mathcal{R}$ satisfied by the model are precisely those that the sort theory entails. Also observe that M and Σ $\mathcal{R}$-correspond if M satisfies Σ and Σ entails every *atomic* instance of $\mathcal{R}$ that is satisfied by M.

Not every satisfiable sort theory has an $\mathcal{R}$-corresponding model. For example, if $\mathcal{R}$ is the set of all atomic restrictions then

$$\Sigma = \{\text{DOG}(ralph) \vee \text{BABY}(ralph)\}$$

$\mathcal{R}$-corresponds to no model. Any model that satisfies Σ would have to satisfy either $\text{DOG}(ralph)$ or $\text{BABY}(ralph)$. In either case, such a model would satisfy a member of $\mathcal{R}$ that is not entailed by Σ. Also observe that if a set of SNF sentences corresponds to some model then it corresponds to a Herbrand model. As we shall now see, those sort theories that $\mathcal{R}$-correspond to some model are of particular interest.

Theorem 5.15 (*Sorted Herbrand Theorem*). [9] *Let α be a set of $\mathcal{R}$-clauses and let Σ be a set of S-clauses that $\mathcal{R}$-corresponds to some model. Then $\alpha \cup \Sigma$ is unsatisfiable if, and only if, $\alpha_{\Sigma_{gr}}$ is.*

Proof.
($\Leftarrow$) $\alpha \cup \Sigma$ entails each element of $\alpha_{\Sigma_{gr}}$. Thus, if $\alpha_{\Sigma_{gr}}$ is unsatisfiable then so must be $\alpha \cup \Sigma$.

($\Rightarrow$) Let M be a Herbrand model that $\mathcal{R}$-corresponds to Σ and satisfies $\alpha_{\Sigma_{gr}}$. I show that M also satisfies $\Sigma \cup (\alpha^N)_{gr}$, and thereby satisfies $\Sigma \cup \alpha$. Clearly M satisfies Σ. I now consider a, an arbitrary sentence in α and show that M satisfies $(a^N)\theta$, an arbitrary ground instance of a^N. $(a^N)\theta$ is of the form $\tau_1(t_1) \wedge \cdots \wedge \tau_n(t_n) \rightarrow \beta$. Consider two cases:

(1) $\Sigma \not\models \tau_1(t_1) \wedge \cdots \wedge \tau_n(t_n)$. Therefore, because M $\mathcal{R}$-corresponds to Σ and each $\tau_i(t_i)$ is in $\mathcal{R}$, M falsifies $\tau_1(t_1) \wedge \cdots \wedge \tau_n(t_n)$. Hence, M satisfies $\tau_1(t_1) \wedge \cdots \wedge \tau_n(t_n) \rightarrow \beta$.

(2) $\Sigma \models \tau_1(t_1) \wedge \cdots \wedge \tau_n(t_n)$. Then β is an element of $\alpha_{\Sigma_{gr}}$ and hence is satisfied by M. □

[9]For simplicity this theorem is stated in terms of clauses. Nonetheless, like the unsorted Herbrand Theorem, it applies to sentences that are in Skolem Normal Form.

What is the effect of requiring Σ to $\mathcal{R}$-correspond to some model? The Correspondence Theorem, which follows, states that the requirement prohibits Σ from containing disjunctive information about the restrictions in $\mathcal{R}$.

Theorem 5.16 (Correspondence Theorem). *A satisfiable set of S-clauses, Σ, $\mathcal{R}$-corresponds to some model if, and only if, Σ entails a finite disjunction of instances of $\mathcal{R}$ only when it entails one of the disjuncts.*

Proof.

($\Leftarrow$) Let $\psi_1, \ldots, \psi_n$ be instances of $\mathcal{R}$ and assume that Σ entails $\psi_1 \vee \cdots \vee \psi_n$. Let M be the Herbrand model that satisfies precisely those ground atomic formulas that follow from Σ. Assuming that Σ entails some ψ_i, I show that M satisfies Σ and therefore $\mathcal{R}$-corresponds to Σ. Let $C = \neg\alpha_1 \vee \cdots \vee \neg\alpha_k \vee \beta_1 \vee \cdots \vee \beta_m$ be an arbitrary clause in Σ_{gr}. If some model of Σ satisfies one $\neg\alpha_i$ then so does M and hence M satisfies C. Otherwise every model of Σ falsifies every $\neg\alpha_i$ and hence $\Sigma \models \beta_1 \vee \cdots \vee \beta_m$. By the assumption, there is an i such that $\Sigma \models \beta_i$. Thus, M satisfies β_i and therefore it also satisfies C. Either way, M satisfies C, an arbitrary member of Σ_{gr}, and therefore M satisfies Σ.

($\Rightarrow$) A model satisfies a disjunction only if it satisfies one of the disjuncts. Hence a theory that $\mathcal{R}$-corresponds to a model entails a disjunction of instances of $\mathcal{R}$ only if it entails one of the disjuncts. $\square$

What happens if Σ $\mathcal{R}$-corresponds to no model? Consider the case where $\mathcal{R}$ is the set of atomic restrictions and

$$\Sigma = \{\text{BABY}(Ralph) \vee \text{DOG}(Ralph)\},$$

$$\alpha = \{\forall x{:}\text{DOG } Annoys(x, Allan), \forall x{:}\text{BABY } Annoys(x, Allan)\}.$$

Because Σ does not entail any atomic sentences, $\alpha_{\Sigma_{gr}}$ is empty. Now, here is the problem: $\Sigma \cup \alpha \models Annoys(Ralph, Allan)$, but $\alpha_{\Sigma_{gr}}$ does not.

Reiter [28] noticed this difficulty in his work on deductive databases. His solution was to insist that Σ satisfies a condition called "τ-completeness"— that for every sort symbol ω and every term t either $\Sigma \models \omega(t)$ or $\Sigma \models \neg\omega(t)$. This condition is equivalent to requiring that Σ has complete information about all sorts. Though Reiter found a sufficient condition, it is overly restrictive; it is not the lack of information that causes problems, but the presence of disjunctive information. What about the condition that Σ must $\mathcal{R}$-correspond to a model? Is it also overly restrictive? The Necessity/Sufficiency Theorem asserts that the condition is indeed necessary. The proof of the theorem demonstrates that for any sort theory that does not $\mathcal{R}$-correspond to a model an example like the above baby-and-dog one can be constructed.

Theorem 5.17 (Necessity/Sufficiency Theorem). *Let Σ be a set of S-clauses and $\mathcal{R}$ be a set of restrictions. It is both necessary and sufficient that Σ $\mathcal{R}$-corresponds to a model for the following statement to hold:*

> *For every set of $\mathcal{R}$-clauses α, $\Sigma \cup \alpha$ is unsatisfiable if, and only if, $\alpha_{\Sigma_{gr}}$ is.*

Proof.

Sufficiency: This is equivalent to the Sorted Herbrand Theorem.

Necessity: I assume that Σ does not $\mathcal{R}$-correspond to any model and construct a set of $\mathcal{R}$-clauses α such that $\alpha \cup \Sigma$ is unsatisfiable but $\alpha_{\Sigma_{gr}}$ is satisfiable. If Σ is unsatisfiable, then let α be any satisfiable set of ground clauses. Then, $\alpha_{\Sigma_{gr}}$ is satisfiable even though $\alpha \cup \Sigma$ is not. If, on the other hand, Σ is satisfiable then the Correspondence Theorem assures us that there is a disjunction of ground atomic S-formulas, $\psi = P_1(t_1) \vee \cdots \vee P_n(t_n)$ such that $\Sigma \models \psi$ and for every $1 \leq i \leq n$, $\Sigma \not\models P_i(t_i)$. Let α be the set of sentences

$$\{\forall x{:}P_i\, Q_i(x) \mid 1 \leq i \leq n\} \cup \{\neg Q_i(t_i) \mid 1 \leq i \leq n\}.$$

It is now easy to verify that $\alpha_{\Sigma_{gr}}$ is satisfiable even though $\alpha \cup \Sigma$ is not. □

An earlier version of this paper [17] is based on SFOPC in which $\mathcal{R}$ contains only atomic restrictions. The paper shows for that language that the necessary and sufficient condition for the Herbrand Theorem is that Σ has a Herbrand model that is least in the partial order defined by:

> $M_1 \leq M_2$ if, and only if, for every predicate symbol or sort symbol P, $[[P]]^{M_1} \subseteq [[P]]^{M_2}$.

This result is demonstrably a special case of the Necessity/Sufficiency Theorem stated above. If $\mathcal{R}$ contains only atomic restrictions then Σ $\mathcal{R}$-corresponds to a model if, and only if, Σ has a least Herbrand model. This equivalence between $\mathcal{R}$-correspondence and least models holds not only when $\mathcal{R}$ is the set of atomic restrictions, but more generally when $\mathcal{R}$ is any set of *positive* restrictions. After defining the notion of a positive formula, the proof of this equivalence is presented.

Definition 5.18 (*Positive and negative formulas*). A formula occurs positively within itself. If α occurs positively (negatively) within γ then α occurs positively (negatively) within $\gamma \wedge \beta$, $\beta \wedge \gamma$, $\beta \vee \gamma$, $\gamma \vee \beta$, $\beta \rightarrow \gamma$, $\gamma \leftrightarrow \beta$ and $\beta \leftrightarrow \gamma$. If α occurs positively (negatively) within γ then α occurs negatively (positively) within $\neg\beta$, $\gamma \rightarrow \beta$, $\gamma \leftrightarrow \beta$ and $\beta \leftrightarrow \gamma$. A formula is said to be positive (negative) if no atomic formulas occur negatively (positively) within it.

Lemma 5.19 (Monotonicity Lemma). *Let ϕ be a positive formula and M and M' be two Herbrand models such that $M \leq M'$. If M satisfies ϕ then so does M'.*

Proof. Looking at any of the standard transformations for putting a quantifier-free formula into Conjunctive Normal Form (CNF), one can observe that an atom occurs positively (negatively) in a formula if, and only if, it occurs positively (negatively) in the Conjunctive Normal Transform (CNT) of the formula. Hence a formula is positive (negative) if, and only if, its CNT is, and therefore it suffices to prove the theorem only for CNF formulas. A CNF formula is positive if, and only if, it contains no negation signs—that is if, and only if, it is a conjunction of disjunctions of atomic formulas. If M satisfies a disjunction of atomic formulas, so does M'. It follows that if M satisfies a conjunction of disjunctions of atomic formulas then so does M'. □

Theorem 5.20. *Let $\mathcal{R}$ contain only positive restrictions. Then a set Σ of S-clauses $\mathcal{R}$-corresponds to some model if, and only if, it has a least Herbrand model.*

Proof.

($\Leftarrow$) If M is the least Herbrand model of Σ then M satisfies Σ, and therefore satisfies all its consequences. For the other half of the correspondence, notice that if M satisfies a positive formula α then, by the Monotonicity Lemma, so do all models greater than M. Since all models of Σ are greater than M, $\Sigma \models \alpha$.

($\Rightarrow$) If Σ $\mathcal{R}$-corresponds to some model then it $\mathcal{R}$-corresponds to some Herbrand model M. If M weren't the least model it would make some atom α true that was false in the least model. Hence, α would not follow from Σ, and thus M and Σ would not correspond. □

6. Example: sorted resolution

This section uses standard resolution to illustrate how the substitutional framework can be used to systematically transform an unsorted deductive system and its proof of completeness into a sorted deductive system and its proof of completeness.

The resolution rule of inference operates on clauses, each of which we shall take to be a set of literals. If L is a set of literals, then $\bar{L}$ denotes the set containing the complement of every literal in L. Assume that L and M are two FOPC clauses whose variables have been standardized apart. If some $l \subseteq L$ and $m \subseteq M$ are such that $l \cup \bar{m}$ is unifiable by a maximally-general unifier θ (which, in this unsorted case, is a most general unifier), then the clause $(L - l)\theta \cup (M - m)\theta$ is a resolvent of L and M. A resolution derivation of a FOPC clause C from a set of FOPC clauses S is a binary tree such that its root is C, each leaf is a member of S, and each nonleaf node is a resolvent of its children. We shall write $S \vdash_{\text{RES}} C$ to assert that there is a resolution derivation of C from S.

It is now straightforward to transform the definition of resolvent to the SFOPC case where the two clauses may contain restricted variables and the resolvent is relative to a set Σ of S-sentences. Such a resolvent is the same as an ordinary resolvent except that the substitution involved, θ, must be a maximally-general Σ-unifier. Let us make this explicit by considering a set Σ of S-sentences and two $\mathcal{R}$-clauses of SFOPC, L and M, whose variables have been standardized apart. If some $l \subseteq L$ and $m \subseteq M$ are such that $l \cup \bar{m}$ are unifiable by a maximally-general Σ-unifier θ, then the clause $(L - l)\theta \cup (M - m)\theta$ is a Σ-resolvent of L and M. The definition of resolution derivation extends in the obvious straightforward manner. A Σ-resolution derivation of $\mathcal{R}$-clause C from a set S of $\mathcal{R}$-clauses is a binary tree such that its root is C, each of its leaves is a member of S, and each of its interior nodes is a Σ-resolvent of its child nodes. We shall write $S \vdash_{\Sigma\text{RES}} C$ to assert that there is a Σ-resolution derivation of C from S.

In unsorted resolution, given two clauses and a particular set of literals to be resolved upon, one need only consider a single resolvent. All other resolvents are variants of it. However, in sorted resolution one may need to consider many resolvents—one for each substitution in a ΣCIU of the literals to be resolved upon. All other resolvents are Σ-variants of these, as shown by the ΣCIU Structure Theorem.

The derivation displayed in Fig. 1 illustrates sorted resolution. It uses the sort theory Σ, also shown in the figure. Clauses (1), (2) and (3) are input clauses. Observe that all three are admissible since $\Sigma \models \text{T1}(a)$ and $\Sigma \models \text{T2}(a)$. Clauses (1) and (2) can be Σ-resolved together. A ΣCIU of $P(x{:}\text{T1})$ and $P(y{:}\text{T2})$ is

$$\{\{\bar{u}{:}\text{T3}/x{:}\text{T1},\ \bar{u}{:}\text{T3}/y{:}\text{T2}\},\ \{f(\bar{w}{:}\text{T3})/x{:}\text{T1},\ f(\bar{w}{:}\text{T3})/y{:}\text{T2}\}\}.$$

Thus, clauses (1) and (2) have two Σ-resolvents, clauses (4) and (5). The variables in clauses (4) and (5) are not shown as parameters because as soon as they are derived the set $\mathcal{V}$ is expanded to include them. Clauses (3) and (5) Σ-resolve using the singleton ΣCIU $\{\{w{:}\text{T3}/z{:}\text{T1}\}\}$. Their Σ-resolvent is clause (6), the empty clause.

Observe that clauses (3) and (4) cannot be Σ-resolved together because $f(z{:}\text{T1})$ and $u{:}\text{T3}$ are not Σ-unifiable. This can be confirmed by noticing that, apart from its Σ-variants, $u{:}\text{T3}$ has only one Σ-instance: a. That is, other than these Σ-instances, there is no other term t such that $\Sigma \models \bar{\forall}\text{T3}(t)$.

$$\Sigma = \{ \forall x \; \text{T3}(x) \rightarrow \text{T1}(x) \wedge \text{T2}(x),$$
$$\forall x \; \text{T1}(x) \rightarrow \text{T1}(f(x)),$$
$$\forall x \; \text{T2}(x) \rightarrow \text{T2}(f(x)),$$
$$\text{T3}(a) \}$$

(1) $\neg P(x{:}\text{T1}) \vee Q(x{:}\text{T1})$ input
(2) $P(y{:}\text{T2})$ input
(3) $\neg Q(f(z{:}\text{T1}))$ input
(4) $Q(u{:}\text{T3})$ from (1) and (2)
(5) $Q(f(w{:}\text{T3}))$ from (1) and (2)
(6) □   from (3) and (5)

Fig. 1. A Σ-resolution derivation.

Because no Σ-instance of $u{:}\text{T3}$ is a Σ-instance of $f(z{:}\text{T1})$, the two terms have no Σ-unifier.

To see how the completeness of sorted resolution is established, first consider how completeness is established for unsorted resolution. The Completeness Theorem for Resolution states that a set S of FOPC clauses is unsatisfiable only if $S \vdash_{\overline{\text{RES}}} \square$. Typically, proofs of this theorem are of the form illustrated in Fig. 2. First one proves the completeness of resolution for the ground case and then one connects this up to the nonground case on the syntactic side and on the semantic side. Assume S is unsatisfiable. Then, on the semantic side, the connection is made by the Herbrand Theorem for FOPC, which tells us that S_{gr} is unsatisfiable. From this, the completeness of ground resolution tells us that $S_{\text{gr}} \vdash_{\overline{\text{RES}}} \square$. Then, on the syntactic side, the connection to the nonground case is made by the Lifting Theorem for Resolution, which tells us that $S \vdash_{\overline{\text{RES}}} \square$.

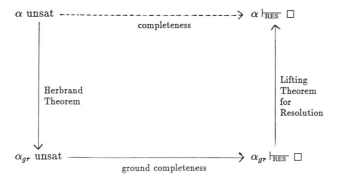

Fig. 2. Completeness proof for resolution

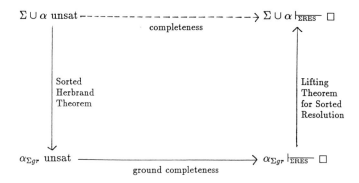

Fig. 3. Completeness proof for sorted resolution.

Many first-order deductive systems that handle variables schematically via unification can be proved complete in this manner. One proves that the system is complete in the ground case and that ground proofs can be lifted. This is then coupled with the Herbrand Theorem to finish the completeness proof.

Now consider the Completeness Theorem for Sorted Resolution.

Theorem 6.1 (Completeness Theorem for Sorted Resolution). *Let α be a set of Σ-admissible $\mathcal{R}$-clauses and Σ be a set of S-clauses that $\mathcal{R}$-corresponds to some model. If $\Sigma \cup \alpha$ is unsatisfiable then $\alpha \vdash_{\overline{\Sigma RES}} \Box$.*

The proof of this theorem, which is illustrated in Fig. 3, parallels the completeness proof for unsorted resolution. Assuming $\Sigma \cup S$ is unsatisfiable, the Sorted Herbrand Theorem tells us that $S_{\Sigma_{gr}}$ is also unsatisfiable. Then the completeness theorem for ground resolution tells us that $S_{\Sigma_{gr}} \vdash_{\overline{\Sigma RES}} \Box$. We know that Σ-resolution is complete for ground clauses because it is the same as ordinary resolution on ground clauses. To complete the proof one uses the Lifting Theorem for Σ-resolution, which tells us that if $S_{\Sigma_{gr}} \vdash_{\overline{\Sigma RES}} \Box$ then $S \vdash_{\overline{\Sigma RES}} \Box$.

So, a completeness proof of the form used for ordinary resolution can be transformed systematically to a completeness proof for the corresponding sorted deduction system. All references to the Herbrand Theorem are replaced with references to the Sorted Herbrand Theorem. The ground completeness theorem remains unchanged. All one needs to do is prove a lifting theorem for the particular sorted deduction system. As we now see, this too can be done in a systematic manner by transforming the lifting theorem of the corresponding unsorted system. Below is the Lifting Theorem for Resolution and its proof, followed by the Lifting Theorem for Sorted Resolution.

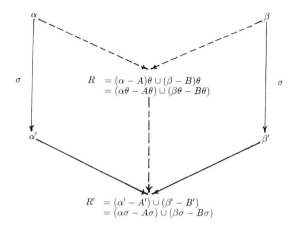

Fig. 4. Lifting proof for resolution

Theorem 6.2 (Lifting Theorem for Resolution). *If S is a set of clauses and C' is a ground clause such that $S_{\mathrm{gr}} \mathop{\vdash}_{\mathrm{RES}} C'$ then there is a clause $C \geq C'$ such that $S \mathop{\vdash}_{\mathrm{RES}} C$.*

Proof. We shall simplify this proof by treating clauses as multisets instead of as sets. By showing that a single application of resolution lifts, it follows that an entire derivation lifts. Let α and β be clauses with no variables in common and let R' be a resolvent of $\alpha' \in \alpha_{\mathrm{gr}}$ and $\beta' \in \beta_{\mathrm{gr}}$. I show that there is a resolvent R of α and β that is more general than R'. Figure 4 illustrates these relationships. Since α and β have no variables in common there is a substitution σ such that $\alpha' = \alpha\sigma$ and $\beta' = \beta\sigma$. Let A' and B' be the literal multisets in α' and β', respectively, that are resolved upon to produce R' and let A and B be the corresponding multisets in α and β. Since $A\sigma = \bar{B}\sigma$ (recall that $\alpha' = \alpha\sigma$ and $\beta' = \beta\sigma$ are resolvable with selected literals $A' = A\sigma$ and $B' = B\sigma$), $A \cup \bar{B}$ has a maximally-general unifier θ that is more general than σ. Thus $R = (\alpha - A)\theta \cup (\beta - B)\theta$ is a resolvent of α and β and is more general than $R' = (\alpha\sigma - A\sigma) \cup (\beta\sigma - B\sigma)$, which is the chosen resolvent of α' and β'. $\square$

Theorem 6.3 (Lifting Theorem for Sorted Resolution). *If Σ is a set of S-sentences, S is a set of Σ-admissible $\mathcal{R}$-clauses, and C' is a ground clause such that $S_{\Sigma_{\mathrm{gr}}} \mathop{\vdash}_{\Sigma\mathrm{RES}} C'$ then there is an $\mathcal{R}$-clause $C \geq_{\Sigma} C'$ such that $S \mathop{\vdash}_{\Sigma\mathrm{RES}} C$.*

As claimed in Section 4, a proof of the Lifting Theorem for Sorted Resolution can be produced by systematically transforming the proof of the Lifting Theorem for Resolution. Simply replace all occurrences of the words "resolvent", "substitution", "maximally-general unifier", "ground instance", and "more general" with the words "Σ-resolvent", "Σ-substitution", "maximally-general Σ-unifier", "Σ-ground instance", and "Σ-more general" respectively. The resulting argument is correct because all properties of substitutions and their use in instantiating and unifying expressions on which the original proof relies are also properties (as established in Section 5.2) of Σ-substitutions and their use in instantiating and unifying expressions. The reader is encouraged to verify this.

7. Conclusions

Though this paper has left unanswered many questions regarding sorted deduction, it has proposed a framework under which such questions can be addressed for an entire class of deduction systems rather than for one system at a time.

As this paper presents sorted deduction in the context of sorted first-order logic, restricted variables are introduced only by quantification. These restricted quantified variables can be treated as restricted schematic variables on the basis of the Sorted Herbrand Theorem. Nonetheless, the substitutional framework can be applied to systems that introduce schematic variables directly. For example, there is no reason why production systems or grammar systems that use unrestricted variables cannot be extended to incorporate restricted variables. The results presented here concerning sorted substitution, sorted unification, and sorted lifting are as applicable in those contexts as in the logic context.

Appendix A. The monomorphic tree restriction and sorted unification

Here we present both a particularly severe restriction on the form of a sort theory and an algorithm that computes a ΣCIU of any two expressions provided that Σ meets the restriction and is finite. We assume that $\mathcal{R}$ contains only atomic restrictions, each of which is Σ-satisfiable. Therefore, every expression is admissible and so the issue of admissibility need not be considered further. The discussion that follows often speaks of the set of all admissible terms that Σ-satisfy a sort τ, so let us define this to be the *satisfaction set* of τ.

The restriction on the sort theory is the combination of two restrictions, the tree restriction and the monomorphism restriction, and hence is called the *monomorphic tree restriction*. A sort theory meeting the tree restriction consists of sentences of two kinds. Sentences of the first kind have the form $\forall x\, \tau(x) \rightarrow \tau'(x)$, where τ and τ' are distinct sort symbols. The tree restriction requires that for any τ there is at most one sentence of the above form. Sentences of the second kind have the form $\bar{\forall}\tau(t)$, where τ is a sort symbol and t is a term. The tree restriction requires that the sort theory does not contain two sentences, $\overline{\forall}\tau(t)$ and $\overline{\forall}\tau'(t')$, such that t and t' are unifiable. The effect of the tree restriction is that if two sort symbols have intersecting satisfaction sets then one satisfaction set is a subset of the other.

The monomorphism restriction imposes on every sentence of the form $\overline{\forall}\tau(t)$ the additional restriction that t must be of the form $f(x_1, ..., x_n)$, where f is an n-ary function symbol for some $n \geq 0$. The effect of this restriction is that if one instance of a nonvariable term satisfies a sort symbol, then so does every instance. Consequently, one can determine whether a nonvariable term satisfies a sort symbol solely on the basis of the term's main function symbol.

If a sort theory Σ meets the monomorphic tree restriction then any two Σ-unifiable expressions have a Σ-most general unifier; in other words, they have a singleton ΣCIU. Notice that in Example 5.8 and Example 5.9, two examples of a nonsingleton ΣCIU, the sort theory violates the tree restriction.

Given two expressions and a sort theory Σ meeting the monomorphic tree restriction the algorithm in Fig. A.1, whose form is based on Martelli and Montanari's [24] algorithm for ordinary unification, determines whether the two expressions are Σ-unifiable, and if so it returns a Σ-most general unifier. Like the Martelli and Montanari algorithm, this algorithm operates by repeatedly transforming a set of equations between expressions to be unified until no more transformations apply, whereupon the most general unifier can be read directly from the equations.

The unsorted unification algorithm uses four transformations, the first three of which are used unadulterated in the sorted algorithm. The fourth unsorted transformation deals with equations in which the left side is a variable and the right side is any term. In the sorted algorithm this transformation is divided in two; Transformation 4 handles those cases in which the right side is not a variable, whereas Transformation 5 handles the cases in which it is. Each of these transformations first checks the well-sortedness of the unifier it is building and, if this succeeds, proceeds as in the unsorted case. Before substituting a term t for a variable $x{:}\tau$, Transformation 4 checks that t Σ-satisfies τ (i.e., whether $\Sigma \models \overline{\forall}\tau(t)$). When Transformation 5 unifies two variables, $x{:}\tau$ and $x'{:}\tau'$, it must check the satisfaction sets of τ and τ'. If the satisfaction set of τ' is a subset of the satisfaction set of τ (i.e., if $\Sigma \models \forall x\, \tau'(x) \rightarrow \tau(x)$) then $x'{:}\tau'$ is substituted for $x{:}\tau$. If the satisfaction set of τ is a subset of the satisfaction set of τ' then $x{:}\tau$ is substituted for $x'{:}\tau'$. If neither satisfaction set is a subset of the other then the unification fails. If Σ is finite, the well-sortedness conditions that these two transformations must test can be decided in finite time by an SLD-resolution procedure that avoids cycles by deleting any clause that is a variant of one of its ancestors.

The final difference between the unsorted and sorted algorithm is that the

Input: Two expressions, s_1 and s_2, and a sort theory Σ meeting the mono-
      morphic tree restriction.
Output: SUCCESS or FAILURE; if SUCCESS then a substitution is also output.

Let X be the singleton set of equations $\{s_1 = s_2\}$
Repeatedly perform any of the following transformations until no transformation
applies:

1. Select any equation of the form $t = x{:}\tau$, where t is not a variable and $x{:}\tau$
   is a variable, and rewrite it as $x{:}\tau = t$.

2. Select any equation of the form $x{:}\tau = x{:}\tau$ where $x{:}\tau$ is a variable and
   erase it.

3. Select any equation of the form $t = t'$ where neither t nor t' is a variable.
   If t and t' are atomic and identical then erase the equation
   Else if t and t' are atomic and different then FAIL
   Else if t is composed of $e_1, \ldots, e_n$ and t' is composed of $e_1', \ldots, e_n'$
       in the same manner
         then replace $t = t'$ by the equations $e_1 = e_1', \ldots, e_n = e_n'$
   Else FAIL.

4. Select any unmarked equation of the form $x{:}\tau = t$ where $x{:}\tau$ is a variable
   and t is not
   If $x{:}\tau$ occurs in t then FAIL
   Else if $\Sigma \models \bar{\forall}\tau(t)$
       then apply the substitution $\{t/x{:}\tau\}$ to all other equations
           (without erasing $x{:}\tau = t$)
           mark $x{:}\tau = t$ "reduced"
   Else FAIL.

5. Select any unmarked equation of the form $x{:}\tau = x'{:}\tau'$ where $x{:}\tau$ and $x'{:}\tau'$
   are distinct variables
   If $\Sigma \models \forall x\, \tau'(x) \to \tau(x)$
   Then apply the substitution $\{x'{:}\tau'/x{:}\tau\}$ to all other equations
         (without erasing $x{:}\tau = x'{:}\tau'$)
       mark $x{:}\tau = x'{:}\tau'$ "reduced"
   Else if $\Sigma \models \forall x\, \tau(x) \to \tau'(x)$
       then replace $x{:}\tau = x'{:}\tau'$ with $x'{:}\tau' = x{:}\tau$
         apply the substitution $\{x{:}\tau/x'{:}\tau'\}$ to all other equations
           (without erasing $x'{:}\tau' = x{:}\tau$)
         mark $x'{:}\tau' = x{:}\tau$ "reduced"
   Else FAIL.

SUCCEED with $\{t_1/x_1, \ldots, t_n/x_n\}$ where $x_1 = t_1, \ldots, x_n = t_n$ are the equations
that remain in X.

Fig. A.1. Sorted Unification Algorithm.

sorted one must check every equation for well-sortedness. If the unsorted
algorithm starts with the single equation $x = f(a)$ then it can halt immediately and report that $\{f(a)/x\}$ is a most general unifier. However, the

sorted algorithm should only report a unifier if $f(a)$ satisfies the sort of x. Thus whenever an equation is checked for well-sortedness it is marked and the algorithm does not report a successful unification until all equations have been marked.

The correctness of this algorithm is not proved here. One appealing way to do this would be to show that the algorithm is a special case of the Universal Sorted Unification Algorithm [18], whose correctness has been proved.

Appendix B. Normal form transformations

Amazingly, the same process that converts an FOPC sentence to prenex form [30] also converts an SFOPC sentence simply by ignoring the restrictions on the variables. Here's why: The conversion process is based on many equivalence schemas, six of which deal with quantification in FOPC. The following theorem gives six corresponding equivalence schemas for SFOPC, which hold for admissible formulas.

Theorem B.1 (Prenex Normal Transform Theorem). *If ψ and ϕ are formulas and ψ has no free occurrences of $x{:}\tau$ then*

(1) $\quad \neg \exists x{:}\tau \, \phi \equiv \forall x{:}\tau \, \neg \phi,$

(2) $\quad \neg \forall x{:}\tau \, \phi \equiv \exists x{:}\tau \, \neg \phi,$

(3) $\quad (\forall x{:}\tau \, \phi) \vee \psi \equiv \forall x{:}\tau \, (\phi \vee \psi),$

(4) $\quad (\exists x{:}\tau \, \phi) \wedge \psi \equiv \exists x{:}\tau \, (\phi \wedge \psi).$

Furthermore, if Σ is a sort theory and τ is Σ-satisfiable then

(5) $\quad \Sigma \cup \{(\forall x{:}\tau \, \phi) \wedge \psi\} \equiv \Sigma \cup \{\forall x{:}\tau \, (\phi \wedge \psi)\},$

(6) $\quad \Sigma \cup \{(\exists x{:}\tau \, \phi) \vee \psi\} \equiv \Sigma \cup \{\exists x{:}\tau \, (\phi \vee \psi)\}.$

Proof.

(1) $\quad \neg \exists x{:}\tau \, \phi \equiv \neg \exists x \, \tau(x) \wedge \phi$
   (definition of restricted quantification)

$\equiv \forall x \, \neg(\tau(x) \wedge \phi)$
   (unsorted equivalence)

$\equiv \forall x \, (\tau(x) \rightarrow \neg\phi)$
   (propositional equivalence)

$\equiv \forall x{:}\tau \, \neg\phi$
   (definition of restricted quantification)

(2)   Dual of above.

(3) $(\forall x{:}\tau\ \phi) \vee \psi \equiv (\forall x\ \tau(x) \rightarrow \phi) \vee \psi$
            (definition of restricted quantification)

        $\equiv \forall x\ ((\tau(x) \rightarrow \phi) \vee \psi)$
            (unsorted equivalence, since x is not free in ψ)

        $\equiv \forall x\ (\tau(x) \rightarrow (\phi \vee \psi))$
            (propositional equivalence)

        $\equiv \forall x{:}\tau\ (\phi \vee \psi)$
            (definition of restricted quantification)

(4)   Dual of above.

(5) $\Sigma \cup \{(\forall x{:}\tau\ \phi) \wedge \psi\} \equiv \Sigma \cup \{(\forall x\ \tau(x) \rightarrow \phi) \wedge \psi\}$
            (definition of restricted quantification)

        $\equiv \Sigma \cup \{(\forall x\ \tau(x) \rightarrow \phi) \wedge (\forall x\ \tau(x) \rightarrow \psi)\}$
            (since τ is Σ-satisfiable)

        $\equiv \Sigma \cup \{(\forall x\ ((\tau(x) \rightarrow \phi) \wedge (\tau(x) \rightarrow \psi)))\}$
            (unsorted equivalence)

        $\equiv \Sigma \cup \{\forall x\ \tau(x) \rightarrow (\phi \wedge \psi)\}$
            (propositional equivalence)

        $\equiv \Sigma \cup \{\forall x{:}\tau\ (\phi \wedge \psi)\}$
            (definition of restricted quantification)

(6)   Dual of above. $\square$

Thus, given a set of SFOPC sentences, $\Sigma \cup \alpha$, where the sentences of α are Σ-admissible, the sentences of α can be transformed to prenex form by moving the quantifiers about as if the restrictions weren't there!

It is necessary that τ be Σ-satisfiable for the fifth and sixth equivalence schemas of the Prenex Normal Transform Theorem to hold. To confirm this assume that some model M satisfies Σ and falsifies both $\exists x\ \tau(x)$ and ψ. Thus τ is not Σ-satisfiable. Now, $\Sigma \cup \{(\forall x{:}\tau\ \phi) \wedge \psi\}$ and $\Sigma \cup \{\forall x{:}\tau\ (\phi \wedge \psi)\}$ are not equivalent since M falsifies the first but satisfies the second. A similar argument shows that τ must be Σ-satisfiable for the sixth equivalence to hold.

Here is a transformation that puts a set of prenex form sentences of SFOPC into Skolem Normal Form and a theorem stating that the transformation preserves satisfiability.

Definition B.2 (*Skolem Normal Transformation*). Let $\alpha \cup \Sigma$ be a set of prenex form sentences of SFOPC. Its Skolem Normal Transform is computed by the following steps.

Step 1. While Σ contains a sentence ϕ that contains an existential quantifier do:

Observe that ϕ is of the form

$$\forall x_1 \forall x_2 \cdots \forall x_n \exists y \; \psi [y]$$

for some $n \geq 0$ and prenex-form formula $\psi[y]$. Choose ξ, some n-ary function symbol that does not occur in $\Sigma \cup \alpha$ and replace ϕ's occurrence in $\Sigma \cup \alpha$ with

$$\forall x_1 \forall x_2 \cdots \forall x_n \; \psi [\xi(x_1, \ldots, x_n)]$$

Step 2. While α contains a sentence ϕ that contains an existential quantifier do:

Observe that ϕ is of the form

$$\forall x_1{:}\tau_1 \forall x_2{:}\tau_2 \cdots \forall x_n{:}\tau_n \exists y{:}\tau_y \; \psi [y] \qquad \text{(B.1)}$$

for some $n \geq 0$ and prenex-form formula $\psi[y]$. Choose ξ, some n-ary function symbol that does not occur in $\alpha \cup \Sigma$ and replace ϕ's occurrence in $\alpha \cup \Sigma$ with

$$\forall x_1{:}\tau_1 \forall x_2{:}\tau_2 \cdots \forall x_n{:}\tau_n \; \psi [\xi(x_1, \ldots, x_n)] \qquad \text{(B.2)}$$

and add

$$\forall x_1, \ldots, x_n$$
$$\tau_1(x_1) \wedge \tau_2(x_2) \wedge \cdots \wedge \tau_n(x_n) \to \tau_y(\xi(x_1, \ldots, x_n)) \qquad \text{(B.3)}$$

to Σ.

Theorem B.3 (Skolem Normal Transform Theorem). *$\alpha \cup \Sigma$ is satisfiable if, and only if, its Skolem Normal Transform is.*

Proof. The transformations made in the first step alter S-sentences, which contain no restricted variables, in exactly the same manner as the unsorted Skolem Normal Transform, which is known to preserve satisfiability.[10]

For the second step, let $\alpha \cup \Sigma$ be the set of sentences at the beginning of any iteration and $\alpha' \cup \Sigma'$ be the sentences at the end of that iteration. It should be clear that (B.2) and (B.3) together entail (B.1). Hence any model that satisfies $\alpha' \cup \Sigma'$ also satisfies $\alpha \cup \Sigma$. We prove the converse by letting M be an arbitrary model that satisfies $\alpha \cup \Sigma$ and constructing a model M' that satisfies $\alpha' \cup \Sigma'$. Since M satisfies (B.1), there is a function

---

[10]Robinson [30] gives a particularly good exposition of the unsorted Skolem Normal Transform.

$F : [[\tau_1]]^M \times \cdots \times [[\tau_m]]^M \longrightarrow [[\tau_y]]^M$ such that M satisfies $\psi[y]$ under any assignment that maps each x_i to a member d_i of $[[\tau_i]]^M$ and y to $F(d_1, \ldots, d_m)$. Let M' be a model that is identical to M except that ξ denotes F. Thus M' satisfies (B.2) and (B.3) because of the way that the denotation of ξ was constructed. None of the other sentences in $\alpha' \cup \Sigma'$ contain ξ and therefore they are satisfied by M', which agrees with M on everything except the denotation of ξ. $\quad \square$

Acknowledgement

I thank the many people with whom I have had fruitful discussions related to this work, especially Tony Cohn. I am also grateful to Fran Evelyn for her support and for her painstaking efforts in proofreading and figure drawing. This work has been partially funded by NASA under grant number NAG 1-613 and by the University of Illinois Research Board.

References

[1] H. Aït-Kaci and R. Nasr, LOGIN: a logic programming language with built-in inheritance, *J. Logic Program.* **3** (1986) 187–215.

[2] J.F. Allen, Towards a general theory of action and time, *Artif. Intell.* **23** (1984) 123–154.

[3] J.F. Allen and B.W. Miller, The rhetorical knowledge representation system: a user's manual (for Rhet Version 14.0), Tech. Report TR 238, Computer Science Department, University of Rochester, Rochester, NY (1988).

[4] J.F. Allen, M. Giuliano and A.M. Frisch, The HORNE reasoning system, Tech. Report TR126 revised, Computer Science Department, University of Rochester, Rochester, NY (1984).

[5] C. Bloch and A.M. Frisch, An examination of the efficiency of sorted deduction (1989).

[6] R.J. Brachman, R.E. Fikes and H.J. Levesque, KRYPTON: a functional approach to knowledge representation, *IEEE Comput.* **16** (10) (1983) 67–73, Special Issue on Knowledge Representation.

[7] J. Cohen, Constraint logic programming languages, *Commun. ACM* **33** (7) (1990) 52–68.

[8] A.G. Cohn, Mechanising a particularly expressive many sorted logic, Ph.D. Thesis, Department of Computer Science, University of Essex, England (1983).

[9] A.G. Cohn, On the solution of *Schubert's Steamroller* in many sorted logic, in: *Proceedings IJCAI-85*, Los Angeles, CA (1985) 1169–1174.

[10] A.G. Cohn, Many sorted logic = unsorted logic + control? in: M. Bramer, ed., *Research and Development in Expert Systems* III (Cambridge University Press, Cambridge, England, 1986) 184–194.

[11] A.G. Cohn, A more expressive formulation of many sorted logic, *J. Autom. Reasoning* **3** (1987) 113–200.

[12] A.G. Cohn, On the appearance of sortal literals: a non substitutional framework for hybrid reasoning, in: R.J. Brachman, H.J. Levesque and R. Reiter, eds., *Proceedings of the First International Conference on Principles of Knowledge Representation and Reasoning*, Toronto, Ont. (1989) 55–66.

[13] A.G. Cohn, Taxonomic reasoning with many-sorted logics, *Artif. Intell. Rev.* **3** (1989) 89–128.

[14] S. Feferman, Applications of many sorted interpolation theorems, in: *Proceedings Symposium on Pure Mathematics* (1974) 102–148.

[15] A.M. Frisch, Knowledge retrieval as specialized inference, Ph.D. Thesis, Computer Science Department, University of Rochester, Rochester, NY (1986).

[16] A.M. Frisch, Parsing with restricted quantification: an initial demonstration, *Comput. Intell.* **2** (1986) 142–150.

[17] A.M. Frisch, A general framework for sorted deduction: fundamental results on hybrid reasoning, in: R.J. Brachman, H.J. Levesque and R. Reiter, eds., *Proceedings of the First International Conference on Principles of Knowledge Representation and Reasoning*, Toronto, Ont. (1989) 126–136.

[18] A.M. Frisch and A.G. Cohn, A universal algorithm for sorted unification, in: *Proceedings Unif'90*, Leeds, England (1990).

[19] A.M. Frisch, J.F. Allen and M. Giuliano, An overview of the HORNE logic programming system, *SIGART Newslett.* **84** (1983) 27–29.

[20] P.J. Hayes, A logic of actions, in: B. Meltzer and D. Michie, eds., *Machine Intelligence* **6** (Edinburgh University Press, Edinburgh, Scotland, 1971) 495–520.

[21] P.J. Hayes, Naive physics 1: ontology for liquids, in: J.R. Hobbs and R.C. Moore, eds., *Formal Theories of the Commonsense World* (Ablex, Norwood, NJ, 1985) 71–107, Chapter 3.

[22] J. Jaffar and J.-L. Lassez, Constraint logic programming, in: *Proceedings 14th ACM Principles of Programming Languages Conference*, Munich, FRG (1987) 111–119.

[23] J. Jaffar, S. Michaylov, P.J. Stuckey and R.H.C. Yap, The CLP($\mathcal{R}$) language and system, Research Report RC 16292 (#72336), IBM T.J. Watson Research Center, Yorktown Heights, NY (1990).

[24] A. Martelli and U. Montanari, An efficient unification algorithm, *ACM Trans. Program. Lang. Syst.* **4** (1982) 258–282.

[25] D. McDermott, A temporal logic for reasoning about processes and plans, *Cogn. Sci.* **6** (1982) 101–155.

[26] J.R. McSkimin and J. Minker, A predicate calculus based semantic network for deductive searching, in: N.V. Findler, ed., *Associative Networks: Representation and Use of Knowledge by Computers* (Academic Press, New York, 1979) 205–238.

[27] P.F. Patel-Schneider, A hybrid, decidable, logic-based knowledge representation system, *Comput. Intell.* **3** (2) (1987) 64–77.

[28] R. Reiter, An approach to deductive question-answering, BBN Tech. Report 3649, Bolt Beranek and Newman, Boston, MA (1977).

[29] R. Reiter, On the integrity of typed first-order data bases, in: H. Gallaire, J. Minker and J.M. Nicolas, eds., *Advances in Data Base Theory* **1** (Plenum, New York, 1981) 137–157.

[30] J.A. Robinson, *Logic: Form and Function* (North-Holland, New York, 1979).

[31] M. Schmidt-Schauß, Unification in many-sorted calculus with declarations, in: *Proceedings Ninth German Workshop on Artificial Intelligence*, Dassel/Solling (1985) 118–132.

[32] M. Schmidt-Schauß, *Computational Aspects of an Order-Sorted Logic with Term Declarations*, Lecture Notes in Computer Science **395** (Springer, Berlin, 1989).

[33] M.E. Stickel, Automated deduction by theory resolution, *J. Autom. Reasoning* **1** (1985) 333–355.

[34] M.E. Stickel, Schubert's Steamroller problem: formulations and solutions, *J. Autom. Reasoning* **2** (1986) 89–101.

[35] P. Van Hentenryk, *Constraint Satisfaction in Logic Programming* (MIT Press, Cambridge, MA, 1989).

[36] M. Vilain, The restricted language architecture of a hybrid representation system, in: *Proceedings IJCAI-85*, Los Angeles, CA (1985) 547–551.

[37] C. Walther, A mechanical solution of Schubert's Steamroller by many-sorted resolution, *Artif. Intell.* **26** (1985) 217–224.

[38] C. Walther, *A Many-Sorted Calculus Based on Resolution and Paramodulation* (Morgan Kaufmann, Los Altos, CA, 1987).

[39] C. Walther, Many-sorted unification, *J. ACM* **35** (1987) 1–17.

Artificial Intelligence 49 (1991) 199–242
Elsevier

Existence assumptions in knowledge representation

Graeme Hirst

Department of Computer Science, University of Toronto, Toronto, Ontario, Canada M5S 1A4

Received November 1989
Revised November 1990

Abstract

Hirst, G., Existence assumptions in knowledge representation, Artificial Intelligence 49 (1991) 199–242.

If knowledge representation formalisms are to be suitable for semantic interpretation of natural language, they must be more adept with representations of existence and nonexistence than they presently are. Quantifiers must sometimes scope over non-existent entities. I review the philosophical background, including Anselm and Kant, and exhibit some ontological problems that natural language sentences pose for knowledge representation. The paraphrase methods of Russell and Quine are unable to deal with many of the problems. Unfortunately, the shortcomings of the Russell–Quine ontology are reflected in most current knowledge representation formalisms in AI. Several alternatives are considered, including some intensional formalisms and the work of Hobbs, but all have problems. Free logics and possible worlds don't help either. But useful insights are found in the Meinongian theory of Parsons, in which a distinction between *nuclear* and *extranuclear* kinds of predicates is made and used to define a universe over which quantification scopes. If this is combined with a naive ontology, with about eight distinct kinds of existence, a better approach to the representation of nonexistence can be developed within Hobbs' basic formalism.

1. Introduction

Most contemporary logics implicitly or explicitly base the semantics of the quantifiers $\exists$ and $\forall$ on the widely-held ontological assumptions of Russell [66,67] and Quine [56]. A small but growing number of philosophers (e.g., Parsons [50], Routley [65], Lambert [32]) believe that these assumptions are mistaken,[1] and have proposed various alternatives. In this paper, I will

---

[1] Introducing his work, Parsons says of the Russell–Quine position that "clear progress is rare in philosophy, and I was pleased to have [it as] an example to cite. But as I thought about it more, I became increasingly dissatisfied" [50, p. xii].

0004-3702/91/$ 03.50 © 1991—Elsevier Science Publishers B.V.

discuss the consequences of the Russell–Quine assumptions for knowledge
representation formalisms, and show that an adequate treatment requires a
multi-faceted view of existence.

My motivation comes from the knowledge representation needs of natural
language understanding. As I have argued elsewhere [20], a knowledge representation (KR) formalism to be used in a natural language understanding
system for unrestricted text must have (at least) the expressive power of
natural language, for otherwise it could not be a target language for semantic
interpretation. Moreover, natural languages reflect genuine properties of the
real world (with different languages possibly highlighting different properties or viewpoints). Thus, AI research may include exhibiting sentences
of natural language and considering how their meaning, and the world it
reflects, may be adequately represented—where "adequately" means that
the representation permits the same inferences to be drawn as the original
sentence. Here, I am concerned with sentences that speak of existence, of
nonexistence, or of nonexistent objects.

2. Three ontological slogans

2.1. "Existence is not a predicate"

Immanuel Kant, in his *Critique of Pure Reason* [26, B.625ff], argued that
existence is *not* a property that may be predicated of an entity the same
way that properties like color and species can be. Kant was responding to
an argument by St Anselm of Canterbury [1, Section II] that purported to
demonstrate the existence of God *a priori*: his "ontological proof". Anselm's
argument was basically this: What we mean by God is, by definition, that
entity that is right up the top end of the scale in all desirable properties: the
entity that is most wise, most good, and so on. On the scale of existence,
clearly actual or necessary existence is better than mere conceptual or possible existence; therefore existence is a defining property of God; therefore
God exists. [2] Descartes [10, Section V] later took much the same approach:
God has all perfections; existence is a perfection; therefore God exists. [3]

Now, being able to define things into existence like this is metaphysically
disturbing, and doesn't really seem possible. Thus, Hume [25, Section IX]
tried to show that it is not possible that an entity exist of necessity, and
Kant took the position described above, which is often characterized by the

---

[2]Compare Smullyan's proof [72, pp. 205–206] that unicorns (or anything else you like)
exist: To prove that unicorns exist, it suffices to prove the stronger statement that existing
unicorns exist. But for existing unicorns to not exist would be a contradiction; therefore existing
unicorns exist; therefore unicorns exist.

[3]For the history of the argument, and a discussion of some of the ontological issues
mentioned below, see Barnes [2].

slogan "Existence is not a predicate" (cf. Moore [47]). This position is now widely accepted in philosophy [27, p. 160; 52, p. 38]. Nevertheless, while it may have the merit of keeping God off our backs, it does raise difficulties in artificial intelligence.

What I want to show in this paper is that existence *can* be predicated, but (lest God be found to be an emergent property of our knowledge representations; no *deus ex machina* here!) it is neither a single predicate nor a predicate of an ordinary kind.

2.2. *"Everything exists"*

An adequate treatment of existence in KR formalisms is complicated not only by the problem described above, but also by a related set of difficulties that derive from a position often summarized by the slogan "Everything exists" (cf. Quine [56, p. 1]). That is, there is nothing that doesn't exist, for if it doesn't exist it isn't anything, and statements apparently about nonexistents are either incoherent or can be explained away. The development of this approach is due mainly to Russell [66,67] and, later, Quine [56]. The Russell–Quine position has become so firmly entrenched in twentieth-century Anglo-American philosophy that it is usually accepted without question [50, pp. 1–5]. If we take the slogan literally, then even if existence can be predicated of an entity, it is no more than a tautology; no entities don't exist. And to assert nonexistence of something would be self-contradictory [47,69]. As we will see, this position too is problematic for knowledge representation.

To a large degree, the question seems to be nothing more than what the word *exist* does mean or should mean, and what status is to be assigned to "nonexistent objects". Quine grants two kinds of existence: concrete, physical existence in the world (the kind that Margaret Thatcher has), and abstract, nonphysical existence (the kind that the number 27 has). "Idea[s] in men's heads" [56, p. 2] are included in one or the other of these categories, and so too, I assume, are events and actions. Clearly, this is a wider definition of existence than the kind that Anselm and Descartes's wished to attribute to God. Presumably they intended some divine equivalent of physical existence—able to have causal interaction with the physical world—and would be unhappy with the idea that God existed only in the way the number 27 does. Likewise, Hume and Kant were using the narrower definition when they attacked necessary existence, for many mathematical objects obviously do exist of necessity (the number 27; the least prime greater than 27). So perhaps existence in this other sense, nonphysical existence without causal connection to the world, *could* be a predicate.

2.3. "There are things that don't exist"

Quine's sense of the word *exist* may be wider than Anselm's and Descartes's, but it is still much narrower than that of Meinong [45], who described his position in an oxymoron: "There are objects of which it is true that there are no such objects" [45, translation, p. 83]. For Meinong (like Brentano before him), every thought or idea, such as the idea of a gold mountain, must be "directed toward" some object, and so all objects of thought have being in some sense, even if not real-world existence. Meinong therefore wanted to give status to objects such as the gold mountain, which is not real, and the round square, which is not even possible, arguing that the gold mountain is just as good an object as Mount Everest, and the fact that it is unreal makes no difference. Note that the question is not about the *concept* or *idea* of the gold mountain and whether that exists; clearly, it does. But when we say that the gold mountain is 1000 metres tall, we aren't just talking about an idea; it is not the idea that is 1000 metres tall but the alleged thing that the idea is about.

Russell pointed out that Meinong's approach got into trouble with objects like "the gold mountain that exists"—which isn't real even though existence is part of its definition (cf. footnote 2). It also troubled him that there was any sense in which there can be such contradictory objects as round squares, sets that contain all the sets that don't contain themselves (sometimes known as "Russell sets"), or objects that are not identical to themselves.[4]

Thus the question to be considered is what, exactly, do quantifiers like $\exists$ and $\forall$ quantify over? If an expression begins with "$\exists x$" or "$\forall x$", then what values may be used or considered for x? Do they include Margaret Thatcher, the number 23, World War II, my putting the cat out last night, the late Alan Turing, Sherlock Holmes, the possibility of rain tomorrow, suavity, fear, the set of round squares, the concept of round squares? In other words, what is in the universe of quantification? What exists?

3. What exists?

3.1. What doesn't exist?

The burden on the Russell–Quine position is to explain the apparent counterexamples—to account for the fact that in ordinary, everyday language we can *talk about* certain things without believing that they exist. In this subsection, I will list many examples of reference in natural language to

---

[4]Parsons [50, pp. 38–42] has argued that a round square is *not* a contradiction in the same way that a nonsquare square is, and that the former is a good object but not the latter. Such distinctions need not concern us in this paper.

seemingly nonexistent entities. My intent is to show that talking about nonexistent objects—and hence representing them, quantifying over them, and reasoning about them—is quite a normal thing to do in natural language. In Section 3.2, I will show how Russell tries to dissolve the problems.

Things that aren't there

Perhaps the simplest apparent counterexample (one that we will see Russell's answer to shortly) is that we can explicitly speak of nonexistence and nonexistent things:

(1)   There's no one in the bathroom.

(2)   The car I need just doesn't exist [spoken after a long and fruitless search for a suitable car] [76, p. 37].

(3)   The perfect chair just doesn't exist.

(4)   There's no such thing as the bogeyman; he doesn't exist, and neither does Margaret Thatcher.

(5)   Nadia doesn't own a dog.

(6)   Round squares are impossible, gold mountains merely unlikely.

We may also speak of events that don't occur and actions that are not taken:

(7)   There are no trains to Saginaw on Sundays [i.e., the event of a train going to Saginaw on a Sunday never occurs].

(8)   Due to maintenance work on the line, the 6:06 to Saginaw will not run on Sunday.

(9)   Today's lecture is cancelled.

(10)   The committee's failure to agree on a budget has prevented renovation of the rectory [i.e., the event of the committee agreeing did not occur, and this in turn caused the event of the renovation to not occur].

(11)   The workers threatened to hold a strike if their pay claims were not met. The company acceded to the demands, and the strike was averted.

(12)   The purpose of the steam-release valve is to prevent an explosion. [5]

---

[5] In qualitative models of systems (such as boilers) for diagnosis and reasoning, there may be entities such as a steam-release valve whose purpose is "to prevent an explosion". The model does not include or predict any explosion, but the purpose of the valve still has to be somehow accounted for. (I am grateful to Ben Kuipers for this example.)

(13)   Nadia refrained from commenting on Ross's new hairstyle.

(14)   Ross failed to notice that Nadia had failed to feed the newt.

We can speak of holes, voids, and vacuums; that is, entities that are seemingly constituted by the absence of anything can be spoken of as if they were material objects:

(15)   There are too many holes in this cheese [cf. [38]].

(16)   Keep your eye on the doughnut, not on the hole.

(17)   The pump serves to create a vacuum in the flask.

(18)   A complete lack of money led to the downfall of the company.

Existence itself as an object
We can seemingly speak of existence as an object, one that need not exist:

(19)   The existence of Pluto was predicted by mathematics and confirmed by observation.

(20)   The existence of Vulcan was predicted by mathematics but disproved by observation.

(21)   It's a good thing that carnivorous cows don't exist [i.e., the nonexistence of carnivorous cows is a good thing].

(22)   A complete lack of money has prevented renovation of the rectory [i.e., the nonexistence of available funds has caused the nonexistence of the renovation].

Claims of reality
We can even (untruly, but not incoherently) assert that unreal objects exist:

(23)   I saw a gold mountain near the freeway this morning.

(24)   Round squares make me seasick—especially the green ones.

(25)   Unreal objects exist.

We can also report such beliefs of others without committing ourselves.

(26)   Nadia believes that a unicorn named Old Ironsides has been intercepting her mail and stealing the fashion magazines.

Claims of possibility

We can speak of possible objects and events without committing ourselves either to their reality or unreality, and of objects and events whose existence is merely contingent upon other things.

(27)   There may be someone in room 23 who can help you.

(28)   If you assemble the parts correctly, you will have created a handsome two-metre model of the CN Tower.

(29)   If Ross's mother had accepted that offer of a job in New York and settled down there and married some nice young businessman, she would probably have had a child that would have turned out just like Nadia.

(30)   It might rain tomorrow.

Existence at other times

We can refer to things that don't now exist, but did or will. We can speak of things now gone:

(31)   Alan Turing was a brilliant mathematician.

(32)   Last night's dinner was disastrous.

Sometimes, we may or even *must* use the present tense for things of the past, suggesting that they have some kind of continuing existence:

(33)   (a) Alan Turing is a celebrated mathematician [after Barnes [2, p. 48]].
       (b) *Alan Turing was a celebrated mathematician[6] [in the sense that he continues to be celebrated].

(34)   (a) Alan Turing is dead.
       (b) *Alan Turing was dead.

And we can talk of things to come:

(35)   Tomorrow's dinner is going to be delicious.

(36)   The baby that Diane is planning to have will surely interfere with her violin lessons.

---

[6] I use the star in the usual way to indicate linguistic ill-formedness.

Fictional and imaginary objects
   We can speak of fictional entities and classes as if they really existed.

   (37)   Dragons don't have fur [52, p. 40].

   (38)   Sherlock Holmes was the protagonist of many stories by Conan
           Doyle.

   (39)   Sherlock Holmes lived in London with his friend, Dr Watson.

And possibly even:

   (40)   Sherlock Holmes is no longer alive.

Indeed, a large part of the study of literature consists of deriving "facts"
about fictional characters that are only implicit in the text:

   (41)   Holmes regards Dr Watson as a mother figure for whom he
           has considerable oedipal attraction.

And we can relate fictional objects to objects that do exist:

   (42)   Nadia models herself upon Sherlock Holmes.

3.2. The Russell–Quine ontology

3.2.1. Paraphrases and the theory of descriptions

   Russell's approach, his *theory of descriptions* [48,66,67], was to regard
apparent assertions of existence and nonexistence as merely paraphrases—in
logic or a literal English rendering thereof—of other forms in which the
assertion is not actually made. Instead, the offending bits are expressed as
variables and quantifiers, and the resulting expression is something that can
legitimately be true or false. Thus, *Dragons exist* is a paraphrase of *There is
at least one thing that is a dragon*:

   (43) $\exists x (dragon(x))$.

Since no such x exists, the sentence is false. Likewise, *Dragons don't exist*
is a paraphrase of the negation of (43):

   (44) $\forall x (\neg dragon(x))$

           "For any x, it is not the case that x is a dragon."

   Attempts to assert properties of nonexistent objects may be handled in a
similar manner:

   (45)   Dragons like baklava.

           $\forall x (dragon(x) \rightarrow likes\text{-}baklava(x))$.

This is vacuously true if there are no dragons [67, p. 229]; but statements about particular dragons would be false:

(46)   My dragon likes baklava.

$\exists x\,(my\text{-}dragon(x) \wedge likes\text{-}baklava(x))$.

This is false because there is no x for which the left-hand side of the conjunction is true. One might instead have used a vacuously true form like that of (45), but the form of (46) reflects Russell's belief that such sentences were false, and also his concerns with definite descriptions (see below).

In the natural language versions of these statements, we have the apparent problem that to even mention dragons seems to give them some sort of existence; to say that *Dragons like baklava* seems to presuppose the existence of the class of dragons. Russell's claim was that on the "correct" reading—the representations above, or literal English glosses of them—the problem dissolves. The logical forms contain no assertion of the existence of a nonempty class of dragons. Moreover, the predicate *dragon* is itself a complex term, and may be regarded as simply an abbreviation for a description such as

(47) $fire\text{-}breathing(x) \wedge leather\text{-}winged(x) \wedge \cdots$.

Definite references may also be paraphrased. Thus:

(48)   The builder of Waverley station was a Scot.

$\exists x\,(built(Waverley, x) \wedge$
$\qquad\qquad \forall y\,(built(Waverley, y) \rightarrow y = x) \wedge Scot(x))$.

"One and only one entity built Waverley station, and that one was a Scot." [66, pp. 113–114]

(If the noun phrase being interpreted does not contain sufficient information to uniquely identify the individual, information from context may be added. Thus (48) could also be the representation of the sentence *The builder is a Scot* if the context made it clear that the builder in question was that of Waverley station.) A similar treatment upon *The present king of France is bald* shows the sentence to be false, like (46), because there is no entity denoted by *the present king of France*.[7]   Quine [56, p. 7] showed

---

[7]The problem here is, of course, presupposition failure—the sentence tries to talk about something that doesn't exist, and does so without any of the "redeeming" characteristics of the sentences about nonexistents that were exhibited in Section 3.1. Russell's position on presupposition was famously disputed by Strawson [75], and is no longer generally accepted. Strawson's position was that the presuppositions of a sentence (or, more precisely, of a particular utterance of a sentence) are distinct from its main assertion, and, unlike the main assertion, are unchanged by sentence negation. If a presupposition is false, then the main

how the method can be extended to include proper names, so that sentences about named fictional entities might be paraphrased:

(49)   Sherlock Holmes is smart.

$\exists x (isHolmes(x) \land smart(x)).$

"There is an x that has the property of being Sherlock Holmes, and x has the further property of being smart."

Again, the result is a sentence that is false, for there is no x in the real world that has the property of being Sherlock Holmes.

3.2.2. Problems with the theory

Paraphrasing in this manner immediately disposes of some of the problems mentioned in Section 3.1, but it does so at some cost.

First, all sentences that assert properties of nonexistents are false if specific and true if generic, and negating such sentences doesn't change their truth value! For example, the negation of (46) is:

(50)   My dragon doesn't like baklava.

$\exists x (my\text{-}dragon(x) \land \neg likes\text{-}baklava(x)).$

This is false for the same reason that (46) is. Likewise, the negation of (45), *Dragons don't like baklava*, is true. The underlying problem here, of course, is that English negation and logical negation aren't the same. If we put a "$\neg$" in front of the logical form of (46), we do change its truth value, but that's not what the English word *not* does. In particular, negation in English (and probably in all natural languages) preserves the presuppositions of the original sentence. In the case of (50), alas, it also preserves Russell's erroneous approach to presuppositions (see footnote 7).

A second problem is a technical one in the nature of the paraphrasing task itself: it destroys, quite deliberately, the similarity between the surface form of the sentence and the representation of its meaning. Ryle [69], for instance, regards "quasi-ontological statements" as "systematically misleading expressions"—expressions whose semantic representations, if they have any at all, are quite unlike those suggested by their surface forms. But, as I have argued elsewhere [18,19], there are many virtues in compositional semantic representations in which each element is a direct reflection of a surface constituent of the sentence. While it may not always be possible to

---

assertion, or the sentence itself, can be neither true nor false; rather, it has no truth value at all. For a review of current approaches to presupposition, see Levinson [34] or Horton [22]. A treatment of presupposition *per se* is beyond the scope of the present paper; for that, see [22,23]. I am concerned here rather with the treatment of the entities that may be felicitously presupposed.

maintain this, the advantages to be gained from it are such that it is not to be given up lightly.

Third, and most seriously, there are, as we saw earlier, sentences about nonexistents for which one's intuition strongly contradicts Russell's theory of descriptions. These include sentences about the defining properties of nonexistents and sentences in which nonexistents seem to have some actual interaction with the real world.

In the first of these classes, we have sentences such as this:

(51) Dragons are small, radish-eating rodents, found mostly in the high Arctic.

$$\forall x (dragon(x) \rightarrow (rodent(x) \land eats\text{-}radishes(x) \land \cdots)).$$

For Russell, this is true, though in any ordinary conversation it would be thought of as false. Likewise, we all agree with Russell and Quine about the falsity of (52):

(52) Sherlock Holmes was stupid.

but we disagree about the reason: in ordinary conversation this sentence is taken as false exactly because its converse is taken as true (cf. Parsons [50, p. 37]).

In the second class are sentences asserting the nonexistence of something. While we might accept representations like (44) for the denial of classes, the denial of the existence of specific entities is trickier. Consider again:

(53) Ross cancelled the lecture.

(54) The (threatened) strike was averted by last-minute negotiations.

On Russell's theory, sentences like these must invariably be false, which is clearly wrong. Notice that paraphrase, in the style of sentence (44), doesn't help here, because these sentences are asserting more than just nonexistence; they are asserting a causal relationship. The expression *The strike was averted* means that the strike never occurred—it did not exist—and that some specific action by someone prevented its occurrence. And which strike was averted? The particular strike that the workers threatened to hold, which has specific properties of time, cause, participants, and so on, that differentiate it from all other real or potential strikes, all properties that could be used when constructing the description in a Russellian paraphrase. But under Russell's view, we cannot truthfully talk about this strike at all, for it does not exist; any sentence that attempts to refer to it will be false. (Note, as before, that we can't get out of this by saying that the reference is to the idea of the strike; it is not the idea that is averted.)

It might be objected that to say *The strike was averted* is a looseness of the English language. One can also use an indefinite reference, and perhaps this is the basic form that should be interpreted:[8]

(55)   (When management capitulated,) a strike was averted.

This would yield a representation such as this:

(56) $\exists y (cause(y, \neg \exists x (strike(x))))$.

         Someone caused that there be no strike.

(We shall blithely allow *cause* as a predicate that takes a proposition in its second argument and asserts that the entity in the first argument caused the second argument to be true.) The problem with this tack is the need to say exactly what didn't happen. After all, there have been a lot of strikes that weren't averted; but (56) says there were no strikes at all. Clearly, some identification from the context is necessary: what was averted was a strike by some particular set of workers at some particular time over some particular claim—so we must identify *the* strike in context, and we're back to where we started.

Another objection might be that the proper paraphrase is *The strike that was planned was averted*, the claim being that the strike does exist, non-physically, like mathematical objects, by virtue of its having been planned. (This would explain why it sounds a bit funny to say *The accident was averted* instead of *An accident was averted* (cf. above), as accidents aren't planned.) The problem with this is that we then have to explain what it would mean to avert an abstract object. Perhaps it means averting the physical realization of this nonphysical object—in effect, the instantiation of a concept. This view follows the lines of Frege's argument that existence *is* a predicatable property, but is a property of concepts, not individuals [13, Section 53, p. 65; 15, pp. 18–19,32,76–66]. To say that something exists is to say of a concept that it has an extension. So, for Frege, the error in Anselm's argument was applying the predicate wrongly—applying it to an extension, God, rather than a concept, the concept of God. On this view, the sentence *Dragons exist* would mean that the set of extensions of the concept of dragons is not empty. And to say that the strike was averted would be to say that there was caused to be no extension that corresponds to the concept of the particular strike in question (specified, in the manner of Russellian paraphrase, in sufficient detail to be unique).

This approach has generally been regarded as philosophically unsatisfactory [73, p. 90].[9] It seems to just sidestep the problem terminologically,

---

[8] Barry Richards, personal communication.

[9] It is simply ignored, for example, by Moore [47] and Prior [54] in their reviews of the problem, and is peremptorily dismissed by Parsons [50, p. 216].

leaving us no wiser as to the nature of the first-order property that all extensions allegedly have—Frege called it "actuality" (*Wirklichkeit*) [13, Section 26, p. 35] (see also [8, p. 194, n. 7])—which, by any name, is the property that we are interested in here. So the problem can't be reduced to one of concepts.

But perhaps we could say that if the strike was planned, it exists as a "future object". To examine this, we must consider the role of time. Russell provides no treatment of existence at times other than the present, but we can speculate on how he would extend his theory to do so.

Let's consider the simpler case first: the past. It is unclear from Russell's account how he would paraphrase, say, *Alan Turing was smart* and *Alan Turing is dead*. That is, would he allow the scope of quantification to include past entities? Doing so would let the first of these sentences be paraphrased like any other, and the past-tense verb would just be an artifact of the pastness of Alan Turing himself, not included in the paraphrase:

(57)   Alan Turing was smart.

$\exists x\,(isTuring(x) \wedge smart(x))$.

This would then be a true sentence, unlike *Sherlock Holmes was smart*. But this doesn't work for the second sentence:

(58)   Alan Turing is dead.

$\exists x\,(isTuring(x) \wedge dead(x))$.

It doesn't work because Turing wasn't dead when he existed, and the verb tense hasn't behaved as in (57). At a minimum, we need to add some notion of time points or intervals such that propositions can be true at some times and not others; thus, (58) would be true today, but false in 1945 and 1862—false in 1945 because Turing was still alive, and false in 1862 because he hadn't then come within the scope of the existential quantifier.

Thus the universe would be seen as travelling through time, collecting up entities into its ontology as it proceeds. Once a thing has started to exist, it never stops. This helps represent sentences (57) and (58), but I don't think this view can be pleasing for the everything-exists gang, for the fact remains that Alan Turing does not now exist in the world any more than the gold mountain does, nor does he seem to exist as a mathematical object. (The idea of Turing continues to exist, but it's not that that's dead.) There doesn't seem to be any good reason why his brief time on earth should give Turing any subsequent ontological advantage over the gold mountain. [10]

[10] A rejoinder that I shall not take very seriously: Alan Turing does in fact still exist, or at least his soul does, in Heaven or Hell or somewhere like that. On this view, one might say that the best paraphrase for *Alan Turing is dead* is one of these:

These problems may be seen even more clearly if we now consider future entities, such as the strike that the faculty are threatening to hold. We can talk about this just as easily as we can about Alan Turing (albeit with less certainty)—it will be long and nasty, it will cause the university president to resign, it may never happen (!). For Quine, certainly (and presumably for Russell—guilt by association), the strike is merely a "possible object", to be kept out of one's ontology at all costs (cf. his arguments against the existence of the "possible man in the doorway" [56]). So now the averted strike is out on two separate counts, each fatal on its own. When it was still a planned strike, it was merely a possible object; after it was averted, it became a past object as well.

But for knowledge representation and natural language understanding, this is simply not acceptable. I have shown above that objects like Alan Turing and the averted strike must be able to be represented, quantified over, and reasoned about just as much as Margaret Thatcher. So the Russell–Quine

(i) Alan Turing's body doesn't exist (or no longer exists).

$\neg \exists x (bodyOfTuring(x))$

(ii) Alan Turing is in the afterlife.

$\exists x \exists y (isTuring(x) \wedge afterlife(y) \wedge in(x,y))$

Form (i) is undoubtedly true, and the truth of form (ii) depends on whether there is an afterlife and if so who's there, issues that I will not solve in this paper.

The value of this particular rejoinder is to draw attention to the cultural bias in the expression of the problem; perhaps we say that Alan Turing *is* dead just because English reflects our long cultural history of belief in a soul and an afterlife. If we are careful to avoid such bias in our language, we will be able to analyze the problem correctly (or so said a large twentieth-century school of philosophy). Notice, for example, that English offers no analogous expressions for the past existence of objects to which we do not (culturally) attribute an afterlife; if my wristwatch has ceased to be, I can say *My wristwatch was destroyed* but not *My wristwatch is destroyed* (and only as a joke or metaphor, *My wristwatch is dead*). Thus when we say that Turing is dead, our paraphrase should be no more than that there is no x such that $isTuring(x)$; and that this statement was false at an earlier time is an implicature of the word *dead*.

I don't think that this argument goes through. There are too many other things we can say about entities of the past that seem to presume their continued existence:

(iii) Alan Turing {is | *was} a celebrated mathematician.

(iv) Nadia models herself upon Alan Turing.

(v) Nadia knows more about NP-completeness than Alan Turing ever did. [Although Turing is referred to in the past tense, the entity *Alan Turing's knowledge of NP-completeness* is available for comparison with an entity, Nadia's knowledge, that exists in the present and did not exist at the time of Turing.]

(vi) Nadia modelled her new sculpture upon my old wristwatch (which was destroyed last year).

(vii) The Flat Earth Society is now disbanded.

position is inadequate. Unfortunately, as I will show next, most knowledge representation formalisms share the Russell–Quine deficiencies.

4. Existence assumptions in KR formalisms

To what extent are knowledge representation formalisms able to deal adequately with existence and nonexistence? The universe of discourse of a system is, of course, circumscribed by what's in its knowledge base; but given that nonexistent entities may have to be included (and, in a full NLU system, *must* be included), how does the average formalism behave?

For the most part, KR formalisms are Russellian in their approach to ontology. To use a term is to assert that it denotes, and, in particular, that it denotes an extant entity [79]. To assert, for example,

   (59)   Ross cancelled the lecture.

        cancelled(Ross, lecture23).

implies for most systems (e.g., KRYPTON [3] and Sowa's conceptual graphs [74]) that *lecture23* exists just as much as *Ross* does, even if the expression says that it doesn't.

4.1. Platonic-universe approaches

Not all KR formalisms impute existence to denotations of their terms. A simple first-order system in which (ignoring all the philosophical wisdom discussed above) existence is a predicate like any other has been proposed by Hobbs [21] in his paper entitled "Ontological promiscuity". The "promiscuity" of the title refers to the Meinong-like inclusion of nonexistent objects, including the reification of events and properties as objects;[11] Hobbs' set of objects is a Platonic universe, "highly constrained by the way the ... material world is" (p. 63). The quantifiers ∃ and ∀ range over this universe, and all variables are assumed to denote some entity in it. In general, the formalism is deliberately simple and "flat", without modals, intensions, or even negation. (Hobbs' aim in the paper is to show that predicates in his system suffice instead.)

In this approach, no object mentioned in a representation is assumed to exist in the real world unless such existence is either explicitly stated

---

[11] Treating events as objects, in the style of Davidson [9], is a position that I have adopted in this paper and assumed to be relatively uncontroversial even for supporters of the Quine–Russell position. Treating properties as objects is a separate question somewhat orthogonal to the concerns of the present paper; suffice it to say here that Quine and Russell would not, I think, approve.

or axiomatically derivable. For example, *Ross worships Zeus* is represented as:

(60) $worship'(E, Ross, Zeus) \wedge Exist(E)$.

The first conjunct says that E is a worshipping by Ross of Zeus, and the second says that E exists in the real world. (Do not confuse the predicate *Exist*, which denotes real-world existence, with the quantifier $\exists$, which ranges over the entire Platonic universe.) The predicate *worship'* is existentially transparent in its second argument but not its third. This means that the real-world existence of E implies the existence of Ross but not that of Zeus. That is, it is an axiom of the system that:

(61) $\forall E \forall x \forall y ((worship'(E, x, y) \wedge Exist(E)) \rightarrow Exist(x))$

Hobbs shows that with an adaptation of Zalta's system of abstract objects [80], this approach is able to deal with several problems of opaque contexts that are usually thought to require higher-order representations, while at the same time remaining (moderately) faithful to the surface form of the English sentence.

Although Hobbs mentions nonexistence only briefly, it is clear that by extending his approach we can account for some of the problems mentioned above. Just as transparent argument positions entail existence, we will allow an argument position to be *anti-transparent*, entailing that the object in that position does *not* exist. (Anti-transparent positions are not to be confused with Hobbs' opaque positions, which entail nothing.) We can then represent the prevention of the occurrence of the strike:

(62)   The strike was averted.

        $strike(s) \wedge \exists x (Exist(E) \wedge avert'(E, x, s))$.

        "s is the strike (identified from context), and in the Platonic universe there is an x such that x averted s, and the averting E really exists."

It would be stipulated that *avert'* is transparent in its second argument and anti-transparent in its third—that is, in (62), the existence of the averting, E, would imply the existence of the averter but the nonexistence of the strike:

(63) $\forall E \forall x \forall y ((avert'(E, x, y) \wedge Exist(E)) \rightarrow$
$$(Exist(x) \wedge not(Exist(y))))).$$

The existence of existence also seems representable. Hobbs has a "nominalization operator", $'$, which turns an n-ary predicate into an $(n + 1)$-ary predicate whose first argument is the condition that holds when the base predicate is true of the other arguments. We saw this above with ternary predicates such as *worship'* (*E, Ross, Zeus*), derived from the binary predicate *worship*(*Ross, Zeus*). Since *Exist* is just another predicate, there is nothing to stop us nominalizing it:

(64)　The existence of carnivorous cows is predicted by GB theory.

$$Exist'\,(E_1, carnivorous\text{-}cows)\,\wedge$$
$$predict'\,(E_2, GB\text{-}theory, E_1)\,\wedge\,Exist(E_2).$$

"E_1 is the existence of carnivorous cows, E_2 is the prediction of E_1 by GB theory, and E_2 exists (though E_1 might not)."

On the other hand, there is no treatment of fictional objects. Nonexistent objects can be mentioned, as we saw in the assertion of *Ross worships Zeus*, but there is nothing that lets us say that Zeus exists in fiction whereas the Giant Cosmic Groundhog (which I just made up) and the averted strike do not. An obvious move is simply to add a predicate *Fictional* to the formalism. Then *worship'* would have the property that its third argument must exist either in the real world (like Nadia, whom Ross also worships) or in fiction (even if only a small fiction in Ross's mind). Hobbs' Platonic universe would now have a tripartite division into the existent, the fictional, and all the rest. [12]

But there is no reason to stop at a tripartite division. Following Fauconnier [11], we can divide the Platonic universe into many different, overlapping ontological spaces, one for each different work of fiction, each theory or hypothesis, each different perception of the world. In Fauconnier's theory, the "reality" [11, p. 17] of some agent is the top-level universe, and each division, or *mental space*, is a subset of the entities in that reality and the relationships in which they participate. A mental space may include any existent or nonexistent entity that the agent thinks about. Fauconnier shows how mental spaces can serve in a semantic theory for natural language, accounting for such phenomena as embedded belief contexts, presuppositions, and counterfactuals. This is compatible, I think, with Hobbs' approach, and indeed is implicit in the approach that I develop in Section 7.1 below.

But so far, this approach doesn't give an adequate treatment of objects like Alan Turing—we can't talk about Turing's different and divergent statuses at different times. Hobbs' notion of time is based on English verb tenses. An assertion can be said to be true in the past or future. So one could say that Alan Turing's existence is true in the past—but it has to be *all* the past. A better approach is developed in the TELOS system of Koubarakis et al. [28,29], in which the truth of an assertion may be limited to any

---

[12]I will resist the temptation to be side-tracked onto the question of characterizing more precisely what it means to be fictional rather than just nonexistent; see [78] for discussion.

time interval, and one can quite literally have objects like *Alan Turing 1912–1954.*[13]

In addition, it seems that Anselm's fallacy is valid in the system. Although Hobbs gives no examples of definitions, it seems that *Exist* can be used directly or indirectly as a defining characteristic, since it's just another predicate. Its direct use in a definition could be prohibited by stipulation; but preventing its indirect use is not possible, as it is a deliberate feature of the system that existence can be axiomatically derived from various assertions—one has to be allowed to define predicates with transparent arguments. Thus, following Descartes's version of the fallacy,[14] one could define the predicate *perfect* to be transparent in its (sole) argument, and then assert that God is, by definition, *perfect*:[15]

---

[13]Hobbs has pointed out (personal communication) that a similar effect could be developed in his system by treating times as entities, and asserting that each particular existence occurs at a particular time.

[14]Anselm's original version, as I glossed it in Section 2.1 above, is second-order and so would not be expressible in Hobbs' system as it presently stands (but see Lewis's first-order possible-world formalization of a slightly different reading of Anselm's argument [36]). Assuming the addition of second-order quantifiers to Hobbs' formalism, we could express Anselm's argument as follows:

(i) $\forall S \forall P (scale(S) \wedge maximum(S,P) \rightarrow P(God))$.

"For any scale S such that P is the property of being at the maximum point on that scale, God has property P; i.e., God is up the top end of the scale in all (desirable) characteristics."

scale(Wisdom),
scale(Lovingness),
scale(Existence).

"Scales include wisdom, lovingness, and existence."

maximum(Wisdom, Omniscience),
maximum(Lovingness, AllLoving),
maximum(Existence, Exist).

"The top end of the wisdom scale is omniscience, of the lovingness scale is being all-loving, of the existence scale is real-world existence." (*Necessary* real-world existence would be an even stronger condition (cf. Section 2.1 above), but Hobbs' standard predicate *Exist* suffices to make the point.)

[15]It might be argued that this is a *virtue* of the system. The system is supposed to represent natural language; we can express Anselm's fallacy in natural language; so the system should be able to represent Anselm's fallacy. This is true; but it doesn't follow that the fallacy should be *valid* in the system; after all, it isn't valid in natural language (but cf. [36]). Just as a formalism should be able to represent entities regardless of their existence, it should be able to represent arguments regardless of their validity—but that goes beyond the scope of this paper.

It might also be suggested that the validity of Anselm's fallacy in the system is nothing more than an example of "garbage in, garbage out". Write some silly axioms and you get a silly answer. One can perform analogous abuses in *any* formalism, such as just directly stating the existence of God (or anything else) as an axiom:

(i) *Exist(God)*,
     Exist(Giant-Cosmic-Groundhog).

(65) $\forall x\,(perfect(x) \rightarrow Omniscient(x))$,
       $\forall x\,(perfect(x) \rightarrow AllLoving(x))$,
       $\forall x\,(perfect(x) \rightarrow Exist(x))$.

"To be perfect is to be omniscient, all-loving, and existent."

perfect(*God*).

"God is perfect."

The same logical cornucopia will produce the perfect armchair, the perfect automobile, and the perfect lover at little extra expense.

4.2. *Intensional approaches*

Although it was important for Meinong that thoughts and ideas could be directed to nonexistent objects, I have said little up to now, except in passing, about ideas, intensions, and concepts. Indeed, both Russell and Hobbs were at pains to avoid the standard Fregean distinction [14] between intension and extension (*Sinn* and *Bedeutung*). But even Quine grants ideas a place in his universe (see Section 2.2 above); so we now turn to this topic. I will use the terms *concept*, *idea*, and *intension* interchangeably below; the technical differences between them will be unimportant. Likewise, I will conflate *extension* with the *denotation*, *realization*, or *instance* of an idea.

An adequate treatment of concepts as "first-class objects" has often eluded knowledge representation systems. By a first-class object, I mean here an object that can be referred to as an individual in its own right, be used in inference, be a component of other objects, and so on. This would be necessary if we were to act on the suggestion (Section 3.2.2 above) that the sentence *The strike was averted* be represented as the prevention of the realization of an instance of the concept of strikes. Now, because concepts are used to define other objects, many systems accord them a special status that precludes their simultaneously acting as ordinary objects or individuals. A typical example is Charniak's FRAIL [6], a language in which concepts are *generic frames*, but inference can be carried out only on *instances* of those frames; it is not possible for a frame to be simultaneously generic and an instance. In KRYPTON [3], which makes a careful separation of

Only a clumsy stipulation could prevent such deliberate abuse of a formalism, and there seems little reason to bother doing so in any practical use of the system.

The point that this objection misses is that Hobbs' system *encourages* the use of transparency axioms such as (61), and a practical system would have many hundreds of them. Situations like that summarized in (65) might arise from an unexpected interaction of scattered axioms and definitions in the system, each of them individually acceptable and intended to do nothing more than to define various concepts and terms. In this connection, it's also worth noting that one of Frege's motivations in [13] was to prevent spurious mathematical objects being "defined into existence" by ill-formed definitions.

"terminological" knowledge (which goes in its "T-box") and assertions about the world (in its "A-box"), it is possible to reason with the terminological knowledge, which can be thought of as statements about concepts, but concepts *per se* can still not be reified as first-class individuals.

Languages in which concepts *are* first-class objects include McCarthy's first-order language [43,44], Shapiro and colleagues' SNePS [40,71], and Sowa's conceptual graphs [74]. Such languages must provide a mechanism to relate objects to the concepts of which they are instances. For example, Sowa's conceptual graphs tie concepts and their extensions together by notational means. Thus [CAT:*] represents the concept of cats, and [CAT:#234] represents some particular cat (namely, cat number 234). The notation [CAT:*x] represents the individual concept of a cat: a single cat, but not any particular known one; the x may be thought of as a variable, so that all occurrences of [CAT:*x] must refer to the same (unknown) cat, but [CAT:*y] might be a different one. These different types may be used interchangeably (with different meaning, of course) in the graph representations that can be built. However, all graphs are implicitly existentially quantified; that is, the ontology is implicitly Russellian.

The SNePS network formalism is of special interest, as Rapaport [63] has suggested that Parsons' theory (Section 6 below) could give it a formal semantics. In SNePS, *all* entities are intensions, and extensions *per se* are not used. This is because SNePS takes representations to be those of the knowledge of an agent rather than representations of the world directly. The intensions are connected to reality only through the agent's perception. Thus SNePS is free of extensions only for an external observer of the system. The SNePS objects used by a computational agent that employs the formalism (such as Rapaport's CASSIE [71]) are the concepts in that agent's "mind", so to the observer they are intensions. To the agent itself, however, they are subjective extensions, identified with its perceptions of reality. Shapiro and colleagues show only individual concepts, such as the node *John* representing the idea of John;[16] I assume that if the agent is to think about the idea of John, it will need a node that represents the idea of the idea.

McCarthy's first-order language adapts the approach taken by Frege (Section 3.2.2 above). McCarthy includes both concepts and extensions as entities in his language, though, unlike Frege, he does not formally distinguish them from one another.[17] A function called *denot* maps concepts to the entities, if any, that they denote. (Thus individual concepts such as *John* are mapped to an individual, and generic concepts like *Dog*, not explicitly mentioned by McCarthy, would presumably be mapped to an appropriate

---

[16]For simplicity, I am ignoring Shapiro's careful distinction between nodes and their names.

[17]The typographical distinctions in McCarthy's formulas are for the reader's convenience, and are not part of the theory.

set of individuals.) Following Frege, the predicate *Exists* is true of those concepts for which there is a denotation.[18] Predicates for concepts may be defined "parallel" to those for denotations. For example, if *ishorse* is a predicate true of horses, then *Ishorse* can be defined as a predicate true both (i) of concepts for which *ishorse* is true of their denotations, and (ii) perhaps also of some concepts that don't have denotations, such as *Pegasus*.

Philosophically, this suffers from the same problems as the Fregean approach upon which it is based. As a representation formalism for AI, it has the advantage of simplicity in being first-order, but also the consequent disadvantage that intensions cannot have any special status. Indeed, generally speaking, knowledge representation formalisms that treat concepts as first-class objects do not formally distinguish them from individuals. (Those that don't, do; they have to, in order to discriminate against them.) I don't know of any principled reason for this. Such systems are *weakly intensional* systems, countenancing intensions but not making anything special of them. In contrast, *strongly intensional* systems take intensions to be not just first-class objects but objects of a distinct kind.[19] Montague semantics [46] is a good (noncomputational) example of a strongly intensional system. A strongly intensional system will be surely necessary for an ontologically adequate treatment of intensions. McCarthy could use his *denot* function to map intensions to their extensions, but going in the opposite direction requires an operator, as in Montague semantics. The examples of Section 3.1 show such operations to be frequently necessary, and the modes of existence to be discussed in Section 7.1 below suggest that a diverse set of operators may be required.

The story so far. We want to represent natural language sentences about existence and nonexistence. Philosophers tell us (with some justification) that we'll get into trouble if we construe existence as a predicate. But following this advice leaves us with a KR formalism too weak to do the job. And so far, even formalisms that ignore the advice are inadequate or troubled.

Next. Some suggested solutions.

[18]So McCarthy's predicate is not to be confused with Hobbs' (Section 4.1 above). McCarthy's *Exists* is a predicate true of concepts that have real-world denotations; Hobbs' *Exist* is true of the real-world objects themselves.

[19]This distinction is due to Graeme Ritchie (personal communication).

5. Free logics and possible-world formalisms

5.1. Free logics

Another way that has been suggested around the Russell–Quine problems is the use of *free logics*. A free logic is a logic that makes no assumptions about existence—specifically, a logic that tolerates terms that have no denotation in its universe, never quantifying over them.[20] For example, Woodruff's system **UE** [77] is a free logic with truth-value gaps (i.e., with the truth values **t**, **f**, and **u**) and a distinction between assertions of truth and assertions of nonfalsity. Nondenoting terms have no interpretation at all, and a predicate need only have truth value **t** or **f** if all its arguments denote. Thus the system is explicitly Strawsonian. In contrast, Schock's free logic [70] has only two truth values, and (in the style of Frege) uses the empty set as the "denotation" of nondenoting terms. Both systems have an "existence" predicate, which is true just of those terms that denote. (See [42] for a survey of free logics and their properties.)

At first sight, free logics seem to be an attractive solution in KR to the problems of Russellianism. Free logics are a conceptually easy extension of classical systems; deduction systems already exist for them; and truth-value gaps are already a focus of research in the field (e.g., Patel-Schneider's four-valued logic [51]). From a natural language perspective, free logics help avoid Russellian paraphrases, thereby leading to a more compositional semantics—we can use any object "as is". So if we want to say that Alan Turing was smart, we can say (66) directly, with no need for an existential quantifier:

(66)   *smart(AlanTuring)*.

But alas, free logics turn out to have most of the same problems for natural language understanding as Russell's standard logic. We are allowed to use the term *AlanTuring*, but Alan Turing himself is still not in the universe for quantification. Sentences like (66) need not be false (at least in Woodruff's logic), but (except in a trivial, unhelpful way) they still can't be true.

5.2. Possible worlds and their populations

Clearly, then, the problem is to somehow bring Alan Turing, the averted strike, Sherlock Holmes, and our other nonexistent entities within the set of entities of which true predications may be made, while not allowing them to be considered existent. One suggestion for this is the use of the concept of

---

[20]Hobbs' system (Section 4.1 above) is not a free logic. While it makes no assumptions about real-world existence, it does assume that all terms denote something in the Platonic universe, and it quantifies over them.

a *possible world*. Then we could say that such entities are members of other possible worlds—including worlds of fiction and worlds of other times—but not members of the actual world. (Notice that possible worlds are themselves nonexistent objects that we can talk about in the real world.)

There are many different versions of the notion of possible worlds, and a complete survey would be beyond the scope of this paper.[21] Generally, however, a world is construed as a maximal, consistent state of affairs. That is, a world is complete, in the sense that nothing is unspecified, and the specifications are not contradictory (e.g., [31, p. 18; 53, p. 44; 78, pp. 103–104]). A world W' is *possible relative to another world* W (or, equivalently, is *accessible from* W) if, intuitively, the state of affairs of W' might possibly have obtained instead of W, where "possibly" may be construed as broadly or narrowly as one likes. For example, one could take it as logical possibility, and so permit, in worlds possible relative to our own, pigs that fly by means of anti-gravity grunting; or one could take it as physical possibility and so require the flying pigs to employ wings; or one might require the worlds to be very similar, and so exclude flying pigs altogether.

Given the notion of possible worlds, the question then arises as to what the individuals that populate the worlds are. On the one hand, we intuitively want to say that, by and large, the same individuals turn up in more than one world, even if they have different properties. So the Margaret Thatcher who won a certain election in the real world is the same individual who lost that same election in a different possible world. Of course, some worlds will have individuals that our world doesn't, such as the baby that Laura had in the world in which the condom broke; and some worlds will lack individuals that ours has, such as Margaret Thatcher in the world in which her parents never met one another. On the other hand, some philosophers, from Leibniz on [53, p. 88], have held that, since individuals in different worlds have different properties (even if only the property of being in some particular world), they must be distinct individuals. David Lewis [35] has proposed that although individuals can be in at most one world, they can have *counterparts* in other worlds—possibly several of them in a single world. The counterparts of an individual are those things, if any, in other worlds that are most similar to that individual. The counterpart relationship is not transitive or symmetric, and can be one-to-many and many-to-one.[22] Taking

[21]Indeed the very notion of a possible world is controversial, as are the quantified modal logics associated with them (see below). The bad guy, once more, is Quine. His objections are given in [57], which is reprinted, with replies from the other side, in [39]. A summary is given by Plantinga in [53].

[22]If we limited counterparts to at most one per world, and made the relationship symmetric and transitive, then we could identify equivalence classes of counterparts with individuals, and the approach would become effectively the same as its competitor; but such limitations are explicitly not Lewis's intent [35, p. 28].

the middle ground between these positions, Chisholm [7] and Purtill [55] have suggested that "small" changes in properties across worlds preserve the identity of an individual, but cumulatively, such changes will eventually lead to it becoming a different individual, even though the transition point may be blurry.

All routes lead to trouble here. If we restrict each individual to a single, independent possible world, we get nowhere with our project in this paper, accounting for the role of nonexistent objects, such as the averted strike, in this (or some) world. Other possible worlds will be quite unconnected to the world under consideration. Lewis's counterpart theory would serve to forge a connection between the worlds, but the theory has many problems (see [31,53]). For example, when we go looking for the averted strike, what are we looking for? An actual strike, presumably, that has no counterpart in the real world. But if it has no counterpart in the real world, how can we identify it? In what sense is it related to the strike that, in the real world, was averted? Presumably, it has the same players, cause, time, location, and so on. But to say that is to reify the averted strike in the real world, and that's exactly what we're trying to *avoid* doing.

But if we allow an individual to turn up in different worlds with different properties, anarchy is not far away. For example, Margaret Thatcher could turn up as a man named István Regoczei who leads a motorcycle gang in Budapest, while Michael Jackson is a woman named Margaret Thatcher who becomes prime minister of the United Kingdom and Ronald Reagan is a palm tree in Florida. [23] This can be prevented if we stipulate that each individual has certain properties, *essences*, that are the same in all worlds; the problem, of course, is in deciding which properties they should be. [24] In most practical AI systems we would want to be quite conservative, and consider the essences to be "important" properties, such as being of a certain natural kind.

5.3. A naive formalization

Let's agree, then, that the same individual may occur in many possible worlds, and that we can constrain the accessibility relation between worlds by stipulating essences. Mathematical objects such as numbers will occur in

[23]Note that an individual's having a different name in different worlds is *not* inconsistent with Kripke's notion of a name as a *rigid designator* that picks out the same individual in all worlds [31]. Kripke is quite explicit [31, pp. 49, 62, 77–78] that a name, when used by us in this world, picks out in other worlds the same individual as it does in this world, regardless of that individual's name in the other worlds.

[24]The literature is divided on whether there really are properties that an individual necessarily has in all logically possible worlds; Plantinga [53] and Lewis [35] say yes; Parsons [49,50] is less certain. Regardless, we can always *stipulate* essences as part of our definition of accessibility between the worlds we wish to consider.

all worlds. We can now see whether this approach will provide an adequate representation of sentences about nonexistent objects. We shall start at a rather naive level with standard, first-order logic, and suggest that instead of asserting the nonexistence of, say, the cancelled lecture, we need merely say that its existence is in some other possible world. For a possible world W, let the *domain* of W, written $D(W)$, be the set of individuals in that world. Let R be the real world. Then we have:

(67) Today's lecture is cancelled.

$$\exists W(W \neq R \wedge \exists x \exists y(x \in D(R) \wedge y \in D(W) \wedge y \notin D(R) \wedge$$
$$person(x) \wedge today's\text{-}lecture(y) \wedge cancel(x,y))).$$

"There exists some world W, not equal to the real world R, among whose individuals there exists a y that isn't among the individuals of R and that is today's lecture, and there exists some individual x in R who is the person who cancelled y."

There are many obvious immediate objections to this. First, it seems to say too much. Someone who asserts *Today's lecture is cancelled* is surely not intending to say anything about the lecture's existence in other possible worlds. So the part of (67) that says $y \in D(W)$ for some $W \neq R$, is just unhelpful, irrelevant baggage. Indeed, it's a tautology, for on the theory that we are trying to apply here, *everything* has that property.[25]

Second, (67) invokes the relation *cancel* between objects that are in different possible worlds. This seems just a little mysterious. How is it possible for a relationship to hold across worlds at all? How exactly was an x in one world able to do something to a y in another? If the cancellation itself is an action in the real world, how can one of its components be in a different world? All these points need clarification.

Third, (67) contains quantification over possible worlds, which are nonexistent objects, and quantification over objects in the domains of possible worlds, some of which exist (because they are also in the real world) and some of which don't. So all of the Russellian problems (Section 3.2.2 above) immediately apply, and the sentence must be false. But this is unfair! The whole point of bringing in possible worlds was so that quantifiers could gain access to the objects in their domains. Clearly, we can't play this game by Russell's rules; we need to consider a system that's more hospitable to possible worlds.

---

[25]That is, *every* object is an individual of some unreal possible world. There is no object that is solely in the real world and no other, for our definition of possible worlds permits worlds that include all the objects of the real world and more.

5.4. Kripke's quantified modal logic

Saul Kripke's semantics for quantified modal logic [30] is undoubtedly the best-known formalization of possible worlds. Kripke defines a quantified model structure as a set W of possible worlds, one of which is the real world R, and a reflexive accessibility relation $\triangleright$ defined over the members of W. The set U is the universe of individuals that turn up in at least one world, and each world W gets some subset of elements of U as its domain of individuals, $D(W)$.

The truth of a formula in this system is always relative to a particular world. In each world W, the *extension* of an n-ary predicate P^n, written $ext(P^n, W)$, is the set of n-tuples of individuals of U for which P^n is true in that world. For example, the extension of *loves* in W might be the set

$$\{\langle John, Ross\rangle, \langle Ross, Ironsides\rangle, \ldots\}.$$

Then $loves(x, y)$ would be true in W iff the pair $\langle a, b\rangle$ is in this set, where a is the individual of U that is assigned to the variable x in W and b is that assigned to y. Given this definition of truth for atomic formulas, operators for conjunction, $\wedge$, and negation, $\neg$, are defined in the usual way; necessity, $\square$, is defined as truth in all accessible worlds. [26]

Note that there is no requirement that the individuals assigned to variables in W or the individuals used in the extensions of predicates in W be restricted to individuals in $D(W)$; rather, any element of U is allowed. Such a restriction does apply, however, in the definition of the quantifier $\forall$, which scopes only over individuals of W. That is, the formula $\forall x P^n(y_1, \ldots, y_{i-1}, x, y_{i+1}, \ldots, y_n)$ is true in W for some assignment of elements of U to the y_i iff it's true in W for any assignment to x from $D(W)$. So the truth in W of a sentence such as *Everyone loves Ross* is not blocked by the mere possibility that someone doesn't.

Because variables and predicate extensions can use individuals from any world, we can express propositions that relate individuals from different worlds. For example, we can say that it's true in the real world that Ross loves Pegasus, even if Ross is in the real world and Pegasus isn't. However, it's clear that Kripke himself considers this to be an infelicity of his approach. He regards it as a mere convention that such sentences have any truth value at all [30, pp. 65–66], and one might just as easily have taken the Strawsonian view (as in Woodruff's **UE** [77]; see above) that their value is undefined. [27] Moreover, if such sentences *are* to be given a truth value,

---

[26] I omit the technical details of these and other aspects of the semantics that will not concern us in this paper. The interested reader can find them in Kripke's paper [30] or textbooks such as [24, pp. 178ff].

[27] In fact, the free logic "existence" predicate, i.e., the predicate true just of terms that denote, is just the unary predicate whose extension is $D(W)$ in each W.

says Kripke [30, footnote 11], then they should always be given the value *false*! It is only for certain technical reasons (related to other concerns of Kripke's) that he does not include in his semantics the stipulation that extensions of predicates in each world W be limited to tuples of individuals in $D(W)$ [30, footnote 11].

If we take this seriously, then we are stuck. We can say that our averted strike exists as a real strike in other possible worlds, and that it has certain properties in those worlds, such as lasting for three days or three weeks. But we still can't speak truly of its properties in the worlds in which it was averted, such as its property of having been proposed by Ross, the union steward, and having been averted by the intervention of Malcolm, the mediator. But despair is unnecessary. Even if he didn't want to, Kripke has given us a formalism in which we can speak truly in one world of objects in another. We can use the formalism for what it's worth, and hope that eventually Kripke will agree that what he thought of as a bug is actually a feature.

So let's try some of our problem sentences in Kripke's logic. First, we shall assume that, in addition to worlds possible relative to the present-moment real world R, we also have worlds of the past available to us. Hence U includes all past objects, and we can talk about Alan Turing:

(68)   Alan Turing is dead.

   dead(*AlanTuring*), where the person Alan Turing is the value
   of the variable *AlanTuring*.

If Turing is included in $ext(dead, R)$, then this is a well-formed sentence, true in the real world, even if Turing $\notin D(R)$. A similar treatment will work for *Alan Turing is a celebrated mathematician* and *Nadia admires Alan Turing*. And although we might feel a little worried about so doing, if we also allow Alan Turing to be in $ext(smart, R)$, the set of objects that are smart in the present real world, then we also have *Alan Turing was smart*.

Can we also say that works of fiction are possible worlds, and thus account for dragons and Sherlock Holmes exactly as we accounted for Alan Turing? Kripke, unfortunately, objects to so doing.[28] On Kripke's view, fictional objects don't occur in any possible world; even if a world happened to contain an individual whose properties were exactly those of Sherlock Holmes, that individual would not *be* Sherlock Holmes. Alvin Plantinga [53, pp. 155–159] has also argued against a possible-world treatment of fiction. For while a possible world is complete, a fictional world is necessarily partial. For example, while it is true that Hamlet had feet, it is neither true

---

[28]In [30] he says otherwise, but later, in the addendum to its reprinting in [39], he explicitly repudiates this; see also [31, pp. 157–158].

nor false that his shoe size was 9B [53, p. 158]. A fiction, therefore, at best specifies a *class* of possible worlds.

But perhaps we can again ignore Kripke's advice, which is really based on a metaphysical argument as to what worlds *ought* to be considered accessible from the real world, and simply stipulate that fictional worlds *will* be considered accessible from R, and their objects *will* be in $\mathcal{U}$. The partial nature of such worlds need not concern us; it is straightforward to develop the idea of specially designated worlds in which formulas will have no truth value if they are not explicitly in accordance with, or contradicted by, the "specifications" of the world. So then we have Sherlock Holmes in $\mathcal{U}$, and it will be true, in the Sherlock Holmes world, that Sherlock Holmes was smart. It will also be true in R if we allow Sherlock Holmes to be in $ext(smart, R)$. This may come down to a matter of ontological taste.

Now let's try the cancelled lecture. Writing $\exists x$ for $\neg \forall x \neg$, we are tempted by the following:

(69)   Today's lecture is cancelled.

$\exists x \exists y (person(x) \land today's\text{-}lecture(y) \land cancel(x, y))$.

But this is not correct! We want x and y to be in different worlds, but the semantics of $\exists$, for reasons crucial to the logic, requires them to both be in the world R of which we are speaking! The formula in (69) says

> "There is something $x \in D(R)$, $x \in ext(person, R)$,
> and something $y \in D(R)$, $y \in ext(today's\text{-}lecture, R)$,
> and $\langle x, y \rangle \in ext(cancel, R)$."

While Kripke's logic allows us to *talk about* entities in other worlds, it doesn't allow us to *quantify* over them. That means that we can't pick them out by means of quantifiers and properties. For Kripke, the only way to pick out an object in another world is to use its name as a rigid designator, as we did with Alan Turing in (68). Now, Kripke does allow [31, pp. 79–80] that a suitably precise description could be a rigid designator, and this might be the case for *today's lecture* in (69), but we can't rely on this always being so:

(70)   Ross cancelled one of his lectures (but I don't know which one).

So while we have, in other worlds, the lectures and strikes that didn't occur in the real world, we can't quantify over them; we can talk about them only if we have rigid designators for them—or if we reify them in the real world.

Not only can't we quantify over individuals in other worlds, but we can't quantify over the worlds themselves either, nor even refer to them explicitly, even though (as our present discussion serves to show!) they too may be objects of discourse:

(71)   There are many possible worlds in which Ross is a Justice of the High Court.

(72)   I have a dream of a better world, in which they are free who here are oppressed, and they are well who here are sick and lame.

The best we can do for (71) is (73), which fails to capture the meaning of *many*, as we can't talk about (the cardinality of) the set of worlds in which a proposition is true. We write $\Diamond$ ("possibly") for $\neg\Box\neg$:

(73) $\Diamond High\text{-}Court\text{-}Justice(Ross)$.

"It is possible that Ross is a Justice of the High Court; there is at least one accessible world in which Ross is a Justice of the High Court."

For (72), we can use the possibility operator $\Diamond$ to implicitly invoke the possible world that is mentioned, but we again run into the problem that quantifiers scope only in a single world. The following is *not* what we want:

(74) $\Diamond\forall x\,((oppressed(x) \rightarrow free(x)) \land (sick(x) \rightarrow well(x)))$.

"There is a world in which everything that is oppressed is simultaneously free and everything that is sick is simultaneously well."

What we want to say for (72) is that everything that is oppressed in the real world R is free in the dream world, everything that is sick and lame in R is well in the other world. The problem is that we cannot, in general, write formulas in which truth in one world depends on truth in another.

We can't fix this just by following Plantinga [53, p. 47] in admitting possible worlds as objects in the universe (even though they are nonexistent!),[29] each occurring in all the worlds from which it is accessible; that is, $W' \in D(W)$ whenever $W \triangleright W'$. This doesn't help, because $W' \in D(W)$ does *not* imply that the objects in $D(W')$ are also in $D(W)$ and hence accessible to quantifiers in W. (If that were to happen, then all worlds would include all individuals.) So we still can't write a formula in W that depends on truth in W'. The following (disregarding the second part of the conjunction) still doesn't give us what we want:

(75) $\exists W'\forall x\,((x \in D(R) \land oppressed(x))$
$\rightarrow (\exists y\,(y \in D(W') \land free(y) \land y = x)))$.

---

[29]Though we *model* them with mathematical objects, possible worlds are not themselves mathematical objects any more than Sherlock Holmes or the cancelled lecture are.

What we would need to carry all this through is a completely different formalization of possible worlds that would allow us to embed quantification in one world within quantification in another, indexing variables and predicates by world.

5.5. *Why possible-world theories don't help*

In summary, then, it seems that while the notion of possible worlds and quantified modal logics such as Kripke's might be useful mechanisms for explicating concepts of possibility and necessity, they aren't really very good with nonexistent objects. It should now be clear why this is so. The intent of Kripke's logic was to divide the universe up into separate worlds in order to constrain quantification in modal contexts, rather than to explicate the notion of nonexistent objects *per se* or to account for true assertions about objects in other worlds. (As we saw, Kripke believed that there are no such assertions.) But we weren't able to make very good use of the logic. Firstly, we used possible worlds as convenient places to store our nonexistent objects, the junk from our metaphysical attic, and not for modal reasoning at all. Secondly, we found ourselves wishing that everything would be in every world anyway, defeating the very purpose of the logic.

To put it another way, what we want to talk about and represent is one particular world, usually the actual world, and the question is therefore how dragons and averted strikes exist in the particular world of interest. It is insufficient to say merely that dragons exist in some different possible world, for so, after all, does Margaret Thatcher. That tells us nothing about the difference between dragons and Margaret Thatcher in the world that we *are* representing.

Perhaps, then, we should take courage and say that, yes, we *will* let everything be in every world and be within the scope of quantification there. Then for most purposes, we'll only need one world; it'll have everything in it that we want. Modal reasoning will still require other possible worlds—worlds in which the same universe of individuals have different properties—but that will be an orthogonal issue.

The story so far. We want to represent natural language sentences about existence and nonexistence. But construing nonexistence as existence in another possible world gets us into trouble with quantification scope and mixtures of truth in different worlds. No matter what we do, everything seems to want to collapse into one world.

Next. A solution in which everything is in one world.

6. Theories of nonexistent objects

Hobbs' scheme implicitly countenanced nonexistent objects, but, as we saw, found itself limited because it tried not to make anything special of the notion of existence. Free logics also accept nonexistent objects, but try their best to ignore them. Quantified modal logics just send them to Siberia. We now turn to an approach that doesn't just accept nonexistent objects—it whole-heartedly embraces them. The approach is that of Parsons [50]; it is explicitly motivated by Meinong's ideas (see Section 2.3 above). Parsons' goal is to define an abundant Meinongian universe that includes nonexistent objects, while excluding incoherent objects (such as those that are not self-identical) that give rise to problems and inconsistencies. [30]

Parsons defines *nuclear properties* as the "ordinary properties" that we regularly attribute to individuals [50, p. 24]. For example, being in New Zealand, being Nadia, and being Sherlock Holmes are nuclear properties, but, as we shall see, existing and being perfect are not. Corresponding to each nuclear property is a *nuclear predicate* that is true of the individuals that have that property. There are also *nuclear relations* of two (or more) places; for example, Nadia and her cat may be in the nuclear relationship that the former feeds the latter.

In Parsons' theory, for each distinct set of nuclear properties, the unique object that has exactly that set of properties is included in the universe over which quantifiers scope. But that's all that's in the universe. There is an object that is green (and has no other nuclear property but that); there is an object that is both green and Nadia; there is even an object that is green and Nadia and Sherlock Holmes. But not all these objects exist in the real world—in some cases because they just happen not to, and in other cases because they are not possible.

Properties and relations that aren't nuclear are said to be *extranuclear*. The prime example is physical existence, written *E*!. Thus, existence is taken as a predicate, but one of a special kind. Some other extranuclear predicates are: being perfect, being possible, being an object in the universe, being worshipped by Ross, and being thought about by Margaret Thatcher. (However, worshipping Zeus and thinking about Margaret Thatcher would

---

[30]Rapaport [59,60,62] has also presented a Meinong-inspired theory of nonexistent objects. Space does not permit discussion of both theories. The main differences between the two are the following:
  (1) Parsons has only one type of object, which may or may not exist, whereas Rapaport distinguishes Meinongian objects ("M-objects") from actual objects ("*sein*-correlates" of M-objects).
  (2) Parsons has two types of predicate, whereas Rapaport has one type that can be applied in two different ways: actual objects "exemplify" their properties, whereas M-objects "are constituted" by their properties.

both be nuclear.) Parsons admits [50, p. 24] to being unable to precisely characterize the distinction between the two types of predicate. He suggests, however, that in any particular case, if there is any doubt or controversy over whether a particular property or relation is nuclear, then it probably isn't. Another clue comes from the fact that nuclear relations may hold only between two existent objects or between two nonexistent objects; any relation that can hold between an existent and a nonexistent object must be extranuclear [50, p. 160]. Thus, *is-taller-than* is an extranuclear relation, because Margaret Thatcher (who exists) is taller than Hercule Poirot (who doesn't) [50, pp. 168–169]. In fact, by a similar argument, any comparative relation is extranuclear, and so are relations like *avert* and *cancel*.[31]

Although the universe is defined in terms of distinct sets of nuclear properties, any object in the universe may also have extranuclear properties. In fact, they all have the extranuclear property of being an object in the universe, for example; and some have the extranuclear property of physical existence.

Now, the tricky part is what to do with objects like the golden mountain and the existent golden mountain. These both have exactly the same set of nuclear properties, i.e., goldenness and mountainhood, and are therefore the "same" object by our earlier definition. This seems undesirable; intuitively, "the X" and "the existent X" are different objects—especially if X isn't itself existent. Yet the existent golden mountain must be accounted for, as we can still talk about it, and the account must not entail its existence. So following Meinong, Parsons introduces the concept of *watering down* extranuclear properties to nuclear ones. Thus for Parsons, there is also an existence property that's nuclear—call it $E!_N$. That's the kind of existence that the existent golden mountain has, and that's how it gets into the universe as a distinct object from the regular golden mountain. Watered-down existence says nothing about real, genuine, full-blown extranuclear existence, and the existent golden mountain still doesn't have the latter. A similar story can be told about the possible round square; its possibility is merely the watered-down variety.

The watering-down operation on an extranuclear predicate creates a new nuclear predicate that among existing objects is true of the same objects of which the original predicate was true. That is, if a given existing object has an extranuclear predicate true of it, it will have the corresponding watered-down nuclear predicate true of it as well; and vice versa. Anything

---

[31] In his formalization, to be discussed below, Parsons excludes extranuclear relations, such as *worship*, *avert*, and *cancel*, that yield a nuclear property when one of their argument positions is closed ("plugged up") and an extranuclear property when the other one is. He claims [50, p. 65] that this is for simplicity, and that there are no theoretical difficulties in including such relations. In Section 7.2, we shall rely on this indeed being so, and assume them to have been added to the formalization.

that exists full-strength also exists in a watered-down way; anything that exists that is full-strength-possible is also watered-down-possible. Among nonexistent objects, however, the extranuclear predicate and its watered-down counterpart may diverge. But it's not clear just what sort of a thing these watered-down properties are. What exactly is it that the watered-down-existent gold mountain has that the regular gold mountain doesn't? Just, it seems, an abstract attribution that has no effect on anything except in serving to distinguish the two.

Parsons develops a formal language, called $\mathcal{O}$, for talking about this universe. $\mathcal{O}$ is a second-order modal language with belief contexts; quantification is explicitly over all objects in the universe. The language distinguishes the two types of predicates, and the extranuclear predicate of existence, $E!$, has special axiomatic properties. The watering-down operation on extranuclear predicates is defined. The modalities of necessity and possibility are defined over a set of possible universes; but each possible universe contains the same objects and differs from the others only in which objects have which properties (including existence). Using Montague-like techniques [46], Parsons shows how $\mathcal{O}$ can act as a semantics for a fragment of English, treating sentences such as:

(76)   The King of France doesn't exist.

$\neg (\iota x)(E!(x) \wedge \textit{King-of-France}(x))[\lambda y E!(y)]$.

Roughly, this says that it is not true that there is—in the actual world—a unique x that both is the King of France and exists in the world; if there is indeed no King of France, this formula is true. Also included in the fragment is the sentence *Every good modern chemist knows more about chemical analysis than Sherlock Holmes* (cf. sentence (v) of footnote 10).

If we are willing to accept Parsons' approach, then a number of our problems are solved. We can talk about Sherlock Holmes and dragons and other fictional objects all we like. (Parsons devotes two chapters to fictional objects.) We also have Alan Turing available, and, presumably, all future objects. And we have lots of useful objects that don't exist, including strikes and lectures that never happened—that is, we have the objects that have exactly the properties required, with no necessity that they exist. And the existence of God is not a theorem, no matter how God is described; "for either the description will be purely nuclear in character, and we will not be able to show that the objects [that] satisfy it exist, or it will be partially extranuclear, and we will not be able to show that *any* object [in the universe] satisfies it" ([50, p. 213], emphasis added).

It should be noted, however, that by the same argument, we are not actually *guaranteed* to have averted strikes or cancelled lectures *per se* in the universe, because being averted and being cancelled are extranuclear properties. What we do have at least are strikes and lectures that have all the exact same nuclear properties as the strikes and lectures of interest, including strikes that have been watered-down-averted and lectures that have been watered-down-cancelled. Whether any particular strike or lecture is genuinely, extranuclearly averted or cancelled will be a matter of contingent fact.

Parsons' approach is not without problems. (See Rapaport [64] for a detailed critique.) For example, while nonexistent strikes and lectures are available as objects, we can't do everything with them that we would like. O can say that an existent Ross stands in a *cancelled* relation to a nonexistent lecture, but it is not possible, I think, to explicate the meaning of this as Ross *causing* the nonexistence; Parsons did not consider such things.

Another problem is the profligate scope of the quantifiers. An insight from free logic and Kripke's quantified modal logic that must be retained is that quantification scope must be restrained. Parsons' universe is much too large to quantify over, because it contains a counterexample to every nuclear proposition, an instance of every set of nuclear properties. For example, in Parsons' universe, the sentences *No pigs fly* and *All marmots are mortal* are false, because the universe includes flying pigs and immortal marmots. The effect is rather like that of the Sorcerer's Apprentice; we wanted to account for just a few nonexistent objects, and now we find hordes of them coming out of the woodwork like cockroaches.

But there is no single correct constraint on quantification. For example, it would normally be silly to quantify over all the unwritten books, unthought ideas, or unlived lives; but sometimes, one might have to do so. (An unwritten book is surely reified in the sentence *Ross is going to start writing a book.*) In KR systems, this may not be a practical problem, for the size of the universe is limited by the size of the knowledge base anyway, and even within that, searches would normally be further constrained. This is not to say that a knowledge base cannot contain (finite representations of) infinite objects—the set of integers, for example—but a practical system will normally limit itself to the entities it already knows about and won't capriciously start generating new ones just to see what turns up.

Despite these problems, we'll see in Section 7.2 below that a number of aspects of Parsons' approach are helpful in our goal of including nonexistent objects in a knowledge representation formalism.

The story so far. We want to represent natural language sentences about existence and nonexistence. But knowledge representation formalisms either impute existence to objects when they shouldn't, or they get into trouble treating existence as a predicate. Free logics and possible-world theories don't help either. Philosophical theories of nonexistent objects offer some hope for a solution.

Next. Naivety to the rescue.

7. Naive ontology: the ontology of natural language

Let's take stock of where we are. We've seen three separate ideas of what the set of things that exist is:

A: the things that physically exist (plus mathematical objects);
B: the things that quantifiers scope over;
C: the things we can talk and think about.

We've seen these ideas related in various ways. The austere view, from Russell and Quine, is that $A = B = C$. The promiscuous view, from Meinong and Hobbs, is that $A \subset B = C$. In between, Kripke and Parsons, in different ways, say that $A \subset B \subset C$—that is, they try to be as promiscuous as possible without actually getting into trouble. I've argued throughout the paper that a generally promiscuous approach is required for an adequate representation of natural language in AI. In this section, now, I want to lay the foundation for such a representation. I'll be taking the promiscuous-but-cautious view, $A \subset B \subset C$, making B as large as possible.

7.1. Different kinds of existence

The real problem with the Russell–Quine position, the free-logic and possible-world approaches, and even Parsons' approach is that they equivocate about existence; they speak as if all things that exist exist in the same way. This is clearly not so. Margaret Thatcher exists, and so does the number 27, but they do so in different ways: one is a physical object in the world, while the other has only abstract existence. But even Quine is willing to grant the existence of mathematical entities—and of concepts in general. If we admit these two kinds of existence, then perhaps we can find even more kinds if we look. And arguments about the nature of one kind—whether it can be a predicate, for example—need not hold true of the others.

In fact, following the style of naive physics [17], we can develop a *naive ontology* that captures the commonsense view of existence that natural language reflects. In doing so, we follow Meinong in not limiting membership in the universe to things in the world, but attributing it to anything that can be spoken of. The commonsense notion that anything that can be spoken of has being of some kind or another may not stand up to intense scrutiny, but is certainly robust enough for our naive approach. (Plantinga [53], for example, shows that the notion is able to withstand quite a number of philosophical challenges, and needs to go to some length before he believes that he can claim that he has defeated it.)

And we go further, by imposing a taxonomy of existence upon the universe, identifying about eight different kinds of existence. In particular, we solve the problems of the cancelled lecture and the averted strike by attributing some kind of being to them (but not physical actuality). Thus all sentences will be about objects that are somewhere in the universe, and will therefore have the potential to be true.

We start by taking the universe to be as Parsons defined it: the set of objects given by all possible distinct nonempty combinations of nuclear properties, including watered-down extranuclear properties. This will give us a large assortment of physical objects, mathematical objects, concepts, and so on. This is the kosher part of the universe. To this, we add a "quarantine" section in which objects live with no nuclear properties at all. These are the *tref* objects that would create inconsistency in Parsons' system: Russell sets, non-self-identical objects, and so on. The various kinds of existence that we identify, all in the kosher part of this universe, are then as follows. All are extranuclear properties:

- Physical existence in the present real world (or that under consideration), with causal interaction. Margaret Thatcher exists this way, and so do events such as Nadia's putting the cat out. This is the same property as that of Parsons' original $E!$ predicate.
- Physical existence in a past world (with causal interaction therein, and some indirect causal connection to the present world). The late Alan Turing, for example, exists in a world of the past; he doesn't exist now, but nevertheless he *is*, in the present, a celebrated mathematician, and likewise he *is* dead (see Section 3.2.2 above).
- Abstract, necessary existence, as of mathematical objects such as 27 and the least prime greater than 27.
- Existence outside a world, but with causal interaction with that world. This is the kind of existence that most Western religions attribute to God.
- Abstract, contingent existence in the real world. Freedom, suavity, and fear would come into this category.
- Existence as a concept, which is abstract but contingent, such as the concept of Margaret Thatcher, which need not have existed. [32]

---

[32] One may wish to combine this category with the previous one, saying that concepts are not ontologically distinct from other abstract entities like suavity. I will not take a position on this. Alternatively, one might argue that the existence of a concept may be necessary or contingent depending on its extension. That is, the concept of Margaret Thatcher is as contingent as Margaret Thatcher is, but the concept of the least prime greater than 27 is necessary because its extension is. The category of existence as a concept would then be split over the three abstract categories above.

- Unactualized existence. [33] This category includes objects that could become actual in the future, objects in counterfactuals, "past" objects that never came into being, and perhaps also impossible objects. Strictly speaking, this category crosses with the previous six. The baby that Diane wants to have has unactualized physical existence; the book that Ross once wanted to write has unactualized past existence; and hypothetical gods have unactualized divine existence. It's not clear to me that unactualized necessary existence is meaningful, unless that's the kind that $\sqrt{-1}$ has. Note that objects in the quarantine section of the universe do not have even unactualized existence.

- Existence in fiction. This is the sense in which Sherlock Holmes and dragons exist. [34] This category, too, crosses with the others. Sherlock Holmes and dragons have fictional physical existence; mythological gods have fictional divine existence; and a story about a counterexample to the four-color theorem invokes fictional necessary existence. [35]

My point here is not to argue for exactly this list of types of existence—that's a topic in philosophy, not artificial intelligence—but rather to demonstrate that however many distinct types of existence there are, it's somewhat more than two. [36] Any knowledge representation formalism that is to be adequate to the task of natural language understanding will need to be able to account for them all—that is, it will treat existence as a set of properties, and, given a particular object's mode of existence, draw inferences accordingly.

It should be clear that the various kinds of existence can't all be accounted for just by organizing the IS-A hierarchy the right way. It is true that one can, at the top, make a distinction between abstract and concrete entities. But

---

[33] I use this horrible term for want of a better one.

[34] "Everyone knows that dragons don't exist. But while this simplistic formulation may satisfy the layman, it does not suffice for the scientific mind. ... The brilliant Cerebron, attacking the problem analytically, discovered three distinct kinds of dragon: the mythical, the chimerical, and the purely hypothetical. They were all, one might say, nonexistent, but each nonexisted in an entirely different way." (Stanisław Lem [33, p. 76])

[35] This still leaves a few loose ends. For example, it could be argued that the fictional physical existence of, say, Sherlock Holmes entails both the fictional existence and the actual existence of the concept of Sherlock Holmes. Are these then two separate entities, or one entity with a dual mode of existence, or what?

[36] Routley [65, p. 441] objects to all "kinds-of-existence doctrines", apparently because they don't have the guts to come right out and say that there are things that just plain don't exist. Routley puts his position by parody rather than argument ("canned peaches exist as grocery supplies"), so his objections remain unclear. But it seems to me that if there is a dispute, it is terminological; to the optimist, an object has "unactualized existence", while to the pessimist, it's simply "nonexistent". Moreover, I think Routley's objections are misdirected. His main aim is to attack the "ontological assumption"—basically, a bias against nonexistence. But our naive ontology here does not include the dreaded ontological assumption, and indeed is consistent with its converse (cf. [61, p. 550n]).

past existence, unactualized existence, and fictional existence are certainly orthogonal to the hierarchy of concrete entities. And it is usual to arrange an IS-A hierarchy as a network in which nodes representing instances are necessarily leaves and those representing concepts are (or can be) interior nodes; there are clear advantages in retaining this structure for reasoning about inheritance of properties, rather than trying to separate concepts and instances as fundamentally different types.

7.2. Using the naive ontology

We can now show how the naive ontology can be used to fix some of the problems of transparency and entailment of existence in Hobbs' system. I will not present a formalization, as many details remain to be worked out.

First, recall that in Parsons' system, nuclear relations could hold only between objects that both existed or both didn't. We can immediately generalize this: nuclear relations may hold only between objects that exist in *the same way*. For example, *instance-of* will not be nuclear, as it can relate concepts, which exist one way, to objects that exist in other ways. As before, *avert, cancel,* and so on will also be extranuclear.

Second, we take the notion of watering-down to mean severely weakening a predicate to the point where it becomes nothing but an abstract attribute with no significant consequences. We do this by prohibiting watered-down properties from entailing anything but other watered-down properties. So, for example, while the extranuclear property of omniscience entails the nuclear property of knowing where Ross is, watered-down omniscience does not.

Third, we prohibit objects in the quarantined section of the universe from doing just about everything. Intuitively, we allow them to be mentioned, but not used. So we can talk about Russell sets, and our use of the term will refer, but that's about all. They may not appear in any axiom, nor participate in any inference. And quantifiers do not scope over them. [37] (Note that these restrictions do not apply to the *concepts* of the *tref* objects; these have healthy, conceptual existence in the kosher section of the universe.)

Next, we extend the notion of transparent argument positions, as in Hobbs' system, so that the existence of various objects can be inferred from assertions about relationships in which they participate. Let's consider simple nuclear relationships first:

(77)   Ross kisses Nadia.

       kiss(Ross, Nadia).

---

[37] Thus with respect to quantifiers, these objects are rather like objects in other possible worlds in Kripke's quantified modal logic (Section 5.4 above); that is, they can be picked out by a rigid designator but not by a quantifier.

Because it is nuclear, both argument positions of *kiss* will be transparent. From this, we will now infer *not* that Nadia and Ross exist, but rather that to the extent that they exist, they do so in the same way—both are physical or fictional or past or whatever. (Presumably real-world physical existence would be a good default assumption if there were no indication to the contrary; and the various kinds of conceptual, abstract, and divine existence would be ruled out by the lexical semantics of *kiss*.) Using Hobbs' style of formalism, we can go further. We must revise Hobbs' basic form, which was (78):

(78) $kiss'(E, Ross, Nadia) \wedge Exist(E)$

to specify what kind of existence E has. It will then follow that Ross and Nadia exist the same way that E does; for example, in (79):

(79) $kiss'(E, Ross, Nadia) \wedge Physically\text{-}exist(E)$

we can infer the physical existence of Ross and Nadia from that of the kissing action.

In the case of extranuclear relationships, such inferences do not go through. As desired, we can infer nothing from (80) about the ontological status of Margaret or Hercule:

(80) $taller\text{-}than(Margaret, Hercule)$.

But some extranuclear relationships admit what we earlier (Section 4.1) called *anti-transparent positions*. Our paradigm case is the averted strike. Even if averting *per se* is extranuclear, the property of being an act of averting seems to be nuclear:

(81) $avert'(E, Ross, Strike) \wedge Exist(E)$,

where *Exist* is now taken to mean existing in one way or another. Because *avert* is extranuclear, no inferences can be automatic here. Rather, it is a matter of the lexical semantics of *avert* that certain limited inferences go through: that Ross exists the way E does and that the strike must have unactualized existence.

Lastly, we are protected against accidentally defining God, or anything else, into real existence. The assertion of a nuclear property allows one to infer only that the individual of which it is predicated exists in some way. For example, the truth of *green(Nadia)* doesn't entail Nadia's physical existence, but only that she is in the universe somewhere. And the assertion of an extranuclear property does still less; the truth of *perfect(God)* doesn't entail that God is even in the unquarantined universe. (A watered-down-perfect God is, but nothing interesting follows from that.)

8. Conclusion

What I've shown in this paper is that knowledge representation formalisms that are to be suitable for use in natural language understanding must take account of the ways that existence and nonexistence can be spoken of in natural language. Neither the traditional approaches of Frege, Russell, and Quine, nor possible-world theories and free logics are adequate.

Intuitively, a better approach seems to require treating existence as a predicate and including nonexistent objects in the universe over which our quantifiers scope—much as Hobbs did. Philosophers have traditionally taken a dim view of such activities, however, and I've tried to show the reasons for their concern. Nevertheless, I think Hobbs' approach is the most promising of those that we've looked at. But developing it further requires developing the notion of a naive ontology. The task is analogous to naive physics and other projects in AI to represent commonsense notions of the world, and in this paper, I've presented a first cut at such an ontology and shown how it could be added to Hobbs' system.

I also see promise in Parsons' Meinongian account. By basing our definition of the universe on his, we were able to give our naive ontology a large supply of useful objects without it lapsing into inconsistency. And Parsons' distinction between nuclear and extranuclear predicates can help strengthen a Hobbs-like approach against the wrath of the philosophers that it scorns. In Section 7.2, I've sketched an outline of how the distinction could be used.

There are many details left to be worked out, of course. However, I will have succeeded in my goals for this paper if I have convinced the reader that nonexistent objects, their representation, and their role in quantification are important concerns in artificial intelligence, but there are no workable, off-the-shelf solutions in philosophy that we can just take and use.

Acknowledgement

A small, early, less-correct version of this paper was presented at the First International Conference on Principles of Knowledge Representation and Reasoning, Toronto, May 1989, and appears in the Proceedings thereof [5].

For discussions on these matters and comments and advice on earlier versions of this paper, I am grateful to Stephen Regoczei, Bill Rapaport, Jeff Pelletier, James Allen, John Barnden, Stephen Bellantoni, Ed Cohen, Chrysanne DiMarco, Jerry Hobbs, Diane Horton, Shalom Lappin, Andrew Malton, Chris Mellish, Terence Parsons, Anonymous Referees, Allen Renear, Barry Richards, Graeme Ritchie, Stuart Shapiro, John Sowa, Joan Talent, Nadia Talent, Eric Wheeler, Bill Woods, Felix Yen, and Włodek Zadrożny.

The foundations of this work were laid while I was at the Department of

Artificial Intelligence, University of Edinburgh, with the support of a Visiting Fellowship from the U.K. Science and Engineering Research Council. The balance of the work was supported by the Natural Sciences and Engineering Research Council of Canada. The final revision was prepared with facilities kindly provided by the Department of Computer Science, University of Rochester, while I was a visitor there.

References

[1] Anselm, *Proslogion* (M.J. Charlesworth, translator) (Clarendon Press, Oxford, 1965).
[2] J. Barnes, *The Ontological Argument* (Macmillan, London, 1972).
[3] R.J. Brachman, R.E. Fikes and H.J. Levesque, KRYPTON: a functional approach to knowledge representation, Tech. Report 16, Fairchild Laboratory for Artificial Intelligence Research, Palo Alto, CA (1983); reprinted in: R.J. Brachman and H.J. Levesque, eds., *Readings in Knowledge Representation* (Morgan Kaufmann, Los Altos, CA, 1985) 411–429.
[4] R.J. Brachman and H.J. Levesque, eds., *Readings in Knowledge Representation* (Morgan Kaufmann, Los Altos, CA, 1985).
[5] R.J. Brachman, H.J. Levesque and R. Reiter, eds., *Proceedings of the First International Conference on Principles of Knowledge Representation and Reasoning*, Toronto, Ont. (Morgan Kaufmann, San Mateo, CA, 1989).
[6] E. Charniak, M.K. Gavin and J.A. Hendler, The Frail/NASL reference manual, Tech. Report CS-83-06, Department of Computer Science, Brown University, Providence, RI (1983).
[7] R.M. Chisholm, Identity through possible worlds: some questions, *Noûs* **1** (1968) 1–8.
[8] G. Currie, *Frege: An Introduction to His Philosophy*, Harvester Studies in Philosophy **11** (Harvester, Brighton, 1982).
[9] D. Davidson, *Essays on Actions and Events* (Clarendon Press, Oxford, 1980).
[10] R. Descartes, Meditations on first philosophy, in: *The Philosophical Works of Descartes* Vol. I (E.S. Haldane and G.R.T. Ross, translators) (Cambridge University Press, Cambridge, 1911).
[11] G. Fauconnier, *Mental Spaces: Aspects of Meaning Construction in Natural Language* (MIT Press, Cambridge, MA, 1985).
[12] H. Feigl and W. Sellars, eds., *Readings in Philosophical Analysis* (Appleton-Century-Croft, New York, 1949).
[13] G. Frege, *Die Grundlagen der Arithmetik* (Wilhelm Köbner, Breslau, 1884); reprinted as: G. Frege, *The Foundations of Arithmetic* (J.L. Austin, translator) (Blackwell, Oxford, 2nd rev. ed., 1953).
[14] G. Frege, Über Sinn und Bedeutung, *Z. Philos. Philos. Kritik* **100** (1892) 25–50; reprinted as: On sense and nominatum (H. Feigl, translator), in: H. Feigl and W. Sellars, eds., *Readings in Philosophical Analysis* (Appleton-Century-Croft, New York, 1949) 85–102; also as: On sense and reference (M. Black, translator), in: P.T. Geach and M. Black, eds., *Translations from the Philosophical Writings of Gottlob Frege* (Blackwell, Oxford, 1952) 56–78.
[15] G. Frege, *On the Foundations of Geometry and Formal Theories of Arithmetic* (E.-H.W. Kluge, translator) (Yale University Press, New Haven, CT, 1971).
[16] P.T. Geach and M. Black, eds., *Translations from the Philosophical Writings of Gottlob Frege* (Blackwell, Oxford, 1952).
[17] P.J. Hayes, The second naive physics manifesto, in: J.R. Hobbs and R.C. Moore, eds., *Formal Theories of the Commonsense World* (Ablex, Norwood, NJ, 1985) 1–36; reprinted in: R.J. Brachman and H.J. Levesque, eds., *Readings in Knowledge Representation* (Morgan Kaufmann, Los Altos, CA, 1985) 468–485.

[18] G. Hirst, *Semantic Interpretation and the Resolution of Ambiguity* (Cambridge University Press, Cambridge, 1987).

[19] G. Hirst, Semantic interpretation and ambiguity, *Artif. Intell.* **34** (1988) 131–177.

[20] G. Hirst, Knowledge representation problems for natural language understanding, Abstract in: H. Trost, ed., *4. Österreichische Artificial-Intelligence-Tagung: Wiener Workshop Wissensbasierte Sprachverarbeitung: Proceedings*, Informatik-Fachberichte **176** (Springer, Berlin, 1988).

[21] J.R. Hobbs, Ontological promiscuity, in: *Proceedings 23rd Annual Meeting of the Association for Computational Linguistics*, Chicago, IL (1985) 61–69.

[22] D.L. Horton, Incorporating agents' beliefs in a model of presupposition, M.Sc. Thesis, Tech. Report CSRI-201, Computer Systems Research Institute, University of Toronto, Toronto, Ont. (1987).

[23] D.L. Horton and G. Hirst, Presuppositions as beliefs, in: *Proceedings International Conference on Computational Linguistics (COLING-88)*, Budapest (1988) 255–260.

[24] G.E. Hughes and M.J. Cresswell, *An Introduction to Modal Logic* (Methuen, London, 1968).

[25] D. Hume, *Dialogues Concerning Natural Religion* (N. Kemp Smith, ed.) (Clarendon Press, Oxford, 1935).

[26] I. Kant, *Critique of Pure Reason* (N. Kemp Smith, translator) (Macmillan, London, 2nd rev. ed., 1933).

[27] W.E. Kennick. Moore on existence and predication, in: A. Ambrose and M. Lazerowitz, eds., *G.E. Moore: Essays in Retrospect* (Allen & Unwin, London, 1970) 160–192.

[28] M. Koubarakis, J. Mylopoulos, M. Stanley and M. Jarke, TELOS: a knowledge representation language for requirements modelling, Tech. Report KRR-89-1, Department of Computer Science, University of Toronto, Toronto, Ont. (1989).

[29] M. Koubarakis, J. Mylopoulos, M. Stanley and A. Borgida, TELOS: features and formalization, Tech. Report KRR-89-4, Department of Computer Science, University of Toronto, Toronto, Ont. (1989).

[30] S.A. Kripke, Semantical considerations on modal logic, *Acta Philos. Fenn.* **16** (Proceedings of a colloquium on modal and many-valued logics) (1963) 83–94; reprinted, with addendum, in: L. Linsky, ed., *Reference and Modality* (Oxford University Press, Oxford, 1971) 63–72 and 172.

[31] S.A. Kripke, *Naming and Necessity* (Harvard University Press, Cambridge, MA, 1980).

[32] K. Lambert, *Meinong and the Principle of Independence* (Cambridge University Press, Cambridge, 1983).

[33] S. Lem, The third sally, or The dragons of probability, in: *The Cyberiad: Fables for the Cybernetic Age* (M. Kandel, translator) (Avon Books, New York, 1976).

[34] S.C. Levinson. *Pragmatics* (Cambridge University Press, Cambridge, 1983).

[35] D. Lewis, Counterpart theory and quantified modal logic, *J. Philos.* **65** (1968) 113–126; reprinted, with addenda, in: D. Lewis, *Philosophical Papers*, Vol. I (Oxford University Press, New York, 1983) 26–46.

[36] D. Lewis, Anselm and actuality, *Noûs* **4** (1970) 175–188; reprinted, with addenda, in: D. Lewis, *Philosophical Papers*, Vol. I (Oxford University Press, New York, 1983) 10–25.

[37] D. Lewis, *Philosophical Papers*, Vol. I (Oxford University Press, New York, 1983).

[38] D. Lewis and S. Lewis, Holes, *Australasian J. Philos.* **48** (1970) 206–212; reprinted in: D. Lewis, *Philosophical Papers*, Vol. I (Oxford University Press, New York, 1983) 3–9.

[39] L. Linsky, ed., *Reference and Modality* (Oxford University Press, Oxford, 1971).

[40] A.S. Maida and S.C. Shapiro, Intensional concepts in propositional semantic networks, *Cognitive Sci.* **6** (1982) 291–330.

[41] J. Margolis, ed., *An Introduction to Philosophical Enquiry* (Knopf, New York, 1968).

[42] J.N. Martin, *Elements of Formal Semantics: An Introduction to Logic for Students of Language* (Academic Press, Orlando, FL, 1987).

[43] J. McCarthy, Epistemological problems of artificial intelligence, in: *Proceedings IJCAI-77*, Cambridge, MA (1977) 1038–1044.

[44] J. McCarthy, First order theories of individual concepts and propositions, in: J.E. Hayes,

D. Michie and L.I. Mikulich, eds., *Machine Intelligence* **9** (Ellis Horwood, Chichester, 1979) 129–147; reprinted in: R.J. Brachman and H.J. Levesque, eds., *Readings in Knowledge Representation* (Morgan Kaufmann, Los Altos, CA, 1985) 523–533.

[45] A. Meinong, Über Gegenstandstheorie, in: A. Meinong, ed., *Untersuchungen zur Gegenstandstheorie und Psychologie* (Barth, Leipzig, 1904); reprinted in: A. Meinong, *Gesamtausgabe*, Vol. II (R. Haller and R. Kindinger, eds.) (Akademische Druck- und Verlaganstalt, Graz, 1969–1978) 481–535; reprinted as: The theory of objects (I. Levi, D.B. Terrell and R.M. Chisholm, translators), in: R.M. Chisholm, ed., *Realism and the Background of Phenomenology* (Free Press, Glencoe, IL, 1960) 76–117.

[46] R. Montague, The proper treatment of quantification in ordinary English, in: K.J.J. Hintikka, J.M.E. Moravcsik and P.C. Suppes, eds., *Approaches to Natural Language: Proceedings 1970 Stanford Workshop on Grammar and Semantics* (Reidel, Dordrecht, 1973) 221–242; reprinted in: R. Montague, *Formal Philosophy: Selected Papers of Richard Montague* (R.H. Thomason, ed.) (Yale University Press, New Haven, CT, 1974) 247–270.

[47] G.E. Moore, Is existence a predicate? in: *What Can Philosophy Determine?*, Proceedings Aristotelian Society, Suppl. Vol. **15** (1936) 175–188; reprinted in: G.E. Moore, *Philosophical Papers* (Allen & Unwin, London, 1959), 115–126; also in: A.G.N. Flew, ed., *Logic and Language* (Second Series) (Basil Blackwell, Oxford, 1953) 82–94.

[48] S. Neale, *Descriptions* (MIT Press, Cambridge, MA, 1990).

[49] T. Parsons, Essentialism and quantified modal logic, *Philos. Rev.* **78** (1969) 35–52; reprinted in: L. Linsky, ed., *Reference and Modality* (Oxford University Press, Oxford, 1971) 73–87.

[50] T. Parsons, *Nonexistent Objects* (Yale University Press, New Haven, CT, 1980).

[51] P.F. Patel-Schneider, A four-valued semantics for frame-based description languages, in: *Proceedings AAAI-86*, Philadelphia, PA (1986) 344–348.

[52] A. Plantinga, *God and Other Minds: A Study of the Rational Justification of Belief in God* (Cornell University Press, Ithaca, NY, 1967).

[53] A. Plantinga, *The Nature of Necessity* (Clarendon Press, Oxford, 1974).

[54] A.N. Prior, Existence, in: P. Edwards, ed., *The Encyclopedia of Philosophy* **3** (Macmillan, New York, 1967) 141–147.

[55] R.L. Purtill, About identity through possible worlds, *Noûs* **2** (1968) 87–89.

[56] W.V.O. Quine, On what there is, *Rev. Metaphys.* **1** (1948) 21–38; reprinted in: *Freedom, Language, and Reality*, Proceedings Aristotelian Society, Suppl. Vol. **25** (1951) 216–233; also in: W.V.O. Quine, *From a Logical Point of View: Logico-Philosophical Essays* (Harvard University Press, Cambridge, MA, 1st ed., 1953; 2nd ed., 1961) 1–19; also in: J. Margolis, ed., *An Introduction to Philosophical Enquiry* (Knopf, New York, 1968) 668–679.

[57] W.V.O. Quine, Reference and modality, in: W.V.O. Quine, *From a Logical Point of View: Logico-Philosophical Essays* (Harvard University Press, Cambridge, MA, 1st ed., 1953; 2nd ed., 1961) 139–157; reprinted in: L. Linsky, ed., *Reference and Modality* (Oxford University Press, Oxford, 1971) 17–34.

[58] W.V.O. Quine, *From a Logical Point of View: Logico-Philosophical Essays* (Harvard University Press, Cambridge, MA, 1st ed., 1953; 2nd ed., 1961).

[59] W.J. Rapaport, Meinongian theories and a Russellian paradox, *Noûs* **12** (1978) 153–180.

[60] W.J. Rapaport, How to make the world fit our language: an essay in Meinongian semantics, *Grazer Philos. Stud.* **14** (1981) 1–21.

[61] W.J. Rapaport, Review of: R. Routley, Exploring Meinong's jungle and beyond: an investigation of noneism and the theory of items (interim ed.), Departmental Monograph 3, Philosophy Department, Research School of Social Sciences, Australian National University, Canberra, ACT (1980), *Philos. Phenomenological Res.* **44** (1984) 539–552.

[62] W.J. Rapaport, Non-existent objects and epistemological ontology, *Grazer Philos. Stud.* **25/26** (1985/86) 61–95.

[63] W.J. Rapaport, Meinongian semantics for propositional semantic networks, in: *Proceedings 23rd Annual Meeting of the Association for Computational Linguistics,*

Chicago, IL (1985) 43–48.

[64] W.J. Rapaport, To be and not to be (Review of: T. Parsons, *Nonexistent Objects* (Yale University Press, New Haven, CT, 1980)), *Noûs* **19** (1985) 255–271.

[65] R. Routley, Exploring Meinong's jungle and beyond: an investigation of noneism and the theory of items (interim ed.), Departmental Monograph 3, Philosophy Department, Research School of Social Sciences, Australian National University, Canberra, ACT (1980).

[66] B. Russell, On denoting, *Mind n.s.* **14** (1905) 479–493; reprinted in: B. Russell, *Essays in Analysis* (D. Lackey, ed.) (Allen & Unwin, London, 1973) 103–119; reprinted in: H. Feigl and W. Sellars, eds., *Readings in Philosophical Analysis* (Appleton-Century-Croft, New York, 1949) 103–115; also in: B. Russell, *Logic and Analysis: Essays 1901–1950* (R.C. Marsh, ed.) (Allen & Unwin, London, 1956) 39–56; also in: J. Margolis, ed., *An Introduction to Philosophical Enquiry* (Knopf, New York, 1968) 631–642.

[67] B. Russell, The philosophy of logical atomism, in: B. Russell, *Logic and Analysis: Essays 1901–1950* (R.C. Marsh, ed.) (Allen & Unwin, London, 1956) 175–281.

[68] B. Russell, *Logic and Analysis: Essays 1901–1950* (R.C. Marsh, ed.) (Allen & Unwin, London, 1956).

[69] G. Ryle, Systematically misleading expressions, *Proceedings Aristotelian Society* **32** (1931–32) 139–170; reprinted in: A.G.N. Flew, ed., *Logic and Language* (First Series) (Basil Blackwell, Oxford, 1950) 11–36.

[70] R. Schock, *Logics without Existence Assumptions* (Almqvist & Wiksell, Stockholm, 1968).

[71] S.C. Shapiro and W.J. Rapaport, SNePS considered as a fully intensional propositional semantic network, in: N. Cercone and G. McCalla, eds., *The Knowledge Frontier: Essays in the Representation of Knowledge* (Springer, New York, 1987) 262–315.

[72] R.M. Smullyan, *What is the Name of This Book?—The Riddle of Dracula and Other Logical Puzzles* (Prentice-Hall, Englewood Cliffs, NJ, 1978).

[73] H.D. Sluga, *Gottlob Frege* (Routledge & Kegan Paul, London, 1980).

[74] J.F. Sowa, *Conceptual Structures: Information Processing in Mind and Machine* (Addison-Wesley, Reading, MA, 1984).

[75] P.F. Strawson, On referring, *Mind n.s.* **59** (1950) 320–344.

[76] C.J.F. Williams, *What is Existence?* (Clarendon Press, Oxford, 1981).

[77] P.W. Woodruff, Logic and truth value gaps, in: K. Lambert, ed., *Philosophical Problems in Logic: Some Recent Developments* (Reidel, Dordrecht, 1970) 121–142.

[78] J. Woods, *The Logic of Fiction: A Philosophical Sounding of Deviant Logic*, De Proprietatibus Litterarum, Series Minor **16** (Mouton, The Hague, 1974).

[79] W.A. Woods, What's in a link: foundations for semantic networks, in: D.G. Bobrow and A.M. Collins, eds., *Representation and Understanding: Studies in Cognitive Science, Language, Thought and Culture: Advances in the Study of Cognition* (Academic Press, New York, 1975) 35–82; reprinted in: R.J. Brachman and H.J. Levesque, eds., *Readings in Knowledge Representation* (Morgan Kaufmann, Los Altos, CA, 1985) 217–241.

[80] E.N. Zalta, *Abstract Objects: An Introduction to Axiomatic Metaphysics*, Synthese Library **160** (Reidel, Dordrecht, 1983).

Artificial Intelligence 49 (1991) 243–279
Elsevier

Hard problems for simple default logics *

Henry A. Kautz

AT&T Bell Laboratories, Murray Hill, NJ 07974, USA

Bart Selman [†]

Department of Computer Science, University of Toronto, Toronto, Ontario, Canada M5S 1A4

Received November 1989
Revised August 1990

Abstract

Kautz, H.A. and B. Selman, Hard problems for simple default logics, Artificial Intelligence 49 (1991) 243–279.

We investigate the complexity of reasoning with a number of limited default logics. Surprising negative results (the high complexity of simple three literal default rules) as well as positive results (a fast algorithm for skeptical reasoning with binary defaults) are reported, and sources of complexity are discussed. These results impact on work on defeasible inheritance hierarchies as well as default reasoning in general.

1. Introduction

It has been suggested that some kind of default inference can be used to simplify and speed commonsense reasoning. Researchers have appealed to default logics as a solution to the problem of generating and reasoning with large numbers of "frame axioms"; as a way of simplifying complex probabilistic calculations; and recently as a way of "vivifying" (filling out) an incomplete knowledge base, thus suppressing the complexities of reasoning with uncertainty [10,11].

---

*This is an expanded version of a paper that appears in the *Proceedings of the First International Conference on Principles of Knowledge Representation and Reasoning*, Toronto, Ontario, Canada, May 15–18, 1989.
[†]Current address: AT&T Bell Laboratories, Murray Hill, NJ 07974, USA

0004-3702/91/$ 03.50 © 1991—Elsevier Science Publishers B.V.

While current formal theories of default inference are computationally much worse than ordinary logic, it has been tacitly assumed that this additional complexity arises from their use of consistency tests. Our interest in fast, special purpose inference mechanisms led us to investigate very simple propositional, disjunction-free systems of default reasoning, where consistency checking is trivial. Here, we thought, default reasoning should shine.

This paper reports a number of surprising complexity results involving restricted versions of Ray Reiter's default logic [13]. We define a partially-ordered space of propositional default theories of varying degrees of generality. For each we determine the complexity of solving the following three problems: finding an extension; determining if a given proposition is true in some extension; and determining if a given proposition is true in all extensions.

All of these problems are NP-hard for propositional, disjunction-free default logic. This shows that consistency checking is *not* the only source of complexity in default reasoning. We show that a condition called "ordering" (which is related to stratification in logic programming) makes finding an extension tractable. The extension membership problems, however, remain intractable for most of the restricted logics. In particular, these questions are NP-complete for the logic that most naturally represents acyclic inheritance hierarchies. Systems whose rules are similar in form to Horn clauses do admit a tractable algorithm for testing membership in some extension. Finally, we present a polynomial algorithm for testing the membership of a proposition in all extensions of the very restricted class of "normal unary" theories, thus settling an open question in work on inheritance.

The next part of the paper presents general reductions of finding an extension to testing membership in some extension, and that to testing membership in all extensions. This shows that for a large class of default theories, it is at least as hard to test the status of a single proposition as to compute a complete extension.

The final part of the paper provides some intuitive characterizations of the sources of complexity in default reasoning. It suggests that the most efficient use of default information is to "flesh out" the missing detail in a knowledge base in a "brave" manner, a process that corresponds to finding an extension.

A note on notation: throughout this paper, the symbols p, q, r, s, and t are used for propositional letters (also called positive literals). The symbols a, b, c, x, y, and z are used for literals (propositional letters and their negations). The greek letters α, β, and γ are used for formulas. The sign $\sim$ is a meta-language operator that maps a positive literal to a negative literal and vice versa. For example, the expression

$$\sim x \in E$$

where E is a set of literals, is equivalent to the lengthy expression

> if $x = p$ for some letter p, then $\neg x \in E$; otherwise, where $x = \neg p$
> for some letter p, it is the case that $p \in E$.

Use of this operator avoids the need to explicitly invoke a rule of negation elimination to convert formulas of the form $\neg\neg p$ to p.

2. Reiter's default logic

Reiter formalized default reasoning by extending first-order logic with default inference rules. This paper will not consider the other nonmonotonic formalisms based on modal logic, circumscription, or model-preference rules, although many of the results it presents have counterparts in those systems. (See [14,15] for a similar analysis of model-preference theories.)

A *default theory* is a pair (D, W) where D is a set of default rules and W a set of ordinary first-order formulas. This paper examines theories containing only *semi-normal default rules*, which are of the form

$$\frac{\alpha : \beta \wedge \gamma}{\beta}$$

where α is the *prerequisite*, β the *conclusion*, and $\beta \wedge \gamma$ the *justification* of a rule, each of them formulas. The rule is intuitively understood as meaning that if α is known, and $\beta \wedge \gamma$ is consistent with what is known, then β may be inferred. If γ is missing, then the rule is *normal*. Default rules are sometimes written as $\alpha : \beta \wedge \gamma / \gamma$ for typographic clarity.

An *extension* is a maximal set of conclusions that can be drawn from a theory. But care must be taken that the justification of each rule used in the construction of an extension be consistent with the complete contents of the extension, not just with the non-default information.

Definition 2.1 (*Extension*). Where E is a set of formulas, $\text{Th}(E)$ is the deductive closure of E. $\mathcal{E}$ is an extension for the theory (D, W) if and only if it satisfies the following equations:

$$E_0 = W,$$

and for $i > 0$,

$$E_{i+1} = \text{Th}(E_i) \cup \left\{ \gamma \,\middle|\, \frac{\alpha : \beta}{\gamma} \in D, \ \alpha \in E_i, \ \text{and} \ \neg\beta \notin \mathcal{E} \right\};$$

$$\mathcal{E} = \bigcup_{i=0}^{\infty} E_i.$$

Note the explicit reference to $\mathcal{E}$ in the definition of E_{i+1}. A theory can have several, one, or no extensions.

Although normal theories have a number of nice theoretical and computational properties, semi-normal rules are often needed to establish a priority among the defaults. For example, two default rules may have conflicting conclusions, yet have their preconditions satisfied in the same situation. If normal rules were used, this kind of situation would lead to two different extensions. One may know, however, that the first rule should always take priority over the second when both apply. This can be encoded by adding the negation of the precondition of the first rule to the justification of the second rule. Formally, given rules δ_1 and δ_2, where

$$\delta_1 = \frac{\alpha_1 : \beta_1 \wedge \gamma_1}{\beta_1}, \qquad \delta_2 = \frac{\alpha_2 : \beta_2 \wedge \gamma_2}{\beta_2},$$

in order to establish δ_1 as being of higher priority than δ_2, replace δ_2 by δ_2':

$$\delta_2' = \frac{\alpha_2 : \beta_2 \wedge \gamma_2 \wedge \neg \alpha_1}{\beta_2}.$$

One kind of priority that this scheme can encode is the "specificity" ordering that intuitively should appear in an inheritance hierarchy. For example, W may include the fact that "penguins are birds",[1] and D defaults that assert that penguins don't fly, and that birds do fly. The first, more specific default can be given priority over the second by encoding the pair as

$$\frac{Penguin : \neg Fly}{\neg Fly}, \qquad \frac{Bird : Fly \wedge \neg Penguin}{Fly}.$$

3. Complexity

Following [8], we shall refer to a problem class as "tractable" if a polynomial-time algorithm can solve all its instances. It is not yet possible to prove that any of the problem classes considered in this paper require exponential time, but many are as hard as any solvable in polynomial time by a nondeterministic computer. Such "NP-hard" problems are considered to be intractable.

This paper only considers worst-case complexity. Since the problem instances that cause a particular algorithm to run the longest time may rarely arise, it would be useful to follow this worst-case analysis by some kind of

---

[1] It remains an open problem to determine if a default theory *must* include this assertion, although a survey of the literature lends strong evidence to the conjecture. Certainly it is true that every *paper* on nonmonotonic reasoning must include this example [5].

"average-case" analysis. Such an analysis would require some characterization of "average" commonsense theories—a significant task in its own right.

Nonetheless, this worst-case analysis is useful in revealing different sources of complexity in default reasoning, and in providing efficient algorithms for certain problem classes. For example, Section 5 includes a polynomial-time algorithm for computing extensions of the special class of ordered default theories. This algorithm is not necessarily correct for more general problem classes; on the other hand, the obvious general algorithm for computing extensions can take exponential time on an ordered theory. Once tractable algorithms are known for a number of useful classes of default theories, a general algorithm can be constructed that first tests to see if any of the special case algorithms apply, and if none does, invokes the intractable general method.

This paper uses the standard terminology of NP-completeness, which is summarized in Appendix A.

4. A taxonomy of default theories

Two sources of complexity in default theories are readily apparent: the inherent complexity of the first-order component (W), and the complexity of determining whether the justification of a default rule is consistent with the currently-derived set of formulas. We will restrict our attention to finite propositional theories in which W is simply a set (conjunction) of literals. The precondition, justification, and consequence of each default rule is also a conjunction of literals. We will call such a theory "disjunction-free" (abbreviated "DF"). Thus determining whether a default rule is applicable to W is trivial: the precondition must be a subset of W, and the intersection of W with the negation of each literal in the justification must be empty. The extended theory is again a set (conjunction) of literals. Although an extension is, by definition, an infinite, deductively closed set of formulas, any extension of a disjunction-free theory is equivalent to the deductive closure of a finite set of literals. Henceforth, when we speak of "computing an extension", we will mean computing such a finite set of literals.

The following functions access the components of default rules of this restricted form.

Definition 4.1 (pre, concl, just*, just). Where

$$\delta = \frac{a_1 \wedge \cdots \wedge a_l : b_1 \wedge \cdots \wedge b_m \wedge c_1 \wedge \cdots \wedge c_n}{b_1 \wedge \cdots \wedge b_m}$$

and none of the c_i are the same as any of the b_i, let

$$\text{pre}(\delta) = \{a_1, \ldots, a_l\},$$

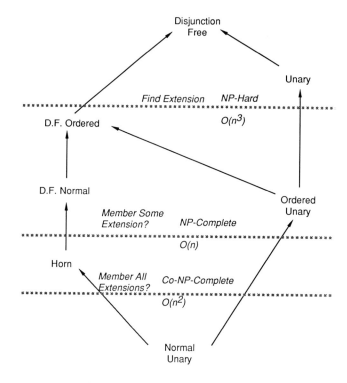

Fig. 1. The hierarchy of default theories.

$$\mathrm{concl}(\delta) = \{b_1, \ldots, b_m\},$$

$$\mathrm{just}^*(\delta) = \{c_1, \ldots, c_n\},$$

$$\mathrm{just}(\delta) = \mathrm{just}^*(\delta) \cup \mathrm{concl}(\delta).$$

Any inferential power such systems possess resides in the default rules; the only non-default inference rules that apply are negation elimination and conjunction-in and -out (to convert, e.g., $\{\alpha, \beta\}$ to $\alpha \wedge \beta$ and vice versa). The reader should remember, in particular, that because the default rules are in fact rules and not axioms, the principle of reasoning by cases does not apply. For example, given a theory with empty W and rules

$$\frac{p : q}{q}, \qquad \frac{\neg p : q}{q},$$

one may *not* conclude q.

Further restrictions on the form of the default rules leads to the hierarchy shown in Fig. 1. The black arrows lead from the more restricted classes to the more general classes. A negative complexity result (that is, a transformation from an NP-hard problem) for a class in the hierarchy applies also to all elements above it. A positive complexity result (that is, a polynomial-time

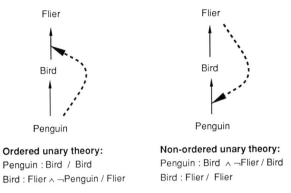

Ordered unary theory:
Penguin : Bird / Bird
Bird : Flier ∧ ¬Penguin / Flier

Non-ordered unary theory:
Penguin : Bird ∧ ¬Flier / Bird
Bird : Flier / Flier

Fig. 2. Ordered and unordered unary default theories.

algorithm) for a class applies also to all classes below it. The classes of theories are as follows:

- *Unary*: These theories restrict the prerequisite to a single letter and the consequence to a single literal. In the case of a positive consequence, the justification may include a single additional negative literal. Unary theories have a simple graphical notation, as shown in Fig. 2. Positive and negative default arcs appear, where optional cancel links may be attached to positive arcs. Note that only positive information enables or cancels the default. Unary theories are a simple example of the kind of graph-based representational systems inspired by Fahlman's work on NETL [7], and are a restricted case of Etherington's "network theories" [6, p. 91].

- *Disjunction-free ordered*: "Ordering" is a syntactic property of default theories developed in [6, p. 86] as a sufficient (but not necessary) condition for a theory to have an extension. The basic idea is to make sure that the application of a default rule can never enable another rule whose conclusion is inconsistent with the justification of the first rule. Formally, given a disjunction-free theory (D, W) and a set *lits* containing the literals in the theory, define $\ll$ and $\leqslant\!\!\!\!\!\leqslant$ to be the smallest relations over *lits* × *lits* such that

  - $\leqslant\!\!\!\!\!\leqslant$ is reflexive,
  - $\leqslant\!\!\!\!\!\leqslant$ is a superset of $\ll$,
  - $\ll$ and $\leqslant\!\!\!\!\!\leqslant$ are transitive,
  - $\ll$ is transitive through $\leqslant\!\!\!\!\!\leqslant$; that is, for literals x, y, and z in *lits*:

  $$[(x \ll y \wedge y \leqslant\!\!\!\!\!\leqslant z) \vee (x \leqslant\!\!\!\!\!\leqslant y \wedge y \ll z)] \supset x \ll z,$$

  - for every $\delta \in D$, and every $a \in \text{pre}(\delta)$, $b \in \text{concl}(\delta)$, and $c \in$

just*(δ):

$a \ll b$, $\sim c \ll b$.

Then (D, W) is ordered if and only if it contains no literal x such that $x \ll x$.[2] Ordered theories are quite expressive, but as we will see also have some nice computational properties. Later we will describe how ordering is a generalization of the notion of *stratification* in logic programming.

- *Ordered unary*: These theories have no cycles involving cancel arcs, as shown in Fig. 2. Of all the classes considered here, ordered unary theories possess the minimum amount of machinery necessary to represent inheritance hierarchies with some notion of priority between rules.
- *Disjunction-free normal*: Normal theories are formally well-behaved, and possess a resolution-based proof procedure. Normal theories are ordered.
- *Horn*: Horn clause non-default theories have proven useful for applications in databases and expert systems. Satisfiability of propositional Horn clauses can be determined in linear time [3]. Therefore in the search for "easy" default theories it is natural to consider default theories whose rules are similar in form to Horn clauses: the literals in the prerequisite are all positive, and the justification and consequence are the same single literal.
- *Normal unary*: This final category falls in the intersection of all the others. Its graphical representation contains only positive and negative default implication arcs. Normal unary theories can represent inheritance hierarchies with no "preemption strategy" between competing paths [16], but are more general, in that the graph need not be acyclic.

Table 1 summarizes the forms of the rules that appear in each kind of theory. In every case, the elements of a rule are optional. For example, the precondition of a rule may be empty.

5. Finding an extension

It is obvious that the question of whether a first-order default theory has an extension is undecidable, because the question of whether the justification of a rule is consistent with an extension is equally undecidable. In the case of disjunction-free theories, however, this consistency test, as well as the test that the precondition of a rule is satisfied, reduce to simple set operations.

---

[2]The definition of $\underset{\sim}{\ll}$ given in [6] does not require that relation to be reflexive or a superset of $\ll$. But the definitions agree on $\ll$, and on whether any particular theory is ordered or not.

Table 1
Forms of default rules in the various classes of theories

Unary	$p : q/q, \qquad p : q \wedge \neg r/p, \qquad p : \neg q/\neg q,$
Disjunction-free ordered	$a_1 \wedge \cdots \wedge a_l : b_1 \wedge \cdots \wedge b_m \wedge c_1 \wedge \cdots \wedge c_n / b_1 \wedge \cdots \wedge b_m$ and for no literal x is $x \ll x$
Ordered unary	$p : q/q, \qquad p : q \wedge \neg r/p, \qquad p : \neg q/\neg q,$ and for no literal x is $x \ll x$
Disjunction-free normal	$a_1 \wedge \cdots \wedge a_l : b_1 \wedge \cdots \wedge b_m / b_1 \wedge \cdots \wedge b_m$
Horn	$p_1 \wedge \cdots \wedge p_n : q/q$ $p_1 \wedge \cdots \wedge p_n : \neg q/\neg q$
Normal unary	$p : q/q, \qquad p : \neg q/\neg q$

Furthermore, the fact that the theories are finite allows an extension to be constructed by the application of one rule at a time. It is straightforward to rewrite the definition of an extension for this special case:

Lemma 5.1 (Extension of a disjunction-free theory). *Let (D, W) be a disjunction-free default theory. Then $\mathcal{E}$ is an extension of (D, W) if and only if there exists a sequence of rules $\delta_1, \delta_2, \ldots, \delta_n$ from D, and a series of sets $E_0, E_1, \ldots, E_n$ such that for all $i > 0$:*

$$E_0 = W,$$

$$E_i = E_{i-1} \cup \text{concl}(\delta_i),$$

$$\text{pre}(\delta_i) \subseteq E_{i-1},$$

$$\neg \exists c \in \text{just}(\delta_i) \, . \sim c \in E_n,$$

$$\neg \exists \delta \in D \, . \, \text{pre}(\delta) \subseteq E_n \wedge \text{concl}(\delta) \not\subseteq E_n$$
$$\wedge \neg \exists c \in \text{just}(\delta). \sim c \in E_n$$

and $\mathcal{E}$ is the deductive-closure of E_n.

This observation makes it possible to construct a nondeterministic algorithm to decide if a disjunction-free theory has an extension. The machine guesses an extension. It then tries to verify the extension by trying to construct it starting with W, and adding the conclusion of any rule whose precondition is contained in the current approximation and whose justification is consistent with the guessed extension. When the loop halts the guess is correct just in case the final approximation is the same as the extension. The first algorithm in Fig. 3 does just this. It takes as input not only the theory but two additional arguments, *In* and *Out*, which restrict

ND-Exists-Extension-Containing(In, Out, D, W)

    input: A disjunction-free theory (D,W) and sets of literals In and Out.

    output: "Yes" iff there exists an extension containing all of In
               but none of Out.

    Guess E, an arbitrary consistent superset of In disjoint from Out
    $E' := W$
    while $[\ \exists \delta \in D \,.\, \text{applicable}(\delta, E', E)\ ]$ **do**
      $E' := E' \cup \text{concl}(\delta)$
    if $[\ E' \neq E\ ]$
      then "no"
      else "yes"
end.

ND-Find-Extension(D, W)

    input: A disjunction-free theory (D,W).

    output: An extension of the theory, or "no" if there is none.

    if $[\neg \text{ ND-Exists-Extension-Containing}(\emptyset, \emptyset, D, W)\ ]$
      then return "no"
    $E := \emptyset$
    for $\delta \in D$ **do**
      if $[\text{ND-Exists-Extension-Containing}(E \cup \text{concl}(\delta), \emptyset, D, W)\ ]$
        then $E := E \cup \text{concl}(\delta)$
    return E
end.

Definitions:

    $\text{applicable}(\delta, E', E)$ iff
        (a) $\text{pre}(\delta) \subseteq E'$,
        (b) $\text{concl}(\delta) \not\subseteq E'$, and
        (c) $\neg \exists p \in \text{just}(\delta) \,.\, \sim p \in E$

Fig. 3. Nondeterministic algorithm to find an extension of a disjunction-free theory.

the extensions that can be guessed. The set operations performed in the subroutine **applicable** run in polynomial time, and in the worst case the inner loop cycles $|D|$ times and in each cycle $|D|$ or fewer rules are checked for applicability, so the algorithm also runs in nondeterministic polynomial time. Therefore the extension existence decision problem is in NP.

The second algorithm in the figure actually computes an extension, building it from the conclusions of rules one rule at a time. The In parameter of **ND-Exists-Extension-Containing** is passed to the current approximation together with the conclusion of the next rule under consideration. If the answer is "yes" then the conclusion is added to the approximation. The main loop in this algorithm iterates $|D|$ times, thus proving our first theorem:

Theorem 5.2. *The problem of computing an extension of a disjunction-free default theory (or determining that none exists) is NP-easy.*

So, finding an extension of a DF propositional theory is not harder than the hardest problem in NP. The question then becomes: is there a *deterministic* polynomial algorithm to compute an extension of a disjunction-free theory? Unless P is NP, the answer is no. In fact, 3SAT can be reduced to the extension existence problem for unary theories. Suppose σ is a formula in 3CNF. We can construct a default theory whose extension, if any, is a model of σ. Four sets of rules are needed. The first adds every letter or its negation to the "candidate" extension. The second adds special letters to stand for negative literals, since negative literals cannot appear in the preconditions of rules. The third group checks that every clause is satisfied. If the negation of every literal in some clause is present in the candidate extension, then a special "failure" letter $\mathcal{F}$ is added. The fourth group contains a special "killer" rule. The precondition of this rule is $\mathcal{F}$, but its conclusion, $\mathcal{Z}$, is inconsistent with the justification of the rule which added $\mathcal{F}$. This kind of "vicious cycle" undermines the candidate extension: it can't be a "real" extension after all! Thus, σ is satisfiable if and only if the theory has an extension; that is, when no sequence of applications of default rules can ever conclude $\mathcal{F}$.

The following makes this reduction precise.

Definition 5.3 (*Mappings from 3CNF to defaults*). Let σ be a propositional 3CNF formula. The function π maps each positive literal to itself, and each negative literal $\neg p$ to a new letter p'. Consider the following groups of default rules:

(A) for each letter p that appears in σ, the rules:

$$\frac{: p}{p}, \qquad \frac{: \neg p}{\neg p};$$

(B) for each letter p that appears in σ, the rules:

$$\frac{p : \neg p'}{\neg p'}, \qquad \frac{: p' \wedge \neg p}{p'};$$

(C)　for each clause $x \vee y \vee z$ of σ, the following three rules, where $\mathcal{F}_{xy}$, $\mathcal{F}_{xyz}$, $\mathcal{F}$, and $\mathcal{Z}$ are new letters:

$$\frac{\pi\,(\sim x) : \mathcal{F}_{xy} \wedge \neg \pi\,(y)}{\mathcal{F}_{xy}},$$

$$\frac{\mathcal{F}_{xy} : \mathcal{F}_{xyz} \wedge \neg \pi\,(z)}{\mathcal{F}_{xyz}},$$

$$\frac{\mathcal{F}_{xyz} : \mathcal{F} \wedge \neg \mathcal{Z}}{\mathcal{F}};$$

(D)　the single rule:

$$\frac{\mathcal{F} : \mathcal{Z}}{\mathcal{Z}}.$$

Thus we see that a 3CNF formula is satisfiable if and only if the default theory consisting of an empty W and a D made up of groups (A), (B), (C), and (D) has an extension. This proves the next theorem:

Theorem 5.4. *The problem of determining whether a unary default theory has an extension is NP-complete. The corresponding problem of computing a set of literals equivalent to an extension (or determining that none exists) is NP-hard.*

As noted earlier, ordered theories cannot fall victim to the kind of vicious cycle used in this reduction. In fact, the extension existence problem is trivial for ordered theories: they always have extensions. One might think that it is possible to construct an extension of an ordered theory by simply applying *any* rule which applies to W, then *any* rule which applies W and the conclusions of the first rule, and so on, until no rules apply. But this is not the case. Consider a theory containing an empty W and just two rules:

$$\delta_1 = \frac{: q \wedge \neg p}{q}, \qquad \delta_2 = \frac{: p}{p}.$$

The rule δ_1 applies to W, but there is no sequence of rule applications beginning with δ_1 that leads to an extension. Intuitively, δ_2 is of higher priority; that rule must be considered for application before δ_1. So what is needed is a way to derive a priority ordering on the *rules* of an ordered theory, given the ordering on its *literals*. The following definition does just that.

Ordered-Find-Extension (D, W)

    input: A disjunction-free ordered theory (D, W)
    output: An extension of the theory.

    Topologically sort D by $\prec$, so that $D[i]$ is the ith rule in the ordering
    $E := W$
    $i := 1$
    while $[\, i \le |D| \,]$ **do**
      if $[\, \text{applicable}(D[i], E, E) \,]$
        then
          begin
            $E := E \cup \text{concl}(D[i])$
            $i := 1$
          end
        else $i := i + 1$
    return E
end.

Fig. 4. Deterministic polynomial-time algorithm to find an extension of a disjunction-free ordered theory.

Definition 5.5 ($\prec$ *over* D). Let (D, W) be a disjunction-free ordered theory, and $\ll$ be defined over the literals of the theory as described above. Then for any $\delta_1, \delta_2 \in D$,

$$\delta_1 \prec \delta_2$$

if and only if

$$\exists b \in \text{concl}(\delta_1), \; c \in \text{just*}(\delta_2) \,.\, b \ll \sim c.$$

Lemma B.1 in the appendix proves that $\prec$ is in fact a partial order. In the example just given, the theory orders $q \ll p$, so that $\delta_2 \prec \delta_1$, as desired. One finds an extension by computing the partial order over the rules, topologically sorting the rules by the order, and then repeatedly firing the lowest ranked rule which is applicable. Figure 4 presents the algorithm, whose proof of correctness appears in Appendix B. The computationally most intensive part of the process turns out to be the transitive closure operation needed to compute $\ll$, which requires cubic time. This leads to the following theorem:

Theorem 5.6. *There is an* $O(n^3)$ *algorithm that finds an extension of a disjunction-free ordered theory, where n is the length of theory.*

This result is significant for several reasons. As we noted before, ordered unary theories can represent default inheritance hierarchies, as was demonstrated by [4]. This gives an efficient algorithm for finding some extension, that is, some consistent interpretation, of such inheritance hierarchies. This form of default inheritance has been called "credulous" reasoning by Touretzky et al. [18]. It is of further interest that the efficiency comes from ordering, and *not* from the fact that the theories are unary, *nor* from the fact that inheritance hierarchies are *completely* acyclic. The requirement that the graphical representation of the inheritance hierarchy be acyclic (a condition imposed by Touretzky [19] and followed in the literature ever since) is a sufficient condition for ordering, but is not necessary. For example, the theory containing just the rules

$$\frac{Penguin : \neg Flier}{\neg Flier}, \qquad \frac{Flier : \neg Penguin}{\neg Penguin}$$

is ordered, but would not be admitted by most definitions of an inheritance hierarchy.

This result is also important because of its relation to logic programming. It has been known for some time [2,12] that stratified logic programs (without "cut") can be mapped into default logic theories, by turning clauses of the form:

$$b \rightarrow a_1, \ldots, a_m, \neg c_1, \ldots, \neg c_n$$

into default rules of the form:

$$\frac{a_1 \wedge \cdots \wedge a_m : \neg c_1, \ldots, \neg c_n}{b}.$$

These rules are not semi-normal, and therefore not ordered. But it is not difficult to show that translation into rules of the form

$$\frac{a_1 \wedge \cdots \wedge a_m : b \wedge \neg c_1 \wedge \cdots \wedge \neg c_n}{b}$$

yields an ordered default theory with the same unique extension. Therefore we also have a polynomial algorithm for propositional stratified logic programming.

Although ordered theories are still quite expressive, some natural situations do map into unordered theories. Consider the "corrupt city government" example illustrated in Fig. 5. We are using default rules to represent the concept "most". This year, most Republican councilmen are running for office, as are most Democratic councilmen. Furthermore, most councilmen running for office are under indictment. The District Attorney is Democratic, and will push the cases against the Republicans much harder than the cases against the Democrats. Therefore most Republican councilmen who are under indictment are *not* running for office. This final condition is most

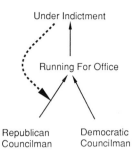

Fig. 5. An unordered default theory.

naturally represented by a justification on the default rule for Republicans running for office, that is,

$$\frac{Republican : Running \wedge \neg UnderIndictment}{Running}.$$

The alternative of making "not Republican" a justification on the "under indictment" rule would leave the theory ordered but would change the meaning of the theory. It is easy to verify that there are worlds where most Republicans who are running for office are under indictment, and yet most Republicans who are under indictment are not running for office.

In summary, finding an extension is tractable for ordered theories and intractable for the non-ordered ones considered in this paper, as shown by the top-most horizontal line in Fig. 1. Intractability is caused by the apparent need to consider all possible sequential orderings of rule applications to see if any do not lead to situations where the conclusion of an applicable rule contradicts the justification of a previously applied rule.

6. Membership in some extension

An extension can be thought of as a complete set of beliefs which is consistent with a given set of defaults. Often one is concerned, however, with the status of only a particular proposition. Asking if a proposition p is a member of *some* extension of a theory is equivalent to asking if it is *reasonable* to believe p; that is, whether there is a good argument for p. The same theory may provide good arguments for both p and $\neg p$; but the complementary literals must appear in different extensions.

Reiter [13] showed that p holds in some extension of a normal theory just in case there is a top-down default proof of p. (A top-down default proof is, roughly, a sequence of non-default proofs; the first proves the goal given W and the conclusions of some set of the default rules; the next proves the antecedents of those defaults, perhaps given the conclusions of another set of default rules; and so on, until a proof that only depends on W is reached.) As we noted above, Touretzky's notion of "credulous" reasoning is similar to finding an extension; he has no notion similar to determining membership in some extension.

The nondeterministic algorithm given in Fig. 3 that solves the generalized version of the extension existence decision problem also solves this problem. The function call

ND-Exists-Extension-Containing $(\{x\}, \emptyset, D, W)$

returns "yes" whenever x appears in some extension . Thus:

Theorem 6.1. *The problem of determining if a given literal appears in some extension of a disjunction-free theory is in NP.*

One might think that checking the status of a single literal is easier than computing an entire extension. Unfortunately, this is not the case. Default logic is "non-local" in the sense that to determine the status of any proposition, one must consider all interactions between all rules and axioms. Is the problem then of equivalent complexity to computing an extension? Surprisingly, the answer is again in general no. While finding an extension is tractable for ordered theories, determining membership in some extension is NP-complete. In fact, we will prove two stronger results, for two special cases of ordered theories: ordered unary and disjunction-free normal.

First, consider the ordered unary case. We will use a reduction like the one used in the proof of Theorem 5.4 above, but will eliminate the "killer" rule (D), which makes the theory unordered. Then we add the following rule, which makes sure that an extension contains a new letter $\mathcal{T}$ whenever it does *not* contain the "failure" letter $\mathcal{F}$:

$$\text{(E)} \quad \frac{: \mathcal{T} \wedge \neg \mathcal{F}}{\mathcal{T}}.$$

The reader can verify that the theory generated by applying mappings (A), (B), (C), and (E) to a 3CNF formula σ is ordered unary. Furthermore, σ is satisfiable if and only if this theory has an extension containing $\mathcal{T}$. Thus:

Theorem 6.2. *Determining if a given literal appears in some extension of an ordered unary theory is NP-complete.*

Next, consider the case of disjunction-free normal theories. Normal theories allow negative literals to appear in the precondition which simplifies the reduction. The default rules in set (A) again are used to guess a truth assignment. A second set of rules checks that each clause in σ is satisfied by the extension:

(F) Let $x_i \vee y_i \vee z_i$ stand for the ith clause of σ. Then for each clause i in σ, the following three rules appear, where T_i is a new letter:

$$\frac{x_i : T_i}{T_i}, \qquad \frac{y_i : T_i}{T_i}, \qquad \frac{z_i : T_i}{T_i}.$$

The third group contains a single rule which simply checks that every clause is simultaneously satisfied; that is, that some extension contains all of the T_i:

(G) where n is the number of clauses in σ, the rule:

$$\frac{T_1 \wedge T_2 \wedge \cdots \wedge T_n : T}{T}.$$

A 3CNF clause σ is satisfiable if and only if the theory given by mappings (A), (F), and (G) has an extension containing T. In other words:

Theorem 6.3. *Determining if a given literal appears in some extension of a disjunction-free normal default theory is NP-complete.*

These reductions demonstrate that in order to determine if a literal appears in some extension it is generally necessary (unless P is NP) to search through *all* possible extensions. This should give pause to those who would consider using default rules to extend ordinary backward-chaining theorem proving, as suggested in Reiter's original paper. Default rules can expand the search space exponentially. If the theorem prover chains backward from the given goal, applying default rules as needed, it can reach a state where some "wrong" default has been applied earlier on, which blocks completion of the proof. The system cannot be sure that there is *no* default proof until it tries all different sequences of the defaults.

Is there any interesting class of default theories which does admit a tractable algorithm? Recall that the preconditions of Horn default rules contain only positive literals. This means that no default rule is enabled by applying a different rule which has a negative conclusion. Therefore, in order to construct a default proof of a positive literal p, you do not need to consider any rules with negative conclusions. Because the justification and conclusions of the remaining rules are all positive, none of them can be mutually inconsistent. It is never necessary to "undo" the application of a default rule during the attempt to prove p. The situation where the literal to be tested is negative differs only in that one also uses a rule whose conclusion is the negative goal literal itself.

The following lemma (whose proof appears in Appendix B) shows how to translate the membership problem for Horn default theories into a deduction problem for a consistent classical Horn theory, but eliminating some of the negative default rules.

Lemma 6.4. *Where* (D, W) *is a Horn default theory and* x *is a literal, let* H *be the following Horn theory:*

$$H = W \cup \left\{ \alpha \supset y \;\middle|\; \begin{array}{l} \alpha : y/y \in D \text{ and} \\ \sim y \notin W \text{ and} \\ [(y \neq \sim x \text{ and } y \text{ is positive}) \text{ or } y = x] \end{array} \right\}$$

Then x *appears in some extension of* (D, W) *iff* $H \vdash x$.

By the results of [3] the problem of determining if a literal follows from a propositional Horn theory can be solved in $O(n)$ time, where n is the length of the theory. The translation can also be done in linear time, so therefore:

Theorem 6.5. *There is an* $O(n)$ *algorithm which determines if a given literal appears in any extension of a Horn default theory, where* n *is the length of the theory.*

Horn default theories may have some practical applications in artificial intelligence, as a language for logic programming with default information. It would be useful to let W contain Horn clauses, instead of simply a set of literals, so that both default and non-default information could be represented. Unfortunately, Stillman [17] shows that this extension makes the membership decision problem NP-complete.

The middle horizontal line in Fig. 1 summarizes the results of this section. Horn and normal unary theories are tractable, and the others intractable.

7. Skeptical reasoning

The final kind of reasoning we examine is determining if a proposition holds in all extensions of a theory. This task has been called "skeptical" reasoning in the inheritance literature [18], because it is the most cautious form of default inference. Intuitively, one may skeptically conclude p only when p appears in all sets of beliefs which are consistent with the default axioms. Skeptical reasoning possesses several attractive properties absent from the other two tasks. First, the set of skeptical conclusions of a theory is closed under ordinary logical deduction, and the composition of this set is fixed for any given theory. This leads to the practical advantage of allowing decomposition in problem solving. For example, a system could employ several processors to compute different parts of the set of skeptical conclusions of a theory in parallel. The answers returned by the processors could be simply conjoined. If the processors were computing what held in different arbitrary extensions, however, it would not make sense to conjoin their answers. Second, the conclusions of skeptical reasoning often match our intuitions more closely than the conclusions reached by the other methods. Consider a case where our default knowledge is truly ambiguous; suppose we believe that berries are by default edible, green fruit is by default poisonous, and we encounter a green berry. It seems more reasonable to withhold judgement until more information is gathered, rather than jump to an arbitrary conclusion, which could leave us either hungry or poisoned. [3] Finally, skeptical reasoning provides the strongest notion of consistency. If the non-default part of the theory is consistent, then one cannot skeptically conclude both p and $\neg p$. On the other hand, there may be *some* extension containing p, and *some other* extension containing $\neg p$.

Note that skeptical reasoning cannot be defined in terms of the test for membership in some extension; that is, one cannot skeptically affirm p if no extension contains $\neg p$. This is because some extensions may contain neither p nor $\neg p$.

Skeptical reasoning falls in the class co-NP, rather than NP. The nondeterministic algorithm for the generalized extension existence problem solves this problem as well. To determine if every extension of a theory contains a literal x, we ask if there is any which does not contain x. That is, if

ND-Exists-Extension-Containing $(\emptyset, \{x\}, D, W)$

returns "yes", then the answer is "no, x does not appear in all extensions".

Theorem 7.1. *The problem of determining if a given literal appears in every extension of a disjunction-free theory is in co-NP.*

One might expect the complexity results for skeptical reasoning to mirror those for the membership problem. Indeed, just as membership in some extension is NP-complete for ordered unary theories, membership in all extensions is co-NP-complete for those theories. The reduction uses the rules in groups (A), (B), and (C) from the analysis of the extension existence problem. Recall that these rules were set up to assert the "failure" letter $\mathcal{F}$ just in case the potential extension did not satisfy the 3CNF formula σ. In other words, σ is unsatisfiable if and only if $\mathcal{F}$ appears in all extensions of the theory containing just those rules. This shows that:

Theorem 7.2. *Determining if a given literal appears in every extension of an ordered unary theory is co-NP-complete.*

---

[3]As we will see below, skeptical reasoning is computationally the most demanding form of default reasoning, so in practice one would like to have some idea of the "cost" of jumping to the wrong conclusion in order to be able to decide what default reasoning strategy is most appropriate.

The analogy between membership in all and in some extensions breaks down, however, when we come to the class of Horn theories. We were able to obtain a polynomial algorithm for testing membership in some extension by throwing out all the default rules with negative conclusions (except those which matched the literal to be tested). This cannot be done when one wants to know if a literal holds in all extensions. We need to consider extensions which contain neither the literal nor its negation; extensions where all proofs of the literal are blocked by the application of rules with negative conclusions. Appendix B includes the proof of the following theorem:

Theorem 7.3. *Determining if a given literal appears in every extension of a Horn default theory is co-NP-complete.*

Intuitively, it is harder to find extensions which leave the truth value of a letter undecided than it is to find ones which assign it true or false. This theorem also illustrates the tradeoff between "caution" and speed in default reasoning: the most conservative kind of reasoning in default logic is also the most complex. The next section of this paper includes a general proof of this observation.

The difficulty in devising complete and tractable algorithms for this kind of skeptical reasoning has led some researchers to suppose that any formulation of reasoning based on an intersection of extensions is intractable. (In particular, the polynomial form of skeptical reasoning developed in [9] is *not* correct according to an intersection of extensions or expansions semantics. Whether it is correct according to our intuitions is, of course, another matter.) An example which demonstrates this point is a version of the "extended Nixon diamond", shown in Fig. 6. Nixon inherits from "Voter" in all three extensions, but through Republican in one, Quaker in the other, and both in the third. (Note that in the default logic formulation, unlike in Touretzky's "path-based" system, no special status given to the links that

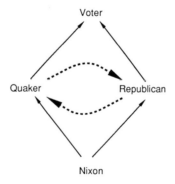

Fig. 6. The extended Nixon diamond.

lead directly out of a leaf node such as Nixon. Touretzky treats such links as representing strict implications, rather than as defaults.)

This problem and others like it can be encoded entirely in a normal unary theory. We have devised the first sound and complete polynomial algorithm for skeptical reasoning in this logic. We will illustrate the central idea behind the algorithm by first considering the restricted case where W is empty, and the literal to be tested is positive. A polynomial algorithm for this case is given in Fig. 7. To determine if a proposition p holds in all extensions, the algorithm attempts to find a complete set of literals containing $\neg p$ which is consistent with some extension that does not contain p.

The reader may gain some understanding of the **Normal-Unary-All-Extensions-Pos** algorithm by "running" it on the extended Nixon diamond example. The set of rules D, where each proposition is abbreviated by its initial letter, is:

$$\frac{n:r}{r}, \qquad \frac{n:q}{q},$$

$$\frac{r:\neg q}{\neg q}, \qquad \frac{q:\neg r}{\neg r},$$

$$\frac{r:v}{v}, \qquad \frac{q:v}{v}.$$

Rather than including n in W, we will simply add a default rule which always adds n. Since no rule adds $\neg n$, this yields exactly the same set of extensions,

$$\frac{:n}{n}.$$

We wish to determine if v holds in all extensions. The three extensions of the theory are:

$$\mathcal{E}_1 \equiv \{n, r, q, v\},$$

$$\mathcal{E}_2 \equiv \{n, r, \neg q, v\},$$

$$\mathcal{E}_3 \equiv \{n, \neg r, q, v\}.$$

Therefore we expect the algorithm to return "yes".

The complete set of literals L is initially set to

$$L_1 = \{n, r, q, \neg v\}.$$

L_1 is positive consistent, and all its elements are grounded. However, $(r, \neg v)$ is negative inconsistent, because a rule with precondition r adds v, and no rule whose precondition holds in L adds $\neg v$. So r is replaced by $\neg r$, yielding the next version of L:

$$L_2 = \{n, \neg r, q, \neg v\}.$$

Normal-Unary-All-Extensions-Pos (p_k, D)

    input: Positive literal p_k and a set D of normal unary
          defaults containing letters $p_1, \ldots, p_n$.
    output: "Yes" iff every extension of $(D, \emptyset)$ contains p_k.

    $L := \{p_1, p_2, \ldots, \neg p_k, \ldots, p_n\}$
    while [pos-consistent (L, D)] **do**
      if [exists $p, \neg q$ in L such that
           ((NOT grounded (p, L, D))
             OR neg-inconsistent $(p, \neg q, L, D)$)]
        then $L := (L - \{p\}) \cup \{\neg p\}$
        else return "no"
    return "yes"
end.

Definitions:

    fixed-pos (p, L, D) iff
          (a) $: p/p \in D$,
          (b) $: \neg p/\neg p \notin D$, and
          (c) $\neg q \in L$, for each rule $q : \neg p/\neg p \in D$
    pos-consistent (L, D) iff
          for all p, if fixed-pos (p, L, D), then $p \in L$
    grounded (p, L, D) iff
          exists a sequence $q_0, q_1, \ldots, q_k = p$ such that
             (a) $q_j \in L$, $0 \le j \le k$,
             (b) $: q_0/q_0 \in D$, and
             (c) $q_{j-1} : q_j/q_j \in D$, $1 \le j \le k$
    neg-inconsistent $(p, \neg q, L, D)$ iff
          (a) p and $\neg q \in L$
          (b) $p : q/q \in D$,
          (c) $: \neg q/\neg q \notin D$, and
          (d) $\neg r \in L$, for each rule $r : \neg q/\neg q \in D$

Fig. 7. Skeptical reasoning algorithm with a positive literal and a set of normal unary defaults as input.

Now the algorithm notices that $(q, \neg v)$ is negative inconsistent, so q is replaced:

$$L_3 = \{n, \neg r, \neg q, \neg v\}.$$

But now $(n, \neg r)$ is negative inconsistent, so n must be replaced by $\neg n$.

$$L_4 = \{\neg n, \neg r, \neg q, \neg v\}.$$

L_4 is not positive consistent, because n is fixed positive. Therefore the algorithm returns "yes"; v holds in all extensions.

An algorithm for the more general case of normal unary skeptical reasoning appears in Fig. 8. It transforms the input theory to the simpler case by replacing literals in W by new rules (as in the example above) and by substituting a new letter for a negative query. A proof of correctness and a complexity analysis of the two algorithms appears in Appendix B. Thus:

Theorem 7.4. *Given a normal unary theory and a literal x, the* **Normal-Unary-All-Extensions algorithm** *returns "yes" if and only if every extension of the theory contains x. The time complexity of the algorithm is* $\mathrm{O}(n^2)$, *where n is the length of the theory.*

In summary, all kinds of skeptical reasoning other than for normal unary theories are intractable, as shown by the lowest horizontal line in Fig. 1. Stein [16] uses normal unary theories to capture so-called "ideally skeptical" inheritance, which is default inheritance without priorities. Thus, our algorithm can be directly applied to handle this, very conservative, form of inheritance. It remains to be seen if there are interesting practical applications of this kind of reasoning.

Normal-Unary-All-Extensions (x, D, W)

    input: A literal x and a normal unary theory (D, W).

    output: "Yes" iff every extension of the theory contains x.

    $D' := \{\delta \in D \mid \sim \mathrm{concl}(\delta) \notin W\} \cup \{: y/y \mid y \in W\}$
    if [x is a positive literal]
      then Normal-Unary-All-Extensions-Pos(x, D')
    else
      begin
        Let p be a new letter
        $D'' := D' \cup \{\mathrm{pre}(\delta) : p/p \mid \delta \in D' \text{ and } \mathrm{concl}(\delta) = \{x\}\}$
                 $\cup \{\mathrm{pre}(\delta) : \neg p/\neg p \mid \delta \in D' \text{ and } \mathrm{concl}(\delta) = \{\sim x\}\}$
        Normal-Unary-All-Extensions-Pos(p, D'')
      end
end.

Fig. 8. Algorithm to determine if a literal holds in all extensions of a normal unary theory.

8. Comparing the reasoning tasks

The complexity results for the specific classes of default theories we considered showed that the task of finding an extension is no harder than determining if a literal holds in some extension of a theory, which in turn is no harder than skeptical reasoning. This section develops general results that show this is true for very broad classes of disjunction-free theories. (These general theorems do not make the previous results redundant; the results limited to the specific classes are stronger.)

First we compare finding an extension to determining if a literal holds in some extension. The first algorithm presented in Fig. 9 reduces the former problem to the latter. The algorithm works by maintaining an approximation to an extension in the variable E. It creates a new default rule whose precondition is the conjunction of all the literals in E, and whose conclusion is a new letter p. The oracle **Some-Extension** determines that some extension of the original theory augmented with this new rule contains p just when some extension of the original theory contains all of E. The main loop of the algorithm makes E maximal, by trying to add each literal to it.

Reduction-Find-To-Some(D, W)

    input: A disjunction-free theory (D, W).

    output: An extension of the theory, or "no" if there is none.

    Let p be a propositional letter not appearing in (D, W)
    if [$\neg$Some-Extension$(p, D \cup \{: p/p\}, W)$]
        then return "no"
    $E := \emptyset$
    for each literal x **do**
      if [Some-Extension$(p, D \cup \{\bigwedge E \wedge x : p/p\}, W)$]
        then $E := E \cup \{x\}$
    return E
end.

Reduction-Some-To-All(x, D, W)

    input: A disjunction-free theory (D, W).

    output: "Yes" if (D, W) has an extension containing x, otherwise "no".

    if [All-Extensions$(\sim x, (D \cup \{: \neg x/\neg x\}, W)$]
      then "no"
      else "yes"
end.

Fig. 9. Turing reductions of reasoning tasks.

Note that a disjunction-free normal default rule is added to the theory. A requirement of this reduction is therefore that the class of default theories under consideration be closed under the addition of such rules. Note that this reduction is not too surprising given our earlier result which showed that the membership question is NP-complete for disjunction-free normal theories.

Theorem 8.1. *For any class of disjunction-free theories that is closed under the addition of a single disjunction-free normal default rule, the problem of finding an extension is Turing-reducible to the problem of determining whether a given literal appears in some extension.*

The second algorithm in Fig. 9 reduces membership in some extension to membership in all extensions. Where x is the literal to be tested, the reduction adds a new default rule with no precondition whose conclusion is $\sim x$. This rule can only fail to be applied to an extension which contains x. Therefore, we see that some extension of the original theory contains x if and only if it is not the case that every extension of the modified theory contains $\sim x$. This reduction applies to any class of theories closed under the addition of the new default rule, which can be characterized as follows:

Theorem 8.2. *For any class of default theories that is closed under the addition of a rule of the form $: \sim x / \sim x$, determining if a given literal appears in some extension is Turing-reducible to the task of determining whether a given literal appears in all extensions.*

These reductions can be used to derive complexity results for classes of default theories not specifically examined in this paper. For example, by Theorem 8.1, any NP-completeness result for the problem of finding an extension will carry over to that of membership in some extension, provided the class of theories under consideration is disjunction-free and closed under the addition of the simple default specified above. Going in the other direction, a polynomial algorithm for finding an extension can be obtained from one for membership in some extension.

The second reduction is even more general, and even applies to infinite and first-order theories. Any lower bound result, such as NP-hardness, PSPACE-completeness, undecidability, and so on, carries over from the problem of membership in some to membership in all extensions. Likewise, a polynomial algorithm or decision procedure for skeptical reasoning immediately gives one for membership in some extension.

9. Conclusions

We have examined a wide range of simple default theories and have uncovered some surprising worst-case complexity results. The problems of deduction and consistency checking are not the only source of difficulties in reasoning with defaults. In the study of finding an extension, the source of complexity can be characterized as the problem of detecting incoherent cycles in the rules, which make it hard to detect if a sequence of rule applications is actually leading toward an extension. In the membership problems, the source of complexity can be characterized as the exponential number of different extensions that can be generated by a set of defaults. One can think of the rules as specifying a nondeterministic computation, and the test for membership of a literal in some or all extensions as picking out a successful computation, or determining that there are none.

Yet we also developed a number of interesting positive results. We presented a polynomial algorithm to find an extension of a propositional ordered theory, and these theories appear to have many uses in AI and logic programming. In particular, this class includes "credulous" reasoning in default inheritance hierarchies, but is strictly more general, in that rules may have any number of positive literals in the preconditions, and the graphic form of rules may include (certain kinds of) cycles. As noted earlier, the syntactic constraints traditionally placed on inheritance hierarchies do not correspond to the constraints actually needed for efficient reasoning. Ordered theories also subsume stratified logic programs, but allow both negative and positive literals to appear anywhere in a rule.

Horn default theories nicely generalize classical Horn theories and retain linear complexity for the problem of membership in some extension. Finally, we developed the first polynomial algorithm for determining the contents of the intersection of all extensions of a default theory—albeit a very restricted class of theories.

Last but not least, the general reductions between the reasoning tasks suggest how default logic may be most efficiently used in problem solving. The riskiest, most credulous form of default reasoning is also the fastest. At least in the propositional case, it is possible to construct an efficient problem solver which simply applies all its default rules to an input problem description, forward-chaining to a complete extension. The abundance of detail in the extension would, one might hope, simplify or trivialize further inference. This is the use of defaults suggested by Levesque in his proposal for "vivid reasoning" [10].

Reiter identified the notion of a "default logic proof" with determining if a formula held in some extension of a theory. The much greater complexity of the problem of determining membership in some extension over finding an arbitrary extension indicates that great care will be needed in augmenting traditional backward-chaining theorem provers with default rules, in order to not fall victim to an exponential expansion of the search space.

Finally, the most conservative use of default logic, skeptical reasoning, may prove too computationally intensive for any application. If default logic is your tool of choice, and you are concerned with the complexity of inference, it appears that you should design your theory so that any extension in fact yields a reasonable set of conclusions, and you should not depend on taking an intersection of extensions to filter out the good from the bad.

Appendix A. Terminology of NP-completeness

For an introduction to the theory of NP-completeness, see [8]. The class *NP* consists of decision problems (ones whose solution is either "yes" or "no") that can be solved by a nondeterministic algorithm that given a problem instance (1) guesses a data structure and (2) deterministically checks in polynomial time whether the answer is "yes" or "no". The algorithm is said to solve the problem if and only if for any "yes"-instance of the decision problem, there exists a data structure that leads to a "yes" answer after checking; whereas for any "no"-instance of the problem, no such structure exists. An *NP-complete* problem is a member of an NP to which *any* problem in NP can be transformed in polynomial time. A problem is in *co-NP* if its complement is in NP, and any such problem can be transformed in polynomial time into a *co-NP-complete* problem. A problem (not necessarily a decision problem) is *NP-hard* if an NP-complete problem can be solved by a deterministic polynomial algorithm that employs an oracle that solves the NP-hard problem. Conversely, a problem is *NP-easy* if it can be solved by a deterministic polynomial algorithm that employs an oracle that solves a problem in NP. Hence an NP-easy problem is essentially "no harder" than any problem in NP. (That is, if $P = \mathrm{NP}$, then any NP-easy problem is polynomial. But in terms of the complexity hierarchy, NP-easy properly includes both NP and co-NP.)

The NP-complete problem *3SAT* is that of determining the satisfiability of a conjunction of three-element clauses in propositional logic (*3CNF*); that is, of a formula of the form:

$$\sigma = (x_1 \vee y_1 \vee z_1) \wedge (x_2 \vee y_2 \vee z_2) \wedge \cdots.$$

The corresponding co-NP-complete problem is determining the unsatisfiability of such a formula.

Appendix B. Proofs

Proof of Lemma 5.1 (Sketch). It is easy to see that the lemma's definition of an extension is equivalent to the original definition (presented in Section 2) if the logical closure operation is applied to the E's on the right-hand side of the expressions in the lemma. For example, $\sim c \in E_n$ becomes $\sim c \in \mathrm{Th}(E_n)$. The original definition allows the application of a number of defaults at each step, while the lemma effectively stretches the applications out into a single sequence. The difference is not significant for finite propositional theories. (The lemma fails for infinite theories, because there may not be any maximal n.)

Let E be a set of literals and x a single literal. Observe that if E is consistent, then $x \in E$ if and only if $x \in \mathrm{Th}(E)$. Furthermore, if W is a consistent set of literals, then applications of semi-normal default rules will maintain consistency. Therefore the definitions are equivalent for consistent disjunction-free theories. On the other hand, if W is an inconsistent set of literals, then both by the lemma and by the original definition the inconsistent theory $\mathrm{Th}(W)$ is the unique extension. So the definitions are fully equivalent for disjunction-free theories.

Note that the lemma fails for non-semi-normal finite propositional theories containing no disjunctions. This is because the application of a non-semi-normal default rule to a consistent set of literals can yield an inconsistent set. $\square$

Lemma B.1. *The relation $\prec$ as defined over D in a disjunction-free ordered theory is a partial order.*

Proof. We show that $\prec$ is transitive and irreflexive over D.

(*transitive*) Suppose $\delta_1 \prec \delta_2$ and $\delta_2 \prec \delta_3$. Then in must be the case that

$$\exists b_1 \in \mathrm{concl}(\delta_1), c_2 \in \mathrm{just}^*(\delta_2) \,.\, b_1 \ll \sim c_2,$$

$$\exists b_2 \in \mathrm{concl}(\delta_2), c_3 \in \mathrm{just}^*(\delta_3) \,.\, b_2 \ll \sim c_3.$$

The rule δ_2 induces the literal ordering

$$\sim c_2 \ll b_2.$$

So $b_1 \ll \sim c_3$, which entails that $\delta_1 \prec \delta_3$.

(*irreflexive*) Suppose it were the case that $\delta \prec \delta$. Then it must be the case that

$$\exists b \in \mathrm{concl}(\delta), c \in \mathrm{just}^*(\delta) \,.\, b \ll \sim c.$$

But this rule induces the literal ordering

$$\sim c \ll b$$

which would imply that $b \ll b$, violating the definition of an ordered theory.

Proof of Theorem 5.6.

(*correctness*) Let E_{FINAL} be the value returned by **Ordered-Find-Extension**(D, W). We claim that the following assertion is true at the end of the **then** clause in the algorithm:

$$\neg \exists c \in \text{just}(D[i]) . \sim c \in E_{\text{FINAL}}.$$

Correctness of the algorithm follows immediately from this assertion and Lemma 5.1.

So suppose the assertion were false. Let E_j represent the value of the variable E after cycle j of the outer loop, and $D[i_j]$ be the rule selected by the **if** statement in cycle j. Suppose the assertion fails when $j = j_0$. Plainly $c \notin \text{concl}(D[i_{j_0}])$, so

$$c \in \text{just*}(D[i_{j_0}])$$

and there must be some $j_1 > j_0$ such that for $j = j_1$,

$$\sim c \in \text{concl}(D[i_{j_1}]).$$

Then by the definition of $\prec$,

$$D[i_{j_1}] \prec D[i_{j_0}]$$

because $\sim c \underset{\approx}{\ll} \sim c$. This implies that

$$i_{j_1} \ll i_{j_0}.$$

Now suppose that $\text{pre}(D[i_{j_1}]) \subseteq E_{(j_0-1)}$. Then the inner loop in cycle j_0 should choose $D[i_{j_1}]$ rather than $D[i_{j_0}]$. But since this is not the case, there must exist some literal a such that

$$a \in \text{pre}(D[i_{j_1}]), \qquad a \notin E_{(j_0-1)}.$$

This a must have been added in either cycle j_0 or in some cycle which follows j_0. First, consider the possibility that a is added in cycle j_0. In that case, $a \in \text{concl}(D[i_{j_0}])$ and thus $\sim c \ll a$. Also, since $a \in \text{pre}(D[i_{j_1}])$ and $\sim c \in \text{concl}(D[i_{j_1}])$, we have that $a \underset{\approx}{\ll} \sim c$. Thus, $\sim c \ll \sim c$, which contradicts the fact that our theory is ordered. Therefore, a must have been added in some cycle j_2 which follows j_0 and precedes j_1:

$$j_0 < j_2 < j_1.$$

Note that $D[i_{j_2}] \prec D[i_{j_0}]$ because

$$a \underset{\approx}{\ll} \sim c, \qquad a \in \text{concl}(D[i_{j_2}]), \qquad c \in \text{just*}(D[i_{j_0}]).$$

Now by the previous argument $\mathrm{pre}(D[i_{j_2}]) \not\subseteq E_{(j_0-1)}$, so there must be some literal a' such that

$$a' \in \mathrm{pre}(D[i_{j_2}]), \qquad a' \notin E_{(j_0-1)}.$$

Again, we can show that a' cannot have been added in cycle j_0. For suppose it was. Then, $a' \in \mathrm{concl}(D[i_{j_0}])$ and thus $\sim c \ll a'$. Also, since $a' \in \mathrm{pre}(D[i_{j_2}])$ and $a \in \mathrm{concl}(D[i_{j_2}])$, we have that $a' \ll a$, and, again from $D[i_{j_1}]$, we have $a \ll \sim c$. Thus, $\sim c \ll \sim c$, which contradicts the fact that our theory is ordered. Therefore, a must have been added by some rule $D[i_{j_3}]$ which fires at a cycle j_3, where

$$j_0 < j_3 < j_2 < j_1.$$

As before, $D[i_{j_3}] \prec D[i_{j_0-1}]$ and $\mathrm{pre}(D[i_{j_3}]) \not\subseteq E_{j_0}$. The argument can be repeated any number of times, leading to an infinite sequence

$$j_0 < \cdots < j_4 < j_3 < j_2 < j_1.$$

But since there are a finite number of rules in D, this is impossible.

(*complexity*) Let us suppose that the propositional letters of the input are represented by the odd integers 1 through $m-1$, and the corresponding negative literals by the integers 2 through m. Note that $n \leq m \leq 2n$, where n is the length of the theory. The variable E is represented by a vector of length m, with $E[i] = 1$ when the literal represented by i is in E. The precondition, justification (just*), and conclusion of each default rule is stored as a list of integers.

The first task is to compute the ordering $\ll$ on the literals. This relation can be stored in an $m \times m$ table, with entry (i, j) equal to 1 just in case literal $i \ll$ literal j. The table is first set to all 0's except for the diagonal (i, i) which is set to all 1's (because $\ll$ is reflective), in $\mathrm{O}(m^2)$ steps. Next the constraints derived from each default rule ($a \ll b$ and $\sim c \ll b$) initialize the table. The constraints on $\ll$ induced by each rule δ can be calculated in $|\delta|^2$ time, so the initialization step requires the following time:

$$\sum_{i=1}^{|D|} |\delta_i|^2 \leq \left(\sum_{i=1}^{|D|} |\delta_i|\right)^2 \leq n^2.$$

Finally the transitive closure of $\ll$ is taken in $\mathrm{O}(m^3)$ time [1]. Thus this task requires $\mathrm{O}(m^2 + n^2 + m^3) = \mathrm{O}(n^3)$ time.

The next task is to compute the ordering $\prec$ on default rules. For each pair of rules, compare each literal in the conclusion of the first rule with each literal in the proper justification (just*) of the second rule. This takes the following time:

$$
\sum_{i,j=1}^{|D|} |\delta_i||\delta_j| = \sum_{i=1}^{|D|} |\delta_i| \left(\sum_{j=1}^{|D|} |\delta_j| \right)
$$
$$
\leq \sum_{i=1}^{|D|} |\delta_i| n = n \sum_{i=1}^{|D|} |\delta_i| \leq n^2.
$$

The result of this task is a list of length less than $|D|^2$ describing the relation $\prec$.

Now we come to the proper algorithm. The topological sort of D is linear in the number of rules plus the number of pairs describing $\leqslant$. So the sort is $\mathrm{O}(|D| + |D|^2)$ or more simply $\mathrm{O}(n^2)$.

Checking that rule $D[i]$ is applicable to E takes $|D[i]|$ time. Checking all the rules to find an applicable one takes

$$
\sum_{i=1}^{|D|} |D[i]| \leq n
$$

steps. Each rule applies at most once, so this check has to be performed at most $|D|$ times. Therefore all the calls to **applicable** require $\mathrm{O}(|D|n) = \mathrm{O}(n^2)$ time. Each union of E with $\mathrm{concl}(D[i])$ also takes $|D[i]|$ time, and again this step is performed at most $|D|$ times, so again the time is $\mathrm{O}(n^2)$.

The total time for the algorithm is therefore $\mathrm{O}(n^3 + n^2 + n^2) = \mathrm{O}(n^3)$. It is interesting to note that the most expensive part of the algorithm is taking the transitive closure of the literal ordering. □

Proof of Lemma 6.4.

($\Rightarrow$) Suppose x appears in some extension $\mathcal{E}$ of (D, W). By Lemma 5.1 there are a finite number of approximations E_i to $\mathcal{E}$. Let E_j be the lowest numbered approximation such that $x \in E_j$. If $j = 0$ then $x \in W$ so of course $H \vdash x$. Otherwise $x \in \mathrm{concl}(\delta_j)$ which implies that $\mathrm{pre}(\delta_j) \supset x \in H$. It is apparent from the construction of E_j that one can extract a forest of default rules all with positive conclusions rooted at $\mathrm{pre}(\delta_j)$ and with leaves in W. All of the Horn clauses corresponding to these rules must be in H as well. Then this forest together with δ_j constitutes a proof of x from H.

($\Leftarrow$) Suppose $H \vdash x$. Note that H must be consistent; therefore there exists a linear resolution style proof tree T of x from H. Traverse T in an order with visits a node after visiting all of its children; the result is a linearization of the Horn clauses used in the proof of x. Eliminate any clause which appears in W or earlier in the sequence. Replace each clause by the corresponding default rule which generates it. It is clear then that the resulting sequence is a prefix of a sequence of rules whose application to W leads to an extension containing x. □

Proof of Theorem 7.3. An arbitrary 3CNF formula σ is unsatisfiable if and only if $\mathcal{F}$ holds in every extension of the theory containing rules in groups (H), (I), and (J) below:

(H) for each letter p which appears in σ, with $p' = \pi(p)$, the four rules:

$$\frac{:p}{p}, \qquad \frac{:p'}{p'}, \qquad \frac{p':\neg p}{\neg p}, \qquad \frac{:\neg p'}{\neg p'};$$

(I) likewise for each letter p, the following rule, where $\mathcal{F}$ is a new letter:

$$\frac{p \wedge p' : \mathcal{F}}{\mathcal{F}};$$

(J) for each clause $x \vee y \vee z$ of σ, the rule:

$$\frac{\pi(\sim x) \wedge \pi(\sim y) \wedge \pi(\sim z) : \mathcal{F}}{\mathcal{F}}.$$

We prove the equivalent statement, that σ is satisfiable if and only if some extension does not contain $\mathcal{F}$.

(*if*) Let $\mathcal{E}$ be an extension not containing $\mathcal{F}$. By the rules in group (H), for any letter p, every extension contains either $\{p, p'\}$, $\{p, \neg p'\}$, or $\{\neg p, p'\}$. Since none of the rules in group (I) applied in $\mathcal{E}$, the first alternative never occurred for any p. Thus p' can be taken to stand for $\neg p$. Thus the fact that no rule in group (J) could have applied in $\mathcal{E}$ means that one of the literals in each clause of σ appeared in $\mathcal{E}$. So $\mathcal{E}$ is a model for σ, and σ is satisfiable.

(*only if*) Suppose M is a truth assignment for σ. Let $\mathcal{E}$ be the deductive closure of the set of literals which hold in M, together with p' or $\neg p'$ for every literal $\neg p$ or p respectively which holds in M. Then $\mathcal{E}$ is an extension of the default theory. Note that $\mathcal{E}$ is grounded by the rules in groups (H), and that none of the rules in groups (I) or (J) apply. In particular, $\mathcal{F}$ does not appear in $\mathcal{E}$. □

Proof of Theorem 7.4. The correctness proof of the **Normal-Unary-All-Extensions-Pos** algorithm is based on the following loop invariant:

Lemma B.2. *Given a set of normal unary defaults D and a positive literal p_k, the following property is maintained each time through the **while** loop in* **Normal-Unary-All-Extensions-Pos(p_k, D)**:

> INV: *If L contains $\neg q$ and $\mathcal{E}$ is an extension of D that does not contain p_k, then $\mathcal{E}$ does not contain q.*

Proof (By induction on the number of times through the loop).

Base case (upon entering the **while** statement). $L = \{p_1, p_2, ..., \neg p_k, ..., p_n\}$. The only negative literal in L is $\neg p_k$. So, INV holds.

Induction step. Let L be the complete set of literals after l times through the body of the loop, and L' the updated L after one additional time through. By the induction hypothesis, L has property INV. Clearly, if the condition in the **if** statement is false, we have $L' = L$. And thus, INV holds for L'. Otherwise, $L' = (L - \{p\}) \cup \{\neg p\}$ where p in L is such that (1) *not* grounded(p, L, D) or (2) neg-inconsistent$(p, \neg q, L, D)$ for some $\neg q$ in L. We will now show by contradiction that INV holds for L'. Assume that L' does not satisfy INV, i.e., there exists an extension $\mathcal{E}^\star$ of D that does not contain p_k but does contain some letter s such that $\neg s$ in L'. If $s \neq p$, then INV would not hold for L either, violating the induction hypothesis. So, $s = p$.

Case 1. *not* grounded(p, L, D). Since p in $\mathcal{E}^\star$, there must exist a sequence of one or more rules that adds p to the extension, i.e., there exists a sequence $q_0, q_1, ..., q_m = p$ such that
 (a) q_j in $\mathcal{E}^\star$, $0 \leq j \leq m$,
 (b) : q_0/q_0 in D, and
 (c) $p_{j-1} : p_j/p_j$ in D, $1 \leq j \leq m$.
Now, by the induction hypothesis, we have p_j in L with $0 \leq j \leq m$, since these positive literals are in an extension $\mathcal{E}^\star$ of D that does not contain p_k. Therefore, grounded(p, L, D). Contradiction.

Case 2. neg-inconsistent$(p, \neg q, L, D)$. From neg-inconsistent$(p, \neg q, L, D)$, it follows that
 (a) p and $\neg q$ in L,
 (b) $p : q/q$ in D,
 (c) : $\neg q/\neg q$ not in D, and
 (d) for each rule $r : \neg q/\neg q$ in D, we have $\neg r$ in L.
By the induction hypothesis it follows that $\mathcal{E}^\star$ does not contain q (since L contains $\neg q$), and neither does $\mathcal{E}^\star$ contain an r with a rule $r : \neg q/\neg q$ in D (since, if $\mathcal{E}^\star$ would contain such an r then, by the induction hypothesis, L contains r and therefore (d) is false). Contradiction. Moreover, since : $\neg q/\neg q$ not in D, it follows that $\mathcal{E}^\star$ does not contain $\neg q$ either. Now, since p in $\mathcal{E}^\star$, it follows that the rule $p : q/q$ in D is applicable. But since neither q nor $\neg q$ is in $\mathcal{E}^\star$, $\mathcal{E}^\star$ violates the fixed point property of a default logic extension [13, Theorem 2.5]. So, no such $\mathcal{E}^\star$ exists. Contradiction.

From the base case and the induction step, it follows by finite induction that INV is maintained.

We will now prove the correctness of the **Normal-Unary-All-Extensions-Pos** algorithm.

Lemma B.3. *Given a set of normal unary defaults D and a positive literal p_k, the algorithm* **Normal-Unary-All-Extensions-Pos** *returns "yes" iff every* *extension of D contains p_k. The time complexity of the algorithm is $O(n^2)$, where n is the length of D.*

Proof. First, we will show that:

The algorithm returns "yes" iff every extension of D contains p_k.

($\Rightarrow$) By contradiction. Assume the algorithm returns "yes" while there exists some extension $\mathcal{E}^\star$ of D that does not contain p_k. Note that L is not pos-consistent upon exiting. So, there exists some q such that $\neg q$ in L with fixed-pos(q,L,D), i.e.,

  (a) : q/q in D,
  (b) : $\neg q/\neg q$ not in D, and
  (c) for each rule of the form $r : \neg q/\neg q$ in D, we have $\neg r$ in L.

Also, by Lemma B.2, L has the property INV. Now, since $\mathcal{E}^\star$ is an extension of D that does not contain p_k, it follows from INV that $\mathcal{E}^\star$ does not contain q. Moreover, by (b), (c), and INV it follows that $\mathcal{E}^\star$ does not contain $\neg q$ either (no rule present or applicable to add $\neg q$ to $\mathcal{E}$). It follows that : q/q in D is applicable. But since $\mathcal{E}^\star$ does not contain q, $\mathcal{E}^\star$ violates the fixed point property of a default logic extension [13, Theorem 2.5]. Therefore, no such $\mathcal{E}^\star$ exists. Contradiction.

($\Leftarrow$) Assume the algorithm returns "no". Therefore, L upon exiting is such that

  (a) pos-consistent(L,D),
  (b) for each letter q in L, we have grounded(q,L,D),
  (c) there do not exist q and $\neg r$ in L such that neg-inconsistent$(q,\neg r,L,D)$, and
  (d) $\neg p_k$ in L.

We will construct a set of literals from L, and show that the deductive closure of this set is an extension of D that does not contain p_k. Thereby, we will have shown the contrapositive of the $\Leftarrow$-direction.

Let neg-supported$(\neg p,L,D)$ iff : $\neg p/\neg p$ in D or there exists a q in L and a rule $q : \neg p/\neg p$ in D, and let $\mathcal{E} = \text{Th}(\{p \mid p \text{ in } L\} \cup \{\neg p \mid \neg p \text{ in } L \text{ and } \text{neg-supported}(\neg p,L,D) \})$. We will now show that $\mathcal{E}$ is an extension of D that does not contain p_k.

First, by (d) and the definition of $\mathcal{E}$ it follows that $\mathcal{E}$ does not contain p_k. From (b) and the definition of $\mathcal{E}$ it also follows that each positive literal in $\mathcal{E}$ is grounded, i.e., for each p in $\mathcal{E}$ there is a sequence of one or more rules starting with a rule of the form : q_0/q_0 that brings in p. Now, consider starting off with the empty set and applying all the rules (and only those) that bring in all positive letters of $\mathcal{E}$, to obtain E_0. Now, by the definition of $\mathcal{E}$ it follows that all negative letters in $\mathcal{E}$ can subsequently be brought in by rules in D that are applicable at E_0. After applying those rules, and only those, in a sequence starting at E_0, we obtain a set E and its deductive closure $\mathcal{E}$. It now remains to be shown that: (1) no subsequent application of rules can undermine the justification of any rule applied so far (i.e., make some previously applied rule non-applicable), and (2) no additional literals can be brought in by any of the rules in D.

Case 1. Follows immediately from the fact that we have only normal defaults in D.

Case 2. By contradiction. Assume more literals can be added to $\mathcal{E}$ by further rule applications. Let r or $\neg r$ be the first such literal that can thus be added. By definition of $\mathcal{E}$ and the fact that L is a complete set of literals, it follows that $\neg r$ must be in L, and therefore, the first new literal that can be brought in must be a positive one, i.e., r (if $\neg r$ could be brought in then we would have neg-supported$(\neg r, L, D)$ and $\neg r$ would already be in $\mathcal{E}$, contradiction). Note that since r is added by a normal default, $\mathcal{E}$ cannot contain $\neg r$. The literal r can only be brought in via one of the following rule applications:

- Application of a rule $: r/r$. Since there are no rules to bring in $\neg r$ (from definition of $\mathcal{E}$), we have $: \neg r/\neg r$ not in D, and for each rule $s : \neg r/\neg r$ in D, we have $\neg s$ in L. From $: r/r$ in D it follows that fixed-pos(r, L, D). And thus, we have that L is not pos-consistent. Contradiction with (a).

- Application of a rule $t : r/r$. As argued above, we again have that $: \neg r/\neg r$ not in D and for each rule $s : \neg r/\neg r$ in D, we have $\neg s$ in L. Now, since $t : r/r$ is applicable in $\mathcal{E}$, t is in $\mathcal{E}$ and thus, t in L. Therefore, we have neg-inconsistent$(t, \neg r, L, D)$ for t and $\neg r$ in L. Contradiction with (c).

It follows that $\mathcal{E}$ is a fixed point of the defaults and grounded. So, $\mathcal{E}$ is an extension of D not containing p_k, and thus, it is not the case that every extension of D contains p_k. This completes the correctness proof of the algorithm.

Finally, we will determine the time complexity of the algorithm. Since the number of positive literals in L is decreased by one each time through the body of the **while** loop with the possible exception of the last time through, it follows from the definitions of grounded and neg-inconsistent that the loop body is executed at most N times (N is the number of distinct propositional letters in the theory). Computing pos-consistent(L, D) can be done in $O(n)$, where n is the length of the theory. And, a pair of letters p, $\neg q$ such that (*not* grounded(p, L, D)) or neg-inconsistent$(p, \neg q, L, D)$) can also be found in time $O(n)$. Therefore, the time complexity of the **Normal-Unary-All-Extensions-Pos** algorithm is $O(n^2)$. $\quad\square$

Proof of Theorem 7.4 (*Continued*). It is not difficult to see that the set of defaults D' is such that a set of formulas $\mathcal{E}$ is an extension of (D, W) if and only if $\mathcal{E}$ is an extension of $(D', \emptyset)$. (New defaults are introduced that add the literals from W into each extension; note that rules which add literals inconsistent with W have to be removed—such rules are not applicable in the original theory.) When the **Normal-Unary-All-Extensions** algorithm is queried with a positive literal, the algorithm directly calls the subroutine **Exists-Ext-Without-Pos-Lits**; a query with a negative literal x is converted into one for a positive literal for the new letter p. The correctness of the algorithm follows from the observation that the default rules added to D' to obtain D'' are such that all extensions of $(D', \emptyset)$ contain the negative literal x *if and only if* all extensions of $(D'', \emptyset)$ contain the positive literal p. This can be seen as follows. If $(D', \emptyset)$ has some extension containing $\sim x$, then there will be some applicable default to add $\sim x$ to the extension, and thus there is some default in the second set of defaults added to D' that can add $\neg p$ to the corresponding extension of $(D'', \emptyset)$. If $(D', \emptyset)$ has some extension that contains neither x nor $\sim x$, then none of the defaults that could add x or $\sim x$ will be applicable, and thus neither p nor $\neg p$ can be added to the corresponding extension of $(D'', \emptyset)$. So, if $(D', \emptyset)$ has an extension that does not contain x, then $(D'', \emptyset)$ has some extension that contains $\neg p$ or one that contains neither p nor $\neg p$. Finally, assume that all extensions of $(D', \emptyset)$ contain x. For each extension containing x, there will be a corresponding extension of $(D'', \emptyset)$ containing p because of the first set of defaults added to D'. Moreover, there are no other extensions of $(D'', \emptyset)$, since if $(D'', \emptyset)$ had an extension containing $\neg p$, then there would exist an extension of $(D', \emptyset)$ containing $\sim x$: contradiction; and, by a similar argument, $(D'', \emptyset)$ cannot have an extension containing neither p nor $\neg p$. Thus, all extensions of $(D', \emptyset)$ contain the negative literal x if and only if all extensions of $(D'', \emptyset)$ contain the positive literal p.

As can be seen from the algorithm, its time complexity is dominated by that of the procedure **Normal-Unary-All-Extensions-Pos**. Therefore, the time complexity of the algorithm is $O(n^2)$, where n is the length of the theory. □

Acknowledgement

We thank Hector Levesque for useful discussions and comments.

References

[1] A.V. Aho, J.E. Hopcroft and J.D. Ullman, *The Design and Analysis of Computer Algorithms* (Addison-Wesley, Reading, MA, 1976).
[2] N. Bidoit and C. Froidevaux, Minimalism subsumes default logic and circumscription in stratified logic programming, Preprint (1986).
[3] W.F. Dowling and J.H. Gallier, Linear time algorithms for testing the satisfiability of propositional Horn formula, *J. Logic Program.* **3** (1984) 267–284.

[4] D.W. Etherington and R. Reiter, On inheritance hierarchies with exceptions, in: *Proceedings AAAI-83*, Washington, DC (1983).

[5] D. Etherington, K. Forbus, M. Ginsberg, D. Israel and V. Lifschitz, Critical issues in non-monotonic reasoning, in: *Proceedings First International Conference on Principles of Knowledge Representation and Reasoning*, Toronto, Ont. (1989).

[6] D. Etherington, *Reasoning with Incomplete Information* (Morgan Kaufmann, Los Altos, CA, 1988).

[7] S.E. Fahlman, *Netl: A System for Representing and Using Real-World Knowledge* (MIT Press, Cambridge, MA, 1979).

[8] M.R. Garey and D.S. Johnson, *Computers and Intractability* (Freeman, New York, 1979).

[9] J.F. Horty, R. Thomason and D.S. Touretzky, A skeptical theory of inheritance in non-monotonic semantic nets, in: *Proceedings AAAI-87*, Seattle, WA (1987).

[10] H. Levesque, Making believers out of computers, *Artif. Intell.* **30** (1986) 81–108.

[11] J. McCarthy, Applications of circumscription to formalizing common-sense knowledge, *Artif. Intell.* **28** (1986) 89–116.

[12] T.C. Przymusinski, On the relationship between logic programming and non-monotonic reasoning, in: *Proceedings AAAI-88*, St. Paul, MN (1988) 444.

[13] R. Reiter, A logic for default reasoning, *Artif. Intell.* **13** (1980) 81–132.

[14] B. Selman and H. Kautz, The complexity of model-preference default theories, in: *Proceedings CSCSI-88* (1988) 102–109; also in: *Non-monotonic Reasoning*, Lecture Notes in Artificial Intelligence **346** (Springer, Berlin, 1989).

[15] B. Selman and H. Kautz, Model-preference default theories, *Artif. Intell.* **45** (1990) 287–322.

[16] L.A. Stein, Skeptical inheritance: computing the intersection of credulous extensions, in: *Proceedings IJCAI-89*, Detroit, MI (1989) 1153.

[17] J. Stillman, It's not my default: the complexity of membership problems in restricted propositional default logic, in: *Proceedings AAAI-90*, Boston, MA (1990).

[18] D.S. Touretzky, R. Thomason and J.F. Horty, A clash of intuitions: the current state of nonmonotonic multiple inheritance systems, in: *Proceedings IJCAI-87*, Milan, Italy (1987) 476–482.

[19] D.S. Touretzky, *The Mathematics of Inheritance Systems* (Morgan Kaufmann, Los Altos, CA, 1986).

Artificial Intelligence 49 (1991) 281–307
Elsevier

The effect of knowledge on belief: conditioning, specificity and the lottery paradox in default reasoning

David Poole

Department of Computer Science, University of British Columbia, Vancouver, BC, Canada V6T 1W5

Received October 1989
Revised June 1990

Abstract

Poole, D., The effect of knowledge on belief: conditioning, specificity and the lottery paradox in default reasoning, Artificial Intelligence 49 (1991) 281–307.

How should what one knows about an individual affect default conclusions about that individual? This paper contrasts two views of "knowledge" in default reasoning systems. The first is the traditional view that one knows the logical consequences of one's knowledge base. It is shown how, under this interpretation, having to know an exception is too strong for default reasoning. It is argued that we need to distinguish "background" and "contingent" knowledge in order to be able to handle specificity, and that this is a natural distinction. The second view of knowledge is what is contingently known about the world under consideration. Using this view of knowledge, a notion of conditioning that seems like a minimal property of a default is defined. Finally, a qualitative version of the lottery paradox is given; if we want to be able to say that individuals that are typical in every respect do not exist, we should not expect to conclude the conjunction of our default conclusions. This paper expands on work in the proceedings of the First International Conference on Principles of Knowledge Representation and Reasoning [38].

1. Introduction

Default reasoning can be seen as jumping to conclusions about some individual based on knowledge about that individual.

Many papers have considered solutions to the so-called "multiple extension problem" [16,26,36,41], where conclusions of different defaults are in

0004-3702/91/$ 03.50 © 1991—Elsevier Science Publishers B.V.

conflict. These solutions usually consider the multiple extension problem where the antecedents of the defaults happen to be true. For example, if we have defaults that Quakers are pacifists and Republicans are not pacifists, we have to consider what to do when we have someone who is both a Quaker and a Republican [41]. Solutions to these problems usually consist of being agnostic when there are competing defaults and having mechanisms for blocking defaults.

This paper concentrates on instances of the multiple extension problem, with the following property: there is some default such that whenever the antecedent of the default is true, there are extensions in conflict with the conclusion of the default. Unless the multiple extension problem is solved in a satisfactory way such defaults will never be used. Many of the standard ways to solve the multiple extension problem, for example deriving conclusions that are in all extensions, render such defaults useless; the defaults can effectively never be used.

There are two cases where this phenomenon occurs. When the competing defaults have equivalent antecedents we have a qualitative version of the lottery paradox [19]. In the other case we have more specific knowledge competing with more general knowledge, and need to prefer more specific defaults if we want them to be usable.

In this paper we appeal to and expand on an intuition of "conditioning" that says "if p's are q's by default, and all we know about individual C is $p(C)$, we should conclude $q(C)$". This is considered to be a minimal property of a default.

For example, suppose there is the default "birds fly", and someone phones me up and says "Tweety is a bird", and that is all I have ever heard about Tweety, then, using this default, I should conclude that Tweety flies. If I were not to use the default in this case, it seems as though this default would never be used. What needs to be in a system to make sure that such a property holds is the basis of this paper.

The results of this paper can be summarised as:

(1) Requiring one to know an exception (e.g., Reiter's Default Logic [40], Autoepistemic Logic [23,28]) is too strong a condition to capture the naive intuition behind defaults. Similarly the idea of explicitly cancelling defaults cannot be used by itself to solve the multiple extension problem in a satisfactory way.

(2) If we want a local interpretation of defaults, we need to have specificity; that is, we should prefer more specific defaults over more general ones when they compete.

(3) We need to distinguish "background" and "contingent" knowledge in order to automatically handle specificity. This is more than a syntactic distinction.

(4) The lottery paradox arises naturally. If we want the ability to conclude that individuals that are typical in every respect do not exist, conditioning is incompatible with logical closure.

When we talk about a system getting the wrong answer, we have two possible meanings. For the "brave systems" that rely on membership in one extension [28,36,40], we mean that there is a wrong conclusion in one of the extensions (as opposed to not being able to derive the correct conclusion in one extension). For the more skeptical systems, such as those that require membership in all extensions [26,27,37] we mean that the desired result cannot be concluded.

By "belief" in the title of this paper, I mean what can be defeasibly concluded based on what one knows about what is true [44].

2. Current logic-based systems

Consider the following example:

Example 2.1. Suppose we are given:

>   All emus are birds.
>   Birds fly, by default.
>   Emus don't fly, by default.

Should we conclude that an arbitrary individual is not an emu?

This is more than a consideration of whether contrapositives should be allowed (e.g., ε-semantics [31] does not allow contrapositives in general, but does answer "yes" to this question). The argument for concluding that an arbitrary individual is not an emu goes something like:

>   If the individual were a bird, we would conclude that the individual flies, and so we are implicitly assuming it is not an emu (as emus don't fly). If it is not a bird, it is not an emu. Thus in either case it is not an emu.

We divide systems into classes as to whether they answer "yes" or "no" to this question. Virtually all of the systems considered do conclude that an arbitrary individual is not an emu [21,26,31,36]. In some systems [23,28,40] the default can be represented so that the answer to the question is either "no" or "yes". The representations that lead to the answer "no", do so by explicitly blocking the side effect. In Section 2.1 we argue that this explicit blocking is unintuitive in most cases. In Section 2.2 it is shown how problems arise with the side effects (e.g., of concluding that arbitrary individuals are not emus in Example 2.1) interacting.

2.1. Having to know an exception

There are a number of representation systems for which one has to "know" an exception before a default is blocked [23,28,40].

As an example, consider a representation of "birds fly, but emus are exceptional" using Reiter's semi-normal defaults where we don't want to conclude that typical birds are not emus:[1]

$$\frac{bird(x) : flies(x) \land \neg emu(x)}{flies(x)}.$$

An equivalent formulation in autoepistemic logic [23,28] can be given by the axiom:

$$L\ bird(x) \land \neg L\neg(flies(x) \land \neg emu(x)) \Rightarrow flies(x).$$

If we augment this with

$$bird(Tweety),$$
$$bird(Polly)$$

we can conclude

$$flies(Tweety) \land flies(Polly)$$

using the default twice (once for $x = Tweety$, and once for $x = Polly$). There is no conclusion about the emuness of Tweety or Polly.

This may be considered as an appropriate answer. If, however, we add

$$emu(Tweety) \lor emu(Polly),$$

we still have the same conclusion: both Tweety and Polly fly, even though the disjunct tells us that one of them is exceptional.

The problem is in the semi-normal nature of the default; having to "know" or "prove" an exception is much too strong. The disjunction is not strong enough to cancel either default (or even cancel the use of both defaults together).

Consider how other information in the knowledge base could prevent the conclusion of the conjunction. To block the conjunction we have to use the disjunction in some way, as without the disjunction we want to conclude the conjunction. To block one of the default instances, we need to conclude that one of the birds is an emu (or does not fly). Consider how to block the default for Tweety. To use the disjunction to conclude $emu(Tweety)$ we need to conclude $\neg emu(Polly)$ (for example, by having $\forall x\ emu(x) \Rightarrow \neg flies(x)$

---

[1] Throughout this paper the convention of having variables, function symbols and predicate symbols in lower case and constants in upper case is used.

as a fact). This is precisely the side effect that the semi-normal defaults do not allow.

Note that this problem is endemic to the use of non-normal defaults. If we have the semi-normal defaults (or instances of semi-normal defaults):

$$\frac{: \alpha \wedge \beta}{\beta}, \qquad \frac{: \gamma \wedge \delta}{\delta},$$

the fact $\neg \alpha \vee \neg \gamma$ does not block the conclusion $\beta \wedge \delta$.

This problem does not require the explicit statement of disjuncts:

Example 2.2. Consider the semi-normal defaults:

$$\frac{bird(x) : flies(x) \wedge \neg dead(x)}{flies(x)},$$

$$\frac{of\_ancient\_species(x) : fossilised(x) \wedge dead(x)}{fossilised(x)}.$$

If we are given the facts

$$bird(Fred) \wedge of\_ancient\_species(Fred),$$

we can conclude

$$flies(Fred) \wedge fossilised(Fred).$$

The semi-normal nature of the defaults does not recognise the implicit assumptions that Fred is both dead and not dead.

Example 2.3. This problem also manifests itself in a different way if we follow Brewka's [4] suggestion of using semi-normal defaults of the form:[2]

$$\frac{: M \ flies(x)}{bird(x) \Rightarrow flies(x)}$$

to allow case analysis on the antecedents [36], and to also block contrapositives. This representation allows us to conclude $flies(Tweety) \vee flies(Polly)$ from $bird(Tweety) \vee bird(Polly)$, and blocks the conclusion of $\neg bird(Sylvester)$ from $\neg flies(Sylvester)$. However, given $\neg flies(Fred) \vee \neg flies(Mary)$, the contrapositive is not blocked and $\neg bird(Fred) \vee \neg bird(Mary)$ is concluded.

---

[2] This is also the form suggested by Levesque [23, p. 291] to represent "birds fly".

Example 2.4. Although this may seem like peculiar behaviour for these default examples, there are examples where this behaviour does seem appropriate [7]. Consider the default that someone who has a motive, and may be guilty, should be a suspect:

$$\frac{has\_motive(x) : suspect(x) \land guilty(x)}{suspect(x)}.$$

This default can be blocked for an individual *John* if we knew ¬*guilty*(*John*).

The disjunctive exceptions also seem reasonable for this example; if we know both Pete and Mary have motives and we know one is not guilty, it is reasonable to conclude that they both are suspects.

This example perhaps shows the distinction between default reasoning and autoepistemic reasoning that was pointed out by Moore [28]. There are cases where not knowing the particular counterexample is important, but these seem to be the exception rather than the rule.

2.2. Concluding exceptions are false

The alternative answer to the question posed at the start of Section 2 is to conclude that exceptions are false (i.e., that the arbitrary individual in Example 2.1 is not an emu).

Example 2.5. Consider the following elaboration of Example 2.1:

> All emus are birds.
> Birds fly, by default.
> Emus don't fly, by default.
> If something looks like an emu, it is an emu, by default.

Suppose we are also told two facts:

> Tweety is an emu.
> Polly looks like an emu.

Intuitively we would like to conclude that Tweety does not fly (as we have the direct default that emus don't fly, and thus are exceptional birds), and, similarly, we would like to conclude that Polly is an emu. This example is considered as two separate cases in the following two sections.

2.2.1. Specificity

There is a very strong intuition that, based on the information in Example 2.5, we should be able to conclude that Tweety does not fly. Although there are two potentially applicable defaults, the one applicable to emus is more specific and thus should be preferred over the more general default about birds (it is a more specific default as it is about a more specific class). This notion of preference for more specific knowledge has been advocated by many authors [11,24,26,31,35,45,46].

If we don't want to conclude Tweety does not fly in Example 2.5, it seems as though the default "emus don't fly" can never be used. Whenever it can be used, the "birds fly" default is also applicable, and competes with this default. Thus, unless we want a default to be useless, we should prefer to use the more specific default.

There are three basic approaches that have been considered to ensure that we conclude that Tweety does not fly:

(1) Force the user to add "cancellation axioms" to stop the use of the more general default [26,36]. For example, we could name the first default "$\neg ab(Birdsfly, x)$" by writing

$$\forall x \; bird(x) \wedge \neg ab(Birdsfly, x) \Rightarrow flies(x)$$

and adding a cancellation axiom

$$\forall x \; emu(x) \Rightarrow ab(Birdsfly, x).$$

In Example 2.5, we would conclude that Tweety does not fly, as we can use the cancellation axiom to prove the "birds fly" default is not applicable to Tweety.

(2) Build a general priority system, and make the user add priorities[3] [3,26]. The user would make the "emu's don't fly" default have higher priority than the "birds fly" default; when they compete, as in this example, the higher priority default would prevail.

(3) Incorporate specificity into the default reasoning system automatically, [1,11,24,29,35,45,46]. This is discussed further in Section 3.

2.2.2. Inheritance of cancellation

Based on the information in Example 2.5, we also want to conclude that Polly, who looks like an emu, is an emu. This is similar to the previous specificity case, in that the direct default "if it looks like an emu, it is an emu" competes with the conclusion that Polly is not an emu using the first two defaults. If we ever want the third default to be used we have to counter the conclusion of Polly not being an emu.

Consider the three proposed solutions to the specificity problem above:

Solution 1. If we are using cancellation, we have to cancel defaults that argue against Polly being an emu. The most direct counterargument uses the cancellation axiom introduced for specificity in Section 2.2.1. By assuming

---

[3]If we want to automatically add these priorities, this is considered to be the third case.

the first default (i.e., $\neg ab(Birdsfly, Polly)$), we can use the cancellation axiom to conclude that Polly is not an emu (even given no explicit facts about Polly). We must block this conclusion to allow only the conclusion that Polly is an emu. To block the conclusion we have to specify something like

$$\forall x \ looks\_like\_emu(x) \Rightarrow ab(Birdsfly, x).$$

In other words, objects that look like emus must inherit the cancellation of the emu class. Similarly some properties that, by default, allow us to conclude that an individual looks like an emu, must also inherit the cancellation of the "birds fly" default.

This is still not right. Suppose we have an individual Fred that is a bird and looks like an emu, but is not an emu. With the above cancellation axioms in effect, we cannot conclude that Fred flies, even though we know that Fred is not a member of the only exceptional class of birds given.

Thus it seems as though "cancellation axioms" do not provide the tools we need to treat even this simple example in a satisfactory way. [4]

Solution 2. The second case is to use some form of prioritisation. For Polly there are three defaults that together are in conflict (no two of which are in conflict). We need the default about looking like an emu to have higher priority than at least one of the other defaults. As the "birds fly" default has lower priority than the "emus do not fly" default, the default about looking like an emu must have higher priority than the "birds fly" default.

Such arguments about the relative priority of defaults can lead to "counter-examples" to the universal applicability of static prioritisation. The following example is constructed in a manner similer to the example for cancellation. It may look complicated, but the idea is simple. We want to create an example where, in order for the defaults to be used, we need some minimal ordering of defaults. We then set into competition two defaults that are not closely related.

Example 2.6. Suppose we want to represent the following defaults:
   (i) Canadians speak English as a native language.
   (ii) Quebecois are Canadians who do not speak English as a native language.

---

[4]Note however, that the use of cancellation advocated here (and in [36]) can solve the problems that motivated the development of prioritised circumscription in [26]. Rather than cancelling the cancellation axioms, as in [26], a simpler idea is to add new defaults for the subclasses. The intuition is that emus, because they are birds, are exceptional beings with respect to flying, and because they are emus, are exceptional birds. They have their own reason for not flying. See [36] for more details. When we try to use these defaults in practice however, they break because of the reasons in the text.

(iii) If someone is in Quebec they are Quebecois.
(iv) If someone says that they are "au Quebec" they are in Quebec.
(v) If Fred says someone said they are "au Quebec", they said they were "au Quebec".

In order for the second default to be applicable, it has to have higher priority than the first default. In order for the third default to be applicable, it has to have higher priority than one of the first and the second, and so must have higher priority than the first. Similarly the fourth and fifth defaults must also have priority over the first in order for them to be applicable.

Suppose we have the facts:

(a) Mary is a Canadian.
(b) Mary is not Quebecois.
(c) Mary is in Quebec.
(d) Fred says that Mary said she was "au Quebec".
(e) If Mary is a native English speaker, she would not have said she is "au Quebec".

We have created a competition between the first and the fifth defaults. Because of the previous considerations, the fifth default must have priority over the first, and thus we conclude that Mary said she was "au Quebec" and so is not a native English speaker. This is very peculiar: the logic tells us that the default about Fred's literal reliability should have priority over the typicality of non-Quebecois Canadians.

There are many questions that arise as to where priorities come from, how do we add priorities, and how does a user know where to add priorities (this is particularly important when we have recursive rules, such as in frame axioms [16]). If we want to be able to automatically infer priorities (e.g., [14]), we need to consider the next case.

Solution 3. The last case is where the system can automatically handle specificity. This is discussed further in Section 3. It is important to note that, as the inheritance of cancellation of Example 2.5 shows, specificity can be more complicated than the (conceptually simple, but still tricky) case discussed in Section 2.2.1. When we have an object that looks like an emu, we need some form of specificity to override the natural tendency to conclude that the object is not an emu.

2.2.3. A qualitative lottery paradox

The previous example and discussion considered cases where there is a default, such that whenever the antecedent of the default is true there are extensions that run counter to the conclusion of the default. In the previous examples, at least some of the competing defaults were more general (there are cases where the more general default is applicable, and the more specific is not), and it was these defaults that needed to be blocked to force the more specific default to apply. There is one case where the problem does not have to do with specificity. This is where the competing defaults all have the same (or equivalent) antecedents. This turns out to form a qualitative lottery paradox. As we can't use all of the defaults, which can or should we use?

The answer to this problem is closely related to the question of whether individuals that are typical in every respect really exist. Are there birds that are typical in all respects? Are there houses that are typical in all respects? While this may be an arguable point, most default reasoning systems take a very strong stand on such questions: not only do they exist, but they are the typical individual. Many of these systems break if we try to say that there are no individuals of a certain type that are typical in every respect.

Saying that typical individuals of a particular class do not exist, far from being an exceptional situation, would seem to be the norm for large knowledge bases. Consider the following elaboration of our familiar ornithological example:

Example 2.7. Suppose we want to build a knowledge base about birds. Suppose also that all we are told about Tweety is that Tweety is a bird.

We first state knowledge about the different birds we are considering:

$$\forall x \; bird(x) \equiv emu(x) \lor penguin(x) \lor hummingbird(x) \lor$$
$$sandpiper(x) \lor albatross(x) \lor \cdots \lor canary(x).$$

We now state defaults about birds (e.g., they fly, are within certain size ranges, nest in trees, etc.). For each sort of bird that is exceptional in some way we will be able to conclude that Tweety is not that sort of bird:

- We conclude that Tweety is not an emu or a penguin because they are exceptional in not flying.
- We conclude that Tweety is not a hummingbird as hummingbirds are exceptional in their size (consider making a bird cage for Tweety; we have to make assumptions about the size of birds).
- We conclude that Tweety is not a sandpiper as sandpipers are exceptional in nesting on the ground. This assumption would be made if we are walking our robot in the outdoors and someone says "look at that bird nest"; the robot would have to make assumptions of where to look first.
- We conclude that Tweety is not an albatross as albatrosses are exceptional in some other way.

If every sort of bird is exceptional in some way, except for say, the canary, we conclude that Tweety is a canary. If the canary is also exceptional, then in all of the systems considered, we can no longer conclude that Tweety flies (or we conclude it and its negation in different extensions). We have thus lost effectively the use of the default "birds fly".

The problem is that lots of seemingly irrelevant information (namely about how different sorts of birds are exceptional in different aspects) can interact to make none of the defaults applicable. For seemingly unrelated statements to interact to produce such side effects seems like a very bad problem.

The reason that we divide the class of birds into subclasses is because each subclass is exceptional in some way. Rather than being a pathological example, this would seem to be the general rule, typical of hierarchies with exceptions.

This problem is analogous to the lottery paradox of Kyburg [19]. In the lottery paradox we have the default that each ticket will not win (as we want to make plans assuming our ticket will not win, and only seriously plan on what to do with the money if we actually win), however we also have the knowledge that one ticket will win. If we conjoin all of the default conclusions, we end up with a contradiction. Most of the default logic systems "solve" this problem by ignoring all of the defaults,[5] rather than the arguably more intuitive idea [19,20] of not conjoining the conclusions to get a contradiction. Given that the user added the defaults, the system is being very presumptive to ignore the explicit defaults, presumably deciding the user was not rational in adding them (as has been advocated by Shoham [43, p. 392]).

One possible patch[6] to fix the problem in this example is to disjoin the class "typical birds" to the other sorts of birds. We thus conclude that Tweety is a typical bird and has all of the typical properties. The disjunction, however, is a strange statement, as the "typical bird" is not another sort of bird like emus and sparrows, but rather is an artifact of the representation. This solution ignores the fact that all birds, even typical birds, are some sort of bird (the bird that is not of some type would indeed be exceptional!). It does not allow us to reason by cases as to properties of birds. Also, the resulting knowledge base would not allow us to reason to the identity of a bird by ruling out other cases.

It is also not clear how to expand this "solution" to cases where the exceptions are not as homogeneous as in the previous example, and where

---

[5] Membership in one extension systems also effectively ignore the defaults. For each default there is an extension containing the negation of the conclusion of the default (by assuming the other defaults). Depending on how the single extension is chosen, each default can have its conclusion or the negation of its conclusion in the extension.

[6] This was suggested to me by Matt Ginsberg, May 1989.

the lack of a typical individual of a certain type is derived not from case analysis, but from, say, physical constraints as in the following example:

Example 2.8. Consider making assumptions about houses (this is done by real-estate sales-people so they can advertise the "features" of a particular house). We need to make an assumption about the size of a house to interpret statements such as "a large house", or "a normal-sized house". We would also make assumptions about the number of bedrooms, the number of other rooms and the size of each typical room. The analogous situation to the lottery paradox occurs if we can conclude that the "typical house" does not exist because the sizes do not add up. We would not expect the sizes to add up, as the typically sized house has some room larger than normal (as a selling point).

In this example we derive the non-existence of a typical house, not by case analysis, but rather by physical constraints. One could imagine adding some buffer in the description, but this would entail that the typical house has some space not in any room, which is physically impossible, or as "ghost" rooms that no house in fact has.

In Section 4, this qualitative lottery paradox is formalised.

3. Different sorts of "knowing"

In much of AI there is an assumption that there is one sort of "knowing"; one knows something if and only if it is a logical consequence of the knowledge base [22]. In this section I argue that such a definition is inadequate for the intuition behind defaults and for any formalisation of default reasoning that incorporates specificity and standard logical connectives (material implication, in particular).

Example 3.1 highlights some differences between different intuitions behind the statement "all I know".

Example 3.1. Suppose we have a large knowledge base that includes the defaults

> Cats purr.
> Mammals live in the wild.

and also includes the fact that cats are mammals, but does not include any directly contradictory knowledge (e.g., that cats don't purr or that mammals don't live in the wild).

Suppose we have never heard about "Fred", and all someone tells us is "Fred is a cat"; there is some notion that "Fred is a cat" is all that we know about that individual.

It seems as though we should be able to conclude

$$purrs(Fred)$$

but not necessarily

$$lives\_in\_wild(Fred)$$

as cats may be exceptional with respect to living in the wild. It is presumable that, depending on the other knowledge in the system, the "mammals live in the wild" default could be blocked for cats, but the "cats purr" default could not be blocked for cats without rendering the default useless.

In another sense [22,23] we "know" other things about Fred:

- We "know" all tautologies mentioning the constant *Fred* are true, for example,

$$green(Fred) \land (green(Fred) \Rightarrow sick(Fred)) \Rightarrow sick(Fred).$$

- We "know" all general knowledge about Fred (i.e., all the knowledge that we know is true for all individuals is true of Fred), for example:

$$square(Fred) \Rightarrow rectangle(Fred),$$

$$cat(Fred) \Rightarrow mammal(Fred).$$

- We also "know" inferred knowledge about Fred, for example, we can derive

$$mammal(Fred)$$

from $\forall x \; cat(x) \Rightarrow mammal(x)$, as we assumed this is in the knowledge base.

There seems to be two very different forms of "know" here. One consists of the logical consequences of what is in the knowledge base (including $cat(Fred)$ and $mammal(Fred)$). Another is that $cat(Fred)$ is different to the other sorts of knowledge; as far as the defaults are concerned, all we know about Fred is $cat(Fred)$ (so the "cats purr" default should be applicable to Fred), but we know more than $mammal(Fred)$ (so the "mammals live in the wild" default is not necessarily applicable to Fred).

The first is the form of "all I know" that was formalised by Levesque [23]. The second is a very different form of "all I know".

Example 3.2. It seems as though there is enough information in the defaults:

Birds fly, by default.
Emus don't fly, by default.

and the facts

Emus are birds.
Edna is an emu.

to conclude that Edna does not fly, using the intuition of specificity. The default that Edna should fly because she is a bird should not be applicable as we have more specific information about Edna.

The facts involved are

$$\forall x \; emu(x) \Rightarrow bird(x),$$

$$emu(Edna).$$

Example 3.3. Suppose we change Example 3.2 by swapping the role of *emu* and *bird* in the facts. We end up with the facts:

$$\forall x \; bird(x) \Rightarrow emu(x)$$

$$bird(Edna).$$

With the defaults as in Example 3.2 and these facts we would, by symmetry, want to conclude *flies*(*Edna*), which is the opposite of the conclusion in Example 3.2.

Observation 3.4. If we just consider the instances of the facts that are relevant to Edna, we find something interesting. The instance of the facts relative to Edna in Example 3.2, namely

$$emu(Edna) \wedge (emu(Edna) \Rightarrow bird(Edna))$$

is logically equivalent to

$$bird(Edna) \wedge (bird(Edna) \Rightarrow emu(Edna))$$

which is the instance of the facts relative to Edna in Example 3.3. These two examples use exactly the same defaults, logically equivalent instances of the facts, but yield different results.

This observation can be summarised in the claim:

Result 3.5. [7] A default reasoning system that uses classical logic for the facts, and

(1) treats defaults modularly (i.e., their representation does not depend on the facts),

(2) considers only the instances of the facts for the individuals under consideration, and

(3) treats logically equivalent facts as the same,

cannot have specificity.

Proof. If the system incorporates specificity, it gets opposite answers in Examples 3.2 and 3.3. However, under the conditions of the result, Examples 3.2 and 3.3 are identical, and so cannot elicit different answers. $\square$

The problem is that there is not enough information in the semantic content of the instances of the facts to handle specificity. Note that the use of cancellation axioms or user-defined priorities violates the modularity of defaults.

If we want to use classical logic for the background facts, we have to be able to exploit some difference between the facts of Examples 3.2 and 3.3 to account for the opposite answers. There seem to be two possible answers:

(1) The difference between $emu(Edna)$ and $\forall x\ emu(x) \Rightarrow bird(x)$ is syntactic. We know Edna is both an emu and a bird, but we have to take into account the universally quantified formula, and somehow the fact that all the other emus are also birds is crucial. This has been advocated by Bacchus [2]. He argues that we need to randomise over the name *Edna*, in order to consider just the typical emu.

(2) There is a difference in kind between the fact $emu(Edna)$ and the fact $\forall x\ emu(x) \Rightarrow bird(x)$. The latter is always true in the domains under consideration ("background knowledge") and the former only happens to be true ("contingent knowledge").

The following example shows that two syntactically identical formulae can produce opposite answers, thus showing that the distinction is more than just syntactic.

Example 3.6. [8] Suppose we are building an expert system with defaults:

---

[7] This is not called a theorem, because it deliberately uses undefined terms. In particular we do not define what it means for a default reasoning system to "have specificity". The one necessary condition is that it concludes that Edna does not fly in Example 3.2.

[8] This argument is due to Hector Geffner; this example is a syntactic variant of an example of Geffner [13].

Professors are not outdoorsy people.

People who live in Vancouver are outdoorsy.

This expert system has nothing to say about professors who live in Vancouver.

Suppose also that we are providing a facility to ask the user for particular knowledge about the case under consideration [5].

Suppose that the system asks the user "who lives in Vancouver?", and the user replies "all of the professors". The user is thus saying

$$\forall x \; professor(x) \Rightarrow lives\_in\_Vancouver(x)$$

is true about their particular world. Suppose they also tell us that Alan is a professor. Should we conclude that Alan is not outdoorsy? Given that we had nothing to say about professors who live in Vancouver, we should not conclude that Alan is not an outdoorsy person just because all of the professors in the domain under consideration happen to live in Vancouver.

If, however, we had designed the knowledge base taking into account the fact that all professors live in Vancouver, then we should conclude by specificity that Alan is not an outdoorsy person. In some sense, the default "Professors are not outdoorsy people" would have already taken into account the fact that professors live in Vancouver.

What is important about this example is that it shows that there is no syntactic distinction between background and contingent knowledge. It is rather a distinction that must be explicit in building the knowledge base. By "syntactic" I mean having to do with the logical representation, rather than any natural language conventions as to whether some formula is background or contingent. For example Pearl [32] argues that the English word "if" conveys pragmatic information that can be used to distinguish between two modes of knowledge. One thing that is interesting about my example is that it goes to lengths to produce a universally quantified implication as contingent knowledge, without expecting the knowledge engineer to write it explicitly.

This distinction between necessary and contingent facts does not reflect differences in the world being represented, but rather differences in the knowledge bases. There is nothing in the domain that prescribes whether "all the professors live in Vancouver" is background or contingent. This choice reflects whether the knowledge base has been constructed taking this fact into account or not.

Background knowledge is about all possible worlds. To say that "all the professors live in Vancouver" is background knowledge says that there could not be a professor who does not live in Vancouver. Contingent knowledge is about the individuals in one particular world. The contingent statement "all the professors live in Vancouver" is about the individuals in one particular world (the particular world that the user is in, presumably). This distinction is similar to the distinction between propositional and statistical probabilities of Bacchus [2].

In summary, this section has argued for the following claim:

Claim 3.7. *We need to distinguish explicitly between background knowledge and contingent knowledge in a default reasoning system.*

This distinction is very common; it can be seen in the following:

(1) the distinction between the network and markers in marker passing systems such as NETL [9];

(2) the difference between the probabilistic knowledge (such as $p(A|B) = 0.345$) and the conditioning knowledge (B in the preceding equation) in probability theory [31] (see Example 3.8 below);

(3) the difference between background knowledge and observations in abduction [37,39].

(4) the distinction between the general knowledge provided by a knowledge engineer and the particular knowledge provided by a user in a typical expert system architecture [5].

This distinction was first used with respect to nonmonotonic reasoning in Poole's 1985 paper on comparing explanations for specificity [35], and more recently in the work of Delgrande [6] and Geffner [11].

This distinction arises very clearly in Bayesian probability theory [30]. There are two ways to say that A is true. The first is to say $p(A) = 1$. The second is to condition on the knowledge A.

Example 3.8. To show how this distinction arises in probability theory consider the following conditional probabilities:

$$p(\mathit{flies}|\mathit{bird}) = 0.87,$$
$$p(\mathit{flies}|\mathit{emu}) = 0.056,$$
$$p(\mathit{bird}|\mathit{emu}) = 1.$$

Suppose we want to determine the probability that an individual who is an emu flies. If we want to say that *emu* is true, we cannot write $p(\mathit{emu}) = 1$. This statement is logically inconsistent with the conditional probabilities above [30].

We need to condition on *emu*, and ask $p(\mathit{flies}|\mathit{emu})$.

It is important to realise how important and subtle this distinction may be. For example, in Pearl [31] where defaults are treated as background knowledge and formulae as contingent knowledge (called "facts"), background sentences such as "emus are birds" must be put in the same category of defaults, despite the non-defeasible nature of these sentences. One simple device [31] for making "emus are birds" non-defeasible is to write $emu \land \neg bird \rightarrow False$ (using the fact that, in many axiomatisations of probability theory, it is not inconsistent to assign 1 to $p(False|False)$). In related papers, "emus are birds" can be specified using a special connective for non-defeasible conditional (as in Goldsmidt and Pearl [15]), or by distinguishing between the "background context", and the given knowledge on the left-hand side of an entailment relation (as in Geffner and Pearl [12]).

This distinction can be compared with the distinction between necessary and contingent knowledge in modal logics [17]. There is one important difference: in typical modal logics of necessity the necessary propositions have a more important status than the contingent ones. If something follows from a contingent proposition it follows from the necessary proposition (as $Lp \rightarrow p$ is an axiom in all modal logics I know of where L is interpreted as "necessary", as opposed to say, "belief"). In the distinction presented here, the contingent facts have a more important status than the necessary (background) facts; making a fact necessary tends to reduce its impact (as Example 3.6 shows). Background facts are passive and can be ignored unless they are needed in the reasoning process; contingent facts demand to be taken into consideration and accounted for.

The distinction argued for in this paper is about knowledge rather than about truth. What is important is what is known about a particular individual or state of the world that sets it apart from other individuals or possible states of the world.

4. Closure and the lottery paradox

In this section, some of the properties outlined in the previous examples are formalised.

I will use the notation "$p(x) \rightarrow q(x)$" is a default to mean "p's are q's by default". No meaning should be placed in this notation. Different systems use different notation and have different semantics; I intend this discussion to include every notation.

The property that seems to be a minimal property for a default is what I call "conditioning".[9]

---

[9]This discussion is in terms of parametrized (open) defaults as it is most natural for this case. However the argument is purely propositional, and covers propositional systems as well as systems allowing defaults with free variables. A similar notion (without the background–contingent distinction) was called the "one step default property" in [38].

Property 4.1 (*Conditioning*). A default reasoning system has the *conditioning property* if whenever "$p(x) \rightarrow q(x)$" is a default and the contingent knowledge is "$p(C)$" (where constant C does not appear in the background knowledge base), it concludes "$q(C)$".

Thus if "p's are q's" by default, and all we know contingently about some object is that p is true of it, we should conclude q is true of the object.

For example, suppose a system has the default "birds fly" and all we tell it about some object is that it is a bird. If a system has the conditioning property it concludes that the bird flies. This seems like a minimal property "birds fly" should have.

Note that this is an extremely weak property. If we know anything else about C, then this property, by itself, does not sanction us to use the default.

This property is the simplest property of many of the recent conditional accounts of default reasoning [31], namely the, seemingly uncontroversial

$$p \vdash_\Delta q \quad \text{if} \quad p \rightarrow q \in \Delta.$$

Property 4.2 (*Finite conjunctive closure*). A system has the (finite conjunctive) closure property if it concludes finite conjunctions of its conclusions.

This property says that if a system concludes α and concludes β then it concludes $\alpha \wedge \beta$. The "finite" condition means that we do not demand that the system can prove $\forall x \, p(x)$ if it can prove $p(C)$ for all C.

The third property is a restriction of minimal representational power:

Property 4.3 (*Horn representability*). The system can at least represent Horn clauses. That is, it can represent implications of the form

$$a_1 \wedge \cdots \wedge a_n \Rightarrow b$$

and restrictions of the form $\neg(a_1 \wedge \cdots \wedge a_n)$.[10]

Property 4.4 (*Consistency*). Defaults do not introduce inconsistencies. If the facts are consistent, the system doesn't conclude anything at odds with the facts.

Property 4.5 (*Arbitrary defaults*). Beyond perhaps making a restriction on non-directly contradicted defaults, whether a default is acceptable does not depend on other facts and defaults.[11]

---

[10]Note that we are using Horn clauses in a way different from the way Prolog uses them: the negated conjunctions are used as facts rather than as queries.

[11]This is set up as a "straw man" in order to consider what constraints on arbitrary defaults are implied by the other conditions.

It is presumed that the defaults make sense to the person adding them. A system with the arbitrary defaults property allows users to add any defaults they think are appropriate. This property makes no claims as to whether $p(x) \rightarrow q(x)$ should be acceptable as a default if either $p(x) \rightarrow \neg q(x)$ is a default or $\forall x \; p(x) \Rightarrow \neg q(x)$ follows from the facts (it does not seem reasonable to want to conclude q as well as $\neg q$ if a p is encountered).

The following is a constraint on systems with these properties.

Result 4.6. A default reasoning system cannot have all of the following properties:
- (i) conditioning,
- (ii) finite conjunctive closure,
- (iii) Horn representability,
- (iv) consistency,
- (v) arbitrary defaults.

Proof. To prove this, it suffices to give one set of inputs which follow the constraints given in (iii) and (v). By showing that properties (i) and (ii) lead to a contradiction with (iv), we demonstrate that a system with all five properties cannot exist.

Suppose

$$p(x) \rightarrow q_i(x)$$

is a default for $i = 1, \ldots, n$, and

$$\forall x \; \neg q_1(x) \vee \neg q_2(x) \vee \cdots \vee \neg q_n(x)$$

is a background fact, and we are given the contingent fact p(C). By (i) we conclude each "$q_i(C)$", and by (ii) we conclude their conjunction, which is inconsistent, contravening (iv).   □

Given that these five intuitive properties are inconsistent, it is interesting to consider which property different systems have given up.

(i) Conditioning is given up in circumscription [26], in any minimal model solution [43] and in systems which require membership in all extensions [27]. This is because they want the expressiveness that property (iii) gives, they need property (ii) by their very nature, and always reject having inconsistent extensions or reducing to no models. This means that they cannot guarantee that "birds fly" can be used when all they are told is that something is a bird.

Geffner [14] defines a partial order on models that ensures the conditioning property but has to give up "arbitrary defaults" or consistency.

Pollock, in his defeasible reasoning system [34], explicitly gives up this property using his "principle of collective defeat", as he wants the property of finite conjunctive closure. Similarly, Gabbay [10] gives up conditioning by his "compatibility of the > rules" property, which is essentially finite conjunctive closure.

(ii) Finite conjunctive closure is given up in many probability-based systems [1,29], and in systems which, for prediction, only require membership in one extension [28,36,40]. These latter systems get the conditioning property for the wrong reason, namely by being able to conclude a proposition and also conclude its negation (albeit in different extensions).

(iii) Horn representability is given up in inheritance systems [45,46]. These allow (i), (ii), (iv) and (v), however they lack the expressiveness of the richer logic-based formalisms.

(iv) Consistency is given up by thresholding probability as a basis for acceptance [19,25], but is not given up by any of the default reasoning systems I know of. It is, however, argued [18,20,33] that commonsense reasoning does indeed require reasoning under inconsistency.

(v) Arbitrary defaults are given up in ε-semantics [12,31]. There is no consistent probability assignment for the defaults and facts given in the proof of Result 4.6. There are two ways to interpret this:

(a) ε-inconsistency [15] captures the case where default reasoning fails. Detecting that a system is not ε-consistent indicates that there is something wrong with the axiomatisation that should be fixed [31, Section 5].

(b) It means we must treat seriously the semantics saying there are only infinitesimally few exceptions. It shows we cannot use the system if the proportion of exceptions does not have measure zero. In particular, this system does not seem appropriate to represent "birds fly", as it is not true there are infinitesimally few birds that don't fly.

Consider now the implication imposed by the other conditions on "arbitrary defaults". We get into problems when the conjunction of the conclusions of the defaults directly following from some contingent knowledge are inconsistent. Requiring the other four conditions is like imposing the condition that not only does the individual that is normal in every respect exist, but the individual that is normal in every respect is the normal individual.

This section relied on the use of conditioning in formalising our version of the lottery paradox. It is not that the lottery paradox only arises when we use conditioning (Example 2.7 was not stated in terms of conditioning), but rather that the use of conditioning helps us understand what is violated in the lottery paradox. Without casting it in terms of background and contingent knowledge it is difficult to give a condition under which it is unreasonable that a default not be applicable (cf. Example 3.1).

5. Related work

5.1. Lottery paradox and default reasoning

Perlis [33] has also discussed how the lottery paradox can arise in default reasoning. He shows that "omnithinkers" who are Socratic (admit that some of their beliefs are wrong), and recollective (can recall all of their default conclusions) cannot be consistent.

Perlis' argument is very different from the one presented here. We do not require either of these assumptions. We are not talking about how a set of derived conclusions are in conflict, but rather about how one conclusion cannot be drawn because the defaults are in conflict.

Whereas Perlis' argument depends on reasoners reasoning in time, and then admitting that they made a mistake, and so being inconsistent, we rely on the argument that a reasoner will not derive even a direct conclusion. Rather than finding that their conclusions lead to a contradiction, the systems under consideration go to extreme lengths to avoid inconsistencies, even to the point of not being able to use their defaults.

Notice also that the argument presented here consists of a "narrow scope" [8] application of defaults. We are only trying to use a default for one individual and not trying to derive conclusions about an entire population (as do typical instances of the lottery paradox [19,20,33]). The problem is not that there is a default that is not applicable for multiple individuals, but rather that there is an individual for which a set of multiple defaults is not applicable.

Thus, intuitively, restricting the scope of individuals [8] is not a viable solution to the instance of the paradox presented here. However we can solve instances of the qualitative lottery example by reifying the defaults [8]. This is done when we use the abnormality notation; we can use $\neg ab(Birdsfly, x)$ to make the constant *Birdsfly* denote the default. The lottery paradox of Example 2.7 can be avoided for the conclusion about whether Tweety flies by restricting the scope to, say, the constants *Birdsfly* and *Tweety*. The question then arises as to how we knew that we wanted "*Birdsfly*" in the scope. Either it had something to do with a query that we were asking the knowledge base, or it didn't. If it has something to do with a query, then, presumably we are giving up finite conjunctive closure. Different queries will have different scopes, and so it should not be expected that their conclusions conjoin. If the scope does not depend on the query, then either all of the contradictory defaults are in the scope, in which case we still have the qualitative lottery paradox, or some are missing in which case there are some conclusions that have direct defaults, but cannot be concluded. This is very much like just ignoring some of the defaults.

When we have to reify the defaults and then specify which individuals are in the scope, we effectively have to specify which defaults we want to use. It is possible to view defaults as possible hypotheses [36], that can be used as implicit premises in logical arguments. If using scope means we have to make these premises explicit, then it should not be surprising that we can add scope to any of the logic based non-monotonic reasoning formalisms [8], as once we have scope we don't need default reasoning.[12]

5.2. Probabilistic systems

One of the main features of probabilistic interpretations of defaults [31], whether they are based on probabilities arbitrarily close to one [12], an increase in probability [29] or simple majority [1], is the use of conditioning.

For example, the first, seemingly uncontroversial, axiom of ε-semantics [12] is

$$\text{If } (p \rightarrow q) \in \Delta, \text{ then } p \models_{<L,\Delta>} q.$$

This corresponds to the conditioning property presented in Section 4, but is, however, slightly stronger.

Example 5.1. Suppose, as background knowledge, we include

$$bird(Big\_bird) \wedge \neg flies(Big\_bird)$$

and have the default $bird(x) \rightarrow flies(x)$ (in [12] this means that the set of all its ground instances is in Δ). The conditioning property does not sanction us to conclude anything given $bird(Big\_bird)$. However, the above axiom of ε-semantics lets us conclude $flies(Big\_bird)$ from $bird(Big\_bird)$.

The above fact and default is, in fact, ε-inconsistent [31]. Geffner and Pearl [12] do not allow explicit exceptions as part of the background knowledge in this way. Semantically, the reason is that the default implies the conditional probability $p(flies(Big\_bird)|bird(Big\_bird))$ is close to one and the background facts about Big_bird imply that it is zero. Syntactically it is because the conditioning rule allows the conclusion of $flies(Big\_bird)$ from $bird(Big\_bird)$, and a deduction axiom (we conclude what logically follows from the facts) lets us conclude $\neg flies(Big\_bird)$.

---

[12]This was pointed out to me by Julian Craddock.

To represent the fact that Big Bird is an exceptional bird Geffner and Pearl would make a predicate $big\_bird(x)$ that is true if x is Big Bird, and write

$$big\_bird(x) \Rightarrow bird(x) \wedge \neg flies(x)$$

as a background fact. Rather than using a constant to denote the individual, we need to use a predicate to say that a particular constant denotes Big Bird. Thus although the conditioning in this paper and the conditioning in ε-semantics are different, in practice this difference would not be encountered.

There is one difference in interpretation that has been suggested for the distinction between contingent and background. Pearl [32] argues that the background knowledge is reserved exclusively for conditional sentences, regardless of whether they are exceptions or not. He wants to use the English word "if" to convey information as to whether knowledge is background or contingent. All ground sentences therefore would be contingent and not background. The distinction I have been arguing for is slightly different. It is a difference between who provides the knowledge; whether the defaults have taken into account some piece of knowledge or not. Whether this is the same distinction or amounts to the same thing in practice remains to be seen.

6. Conclusion

The unifying theme between the specificity and the lottery paradox problems, is to consider what happens when there are always multiple extensions when the antecedent of a default is true. That is, to consider the case when $p(x) \rightarrow q(x)$ is a default such that whenever $p(C)$ is true for any C, there are competing defaults that do not allow the conclusion of $q(C)$ (or also allow the conclusion $\neg q(C)$). If we do not handle the multiple extensions appropriately, the default becomes useless. We do not like defaults that can never be used; if a user didn't want a default to be used they would not have added the default in the first place.

It was argued that solutions to the multiple extension problem that rely on "knowing" exceptions do not work. It was shown why we need to distinguish between "background" and "contingent" knowledge, and why we should not expect to have conjunctive closure of our default conclusions.

The qualitative lottery paradox was discovered using our Theorist system [36] on (pseudo-real) problems. It was surprising to me to find out how naturally it arises in practice, and how difficult it is to get specificity working satisfactorily beyond trivial examples. There is much work that remains to be done on what problems arise in practice. We don't want to be like the intellectuals in Galileo's time [42, p. 520], and mistakenly think we know what the phenomena are that we are trying to formalise. We need to look at real representational problems and build more experiments to determine what these things we call defaults really are.

Acknowledgement

Thanks to all of the people at the Second International Workshop on Nonmonotonic Reasoning, and the International Conference on Representation and Reasoning who were involved in sharpening my ideas on this problem. Special thanks to Hector Geffner, Eric Neufeld, Judea Pearl and the anonymous reviewers for helping me to get these ideas straight. This research was supported under NSERC grant OGPOO44121.

References

[1] F. Bacchus, A modest, but semantically well founded inheritance reasoner, in: *Proceedings IJCAI-89*, Detroit, MI (1989) 1104–1109.

[2] F. Bacchus, *Representing and Reasoning with Probabilistic Knowledge* (MIT Press, Cambridge, MA, 1990).

[3] G. Brewka, Preferred subtheories: an extended logical framework for default reasoning, in: *Proceedings IJCAI-89*, Detroit, MI (1989) 1043–1048.

[4] G. Brewka, Nonmonotonic reasoning: from theoretical foundation towards efficient computation, Ph.D. Thesis, University of Hamburg (1989).

[5] B.G. Buchanan and E.H. Shortliffe, *Rule-Based Expert Systems* (Addison-Wesley, Reading, MA, 1984).

[6] J. Delgrande, An approach to default reasoning based on a first-order conditional logic: revised report, *Artif. Intell.* **36** (1988) 63–90.

[7] D. Etherington, Reasoning from incomplete information, in: Research Notes in AI (Pitman, London, 1987).

[8] D. Etherington, S. Kraus and D. Perlis, Nonmonotonicity and the scope of reasoning: preliminary report, in: *Proceedings AAAI-90*, Boston, MA (1990) 600–607.

[9] S. Fahlman, *NETL: A System for Representing and Using Real-World Knowledge* (MIT Press, Cambridge, MA, 1979).

[10] D.M. Gabbay, Theoretical foundations for non-monotonic reasoning systems, in: K.R. Apt, ed., *Logics and Models of Concurrent Systems* (Springer, Berlin, 1985) 439–457.

[11] H. Geffner, On the logic of defaults, in: *Proceedings AAAI-88*, St. Paul, MN (1988) 449–454.

[12] H. Geffner and J. Pearl, A framework for reasoning with defaults, in: H.E. Kyburg Jr et al., eds., *Defeasible Reasoning and Knowledge Representation* (Kluwer, Dordrecht, Netherlands 1990).

[13] H. Geffner, Personal Communication (May 1989).

[14] H. Geffner, Conditional entailment: closing the gap between defaults and conditionals, in: *Preprints of Third Workshop on Nonmonotonic Reasoning*, Lake Tahoe CA (1990) 58–72.

[15] M. Goldszmidt and J. Pearl, Deciding consistency of databases containing defeasible and strict information, in: M. Henrion et al., eds., *Uncertainty in Artificial Intelligence* **5** (North-Holland, Amsterdam, 1990) 87–97.

[16] S. Hanks and D. McDermott, Default reasoning, nonmonotonic logics and the frame problem, in: *Proceedings AAAI-86*, Philadelphia, PA (1986) 328–333.

[17] G.E. Hughes and M.J. Cresswell, *An Introduction to Modal Logic* (Methuen, London, 1968).

[18] D.J. Israel, What's wrong with non-monotonic logic, *Proceedings AAAI-80*, Stanford, CA (1980) 99–101.

[19] H.E. Kyburg Jr, *Probability and the Logic of Rational Belief* (Wesleyan University Press, Middletown, 1961).

[20] H.E. Kyburg, Jr, Probabilistic inference and non-monotonic inference, in: *Proceedings Fourth Workshop on Uncertainty in Artificial Intelligence*, Minneapolis, MN (1988) 221–228.

[21] D. Lehmann, What does a conditional knowledge base entail?, in: *Proceedings First International Conference on Principles of Knowledge Representation and Reasoning*, Toronto, Ont. (1989) 212–222.

[22] H.J. Levesque, Foundations of a functional approach to knowledge representation, *Artif. Intell.* **24** (1984) 155–212.

[23] H.J. Levesque, All I know: a study in autoepistemic logic, *Artif. Intell.* **43** (1990) 263–309.

[24] R.P. Loui, Defeat amongst arguments: a system of defeasible inference, *Comput. Intell.* **3** (1987) 100–106.

[25] R.P. Loui, Real rules of inference: acceptance and non-monotonicity in AI, Tech. Report TR-191, University of Rochester, NY (1986).

[26] J. McCarthy, Applications of circumscription to formalising common-sense knowledge, *Artif. Intell.* **28** (1986) 89–116.

[27] D.V. McDermott and J. Doyle, Non-monotonic logic 1, *Artif. Intell.* **13** (1980) 41–72.

[28] R.C. Moore, Semantical Considerations on nonmonotonic logic, *Artif. Intell.* **25** (1985) 75–94.

[29] E. Neufeld and D. Poole, Probabilistic semantics and defaults, in: *Proceedings Fourth Workshop on Uncertainty in Artificial Intelligence*, Minneapolis, MN (1988) 275–282.

[30] J. Pearl, *Probabilistic Reasoning in Intelligent Systems: Networks of Plausible Inference* (Morgan Kaufmann, Los Altos, CA, 1988).

[31] J. Pearl, Probabilistic semantics for nonmonotonic reasoning: a survey, in: *Proceedings First International Conference on Principles of Knowledge Representation and Reasoning*, Toronto, Ont. (1989) 505–516.

[32] J. Pearl, Jeffrey's rule, passage of experience and neo-Bayesianism, in: H.E. Kyburg Jr et al., eds., *Defeasible Reasoning and Knowledge Representation* (Kluwer, Dordrecht, 1990) 245–265.

[33] D. Perlis, On the consistency of commonsense reasoning, *Comput. Intell.* **2** (1987) 180–190.

[34] J.L. Pollock, Defeasible reasoning, *Cogn. Sci.* **11** (1987) 481–518.

[35] D. Poole, On the comparison of theories: preferring the most specific explanation, *Proceedings IJCAI-85*, Los Angeles, CA (1985) 144–147.

[36] D. Poole, A logical framework for default reasoning, *Artif. Intell.* **36** (1988) 27–47.

[37] D. Poole, Explanation and prediction: an architecture for default and abductive reasoning, *Comput. Intell.* **5** (1989) 97–110.

[38] D. Poole, What the lottery paradox tells us about default reasoning, in: *Proceedings First International Conference on Principles of Knowledge Representation and Reasoning*, Toronto, Ont. (1989) 333–340.

[39] H.E. Pople Jr, On the mechanization of abductive logic, *Proceedings IJCAI-73*, New York (1973) 147–152.

[40] R. Reiter, A logic for default reasoning, *Artif. Intell.* **33** (1980) 81–132.

[41] R. Reiter and G. Criscuolo, On interacting defaults, in: *Proceedings IJCAI-1981*, Vancouver, BC (1981) 270–276.

[42] B. Russell, *A History of Western Philosophy* (Counterpoint, London, 1984) (first published 1945).

[43] Y. Shoham, Nonmonotonic logics: meaning and utility, in: *Proceedings IJCAI-87*, Milan, Italy (1987) 388–393.

[44] Y. Shoham and Y. Moses, Belief as defeasible knowledge, in: *Proceedings IJCAI-89*, Detroit, MI (1989) 1168–1173.

[45] R.H. Thomason and J.F. Horty, Logics for inheritance theory, in: *Proceedings Second International Workshop on Non-Monotonic Reasoning*, Lecture Notes in Artificial Intelligence **346** (Springer, Berlin, 1988) 220–237.

[46] D.S. Touretzky, *The Mathematics of Inheritance Theory* (Pitman, London/Morgan Kaufmann, Los Altos, CA, 1986).

Artificial Intelligence 49 (1991) 309–343
Elsevier

Three-valued nonmonotonic formalisms and semantics of logic programs

Teodor Przymusinski*

Department of Mathematical Sciences, The University of Texas at El Paso, El Paso, TX 79968, USA

Received 1 November 1989
Revised October 1990

Abstract

Przymusinski, T., Three-valued nonmonotonic formalisms and semantics of logic programs, Artificial Intelligence 49 (1991) 309–343.

We introduce *three-valued extensions* of major nonmonotonic formalisms and we prove that the recently proposed *well-founded semantics* of logic programs is equivalent, for *arbitrary* logic programs, to three-valued forms of McCarthy's circumscription, Reiter's closed world assumption, Moore's autoepistemic logic and Reiter's default theory. This result not only provides a further justification of the well-founded semantics as a natural extension of the perfect model semantics from the class of stratified programs to the class of all logic programs, but it also establishes the class of *all logic programs* as a large class of theories, for which *natural forms of all four nonmonotonic formalisms coincide*. It also paves the way for using efficient computation methods, developed for logic programming, as inference mechanisms for nonmonotonic reasoning.

1. Introduction

A precise meaning or *semantics* must be associated with any logic program or a deductive database in order to provide its declarative specification, in a manner, which is independent of procedural considerations, context-free, and easy to manipulate, exchange and reason about. The problem of finding a suitable declarative or intended semantics is one of the most

*The author acknowledges support from the National Science Foundation under grant #IRI-89-10729 and from the Army Research Office under grant #27079-MA-SAH.

0004-3702/91/$03.50 © 1991—Elsevier Science Publishers B.V.

important and difficult problems in the theory of logic programming and deductive databases. It also reveals a close relationship existing between logic programming and nonmonotonic reasoning (see [24,26,28]). On the one hand, due to the nonmonotonic character of negation operators used in logic programs and deductive databases, any such intended semantics of a program *P* must be *nonmonotonic* and therefore the problem of finding a proper semantics for logic programs and deductive databases can be viewed as the problem of finding a suitable *nonmonotonic formalization* of the type of reasoning used in logic programming. On the other hand, precisely because of its nonmonotonic character, logic programming can often be used as an *efficient inference engine* for other nonmonotonic formalisms [35].

Recently, the *perfect model semantics* of logic programs has been introduced [1,25,37] and shown to provide an attractive alternative to the traditionally used semantics of logic programs based on *Clark's predicate completion* of the program [4,5,13,18], while at the same time eliminating some serious drawbacks of the latter [29]. The perfect model semantics is not only intuitive, but it also has been shown (see [26]) to be equivalent to suitable forms of all four major formalizations of nonmonotonic reasoning—McCarthy's circumscription [20,21], Reiter's closed world assumption, CWA [33], Moore's autoepistemic logic [22] and Reiter's default theory [34]—thus underlying the close linkage between the areas of logic programming and nonmonotonic reasoning and describing an important class of theories for which natural forms of different nonmonotonic formalisms coincide.

The perfect model semantics, however, is defined only for a relatively narrow class of logic programs, including the class of *stratified* programs [1,3,37]. Subsequently, three different extensions of the perfect model semantics have been proposed:

- *the stable model semantics* [8] based on autoepistemic logic [6] (equivalent to the default model semantics [2] based on default logic);
- *the weakly perfect model semantics* [23] based on circumscription and CWA;
- *the well-founded model semantics* [38].

The *well-founded* semantics is three-valued and, as opposed to the remaining two semantics, is defined for *all* logic programs. Moreover, the author showed [27] that it has properties entirely analogous to the properties of the perfect model semantics. In particular, well-founded models are *minimal models* of the program, as well as *iterated fixed points* of natural operators, *iterated least models* of the program and *preferred models*, with respect to a natural priority relation. Moreover, the least fixed point definition of the well-founded model leads to a natural notion of *dynamic stratification* of an *arbitrary* logic program. Finally, in [30] the author introduced a three-valued version of the stable model semantics and showed that it also *coincides* with the well-founded semantics.

In summary, the well-founded semantics appears to be the *most suitable semantics* for logic programs (see [24] for an overview), avoiding various drawbacks of Clark's predicate completion semantics. The latter, however, can be viewed as a natural and computationally less expensive *approximation* to the well-founded semantics, in the sense that any answers given by the Fitting–Kunen three-valued extension of Clark's semantics [5,13] (or by SLDNF-resolution) are *correct* with respect to the well-founded semantics (but not vice versa).

However, due to the fact that its original definition was not based on any particular nonmonotonic formalism, initially the relationship of well-founded semantics to nonmonotonic formalisms was unclear. Moreover, the fact that well-founded semantics was different from the other two, also mutually distinct, semantics based on various nonmonotonic formalisms, seemed to preclude the possibility of establishing the equivalence of the well-founded semantics to all major nonmonotonic formalisms in classes of programs much broader than the class of stratified programs.

In this paper we show, however, that the well-founded model semantics is also *equivalent* to suitable forms of *all four major formalizations of nonmonotonic reasoning*. However, in order to achieve this equivalence, *three-valued extensions* of nonmonotonic formalisms are needed, which is natural in view of the fact that the well-founded semantics is, in general, three-valued. Accordingly, we define such three-valued extensions of all four nonmonotonic formalisms and we prove that the well-founded semantics is equivalent to suitable three-valued forms of McCarthy's circumscription, Reiter's closed world assumption, Moore's autoepistemic logic and Reiter's default theory.

These results not only provide a further justification of the well-founded semantics, as a suitable semantics for the class of *all* logic programs, but they also establish a large class of theories—namely the class of all logic programs—for which natural forms of all four nonmonotonic formalisms coincide. They also pave the way for using efficient computation methods, developed for logic programming, as *inference mechanisms* for nonmonotonic reasoning.

The author has shown in [27,29] that the well-founded semantics has a *sound and complete procedural mechanism*, called *SLS-resolution* and work has already begun on its effective implementation [10,36,39]. The most significant seems to be the work of Warren on the *Extended Warren Abstract Machine* (XWAM) and a Prolog interpreter which computes the well-founded (or three-valued stable) semantics of logic programs rather than the traditional Clark's predicate completion semantics (see [32] for more details).

The equivalence of semantics implies that SLS-resolution, or any other similar mechanism, can be used as an efficient inference engine for all four nonmonotonic formalisms in the class of logic programs. Moreover, since nonmonotonic theories which are originally *not* given as logic programs, can be often translated (compiled) into logic programs [7], the domain of applicability of SLS-resolution extends much beyond the class of nonmonotonic theories having the form of logic programs.

The extended formalizations of nonmonotonic reasoning introduced in this paper are also likely to prove useful and important in their own right. To illustrate this point, let us consider the following simple autoepistemic theory:

$$\neg \mathbf{L}\textit{tired} \rightarrow \textit{work},$$
$$\neg \mathbf{L}\textit{work} \rightarrow \textit{sleep},$$
$$\neg \mathbf{L}\textit{sleep} \rightarrow \textit{tired},$$
$$\textit{work} \wedge \neg \mathbf{L}\textit{paid} \rightarrow \textit{angry},$$
$$\textit{paid},$$

where "**L**" stands for Moore's *autoepistemic belief operator*. On the one hand, it seems clear that we should believe in *paid* (i.e., **L***paid* must be true) and therefore we should disbelieve *angry* (i.e., **L***angry* must be false). On the other hand, it appears that the first three rules describe only *mutual relationships* between propositions *tired*, *work* and *sleep*, without providing sufficient information to justify either believing or disbelieving them. Depending on the point of view, we could describe our knowledge about propositions *tired*, *work* and *sleep* as either incomplete or perhaps even confusing. It seems therefore that the given theory does not determine our beliefs as far as propositions **L***tired*, **L***work*, **L***sleep* are concerned. Observe, however, that there is nothing unusual about it. In classical logic (as well as in common-sense reasoning) most theories are *incomplete*, i.e., they often neither imply a given formula nor its negation. There is no reason why we should have a different situation as far as beliefs are concerned and be always "forced" to either believe that something is true or believe that it is false. It is quite natural to believe *neither*. This leads naturally to the unique autoepistemic expansion $\mathcal{E}(T)$ of the theory T in which **L***paid* is true, **L***angry* is false but neither the beliefs **L***tired*, **L***work*, **L***sleep* nor their negations are provable from $\mathcal{E}(T)$. If we later learn, e.g., that *work* is actually true then we will conclude that we disbelieve *sleep* and believe in *tired*, but our beliefs about *paid* and *angry* will remain unchanged.

Unfortunately, the above described expansion is *not* a stable autoepistemic expansion in the standard autoepistemic logic AEL. In fact, the above theory does *not* have any autoepistemic expansions in AEL and therefore, from the standpoint of AEL it is *inconsistent*. Consequently, had we decided to use the standard autoepistemic logic, we not only would have been unable to find out that we have an *incomplete* information about properties *tired, work* and *sleep*, but also, perhaps more importantly, we would have been unable to establish the well-determined beliefs about properties *paid* and *angry*.

The above example stresses one of the basic differences between our extended notion of a stable expansion and standard stable expansions. Namely, standard autoepistemic expansions always imply either L*A* or ¬L*A*, for all formulae *A*, i.e., stable expansions always *completely decide* all our beliefs, disallowing the situation, typically occurring in logic (and in commonsense reasoning), that a theory neither implies some formula nor its negation. In particular, autoepistemic expansions do not allow us to believe (or disbelieve) either *A* or *C*, without specifically believing *A* or believing *B*, i.e., they never imply a disjunctive belief formula L*A* ∨ L*C*, without implying either L*A* or L*C*. This is because in the definition of stable expansions we believe in *A* whenever it is provable from the theory and we disbelieve it otherwise, i.e., we always believe a formula or disbelieve it. This appears to be a *serious drawback* of stable expansions resulting in a less expressive logic, which for many reasonable theories is inconsistent and lacks the ability to be effectively computed even within natural classes of theories.

It is important to stress that, while in this paper we use three-valued logic to define the extended nonmonotonic formalisms, *three-valued logic is not necessary* for this purpose and formalisms with analogous properties can be defined *in terms of classical two-valued logic*. In particular, in [31] the author introduces new Autoepistemic Logics of Closed Beliefs whose special case coincides with the three-valued autoepistemic logic defined in this paper, and yet its definition does *not* use three-valued logic.

The above discussion applies equally well to logic programs or deductive databases which may contain, in addition to predicates whose truth value is *fully determined* by the program, also predicates whose truth or falsity is *not* fully determined by the program. For example, consider the logic program *P* naturally corresponding to the above autoepistemic theory *T* [6]:

$$work \leftarrow \neg tired,$$
$$sleep \leftarrow \neg work,$$
$$tired \leftarrow \neg sleep,$$
$$paid \leftarrow,$$
$$angry \leftarrow \neg paid, work.$$

Again, the truth or falsity of predicates *work, sleep* and *tired* is not fully determined by the program, yet, regardless of the status of those predicates, *paid* must be true and thus *angry* must be false. Had we decided to use, e.g., the stable semantics of logic programs, we would have been unable to assign any meaning to this program and thus we would have to view it as *inconsistent*.

It is hoped that the results obtained in this paper will contribute to a better understanding of relations existing between nonmonotonic reasoning and logic programming as well as relations existing between various formalizations of nonmonotonic reasoning and thus to the eventual discovery of deeper underlying principles of nonmonotonic reasoning.

The paper is organized as follows. In Section 2 we define three-valued models of first-order theories. In Section 3 we discuss logic programs and their three-valued models and we define the well-founded semantics. In Section 4 we introduce three-valued circumscription and we prove the equivalence of circumscriptive and well-founded semantics. In Section 5 we define three-valued autoepistemic logic and we show the equivalence of autoepistemic and well-founded semantics. In Section 6 we point out that analogous results can be obtained for Reiter's default theory and CWA.

2. Three-valued models

In this section we define three-valued models of first-order theories. We closely follow the approach developed in [24,27].

By an *alphabet* $\mathcal{A}$ of a first-order language $\mathcal{L}$ we mean a (finite or countably infinite) set of *constant*, *predicate* and *function* symbols.[1] In addition, any alphabet is assumed to contain a countably infinite set of *variable* symbols, connectives $(\wedge, \vee, \neg, \leftarrow)$, quantifiers $(\exists, \forall)$ and the usual punctuation symbols. A *term* over $\mathcal{A}$ is defined recursively as either a variable or a constant or an expression of the form $f(t_1, \ldots, t_k)$, where f is a function symbol and the t_i are terms. An *atom* over $\mathcal{A}$ is an expression of the form $p(t_1, \ldots, t_k)$, where p is a predicate symbol and the t_i are terms. The *first-order language* $\mathcal{L}$ over the alphabet $\mathcal{A}$ is defined as the set of all well-formed first-order formulae that can be built starting from the atoms and using connectives, quantifiers and punctuation symbols in a standard way. A *literal* is an atom or its negation. An atom A is called a *positive literal* and its negation $\neg A$ is called a *negative literal*. An expression is called *ground* if it does not contain any variables. The set of all ground atoms of $\mathcal{A}$ is called the *Herbrand base* $\mathcal{H}$ of $\mathcal{A}$. If G is a quantifier-free formula, then by its *ground instance* we mean any ground formula obtained from G by (consistently) substituting ground terms for all variables. For a given formula G of $\mathcal{L}$ its *universal closure* or just *closure* $(\forall)G$ is obtained by universally quantifying all variables

---

[1] The set of function symbols may be empty while the sets of constant and predicate symbols are assumed to be nonempty.

in G which are not bound by any quantifier. A closed formula is called a *sentence*. Unless otherwise stated, all formulae are assumed to be *closed*.

Definition 2.1. By a *three-valued Herbrand interpretation* I of the language $\mathcal{L}$ we mean any pair $\langle T; F \rangle$, where T and F are disjoint subsets of the Herbrand base $\mathcal{H}$. The set T contains all ground atoms true in I, the set F contains all ground atoms false in I and the truth value of the remaining atoms in $U = \mathcal{H} - (T \cup F)$ is unknown (or undefined). A three-valued interpretation is two-valued iff $\mathcal{H} = T \cup F$ or, equivalently, iff $U = \emptyset$.

Throughout the paper, we restrict ourselves to Herbrand models, but our definitions and most of the results can be easily extended to the non-Herbrand case (cf. [24]). Any interpretation $I = \langle T; F \rangle$ can be equivalently viewed as a function $I : \mathcal{H} \rightarrow \{0, \frac{1}{2}, 1\}$, from the Herbrand base $\mathcal{H}$ to the three-element set $\mathcal{V} = \{0, \frac{1}{2}, 1\}$, defined by:

$$I(A) = \begin{cases} 0, & \text{if } A \in F, \\ \frac{1}{2}, & \text{if } A \in U, \\ 1, & \text{if } A \in T. \end{cases}$$

We now extend the function (interpretation) $I : \mathcal{H} \rightarrow \mathcal{V}$ recursively to the truth valuation $\hat{I} : \mathcal{C} \rightarrow \mathcal{V}$ defined on the set $\mathcal{C}$ of all closed formulae of the language.

Definition 2.2. If I is an interpretation, then the *truth valuation* $\hat{I}$ corresponding to I is a function $\hat{I} : \mathcal{C} \rightarrow \mathcal{V}$ from the set $\mathcal{C}$ of all (closed) formulae of the language to $\mathcal{V}$ recursively defined as follows:
- If A is a ground atom, then $\hat{I}(A) = I(A)$.
- If S is a closed formula then $\hat{I}(\neg S) = 1 - \hat{I}(S)$.
- If S and V are closed formulae, then

$$\hat{I}(S \wedge V) = \min(\hat{I}(S), \hat{I}(V));$$
$$\hat{I}(S \vee V) = \max\{\hat{I}(S), \hat{I}(V)\};$$
$$\hat{I}(V \leftarrow S) = \begin{cases} 1, & \text{if } \hat{I}(V) \geq \hat{I}(S), \\ 0, & \text{otherwise.} \end{cases}$$

- For any formula $S(x)$ with one unbound variable x:

$$\hat{I}(\forall x\, S(x)) = \min\{\hat{I}(S(A)): A \in \mathcal{H}\};$$
$$\hat{I}(\exists x\, S(x)) = \max\{\hat{I}(S(A)): A \in \mathcal{H}\};$$

where the maximum (respectively minimum) of an empty set is defined as 0 (respectively 1).

We can now define the remaining connectives $\Rightarrow$, $\leftrightarrow$, $\Leftrightarrow$ in the usual way:

$$S \Rightarrow V \equiv V \vee \neg S;$$

$$S \leftrightarrow V \equiv (S \to V) \wedge (V \to S);$$

$$S \Leftrightarrow V \equiv (S \Rightarrow V) \wedge (V \Rightarrow S).$$

Our definition of the truth valuation $\hat{I}$ for the connectives $\vee$, $\wedge$, $\neg$ and for the quantifiers $\forall$, $\exists$ uses the so-called (strong) Kleene tables [11]. The truth valuation for the connective $\leftarrow$ is modeled after the approach proposed in [5,13]. There the connective $\leftrightarrow$ is introduced and used to to define three-valued extensions of the Clark predicate completion semantics. The motivation behind the definition of the truth valuation for the implication $V \leftarrow S$ is that the truth value of the consequent V is supposed to be greater than or equal to the truth value of the premise S.

Remark 2.3. Although the two implication connectives $\to$ and $\Rightarrow$ coincide in two-valued logic, they are in general different in three-valued logic. For example, $\mathrm{val}_I(S \to S) = 1$, regardless of the truth value of S, but $\mathrm{val}_I(S \Rightarrow S) = \frac{1}{2}$, if $\mathrm{val}_I(S) = \frac{1}{2}$. This is a reflection of the fact that in three-valued logic we have several different notions of implication, all of which are natural and applicable in different contexts. Similar remarks apply to the two equivalence connectives $\leftrightarrow$ and $\Leftrightarrow$. For example, in [5,13] the equivalence connective "$\leftrightarrow$" represents the equivalence relation needed to build Clark's completion of the program P, while the equivalence connective "$\Leftrightarrow$" is used in the program P itself.

Truth valuations assign to every formula F a number $0, \frac{1}{2}$ or 1, which reflects the *degree of truth* of F, ranging from the lowest, namely *false* (0), through *unknown* ($\frac{1}{2}$), to the highest, namely *true* (1).

Definition 2.4. A *theory* over $\mathcal{L}$ is a (finite or countably infinite) set of closed formulae (sentences) of $\mathcal{L}$. An interpretation I is a (two-valued or three-valued) *model* of a theory R if $\hat{I}(S) = 1$, for all formulae S in R.

There are *two natural orderings* between three-valued interpretations, one of them, $\preceq$, is called the *standard ordering* and the other, $\preceq_F$, is called the *F-ordering* (or Fitting-ordering).

Definition 2.5 [27] Suppose that $I = \langle T; F \rangle$ and $J = \langle T'; F' \rangle$ are two interpretations. We say that $I \preceq J$ if

$$T \subseteq T' \quad \text{and} \quad F \supseteq F'.$$

We say that $I \preceq_F J$ if

$$T \subseteq T' \quad \text{and} \quad F \subseteq F'.$$

Models which are $\preceq$-minimal or $\preceq$-least will be just called minimal or least, respectively. On the other hand, models which are $\preceq_F$-minimal or $\preceq_F$-least will be called F-minimal or F-least, respectively. If $I \preceq J$ (respectively $I \preceq_F J$) and $I \neq J$, then we write $I \prec J$ (respectively $I \prec_F J$).

It is easy to verify that $I \preceq J$ if and only if for all atoms A:

$$I(A) \leq J(A) \quad \text{(or, equivalently, } \hat{I}(A) \leq \hat{J}(A)\text{)},$$

i.e., if and only if $I \preceq J$ in the sense of the usual *pointwise ordering* between functions. The notions of *minimal* and *least* models are clearly different from the notions of *F-minimal* and *F-least* models. While minimal and least models of a theory minimize the *degree of truth* of their atoms, by minimizing the set T of true atoms and maximizing the set F of false atoms F, F-minimal and F-least models minimize the *degree of information* of their atoms, by jointly minimizing the sets T and F of atoms which are either true or false and thus maximizing the set U of unknown atoms. For example, the F-least model of the theory $p \leftarrow p$ is obtained when p is undefined, while the least model of P is obtained when p is false.

3. Logic programs and the well-founded semantics

In this section we define logic programs and their three-valued models [27]. We also introduce the well-founded models and the well-founded semantics [38].

By a *logic program* we mean a (finite or countably infinite) set of universally closed *clauses* of the form

$$A \leftarrow L_1 \wedge \cdots \wedge L_m,$$

where $m \geq 0$, A is an atom and the L_i are literals. Literals L_i are called *premises* and the atom A is called the *head* of the clause. Conforming to a standard convention, conjunctions are replaced by commas and therefore clauses are written in the form

$$A \leftarrow L_1, \ldots, L_m.$$

A program is called *positive* if all of its clauses have only positive (atomic) premises.

Remark 3.1. Notice, that in the definition of a program clause we use the implication symbol $\leftarrow$ rather than $\Leftarrow$, because the satisfaction of the condition that $val_I(S \leftarrow S) = 1$, regardless of the truth value of S (see Remark 2.3), is essential for logic programming.

If P is a program then, unless stated otherwise, we will assume that the alphabet $\mathcal{A}$ used to write P consists precisely of all the constant, predicate and function symbols that explicitly *appear* in P and thus $\mathcal{A} = \mathcal{A}_P$ is completely determined[2] by the program P. We can then talk about the first-order *language $\mathcal{L} = \mathcal{L}_P$ of the program P and the Herbrand base $\mathcal{H} = \mathcal{H}_P$ of the program.*

Clearly, every program P is a theory and the following proposition is straightforward:

Proposition 3.2 [27] *A (Herbrand) interpretation M is a model of a program P if and only if for every ground instance*

$$A \leftarrow L_1, \ldots, L_m$$

of a program clause we have

$$\hat{M}(A) \geq \min\{\hat{M}(L_i): i \leq m\}.$$

Thus, M is a model of a program if and only if the degree of truth of the head of every clause is at least as high as the degree of truth of the conjunction of its premises.

By a *ground instantiation* of a logic program P we mean the (possibly infinite) theory consisting of all ground instances of clauses from P. The following proposition is obvious.

Proposition 3.3. *A (Herbrand) interpretation M is a model of a program P if and only if it is a model of its ground instantiation.*

The above proposition shows that for model-theoretic purposes (as long as only Herbrand interpretations are considered) one can identify any program P with its ground instantiation. Whenever convenient, we will assume, without further mention, that the program P has already been instantiated.

[2]If there are no constants in P, then one is added to the alphabet.

3.1. Well-founded models

We now recall the definition of well-founded models. We combine here the definitions given in [27,38]. Suppose that P is a logic program and I is a three-valued interpretation. We define two subsets T_I and F_I of the Herbrand base as follows:

- T_I is the smallest set of atoms A with the property that A is in T_I if there is a clause $A \leftarrow L_1, \ldots, L_n$ in P such that, for all $i \leq n$, either $\hat{I}(L_i) = 1$ or $L_i = B_i$ is an atom and B_i is in T_I.
- F_I is the largest set of atoms A with the property that if A is in F_I then for every clause $A \leftarrow L_1, \ldots, L_n$ in P there is an $i \leq n$ such that either $\hat{I}(L_i) = 0$ or $L_i = B_i$ is an atom and B_i is in F_I.

The sets T_I and F_I always exist. Intuitively, the set T_I contains all atomic facts which can be derived from P using all true or false facts in the interpretation I. The set F_I, on the other hand, contains all atomic facts which can be assumed false knowing P and all true or false facts in I.

The well-founded model is defined recursively as follows. Let $M_0 = \langle \emptyset; \emptyset \rangle$ and suppose that for every $\alpha < \beta$ interpretations $M_\alpha = \langle T_\alpha; F_\alpha \rangle$ are already defined. Define

$$M_\beta = \langle T_{M_\alpha}; F_{M_\alpha} \rangle$$

if $\beta = \alpha + 1$ is a successor ordinal and

$$M_\beta = \left\langle \bigcup_{\alpha < \beta} T_\alpha; \bigcup_{\alpha < \beta} F_\alpha \right\rangle$$

if β is a limit ordinal. One can show that the transfinite sequence M_α is increasing and therefore there must exist a first ordinal δ such that $M_{\delta+1} = M_\delta$. The fixed point interpretation

$$M_P = M_\delta = \langle T_\delta; F_\delta \rangle = \langle T_{M_\delta}; F_{M_\delta} \rangle$$

can be shown to be a minimal model of P and is called the *well-founded model* of P.

Intuitively, we start with the empty interpretation $M_0 = \langle \emptyset; \emptyset \rangle$ and then at every successor level $\beta = \alpha + 1$ we define the interpretation M_β to contain all atomic facts which can be derived from P knowing M_α and negations of all atomic facts which can be assumed false knowing P and M_α. At every successor level β we add up all the previously obtained interpretations M_α, for $\alpha < \beta$, and we stop at the level δ if nothing new can be obtained.

The *well-founded semantics* of a logic program P is determined by the unique well-founded model M_P of P. We will now use the definition of the well-founded model given above to introduce the *dynamic stratification* of an *arbitrary* logic program P [27]. In the next section, we will show that the well-founded semantics of P is equivalent to the three-valued circumscriptive semantics of P with respect to priorities induced by the dynamic stratification. The dynamic stratification $\{S_\beta : 0 \leq \beta \leq \delta\}$ of P is a decomposition of the Herbrand base $\mathcal{H}_P$ of the program into disjoint strata S_β and has properties similar to the properties of standard stratification and local stratification [1,25,37].

Definition 3.4 [27] For $\beta < \delta$ the β's *dynamic stratum* S_β of P is defined recursively as follows:

$$S_0 = T_{M_0} \cup F_{M_0},$$

$$S_\beta = T_{M_\beta} \cup F_{M_\beta} - \bigcup_{\alpha < \beta} S_\alpha.$$

Moreover, the δ's stratum of P is defined as

$$S_\delta = \mathcal{H}_P - \bigcup_{\alpha < \delta} S_\alpha.$$

The β's stratum S_β of P is therefore defined at level $\beta < \delta$ as the set of all ground atoms that were *newly added* to the interpretation M_β in order to obtain $M_{\beta+1}$ (i.e., those atoms whose truth or falsity was determined at this very level). The last stratum S_δ contains all the remaining atoms, i.e., all atoms whose truth value is undefined in M_P. Therefore, the well-founded model M_P is two-valued if and only if its last stratum S_δ is empty.

4. Three-valued circumscription

In this section we define *three-valued (parallel and prioritized) circumscription* and we show that the well-founded semantics of logic programs is equivalent to the semantics of three-valued prioritized circumscription (with respect to priorities determined by the *dynamic stratification* of the program). This result extends earlier results [16,25,29] showing that the perfect model semantics of *stratified* logic programs is equivalent to the semantics of (two-valued) prioritized circumscription (with respect to priorities determined by standard stratification).

We use a model-theoretic definition of circumscription and we limit our attention to Herbrand models, but our definitions can be easily extended to non-Herbrand models. The only difference between the (model-theoretic) definition of two-valued circumscription [14,15,20,21] and our definition of three-valued circumscription lies in the fact that the former uses only two-valued minimal models while the latter uses all *three-valued minimal models* of the circumscribed theory.

As we mentioned in Section 2, any three-valued interpretation or model M can be viewed as a function

$$M : \mathcal{H}_{\mathcal{L}} \to \{0, \tfrac{1}{2}, 1\}$$

defined on the Herbrand base $\mathcal{H}_{\mathcal{L}}$ of the language with values in the set $\mathcal{V} = \{0, \tfrac{1}{2}, 1\}$. If S is a subset of the Herbrand base, then by $M|S$ we will denote the *restriction* of the interpretation M (viewed as a function) to the set S, i.e.,

$$M|S : S \to \{0, \tfrac{1}{2}, 1\}.$$

By $\prec$ and $\preceq$ we will denote the usual (strict or not) *pointwise ordering* between functions. This ordering coincides with the *standard ordering* between interpretations given in Definition 2.5.

Suppose now that P is a theory over the language $\mathcal{L}$ and suppose that R and Z are two disjoint subsets of the Herbrand base $\mathcal{H}_{\mathcal{L}}$ of $\mathcal{L}$. Atoms in R are called *minimized atoms* and atoms in Z are called *variable atoms*. The remaining atoms in the set $Q = \mathcal{H}_{\mathcal{L}} - (R \cup Z)$ are called *parameters*. We now define three-valued (R, Z)-minimal models of P.

Definition 4.1. We will say that a model M of a theory P is (R, Z)-*less* than a model N if:
  (i) $M|Q = N|Q$;
  (ii) $M|R \prec N|R$.
We denote this fact by $M \prec_{(R,Z)} N$. We say that a model N of P is (R, Z)-*minimal* if there is no model M such that $M \prec_{(R,Z)} N$.

In other words, $M \prec_{(R,Z)} N$ if both models coincide on parameters Q and if the model M restricted to the set R of minimized atoms is strictly smaller than the model N restricted to R. In the special case when *all* atoms are minimized, i.e., when $R = \mathcal{H}_{\mathcal{L}}$, the above ordering $\prec_{(R,Z)}$ coincides with the standard ordering $\prec$ between interpretations and the notion of an (R, Z)-minimal model coincides with the notion of a minimal model.

We now give a model-theoretic definition of three-valued parallel circumscription.

Definition 4.2. A structure M is called a model of *three-valued parallel circumscription* CIRC3$(P; R; Z)$ *of* P, with atoms in R minimized and atoms in Z varied, if and only if M is a three-valued (R, Z)-minimal model of P. A sentence K is said to be *implied* by parallel circumscription CIRC3$(P; R; Z)$ if and only if it is true in all of its models. We denote this fact by

$$\text{CIRC3}(P; R; Z) \models K.$$

In the special case when *all* atoms are minimized, i.e., when $R = \mathcal{H}_\mathcal{L}$, instead of CIRC3($P; R; Z$) we will simply write CIRC3(P). Clearly, M is a model of CIRC3(P) if and only if M is a minimal model of P.

We now turn to three-valued prioritized circumscription. Suppose that $\{S_\beta\}_{0 \leq \beta < \lambda}$ are disjoint subsets of the Herbrand base $\mathcal{H}_\mathcal{L}$ of $\mathcal{L}$ and suppose that Z is a subset of $\mathcal{H}_\mathcal{L}$ disjoint from all the sets S_β. The collection $\{S_\beta\}$ can be thought of as assigning different *priorities* for minimization to the elements of the Herbrand base, with the highest priority given to the atoms in S_0, the next highest to the atoms in S_1, etc. Elements of Z will be called, as before, variable atoms and the remaining atoms (forming the set Q) are parameters.

Definition 4.3. A structure M is called a model of *three-valued prioritized circumscription* CIRC3($P; S_0 > S_1 > \cdots; Z$) *of P*, with respect to priorities $S_0 > S_1 > \cdots$ and variables Z if and only if for every $\beta < \lambda$, M is an $(S_\beta, Z \cup \bigcup_{\gamma > \beta} S_\gamma)$-minimal model of P. A sentence K is said to be *implied* by prioritized circumscription CIRC3($P; S_0 > S_1 > \cdots; Z$) if it is true in all of its models. We denote this fact by CIRC3($P; S_0 > S_1 > \cdots; Z$) $\models K$.

Therefore, to obtain a model M of prioritized circumscription we have to minimize, for all $\beta < \lambda$, atoms in S_β, while varying atoms in $Z \cup \bigcup_{\gamma > \beta} S_\gamma$ and keeping all the remaining atoms, including atoms in $\bigcup_{\gamma < \beta} S_\gamma$, unchanged. If $Z = \emptyset$, then CIRC3($P; S_0 > S_1 > \cdots; Z$) will be simply denoted by CIRC3($P; S_0 > S_1 > \cdots$).

It is clear that parallel circumscription is a special case of prioritized circumscription. The following example illustrates the differences between two-valued and three-valued circumscription.

Example 4.4. Suppose that a theory P is given by:

> *Runs* ← ¬*Abnormal*,
>
> *SendForRepairs* ← ¬*Runs*, *CantFixIt*,
>
> *CantFixIt* ← ¬*CantFixIt*,

and suppose that we are interested in prioritized circumscription of P with respect to priorities:

> *Abnormal > Runs > SendForRepairs > CantFixIt.*

We first minimize *Abnormal* while varying everything else. We conclude that *Abnormal* is false. Then, assuming *Abnormal* is false, we minimize *Runs*, while varying *SendForRepairs* and *CantFixIt*. We conclude that *Runs* is true. Now, assuming *Abnormal* is false and *Runs* is true we minimize *SendForRepairs*, while varying *CantFixIt*. We conclude that *SendForRepairs* is false. Finally, assuming that *Abnormal* and *SendForRepairs* are false and *Runs* is true, we minimize *CantFixIt*. Here, however, different results are obtained depending on whether two-valued or three-valued circumscription is being used. In the only two-valued model M of P, satisfying those constraints and the clause *CantFixIt* $\leftarrow \neg$*CantFixIt*, the atom *CantFixIt* is true, while there is a three-valued model N of P in which *CantFixIt* is undefined. Moreover, $N \prec M$. Therefore, M is the only (two-valued) model of

$$\text{CIRC}(P; Abnormal > Runs > SendForRepairs > CantFixIt);$$

in M atoms *Abnormal* and *SendForRepairs* are false and *Runs* and *CantFixIt* are true. On the other hand, N is the only (three-valued) model of $\text{CIRC3}(P; Abnormal > Runs > SendForRepairs > CantFixIt)$; in N atoms *Abnormal* and *SendForRepairs* are false, *Runs* is true and *CantFixIt* is undefined.

Consequently,

$$\text{CIRC}(P; Abnormal > Runs > SendForRepairs > CantFixIt)$$

implies *CantFixIt*, while

$$\text{CIRC3}(P; Abnormal > Runs > SendForRepairs > CantFixIt)$$

views the information about *CantFixIt* as uncertain or confusing and consequently assigns the unknown value to *CantFixIt*. In essence, two-valued circumscription forces us to view the clause *CantFixIt* $\leftarrow \neg$*CantFixIt* as a disjunction *CantFixIt* $\vee$ *CantFixIt*, while three-valued circumscription does not. The right choice clearly depends on the application. It is clear, however, that in many domains, e.g., in logic programming, viewing the clause as a disjunction may not be acceptable (observe that the theory uses the implication symbol $\leftarrow$ rather than $\Leftarrow$).

We should also point out that the autoepistemic theory

$$Runs \leftarrow \neg L Abnormal,$$
$$SendForRepairs \leftarrow \neg L Runs, CantFixIt,$$
$$CantFixIt \leftarrow \neg L CantFixIt,$$

naturally corresponding to P [6] does not have any two-valued autoepistemic expansions, whereas its unique three-valued autoepistemic expansion (see Example 5.6) coincides with three-valued circumscription.

4.1. Equivalence of well-founded and circumscriptive semantics

We now proceed to the main theorem of this section showing that the well-founded semantics of logic programs is always equivalent to three-valued prioritized circumscription, with respect to priorities determined by the dynamic stratification of the program.

Theorem 4.5 (Equivalence of well-founded and circumscriptive semantics). *Suppose that P is a logic program and $\{S_\beta\}_{\beta \le \delta}$ is its dynamic stratification. The well-founded model semantics of P coincides with the three-valued prioritized circumscription $\mathrm{CIRC3}(P; S_0 > S_1 > \cdots > S_\delta)$ of P in the sense that for any*[3] *formula F:*

$$M_P \models F \quad \equiv \quad \mathrm{CIRC3}(P; S_0 > S_1 > \cdots > S_\delta) \models F;$$

$$M_P \models \neg F \quad \equiv \quad \mathrm{CIRC3}(P; S_0 > S_1 > \cdots > S_\delta) \models \neg F.$$

Proof. We prove the theorem for literals F only. The general case is proved similarly. We will first prove that the well-founded model $M = M_P$ is a model of prioritized circumscription $\mathrm{CIRC3}(P; S_0 > S_1 > \cdots > S_\delta)$ of P. By definition, we have to show that for every $\beta \le \delta$, M is an $(S_\beta, \bigcup_{\gamma > \beta} S_\gamma)$-minimal model of P.

Suppose first that β is any ordinal less than δ. We have to show that M is a model of P that minimizes atoms in $S_\beta = T_{M_\beta} \cup F_{M_\beta}$, keeps all the atoms in

$$S^- = \bigcup_{\alpha < \beta} S_\alpha = \bigcup_{\alpha < \beta} (T_{M_\alpha} \cup F_{M_\alpha})$$

unchanged, while varying all the remaining atoms.

Suppose that N is a model of P such that

$$N|S_\beta < M|S_\beta, \qquad N|S^- = M|S^-.$$

First, recall that if β is a limit ordinal, then

$$M_\beta = \left\langle \bigcup_{\alpha < \beta} T_{M_\alpha}; \bigcup_{\alpha < \beta} F_{M_\alpha} \right\rangle$$

and if $\beta = \alpha + 1$, then

$$M_\beta = \langle T_{M_\alpha}; F_{M_\alpha} \rangle.$$

Since $N|S^- = M|S^-$ we infer that all atoms that are true (respectively false) in M_β must also be true (respectively false) in N.

---

[3] Not containing the connectives $\leftarrow$ and $\leftrightarrow$.

By definition, T_{M_β} is the smallest set of atoms A with the property that A is in T_{M_β} if there is a clause $A \leftarrow L_1, \ldots, L_n$ in P such that, for all $i \leq n$, either $\hat{M}_\beta(L_i) = 1$ or $L_i = B_i$ is an atom and B_i is in T_{M_β}. Thus the set T_{M_β} contains all atomic facts which can be derived from P using all true or false facts in the interpretation M_β. Since all such facts are also true (respectively false) in N, we conclude that all atoms contained in T_{M_β} must be true in N. Since all the remaining atoms in S_β, namely the atoms in F_{M_β}, are false in M_β and thus in M, we infer that $N|S_\beta \geq M|S_\beta$, which is a contradiction.

Suppose now that $\beta = \delta$. Then S_β is the set of all atoms undefined in M. Since $N|S^- = M|S^-$, the two models coincide on all atoms which are either true or false in M. Let F be the set of all atoms which are false in N. Therefore, for every clause $A \leftarrow L_1, \ldots, L_n$ in P there must exist an $i \leq n$ such that $\hat{N}(L_i) = 0$. Moreover, if $L_i = \neg B_i$ is negative, then B_i must be true in N and thus also in M and hence also in M_δ. Therefore F must be contained in F_{M_δ}, which was defined as the largest set of atoms A with the property that if A is in F_{M_δ} then for every clause $A \leftarrow L_1, \ldots, L_n$ in P there is an $i \leq n$ such that either $\hat{M}_\delta(L_i) = 0$ or $L_i = B_i$ is an atom and B_i is in F_{M_δ}. This means that F is contained in the set of atoms false in M, which again shows that $N|S_\delta \geq M|S_\delta$ and is a contradiction.

This completes the proof that the well-founded model is a model of prioritized circumscription. Now we will show that every model N of prioritized circumscription coincides with M_P on all atoms which are either true or false in M_P, i.e., that $M_P \preceq_F N$.

The proof is by induction on the strata S_β of P. Suppose that $\beta < \delta$ and that we already know that $N|S^- = M|S^-$. The argument given above applies almost verbatim to show that all atoms in T_{S_β} must be true in N. Since N minimizes atoms in S_β it is immediate that all atoms in F_{S_β} must therefore be false in N, which completes the inductive proof.

Now suppose that K is a literal. Since the well-founded model $M = M_P$ is a model of prioritized circumscription $CIRC3(P; S_0 > S_1 > \cdots > S_\delta)$ of P, if $CIRC3(P; S_0 > S_1 > \cdots > S_\delta) \models K$, then also $M_P \models K$. Conversely, if $M_P \models K$, then the corresponding atom is either true or false in M_P and therefore it must be also true (respectively false) in all models of prioritized circumscription, which shows that $CIRC3(P; S_0 > S_1 > \cdots > S_\delta) \models K$ and completes the proof. $\square$

Observe that—as it was the case for stratified programs—the prioritization of the Herbrand universe of the program P, and thus the circumscription policy used with the theory P, is given by the (dynamic) stratification of P and thus is automatically determined by the *syntax* of the program.

Example 4.6. The dynamic stratification of the program from Example 4.4 is given by

$$S_0 = \{Abnormal\}, \qquad S_1 = \{Runs\},$$
$$S_2 = \{SendForRepairs\}, \qquad S_3 = \{CantFixIt\},$$

with $\delta = 3$. Therefore, it leads precisely to the prioritization

$$Abnormal > Runs > SendForRepairs > CantFixIt$$

discussed in Example 4.4. The model N is the well-founded model of P and, as we have seen, it is also the only model of

$$CIRC3(P; Abnormal > Runs > SendForRepairs > CantFixIt).$$

Thus three-valued circumscription

$$CIRC3(P; Abnormal > Runs > SendForRepairs > CantFixIt)$$

of P coincides with the well-founded semantics of P, while it is different from two-valued circumscription

$$CIRC(P; Abnormal > Runs > SendForRepairs > CantFixIt)$$

of P.

Now we consider the program discussed in the introduction.

Example 4.7. Let P be as follows:

$$work \leftarrow \neg tired,$$
$$sleep \leftarrow \neg work,$$
$$tired \leftarrow \neg sleep,$$
$$paid \leftarrow,$$
$$angry \leftarrow \neg paid, work.$$

Its dynamic stratification is given by

$$S_0 = \{paid\},$$
$$S_1 = \{angry\},$$
$$S_2 = \{work, sleep, tired\},$$

with $\delta = 2$. Its well-founded model is $M_P = \langle\{paid\}; \{angry\}\rangle$; thus in M_P the atom *paid* is true, *angry* is false and *work*, *sleep* and *tired* are undefined. To compute three-valued prioritized circumscription

$$CIRC3(P; paid > angry > \{work, sleep, tired\})$$

of P we have to first minimize *paid* while varying everything else. We conclude that *paid* must be true. Then, assuming *paid* is true, we minimize *angry*, while varying *work, sleep, tired*, concluding that *angry* is false. Finally, assuming *paid* is true and *angry* is false, we minimize *work, sleep, tired* obtaining four different models of

$$CIRC3(P; paid > angry > \{work, sleep, tired\}),$$

namely,

$$M_1 = \langle \{paid, work, sleep\}; \{angry, tired\} \rangle,$$
$$M_2 = \langle \{paid, work, tired\}; \{angry, sleep\} \rangle,$$
$$M_3 = \langle \{paid, sleep, tired\}; \{angry, work\} \rangle,$$
$$M_4 = M_P = \langle \{paid\}; \{angry\} \rangle.$$

The first three models are two-valued and they are the only models of two-valued circumscription $CIRC(P; paid > angry > \{work, sleep, tired\})$ of P.

It is easy to see that the set of sentences implied by three-valued circumscription, i.e., the set of sentences [4] satisfied in all four models M_1–M_4, coincides with the set of sentences satisfied in the model $M_4 = M_P$ and thus it coincides with the well-founded semantics of P. Observe that the two-valued circumscription is again different from three-valued circumscription, because, e.g., it implies the disjunction *work* $\vee$ *sleep* $\vee$ *tired*, whereas three-valued circumscription views the information about *work, sleep* and *tired* as uncertain or confusing and assigns to *work, sleep, tired* and to *work* $\vee$ *sleep* $\vee$ *tired* the undefined value.

Again, we point out that the autoepistemic theory

$$work \leftarrow \neg \mathbf{L} tired,$$
$$sleep \leftarrow \neg \mathbf{L} work,$$
$$tired \leftarrow \neg \mathbf{L} sleep,$$
$$paid \leftarrow,$$
$$angry \leftarrow \neg \mathbf{L} paid, work.$$

naturally corresponding to P [6] does not have any two-valued autoepistemic expansions, whereas its unique three-valued autoepistemic expansion (see Example 5.6) corresponds to three-valued circumscription.

---

[4] Not using connectives $\leftarrow$ and $\leftrightarrow$.

5. Three-valued autoepistemic logic

In this section we define three-valued autoepistemic logic and we show that the well-founded semantics of logic programs is equivalent to the semantics of three-valued autoepistemic logic. This result extends an earlier result [6] showing that the perfect model semantics of a *stratified* logic program P is equivalent to the semantics of (two-valued) autoepistemic logic. As we mentioned in the Introduction, while in this section we use three-valued logic to define the extended autoepistemic logic, *three-valued logic is not really necessary* for this purpose. In [31] the author introduces new Autoepistemic Logics of Closed Beliefs whose special case coincides with the three-valued autoepistemic logic defined in this paper and yet its definition does *not* use three-valued logic.

Since autoepistemic logic is well-defined only for propositional theories, in this section we will restrict ourselves to (possibly infinite) *propositional theories*. Since any logic program can be always instantiated to a (possibly infinite) ground program, this restriction, at least in the context of Herbrand models, is not essential.

We will denote by **L** the autoepistemic *belief symbol* [22], also called the *belief operator*. By an *autoepistemic language* we mean any language $\mathcal{L}$ with the property that its alphabet contains a propositional symbol **L**S for any sentence S of the language. [5] We will denote the set of all propositions **L**S, where S is a sentence, by B:

$$B = \{\mathbf{L}S: S \text{ is a sentence}\}$$

and we will call them *belief propositions*. By an *autoepistemic theory* we mean a theory over an autoepistemic language. Observe that our autoepistemic language allows arbitrarily deep *nesting of beliefs*.

Before proceeding with the definition of three-valued stable autoepistemic expansions, we first need to look at the two-valued definition from a slightly different, model-theoretic angle. Following is the standard definition of two-valued stable autoepistemic expansions. [6]

Definition 5.1 [22] An *autoepistemic expansion* of an autoepistemic theory

---

[5]Here by **L**S we simply mean a string denoting a propositional symbol, which begins with an **L** followed by the sentence S, e.g. the string "**L**$A \wedge B$". However, to avoid notational confusion, we sometimes use "**L**$(A \wedge B)$" instead. It is important to point out that propositions **L**S are treated here in the same way as all the other propositional symbols and that **L** does *not* represent a modal operator.

[6]In the rest of the paper we will just say autoepistemic expansion instead of *stable* autoepistemic expansion.

P is any consistent theory $\mathcal{E}$ satisfying the following fixed point condition:

$$\mathcal{E} = \mathrm{Cn}(P \cup \{\mathbf{L}S\colon \mathcal{E} \models S\} \cup \{\neg\mathbf{L}S\colon \mathcal{E} \not\models S\}),$$

where S ranges over all sentences and $\mathrm{Cn}(W)$ denotes the set of all logical consequences of a theory W.

In other words, a consistent theory $\mathcal{E}$ is an autoepistemic expansion of P if it coincides with the theory obtained by:

- adding to P all belief propositions $\mathbf{L}S$ for which $\mathcal{E} \models S$;
- and negations of all belief propositions $\mathbf{L}S$ for which $\mathcal{E} \not\models S$;
- and closing the theory under logical consequence.

It is clear that any (two-valued) autoepistemic expansion $\mathcal{E}$ of a theory P is *fully determined* by specifying which belief propositions $\mathbf{L}S$ are true in $\mathcal{E}$ and which belief propositions $\mathbf{L}S$ are false in $\mathcal{E}$. Therefore, any autoepistemic expansion $\mathcal{E}$ can be identified with a unique two-valued *belief interpretation* $E_{\mathcal{E}}$, i.e., with an assignment

$$E_{\mathcal{E}} : B \to \{0, 1\}$$

of truth values (0 or 1) to *belief propositions* $\mathbf{L}S \in B$ defined by:

$$E_{\mathcal{E}}(\mathbf{L}S) = 1 \quad \text{iff} \quad \mathbf{L}S \in \mathcal{E}.$$

Conversely, to every two-valued belief interpretation $E : B \to \{0, 1\}$ there corresponds a unique theory $\mathcal{E}_E$ extending P and defined by:

$$\mathcal{E}_E = \mathrm{Cn}(P \cup \{\mathbf{L}S\colon E(\mathbf{L}S) = 1\} \cup \{\neg\mathbf{L}S\colon E(\mathbf{L}S) = 0\}).$$

Moreover, it is clear that

$$E_{\mathcal{E}_E} = E \quad \text{and} \quad \mathcal{E}_{E_{\mathcal{E}}} = \mathcal{E}.$$

However, in general, if E is an arbitrary belief interpretation then $\mathcal{E}_E$ does *not* have to be an autoepistemic expansion of P and, in fact, it does not even have to be consistent. We will now characterize those belief interpretations $E : B \to \{0, 1\}$ which *exactly correspond* to autoepistemic expansions of P, thus obtaining a *model-theoretic definition of autoepistemic expansions*, which we will later use to define three-valued autoepistemic expansions. We should point out that our model-theoretic characterization of autoepistemic expansions and the concept of *autoepistemic belief models* defined below, are essentially different (although, naturally, related to) from the concept of autoepistemic models considered in [22].

For a given two-valued belief interpretation $E : B \to \{0, 1\}$ we will denote by Mod_E the set of all two-valued models $M : \mathcal{H} \to \{0, 1\}$ of the autoepistemic theory P which extend E, i.e., such that $M|B = E$. Therefore:

$$\mathrm{Mod}_E = \{M : \mathcal{H} \to \{0, 1\} : M \models P, \; M|B = E\}.$$

We recall that $\mathcal{H} = \mathcal{H}_{\mathcal{L}}$ denotes the Herbrand base of P (i.e., the set of all propositions) and $B \subseteq \mathcal{H}$ is the set of all belief propositions $\mathbf{L}S$, where S is a sentence. Assuming that the set Mod_E is not empty, we define, for any sentence S, the truth valuation $\mathrm{Val}_E(S)$ induced by E as follows:

$$\mathrm{Val}_E(S) = \min\{\hat{M}(S) : M \in \mathrm{Mod}_E\}.$$

Otherwise $\mathrm{Val}_E(S)$ is not defined. Thus, $\mathrm{Val}_E(S)$ represents the *minimum truth value* assigned to the sentence S by all models M of P, which extend E, i.e., by those models which are *compatible* with the belief interpretation E. It can therefore be viewed as the most *skeptical* or *minimalistic* assessment of the truth value of S in all models of P compatible with beliefs E.

Definition 5.2. We will say that a belief interpretation $E : B \to \{0, 1\}$ is a (two-valued) *autoepistemic belief model* of P if it satisfies the condition:

$$E(\mathbf{L}S) = \mathrm{Val}_E(S),$$

for every sentence S.

Autoepistemic belief models of a theory P have a natural interpretation. They describe *possible sets of beliefs E* of a rational agent, i.e., sets of beliefs E with the property that, for any sentence S, an agent believes S (i.e., $\mathbf{L}S$ is true in E) if and only if S is true in all models of P, which extend the set E of his beliefs and, thus, are *compatible* with his beliefs. That means that *an agent believes S if and only if S is logically implied by his beliefs E.*

The following theorem (cf. also [12]) gives a model-theoretic definition of autoepistemic expansions by showing that (two-valued) autoepistemic belief models are exactly those belief interpretations E that correspond to autoepistemic expansions $\mathcal{E}_E$ of P. It establishes therefore a one-to-one correspondence between (two-valued) autoepistemic expansions and autoepistemic belief models.

Theorem 5.3 (Model-theoretic characterization of autoepistemic expansions). *If $\mathcal{E}$ is an autoepistemic expansion of P, then $E_{\mathcal{E}}$ is a (two-valued) autoepistemic belief model and $\mathcal{E}_{E_{\mathcal{E}}} = \mathcal{E}$.*

Conversely, if E is a (two-valued) autoepistemic belief model then $\mathcal{E}_E$ is an autoepistemic expansion of P and $E_{\mathcal{E}_E} = E$.

Moreover,

$$\mathcal{E}_E = \{S\text{:} S \text{ is a sentence and } \forall M \in \mathrm{Mod}_E, M \models S\}$$

or, equivalently,

$$\mathcal{E}_E = \{S\text{:} S \text{ is a sentence and } \mathrm{Val}_E(S) = 1\}.$$

Proof. If $\mathcal{E}$ is an autoepistemic expansion of P, then

$$\mathcal{E} = \mathrm{Cn}(P \cup \{\mathbf{L}S \in B : \mathcal{E} \models S\} \cup \{\neg\mathbf{L}S \in B\text{:} \mathcal{E} \not\models S\}).$$

We defined

$$E_{\mathcal{E}}(\mathbf{L}S) = 1 \quad \text{iff} \quad \mathbf{L}S \in \mathcal{E}.$$

Let M be any two-valued model of P which extends $E_{\mathcal{E}}$. Then M is a model of $\mathcal{E}$ and therefore if $E_{\mathcal{E}}(\mathbf{L}S) = 1$ then $M \models S$, which shows that $\mathrm{Val}_{E_{\mathcal{E}}}(S) = 1$. On the other hand, if $E_{\mathcal{E}}(\mathbf{L}S) = 0$ then there must exist a model M of $\mathcal{E}$ such that $M \not\models S$. Clearly, M is a model of P extending $E_{\mathcal{E}}$. Thus $\mathrm{Val}_{E_{\mathcal{E}}}(S) = 0$, which shows that $E_{\mathcal{E}}$ is an autoepistemic belief model of P. The equality $\mathcal{E}_{E_{\mathcal{E}}} = \mathcal{E}$ is obvious.

Suppose now that E is an autoepistemic belief model and

$$\mathcal{E}_E = \mathrm{Cn}(P \cup \{\mathbf{L}S\text{:} E(\mathbf{L}S) = 1\} \cup \{\neg\mathbf{L}S\text{:} E(\mathbf{L}S) = 0\}).$$

Suppose that $E(\mathbf{L}S) = 1$ and let M be any model of $\mathcal{E}_E$. Then clearly M is a model of P extending E. Therefore $\mathrm{Val}_E(S) = 1$ and consequently $M \models S$, which proves that $\mathcal{E}_E \models S$. On the other hand, suppose that $E(\mathbf{L}S) = 0$. Then $\mathrm{Val}_E(S) = 0$ and there must exist a model M of P extending E such that $M \not\models S$. Then M is a model of $\mathcal{E}_E$, which proves that $\mathcal{E}_E \not\models S$. The equality $E_{\mathcal{E}_E} = E$ is obvious.

To prove

$$\mathcal{E}_E = \{S\text{:} S \text{ is a sentence and } \forall M \in \mathrm{Mod}_E, M \models S\}$$

it suffices to observe that a sentence S belongs to

$$\mathrm{Cn}(P \cup \{\mathbf{L}S\text{:} E(\mathbf{L}S) = 1\} \cup \{\neg\mathbf{L}S\text{:} E(\mathbf{L}S) = 0\})$$

if and only if it is true in all models of

$$P \cup \{\mathbf{L}S\text{:} E(\mathbf{L}S) = 1\} \cup \{\neg\mathbf{L}S\text{:} E(\mathbf{L}S) = 0\},$$

or, equivalently, in all models of P which extend E. $\quad\square$

In virtue of the above result establishing a one-to-one correspondence between (two-valued) autoepistemic expansions and autoepistemic belief models, the two concepts can be viewed as *equivalent*.

Example 5.4. Suppose that the theory P is given by

$$Fly \leftarrow \neg \mathbf{L} Abnormal.$$

The belief interpretation E assigning the value 1 to $\mathbf{L}Fly$ and value 0 to $\mathbf{L}Abnormal$ is the unique autoepistemic belief model of P. It corresponds to the unique autoepistemic expansion $\mathcal{E}_E$ of P given by:

$$\mathcal{E}_E = \mathrm{Cn}(P \cup \{\mathbf{L}Fly, \neg \mathbf{L}Abnormal\}).$$

(In this and following examples, for simplicity, we will ignore more complex belief propositions, such as nested beliefs, which naturally also belong to the autoepistemic expansion.) Indeed, there are two (two-valued) models of the theory P which extend E, namely models

$$M_1 = \langle \{Fly, \mathbf{L}Fly\}; \{Abnormal, \mathbf{L}Abnormal\} \rangle$$

and

$$M_2 = \langle \{Fly, \mathbf{L}Fly, Abnormal\}; \{\mathbf{L}Abnormal\} \rangle.$$

Therefore,

$$\mathrm{Val}_E(Fly) = 1 = E(\mathbf{L}Fly),$$

$$\mathrm{Val}_E(Abnormal) = 0 = E(\mathbf{L}Abnormal),$$

which shows that E is an autoepistemic belief model.

On the other hand, the belief interpretation E assigning the value 1 to $\mathbf{L}Abnormal$ and value 0 to $\mathbf{L}Fly$ is not an autoepistemic belief model of P and therefore the corresponding theory $\mathcal{E}_E$ given by:

$$\mathcal{E}_E = \mathrm{Cn}(P \cup \{\mathbf{L}Abnormal, \neg \mathbf{L}Fly\})$$

is not an autoepistemic expansion. Indeed, any interpretation of P which extends E is a model of P and therefore, $\mathrm{Val}_E(Fly) = 0 = E(\mathbf{L}Fly)$, but $\mathrm{Val}_E(Abnormal) = 0 \neq 1 = E(\mathbf{L}Abnormal)$, which shows that E is not an autoepistemic belief model.

Once we have a model-theoretic definition of two-valued autoepistemic expansions we can easily extend it to the three-valued case, thus obtaining a definition of three-valued autoepistemic expansions.

By a *three-valued belief interpretation E* we mean any three-valued interpretation of belief propositions, i.e., an assignment

$$E : B \to \{0, \tfrac{1}{2}, 1\}$$

of truth values (0, $\tfrac{1}{2}$ or 1) to *belief propositions* $\mathbf{L}S \in B$. For a given three-valued belief interpretation E we will denote by $\mathrm{Mod3}_E$ the set of all three-valued models $M : \mathcal{H} \to \{0, \frac{1}{2}, 1\}$ of the autoepistemic theory P which extend E, i.e., such that $M|B = E$. Therefore,

$$\mathrm{Mod3}_E = \{M : \mathcal{H} \to \{0, \tfrac{1}{2}, 1\} : M \models P, \ M|B = E\}.$$

Assuming that the set $\mathrm{Mod3}_E$ is not empty, we define, for any sentence S, the truth valuation $\mathrm{Val3}_E(S)$ induced by E as follows:

$$\mathrm{Val3}_E(S) = \min\{\hat{M}(S) : M \in \mathrm{Mod3}_E\}.$$

Otherwise $\mathrm{Val3}_E(S)$ is not defined. Again, $\mathrm{Val3}_E(S)$ represents the *minimum truth value* assigned to the sentence S by all three-valued models M of P, which are *compatible* with the belief interpretation E. It can therefore be viewed as the most *skeptical* assessment of the truth value of S in all three-valued models of P compatible with E.

Definition 5.5. We will say that a three-valued belief interpretation E is a (three-valued) *autoepistemic belief model* of P if it satisfies the condition:

$$E(\mathbf{L}S) = \mathrm{Val3}_E(S),$$

for every sentence S.

Three-valued autoepistemic belief models of a theory P have the same natural interpretation as two-valued belief models. They describe three-valued *possible sets of beliefs E* of a rational agent, i.e., sets of beliefs E satisfying the condition that for any sentence S:

- An agent believes S (i.e., $\mathbf{L}S$ is true in E) if and only if S is true in all models of P which extend the set of beliefs E, i.e., in all models *compatible* with E. In other words, an agent believes S if and only if S is *logically implied* by his beliefs E.
- An agent *disbelieves* S (i.e., $\neg\mathbf{L}S$ is true in E) if and only if S is false in *at least one* model of P, which is compatible with E. In other words, an agent disbelieves S if and only if $\neg S$ is *consistent* with his beliefs E.
- Otherwise, his beliefs about S are *undefined*. This represents the case when the agent is uncertain of what he believes in or when the information that he possesses about S is incomplete or confusing.

Three-valued autoepistemic belief models should be viewed as *three-valued counterparts of (two-valued) autoepistemic expansions*. In fact, the model-theoretic definition of autoepistemic expansions seems to allow *more flexibility and expressiveness* than the usual proof-theoretic definition. For example, a closer look at the model-theoretic definition suggests one *natural variation* of the definition of autoepistemic expansions, namely, the additional requirement (cf. also [12]) that autoepistemic belief models be *minimal* belief models. This would, e.g., ensure that the autoepistemic theory $a \leftarrow \mathbf{L}a$, which essentially says "a is true if it is believed" has only one expansion in which $\mathbf{L}a$ is false, rather than also having the additional expansion in which $\mathbf{L}a$ is true. In the latter, a is forced to be true exclusively by our belief in it, which does not seem to correctly model our usual commonsense reasoning, in which we usually need some *grounds* for our beliefs, other than those beliefs themselves.

It is not difficult to give a proof-theoretic definition of three-valued autoepistemic expansions. Indeed, to every three-valued autoepistemic belief model E there corresponds a unique expansion $\mathcal{E}_E$ of the theory P given by:

$$\mathcal{E}_E = \{S: S \text{ is a sentence and } \forall M \in \mathrm{Mod3}_E, \ M \models S\}$$

or, equivalently,

$$\mathcal{E}_E = \{S: S \text{ is a sentence and } \mathrm{Val3}_E(S) = 1\},$$

which, according to Theorem 5.3, can be viewed as the three-valued *proof-theoretic* counterpart of a two-valued *autoepistemic expansion*. Conversely, given $\mathcal{E}_E$, one can easily reconstruct E itself, by setting

$$E(\mathbf{L}S) = \begin{cases} 1, & \text{if } \mathbf{L}S \in \mathcal{E}_E, \\ 0, & \text{if } \neg \mathbf{L}S \in \mathcal{E}_E, \\ \frac{1}{2}, & \text{otherwise.} \end{cases}$$

Thus the two concepts, the model-theoretic one and the proof-theoretic one, are again equivalent and therefore in the rest of the paper they will be used interchangeably.

Example 5.6. Let us first consider the autoepistemic theory P naturally corresponding to the circumscriptive theory discussed in the previous section (see Example 4.4):

> $Runs \leftarrow \neg\mathbf{L}Abnormal,$
> $SendForRepairs \leftarrow \neg\mathbf{L}Runs, CantFixIt,$
> $CantFixIt \leftarrow \neg\mathbf{L}CantFixIt.$

This theory does not have any two-valued autoepistemic expansions. It has, however, a unique three-valued autoepistemic expansion or, equivalently, a unique three-valued autoepistemic belief model, namely the model E in which $\mathbf{L}Abnormal$ and $\mathbf{L}SendForRepairs$ are false, $\mathbf{L}Runs$ is true and $\mathbf{L}CantFixIt$ is undefined. Indeed, an interpretation of P extending E is a model of P if and only if $Runs$ is true in it and $SendForRepairs$ is at least undefined. Therefore,

$$\mathrm{Val3}_E(Abnormal) = \mathrm{Val3}_E(SendForRepairs) = 0,$$

$$\mathrm{Val3}_E(\mathit{Runs}) = 1,$$

$$\mathrm{Val3}_E(\mathit{CantFixIt}) = \tfrac{1}{2}.$$

Since $\mathrm{Val3}_E(A) = E(\mathbf{L}A)$, for any atom A, the belief interpretation E is an autoepistemic belief model.[7] It is easy to see that there are no other belief models of P.

Example 5.7. Now we consider the autoepistemic theory P discussed in the introduction (see also Example 4.7):

> *work* ← ¬L*tired*,
>
> *sleep* ← ¬L*work*,
>
> *tired* ← ¬L*sleep*,
>
> *paid* ←,
>
> *angry* ← ¬L*paid*, *work*.

This example also does not have any two-valued autoepistemic expansions. It has, however, a unique three-valued autoepistemic expansion (autoepistemic belief model), namely the model E in which L*angry* is false, L*paid* is true and L*work*, L*sleep* and L*tired* are undefined. Indeed, an interpretation of P extending E is a model of P if and only if *paid* is true in it and *work*, *sleep* and *tired* are at least undefined. Therefore,

$$\mathrm{Val3}_E(\mathit{angry}) = 0,$$

$$\mathrm{Val3}_E(\mathit{paid}) = 1$$

and

$$\mathrm{Val3}_E(\mathit{work}) = \mathrm{Val3}_E(\mathit{sleep}) = \mathrm{Val3}_E(\mathit{tired}) = \tfrac{1}{2}.$$

Since $\mathrm{Val3}_E(A) = E(\mathbf{L}A)$, for any atom A, the belief interpretation E is an autoepistemic belief model. It is easy to see that there are no other belief models of P.

The above examples show that three-valued autoepistemic expansions are strictly *more expressive* than two-valued expansions, by allowing us to assign rational sets of beliefs to *much wider classes of theories*. Moreover, as will be seen in Example 5.16 below, even if a theory has both two-valued and three-valued autoepistemic expansions, the set of all three-valued expansions seems to provide a *more intuitive* set of rational beliefs than just the two-valued expansions. From now on, unless stated otherwise,

---

[7] It is easy to obtain an extension of E to the set of all belief propositions LS, where S is an arbitrary sentence, possibly including nested beliefs.

by an autoepistemic expansion we will mean a three-valued autoepistemic expansion (autoepistemic belief model).

With any (three-valued) autoepistemic expansion E of P, one can associate sets of sentences which are believed, disbelieved or undefined in E.

Definition 5.8. Let E be a three-valued autoepistemic belief model. A sentence S for which $\text{Val3}_E(S) = 1$ (respectively $\text{Val3}_E(S) = 0$; respectively $\text{Val3}_E(S) = \frac{1}{2}$) is said to be *believed* (respectively *disbelieved*; respectively undefined) in E.

The following proposition is a simple consequence of introduced definitions:

Proposition 5.9. *For a sentence S and a three-valued autoepistemic belief model E the following holds*:

   (i) *S is believed in E iff $\mathbf{L}S$ is believed in E iff $E(\mathbf{L}S) = 1$ iff $\neg\mathbf{L}S$ is disbelieved in E.*

   (ii) *S is disbelieved in E iff $\mathbf{L}S$ is disbelieved in E iff $E(\mathbf{L}S) = 0$ iff $\neg\mathbf{L}S$ is believed in E.*

   (iii) *S is undefined in E iff $\mathbf{L}S$ is undefined in E iff $E(\mathbf{L}S) = \frac{1}{2}$ iff $\neg\mathbf{L}S$ is undefined in E.*

Proof. Let S be any sentence. Then, by definition, S is believed in an autoepistemic belief model E if and only if $\text{Val3}_E(S) = 1$, which holds if and only if $E(\mathbf{L}S) = 1$ which is equivalent to $\text{Val3}_E(\mathbf{L}S) = 1$, which in turn means that $\mathbf{L}S$ is believed in E. Moreover, $E(\mathbf{L}S) = 1$ is equivalent to $E(\neg\mathbf{L}S) = 0$, which is equivalent to $\text{Val3}_E(\neg\mathbf{L}S) = 0$, which in turn means that $\neg\mathbf{L}S$ is disbelieved in E.

This proves the first equivalence (i). The remaining two equivalences can be proved in a completely analogous way.   □

A given autoepistemic theory P may, in general, have more than one three-valued autoepistemic expansion. In this case, a rational agent may decide to believe (respectively disbelieve) only those facts which are believed (respectively disbelieved) in all the expansions (possible belief models). This leads to the following definition:

Definition 5.10. Suppose that an autoepistemic theory P has at least one three-valued autoepistemic expansion. We say that a sentence S is *believed* (respectively *disbelieved*) in P if S is believed (respectively disbelieved) in *all* three-valued autoepistemic expansions E of P; otherwise we say that S is *undefined* in P.

The following corollary is an immediate consequence of the previous proposition:

Corollary 5.11. *Suppose that an autoepistemic theory P has at least one three-valued autoepistemic expansion. For a sentence S the following holds:*

(i) *S is believed in P iff* $\mathbf{L}S$ *is believed in P iff* $\neg\mathbf{L}S$ *is disbelieved in P.*

(ii) *S is disbelieved in P iff* $\mathbf{L}S$ *is disbelieved in P iff* $\neg\mathbf{L}S$ *is believed in P.*

Observe that using three-valued autoepistemic logic we are able to talk about *uncertain* or *undefined* beliefs at the level of *individual expansions*. In particular, a theory with a unique expansion does not automatically force us to have all of our beliefs fully determined.

5.1. Equivalence of well-founded and autoepistemic semantics

We now proceed to the main theorem of this section showing that the well-founded semantics of logic programs is always equivalent to the semantics determined by three-valued autoepistemic expansions.

By an *autoepistemic logic program* we mean an autoepistemic theory consisting of (possibly infinitely many) clauses of the form

$$A \leftarrow B_1 \wedge \ldots \wedge B_m \wedge \neg\mathbf{L}C_1 \wedge \ldots \wedge \neg\mathbf{L}C_n)$$

where $m, n \geq 0$ and A, B_i and C_j are atoms (propositions). Observe that autoepistemic logic programs are special types of logic programs and therefore such clauses will also be denoted by

$$A \leftarrow B_1, \ldots, B_m, \neg\mathbf{L}C_1, \ldots, \neg\mathbf{L}C_n.$$

In order to show the equivalence between the well-founded semantics of logic programs and the three-valued autoepistemic semantics, we first need to translate standard logic programs into autoepistemic logic programs. We follow the approach proposed by Gelfond [6].

Definition 5.12 [6] Let P be a logic program. The autoepistemic logic program $\hat{P}$, which we call the *autoepistemic translation of P*, consists of all clauses of the form:

$$A \leftarrow B_1, \ldots, B_m, \neg\mathbf{L}C_1, \ldots, \neg\mathbf{L}C_n,$$

for all possible (ground instances of) clauses:

$$A \leftarrow B_1, \ldots, B_m, \neg C_1, \ldots, \neg C_n$$

from P.

Now we can state the main theorem of this section:

Theorem 5.13   (Equivalence of well-founded and autoepistemic semantics).
*Suppose that P is a logic program, M_P is its well-founded model and $\hat{P}$ is
the autoepistemic translation of P. Then $\hat{P}$ has at least one three-valued
autoepistemic expansion and for any[8] formula F the following holds:*
  (i)   *F is true in M_P iff F is believed in $\hat{P}$;*
  (ii) *F is false in M_P iff F is disbelieved in $\hat{P}$;*
  (iii) *F is undefined in M_P iff F is undefined in $\hat{P}$.*

Proof. We prove it only for literals F. The general case is handled analogously. In [30] the author defined three-valued stable models of a logic
program (extending the concept of stable models introduced in [8]) and
proved that every logic program P has at least one three-valued stable model.
Namely, the well-founded model M_P of P is the F-*least* stable model of P.

It is easy to show that a belief interpretation E is a three-valued autoepistemic belief model of $\hat{P}$ if and only if the corresponding interpretation M
of P defined by:

$$M(A) = E(\mathbf{L}A),$$

for any atom A, is a three-valued stable model of P. The proof is analogous
to the corresponding proof for the case of two-valued stable models [6].

Now, suppose that P is any logic program. From the facts discussed above
we infer that the belief interpretation corresponding to the well-founded
model M_P of P is a three-valued autoepistemic belief model of $\hat{P}$.

Suppose that atom A is true in M_P. Then, since M_P is the F-least stable
model of P, A is also true in all three-valued stable models of P. Therefore,
$E(\mathbf{L}A) = 1$, for all three-valued belief models E of $\hat{P}$. By Proposition
5.9, A is believed in all autoepistemic belief models E of $\hat{P}$ and therefore
A is believed in $\hat{P}$. Conversely, suppose that A is believed in $\hat{P}$. Then
$E(\mathbf{L}A) = 1$, for all three-valued belief models E of $\hat{P}$ and therefore A is
true in all stable models of P. In particular, it is true in M_P.

This proves the equivalence (i). The remaining two equivalences are
proved in a completely analogous way.   □

The above result generalizes the result from [6] stating that the perfect
model semantics coincides with the two-valued autoepistemic semantics
(or—equivalently—with the stable model semantics [8]) for *stratified* logic
programs. More generally, it also extends the result from [38] stating that

---

[8]Not containing any belief propositions or connectives ← and ↔.

two-valued well-founded models coincide with stable models. Observe, that—as opposed to circumscription—no explicit "prioritization" of ground atoms was necessary to obtain the equivalence of the two semantics.

As a byproduct of the main theorem we obtain the following important result:

Corollary 5.14. *Every autoepistemic logic program has at least one three-valued autoepistemic expansion.*

Proof. It is clear that any autoepistemic logic program can be obtained as an autoepistemic translation of the corresponding logic program. In view of the previous theorem, it must therefore have at least one three-valued autoepistemic expansion. □

An analogous result is clearly false for two-valued autoepistemic expansions, since, as we have seen, both autoepistemic logic programs discussed in Examples 5.6 and 5.7 do not have any two-valued autoepistemic expansions.

Example 5.15. The autoepistemic theories P_1 and P_2 studied in Examples 5.6 and 5.7 are clearly autoepistemic logic programs obtained as autoepistemic translations of the corresponding logic programs given in Examples 4.4 and 4.7. Both of them have exactly one three-valued autoepistemic expansion E_i and therefore an atomic formula A is believed (respectively disbelieved) in P_i if and only if it is believed (respectively disbelieved) in E_i. It is easy to see that atoms believed (respectively disbelieved) in P_i exactly coincide with atoms which are true (respectively false) in the well-founded models of the corresponding logic programs (see Examples 4.6 and 4.7). They therefore also coincide with atoms which are true (respectively false) under three-valued circumscription.

We will now give an example of a logic program P, whose autoepistemic translation $\hat{P}$ has a unique two-valued autoepistemic expansion and yet the set of all three-valued autoepistemic expansions seems to provide a more intuitive set of rational beliefs about $\hat{P}$ than the unique two-valued expansion.

Example 5.16 (Van Gelder et al. [38]). Let the program P be given by

$$a \leftarrow \neg b,$$
$$b \leftarrow \neg a,$$
$$p \leftarrow \neg p,$$
$$p \leftarrow \neg a.$$

Thus its autoepistemic translation $\hat{P}$ is given by

$$a \leftarrow \neg \mathbf{L}b,$$
$$b \leftarrow \neg \mathbf{L}a,$$
$$p \leftarrow \neg \mathbf{L}p,$$
$$p \leftarrow \neg \mathbf{L}a.$$

The program $\hat{P}$ has three three-valued autoepistemic expansions (belief models) E_1, E_2 and E_3, defined by:

$$E_1(\mathbf{L}a) = 0, \quad E_1(\mathbf{L}b) = 1, \quad E_1(\mathbf{L}p) = 1,$$
$$E_2(\mathbf{L}a) = \tfrac{1}{2}, \quad E_2(\mathbf{L}b) = \tfrac{1}{2}, \quad E_2(\mathbf{L}p) = \tfrac{1}{2},$$
$$E_3(\mathbf{L}a) = 1, \quad E_3(\mathbf{L}b) = 0, \quad E_3(\mathbf{L}p) = \tfrac{1}{2}.$$

Accordingly, our beliefs in propositions a, b and p are undefined, as they should be, according to the well-founded semantics. However, since only the first expansion E_1 is two-valued, the two-valued autoepistemic semantics (or, equivalently, the stable model semantics [8]) forces us to believe b and p and to disbelieve a. It appears [24,38] that these conclusions can hardly be justified. The first three clauses of the program describe rather unclear and confusing information about a, b and c and the last clause certainly does not clarify the already murky picture. It seems that the only reason why we are forced (by the two-valued autoepistemic semantics) to believe in the truth of b and p and falsity of a is the fact that *we must somehow fit a two-valued set of beliefs* to completely describe a given situation, in spite of the fact that the information provided to us is unclear, incomplete or even confusing and therefore it should warrant a more noncommittal stance.

6. Three-valued default theory and CWA

Due to the close relationship existing between autoepistemic logic and default theory [2,12,19], three-valued default theory can be introduced in a manner fairly similar to three-valued autoepistemic logic. Analogously, due to the close relationship existing between circumscription and the closed world assumption [9], three-valued closed world assumption can be defined similarly to three-valued circumscription. Then the well-founded semantics can be proven equivalent to natural forms of three-valued default theory and CWA.

Similar remarks apply to the so-called *introspective circumscription* recently introduced in [17]. More precisely, as pointed out by Halina Przymusin-ska, two-valued autoepistemic belief models introduced in this paper are in one-to-one correspondence with (also two-valued) models of introspective circumscription. Consequently, their three-valued extension can be also viewed as a *three-valued extension of introspective circumscription*, which therefore adds introspective circumscription to the list of four formalisms which coincide with the well-founded semantics in the class of all logic programs. As a byproduct, it also proves (for propositional theories) the equivalence between autoepistemic logic and introspective circumscription (first proved by Michael Gelfond and Halina Przymusinska).

Acknowledgement

The author is grateful to two anonymous referees for their helpful comments.

References

[1] K. Apt, H. Blair and A. Walker, Towards a theory of declarative knowledge, in: J. Minker, ed., *Foundations of Deductive Databases and Logic Programming* (Morgan Kaufmann, Los Altos, CA, 1988) 89–142.

[2] N. Bidoit and C. Froidevaux, General logical databases and programs: default logic semantics and stratification, *J. Inf. Comput.* (1988).

[3] A. Chandra and D. Harel, Horn clause queries and generalizations, *J. Logic Program.* **1** (1985) 1–15.

[4] K.L. Clark, Negation as failure, in: H. Gallaire and J. Minker, eds., *Logic and Data Bases* (Plenum, New York, 1978) 293–322.

[5] M. Fitting, A Kripke–Kleene semantics for logic programs, *J. Logic Program.* **2** (1985) 295–312.

[6] M. Gelfond, On stratified autoepistemic theories, in: *Proceedings AAAI-87*, Seattle, WA (1987) 207–211.

[7] M. Gelfond and V. Lifschitz, Compiling circumscriptive theories into logic programs, in: *Proceedings Second Workshop on Nonmonotonic Reasoning*, Munich, FRG (1988).

[8] M. Gelfond and V. Lifschitz, The stable model semantics for logic programming, in: R. Kowalski and K. Bowen, eds., *Proceedings Fifth Logic Programming Symposium* (MIT Press, Cambridge, MA, 1988) 1070–1080.

[9] M. Gelfond, H. Przymusinska and T. Przymusinski, On the relationship between circumscription and negation as failure, *Artif. Intell.* **38** (1989) 75–94.

[10] D. Kemp and R. Topor, Completeness of a top-down query evaluation procedure for stratified databases, in: R. Kowalski and K. Bowen, eds., *Proceedings Fifth Logic Programming Symposium* (MIT Press, Cambridge, MA, 1988) 178–194.

[11] S.C. Kleene, *Introduction to Metamathematics* (Van Nostrand, Princeton, NJ, 1952).

[12] K. Konolige, On the relation between default theories and autoepistemic logic, Research Report, SRI International, Menlo Park, CA (1987).

[13] K. Kunen, Negation in logic programming, *J. Logic Program.* **4** (1987) 289–308.

[14] V. Lifschitz, Computing circumscription, in: *Proceedings IJCAI-85*, Los Angeles, CA (1985) 121–127.

[15] V. Lifschitz, On the satisfiability of circumscription, *Artif. Intell.* **28** (1986) 17–27.

[16] V. Lifschitz, On the declarative semantics of logic programs with negation, in: J. Minker, ed., *Foundations of Deductive Databases and Logic Programming* (Morgan Kaufmann, Los Altos, CA, 1988) 177–192.

[17] V. Lifschitz, Between circumscription and autoepistemic logic, Research Report, Stanford University, Stanford, CA (1989).

[18] J.W. Lloyd, *Foundations of Logic Programming* (Springer, New York, 1st ed., 1984).

[19] W. Marek and M. Truszczynski, Relating autoepistemic and default logics, Research Report, University of Kentucky, Lexington, KY (1989).

[20] J. McCarthy, Circumscription—a form of non-monotonic reasoning, *Artif. Intell.* **13** (1980) 27–39.

[21] J. McCarthy, Applications of circumscription to formalizing common-sense knowledge, *Artif. Intell.* **28** (1986) 89–116.

[22] R.C. Moore, Semantic considerations on nonmonotonic logic, *Artif. Intell.* **25** (1985) 75–94.

[23] H. Przymusinska and T. Przymusinski, Weakly perfect model semantics for logic programs, in: R. Kowalski and K. Bowen, eds., *Proceedings Fifth Logic Programming Symposium* (MIT Press, Cambridge, MA, 1988) 1106–1122.

[24] H. Przymusinska and T. Przymusinski, Semantic issues in deductive databases and logic programs, in: R. Banerji, ed., *Formal Techniques in Artificial Intelligence* (North-Holland, Amsterdam, 1990) 321–367.

[25] T. Przymusinski, On the declarative semantics of stratified deductive databases and logic programs, in: J. Minker, ed., *Foundations of Deductive Databases and Logic Programming* (Morgan Kaufmann, Los Altos, CA, 1988) 193–216.

[26] T. Przymusinski, On the relationship between non-monotonic reasoning and logic programming, in: *Proceedings AAAI-88*, St. Paul, MN (1988) 444–448; Full version of this paper appeared as: Non-monotonic reasoning vs. logic programming: a new perspective, in: D. Partridge and Y. Wilks, eds., *The Foundations of Artificial Intelligence. A Sourcebook* (Cambridge University Press, London, 1990) 49–71.

[27] T. Przymusinski, Every logic program has a natural stratification and an iterated fixed point model, in: *Proceedings Eighth Symposium on Principles of Database Systems* (1989) 11–21.

[28] T. Przymusinski, Non-monotonic formalisms and logic programming, in: G. Levi and M. Martelli, eds., *Proceedings Sixth International Logic Programming Conference*, Lisbon, Portugal (1989) 655–674.

[29] T. Przymusinski, On the declarative and procedural semantics of logic programs, *J. Autom. Reasoning* **5** (1989) 167–205.

[30] T. Przymusinski, The well-founded semantics coincides with the three-valued stable semantics, *Fund. Inf.* **13** (1990) 445–464.

[31] T.C. Przymusinski, Autoepistemic logics of closed beliefs and logic programming, in: *Proceedings First International Workshop on Nonmonotonic Reasoning and Logic Programming*, Washington, DC (1991).

[32] T.C. Przymusinski and D.S. Warren, Well-founded semantics: theory and implementation, Research Report, University of Texas, El Paso, TX and SUNY at Stony Brook, NY (1991).

[33] R. Reiter, On closed-world data bases, in: H. Gallaire and J. Minker, eds., *Logic and Data Bases* (Plenum, New York, 1978) 55–76.

[34] R. Reiter, A logic for default theory, *Artif. Intell.* **13** (1980) 81–132.

[35] R. Reiter, Nonmonotonic reasoning, in: *Annual Reviews of Computer Science* (Annual Reviews, Palo Alto, CA, 1986).

[36] H. Seki and H. Itoh, A query evaluation method for stratified programs under the extended CWA, in: R. Kowalski and K. Bowen, eds., *Proceedings Fifth Logic Programming Symposium* (MIT Press, Cambridge, MA, 1988) 195–211.

[37] A. Van Gelder, Negation as failure using tight derivations for general logic programs, *J. Logic Program.* **6** (1989) 109–133; Preliminary version in: *Proceedings Third IEEE Symposium on Logic Programming*, Salt Lake City, UT (1986); also in: J. Minker, ed., *Foundations of Deductive Databases and Logic Programming* (Morgan Kaufmann, Los Altos, CA, 1988).

[38] A. Van Gelder, K.A. Ross and J.S. Schlipf, The well-founded semantics for general logic programs, *J. ACM* (1990); Preliminary abstract in: *Proceedings Seventh ACM Symposium on Principles of Database Systems* (1988) 221–230.

[39] D.S. Warren, The XWAM: a machine that integrates Prolog and deductive database query evaluation, Tech. Report #25, SUNY at Stony Brook, NY (1989).

Artificial Intelligence 49 (1991) 345–360
Elsevier

On the applicability of nonmonotonic logic to formal reasoning in continuous time*

Manny Rayner**

Swedish Institute of Computer Science, Box 1263, S-164 28 Kista, Sweden

Received October 1989
Revised July 1990

Abstract

Rayner, M., On the applicability of nonmonotonic logic to formal reasoning in continuous time, Artificial Intelligence 49 (1991) 345–360.

The paper criticizes arguments recently advanced by Shoham, McDermott and Sandewall, which purport to demonstrate the relevance of nonmonotonic logic to the formalization of reasoning about the evolution of mechanical systems in continuous time. The first half of the paper examines the "Extended Prediction Problem" of Shoham and McDermott; reasons are given to support the claim that the "problem" is the product of a mistaken understanding of the formal basis of Newtonian mechanics, and has no real existence. An example is given showing how, contrary to Shoham and McDermott's arguments, it is possible to formalize reasoning about the evolution of physical systems in continuous time using only classical logic and differential calculus. The second half then reviews Sandewall's nonmonotonic logic for almost-continuous systems. Here it is argued that the proposed framework offers only very marginal advantages in compactness of notation, and generally tends to collapse back into classical logic. In summary, I conclude that there is as yet no good reason to believe that nonmonotonic logic will be a useful tool in this area.

1. Introduction

AI researchers have been trying to formalize temporal reasoning in a computationally tractable way for a while, but most attempts so far have assumed a discrete model of time. Recently, however, there has been growing

---

*Sections 2, 3 and 4 of this paper appeared in substantially the same form under the title "Did Newton Solve the "Extended Prediction Problem"?", in: R.J. Brachmann, H. Levesque and R. Reiter, eds., *Proceedings First International Conference on Principles of Knowledge Representation and Reasoning* (Morgan Kaufmann, Los Altos, CA, 1989). The material in Section 5 has not been previously published.
**Present address: SRI International, Cambridge Computer Science Research Centre, 23 Millers Yard, Cambridge CB2 1RQ, UK.

0004-3702/91/$03.50 © 1991 — Elsevier Science Publishers B.V.

interest in continuous temporal reasoning, partly generated by its intrinsic theoretical interest and partly by the desire to incorporate AI methods in robots, autonomous vehicles, and other systems which carry out intelligent real-time interactions with the exterior world. I shall not attempt to define the meaning of the phrase *continuous time* in the most general possible way (those interested may wish to consult [6]); in the remainder of the paper it will be quite sufficient to interpret it as meaning that time will be isomorphic to the real numbers.

If the formalism is going to be logic-based in some way (and many people seem to agree on this), then it is clearly important to decide what kind of logic should be used. At the moment, considerable attention is being paid to suggestions by Shoham, McDermott and Sandewall, to the effect that some kind of nonmonotonic logic is either necessary (Shoham and McDermott), or at least offers clear advantages over classical logic (Sandewall). However, a close examination of the arguments used to justify this point of view reveals that they are in fact anything but convincing. The main purpose of the current paper is to argue the contrary position: namely, that nonmonotonic logic may well have nothing to offer here, and that attention should be focussed instead on the much better-understood framework of classical logic.

The rest of the paper is organized as follows. I will first examine Shoham and McDermott's claims: in Section 2, I summarize their arguments concerning the so-called "Extended Prediction Problem" in continuous-time temporal reasoning, which they claim is not amenable to solution within the framework of classical logic and infinitesimal calculus. In Section 3, I point out a number of logical errors in their analysis, and in Section 4 present a concrete counter-example, a simple problem in Newtonian kinematics which I demonstrate can be solved entirely within classical logic. In Section 5, I discuss Sandewall's ideas, and once again use a simple problem in kinematics as an illustration of my objections; this time, I show how a few additional axioms force the framework to collapse to the classical one, which I claim will in general be the case. In the last section I sum up my conclusions.

2. Shoham and McDermott: the "Extended Prediction Problem"

I will start by examining the work of Yoav Shoham and Drew McDermott [5] (hereafter S&McD). S&McD take as their point of departure the notorious "Frame Problem", and pay particular attention to the question of formulating it in continuous time. They begin by suggesting that it may best be dealt with by dividing it up into two distinct subproblems, which they refer to as the "qualification problem" and the "extended prediction problem". It is the second of these that will be my primary concern here: I begin by summarizing S&McD's arguments.

S&McD's claim is that there is a problem, the "extended prediction problem" (EPP). This is supposed to be the fact that it is difficult to formalize the process of making predictions over extended periods of time, if the axioms of a temporal theory are expressed as differential equations; S&McD claim moreover that the problem is not the product of a particular temporal formalism, but is general in nature. To substantiate this statement, they present arguments purporting to show that the problem occurs, not only in a conventional framework, but also in the Hayes "histories" formalism. In a later paper, Shoham [4] then goes on to describe his logic of "Chronological Ignorance" (CI), which (among other things) is supposed to provide a solution to the EPP.

What is the actual problem supposed to be? S&McD are happy to agree that Newtonian mechanics is *in principle* capable of describing the behaviour of dynamic systems in continuous time (pp. 52–53)[1]; however, they also claim that there is no well-defined associated *computational mechanism* which formalizes the process of making predictions. Considering the concrete problem of predicting the collision of two billiard balls, they write (p. 54):

> The "prediction," however, is purely model theoretic. No attention was paid to the problem of actually *computing* the point of collision. In fact, it is very unclear how to perform the computation, since all axioms refer to time *points*. Somehow we must identify the "interesting" points in time or space, and interpolate between them by integrating differentials over time. The problem seems a little circular, though, since the identity of the interesting points *depends* on the integration. For example, understanding where the two balls are heading logically precedes the identification of the collision: if we don't know that the two balls are rolling towards each other, there is no reason to expect something interesting at the actual collision point.
>
> How do people solve such physics problems? The inevitable answer seems to be that they "visualize" the problem, identify a solution in some mysterious ("analog") way, and only then *validate* the solution through physics... (italics as in original)

I will take the two paragraphs just quoted as the kernel of S&McD's claim. Before saying anything else, I think that it is important to point out that it is an extremely *strong* claim: all sorts of people are in the business of doing temporal reasoning using differential equations, and many of them would be prepared to defend themselves against the accusation that they are doing anything that couldn't be formalized. When the accusation is moreover exemplified in the trivial problem of predicting the collision of two billiard balls, the feeling that one is on theoretically secure ground is so strong as to more or less amount to

---

[1] All page references in Sections 2–4 are to [5] except where otherwise stated.

certainty. Although I naturally don't mean to imply that a feeling of certainty *proves* anything, this is worth saying, since it motivates most of the reasoning in the sequel. My counter-claim, then, will be that there is actually nothing mysterious about the process of making predictions about continuous-time processes, and that these can readily be formalized with no more theoretical apparatus than is afforded by classical logic, together with the differential and integral calculus. I will first point out what I regard as several concrete logical errors in S&McD's analysis of the EPP, both in the classical and the "histories" frameworks; later I will go further to sketch how it is in fact perfectly possible to predict billiard-ball collisions, using only classical logic and well-defined and unmysterious methods of inference.

3. Specific criticism of Shoham and McDermott's arguments

I will start with S&McD's treatment of the classical framework. Firstly, in several places in the argument, it certainly appears as though S&McD are committing the cardinal sin of confusing "infinitesimal" with "very small". Look, for example, at the following passage from p. 59:

> The most conservative prediction refers to a very short interval of time, in fact an instantaneous one, but that makes it very hard to reason about more lengthy future periods. For example, if on the basis of observing a ball rolling we predict that it will roll just a little bit further, in order to predict that it will roll a long distance we must iterate this process many times (in fact, an infinite number of times). We will call this the *extended prediction* problem.

Now at risk of stating the obvious, it is not correct to say that a differential equation licences prediction "a little bit forwards", and then talk about doing this "many times—in fact an infinite number of times". Differential equations say things about the instantaneous rate of change of functions; to make predictions about extended periods they must be *integrated*. The integration will hold over a period if the differential equation holds over the same period, but the *length* of the period is completely irrelevant.

This is not mere pedantry; S&McD's lack of precision in expressing themselves is obscuring a crucial point. Since the differential equations don't directly allow forward prediction in the first place, the problem is not one of making an inefficient process more effective, predicting over a long interval rather than a short one. The problem is rather how we can justify prediction over any period at all. This is very much at odds with, for example, the following passage from p. 60 (my italics):

> To summarize, the general extended prediction problem is that although we may be able to make predictions about *short* future

intervals, we might have to make a *whole lot of them* before we can predict anything about a substantial part of the future.

All right, so why don't we just integrate the differential equations then? Now S&McD have another argument in reserve; as we have already seen in the passage quoted in Section 1 above, they claim that we don't know what interval to integrate over. My second point is, very simply: *This is not a problem*. All that needs to be done is to perform the integration over an interval whose bounds are left unspecified, except by the restriction that the differential equation should hold within them; this is exactly what applied mathematicians normally do in practice. Say our bounds are t_1, t_2: then what we get is a logical formula of the form

> conditions on what holds at t_1 &
> the differential equations hold between t_1 and $t_2 \rightarrow$
> conditions on what holds at each point between t_1 and t_2.

By using these formulas, together with other facts, we can deduce the maximal t_1 and t_2 over which the integration is valid. In the next section I will illustrate how this is done for the problem with the billiard balls.

My third point concerns the notion of "potential history", which is, I claim, a somewhat misleading concept. Instead of talking about "the way things would turn out if nothing happened" (Shoham's definition of a "potential history"), it will be quite enough to take "the way things *actually* turn out *until* something happens". Then it will be possible to reason that either

   (i) nothing ever does "happen",
   (ii) there is a first thing that "happens".

In case (ii), we will be able to deduce things about when the aforementioned "first thing" occurs. If this sounds cryptic, the example in Section 4 should make things clearer.

I now move on to the reformulation of the problem in Hayes' "histories" framework, dealt with by S&McD in their Section 1.2. The logical fallacies here are of a similar type to those I have just pointed out, but since the integration has in effect already been performed, they are of a more transparent nature.

In one sentence: the way in which S&McD use histories to express the problem isn't the right one. To back up this claim, let's start by reviewing the problem. The initial data is that there are two ROLLING histories, H11 and H21, of which we are given the prefixes, H11′ and H21′. (See Figs 1–3, adapted from S&McD's Figs. 3–5.)

S&McD don't actually define exactly what they mean by a "prefix", but I suggest the following: it is the intersection of the history with some suitable given portion S of space–time. A simple way of defining S would be to let it be

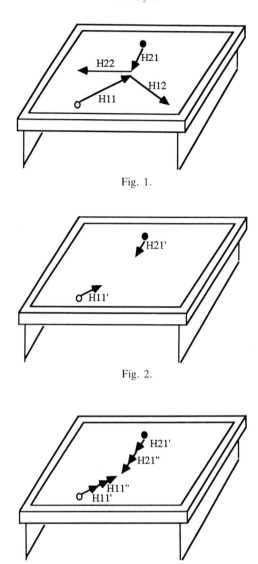

Fig. 1.

Fig. 2.

Fig. 3.

bounded above and below in time by two closely-spaced instants near the beginning of the period under consideration. Anyway, S&McD now go on to say that we want to predict two "new" ROLLING histories. They then inquire what these new histories should look like: either they will extend up to the collision point, or they won't. I agree with their objection that the second alternative merely postpones the problem one step, but their analysis of the first alternative quite fails to hold water.

S&McD's point here is that what we want to say intuitively is that "the histories persist for as long as possible"—i.e. until they collide with something—and that "there only are two histories". They claim that there is a difficulty with the second part; that there are, actually, a lot more histories lying around, like for example the histories H11″ and H21″ which follow just after H11′ and H21′. But this is just playing with words; obviously, every history contains an infinite number of subhistories, so counting all histories can never get us anywhere. What we are interested in are the *maximal* histories in a given bounded chunk of space–time, which in this domain *are* going to be finite in number. Now we can say that there are exactly two maximal histories in S (the chunk we intersected with in the last paragraph to define our prefixes); these are by construction H11′ and H21′.

If we then move on to consider a larger chunk of space–time (call it S'), H11′ and H21′ are in general no longer going to be maximal. They will, however, be included in two unique maximal histories,[2] which in a sufficiently large S' will be precisely H11 and H21. It is then fairly clear how to express our laws of physics so as to make things work. The rule we need is going to be something like the following:

> Let t_1 and t_2 (with $t_1 < t_2$) be two times, and let S be the region of space–time bounded by t_1 and t_2. Assume that all the maximal histories in S are ROLLING histories, which touch both boundaries and not each other, and that there are exactly N such histories. If there are any collisions after t_2, call the earliest time at which one occurs T, and call the region on space–time bounded by t_1 and T, S'. Then there are exactly $N + M$ maximal histories in S', of which M are COLLISION histories and N are ROLLING histories. $M < N$, the intersection of each of the ROLLING histories with S is a distinct maximal history in S, and each of the COLLISION histories occurs at time T.

Together with the rule that COLLISION histories occur precisely when ROLLING histories meet, this will enable us to predict when the first collision occurs, using methods that essentially consist of little more than geometrical calculations in a three-dimensional Euclidean space.

4. Reasoning in continuous time with classical logic: an example

Consider the situation illustrated in Fig. 4. (A propos S&McD's remarks above about "visualization" (p. 54): the diagram is purely for the benefit of human readers, and, as will be seen, contributes nothing to the proof.) We have a billiard table, on which a system of Cartesian coordinates is defined. At

---

[2] Proving the truth of this statement would demand a full axiomatization of the histories framework, something that is obviously impractical here. However, the key step would presumably be an axiom to the effect that the union of two connected histories of the same kind was a history.

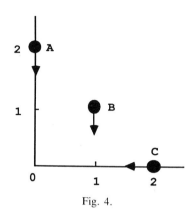

Fig. 4.

time $t = 0$ there are three balls: A at $(0, 2)$ with velocity vector $(0, -2)$; B at $(1, 1)$ with velocity vector $(0, -2)$; and C at $(2, 0)$ with velocity vector $(-2, 0)$. We will assume that balls are point objects which collide iff their positions coincide, and that the only forces on balls are those obtaining at times of collision. Given these assumptions, we want to know whether there will be any collisions, and if so when the first one will occur. Since we aren't going to reason past this point, we don't need to say anything about how balls behave after a collision, whether they bounce, stick together, smash or whatever. We reason as follows:

(1) Either no collision will occur, or else there will be a first collision. In this case, one of the following will be true; A and B will be involved in it, B and C will be involved in it, or C and A will be involved in it. We refer to these four possibilities as No_collision, AB_first, BC_first and AC_first, and we refer to the time of the first collision as t_c with the convention that $t_c = \infty$ if No_collision obtains. (This is only to make the proof a little more elegant.)

(2) For $0 \leqslant t < t_c$ no force acts on the balls. So by Newton's laws, their velocities will be constant during this period, and thus by performing an elementary integration we have that A's position at time t is $(0, 2 - 2t)$, B's is $(1, 1 - 2t)$ and C's is $(2 - 2t, 0)$, $0 \leqslant t \leqslant t_c$.

(3) We want to prove that No_collision doesn't hold, so we use reduction ad absurdum and assume that it does. Thus the positions are as given in (2) for all positive t. We now want to prove that a collision *does* take place to get our contradiction; specifically, we try to prove that A will collide with C. This will be so if we can find a positive t such that

$$(0, 2 - 2t) = (2 - 2t, 0).$$

Elementary algebra shows that $t = 1$ is a (in fact, the only) solution. So No_collision doesn't hold.

(4) We now prove that AB_first doesn't hold. Again, suppose it did. Then the moment of collision is given by the equation

$$(0, 2 - 2t_c) = (1, 1 - 2t_c).$$

This gives us that $0 = 1$, a contradiction. So AB_first doesn't hold either.

(5) Now prove that AC_first doesn't hold. Once more, suppose it did. Then just as above, we have that t_c is given by

$$(0, 2 - 2t_c) = (2 - 2t_c, 0).$$

Algebra gives us that $t_c = 1$. We must now establish that some other collision occurred at some earlier time, to obtain our contradiction. Specifically, we try to prove that B will collide with C. This will be so if we can find a t' such that

$$(1, 1 - 2t') = (2 - 2t', 0).$$

and $0 \leq t' < 1$. But $t = 0.5$ is such a solution, and once again we have a contradiction.

(6) We have proved that there will be a collision, so there must be a first collision. Since AB_first and AC_first have been proved impossible, by elimination we have BC_first. Doing the same bit of algebra as in (5) shows that it occurs at $t = 0.5$.   QED

Let us consider the structure of this proof. First, in (1), we hypothesize a time point t_c, which is when the first thing is going to "happen". The important thing to notice here is that we don't yet say what t_c's *value* is; we define it in terms of its properties, namely that a collision occurs then, and that none occur before. Then, in (2), we integrate the differential equations to get the interval-based information that will allow us to make predictions. If we had been working in a histories formalism, the equations would, as indicated earlier, "already be integrated", and this step would have been superfluous. Having got this far, the remaining steps (3) to (6) are just ordinary monotonic classical logic, and consist of a proof that t_c as described actually does exist, together with a computation of its value. It is clear that the methods used are quite general, and in no way make special use of the billiard-ball scenario. One incidental point is also worth noting explicitly: the collision is shown to have occurred at $t = 0.5$, showing that we really have moved outside the integers.

To point the moral, the proof above demonstrates that classical logic and differential calculus are at any rate *sufficient* to solve problems of this kind. Shoham (personal communication) has however advanced another criticism: he claims that, although the approach I have just demonstrated is possible, it is less *efficient* than using CI.

My answer to Shoham's objection is twofold. Firstly, this is not what is being said in the original paper; it is a separate issue, which as far as I can see has nothing to do with the EPP. Secondly, Shoham has still to demonstrate that proofs of this kind can be carried out *at all* in CI. As he admits himself [4, p. 320], the methods he has so far developed are completely dependent on the use of a discrete model of time; doing CI in continuous time would require the use of different algorithms, the complexity of which is thus completely unknown. Shoham might be right, but he has to present evidence to prove it; to use a metaphor from another game, the ball is now back in his court.

Before concluding this part of the paper, I hope that the reader will pardon a short historical digression. First, I would like to stress that the arguments presented above should not in any way be regarded as startling or unexpected; they are simply the defence of what most mathematicians and physicists would unhesitatingly call the common-sense view, namely that there is no longer anything mysterious about the EPP. If we adopt a broader perspective, however, we can see that the EPP *used* to be a major problem. It is in fact closely related to Zeno's paradox, something that caused philosophers difficulties from Zeno's time until the seventeenth century; until then, nobody even came close to explaining how it was possible to use logic to reason rigorously about continuous change. Indeed, many prominent thinkers went on record as claiming that such things were impossible in principle.

The first person to give a plausible account of mathematical reasoning about continuous processes was Newton, and even *he* was unable to do this in a satisfactorily formal way; this was not achieved until the nineteenth century analysts—people like Bolzano, Dedekind, Riemann and Cauchy—finally managed to put real analysis onto a sound logical footing. Not being an expert on the history of mathematics, I can't say with confidence just when the whole enterprise was completed; but I would be prepared to guess that Russell and Whitehead still had to tie up a few loose ends in the *Principia Mathematica*. The whole process, in other words, took over two hundred years.

To sum up, then, the EPP is undoubtedly an extremely important and difficult problem. It is, however, a problem that has been *solved*, at least to the extent of transferring it from the province of philosophy to that of science, mathematics and logic: completing this task was exactly the achievement of the program sketched above. Nonetheless, we still have the important question of *efficiency* left to consider; this brings us to the following section.

5. Sandewall: reasoning about almost continuous systems

We now move on to discuss Sandewall's work [2, 3]. In contrast to Shoham and McDermott, Sandewall is quite willing to countenance the use of the infinitesimal calculus to model continuous physical processes. He contends, however, that calculus on its own is not enough, since it cannot easily describe the behaviour of the system at points where the values of parameters become discontinuous. Such discontinuities will in general arise in interesting physical problems, and it seems most natural to model them using some sort of discrete logic. So far, Sandewall's arguments seem eminently reasonable: however, his next step is to suggest that the most suitable logic will be a nonmonotonic one, which he refers to as *chronological minimization of discontinuities* (CMD). His argument justifying this decision is as follows:

> ... a nonmonotonic logic is used, since we need to state a default that the left limit value and the right limit value [of a parameter] are equal even in the breakpoints, if it is consistent with the axioms for them to be so ... The proposed preference criterion can be viewed as a generalization of frame-problem persistence, from the classical view in AI of a discrete time-axis and discrete properties, to our approach using real-valued time and real-valued, piecewise continuous parameters. (p. 412)[3]

From this passage, it is not entirely clear why a nonmonotonic logic is deemed to be necessary. Another quote from a later paper expands on the point to some extent:

> Of course the criterion for a proposed definition of semantic entailment is not that it in itself obtains the correct model set, since what models are obtained depends also on the axioms. For the conventional "frame problem", for example, it is perfectly possible to obtain the correct model set with standard, monotonic entailment, but the problem is that it may be very cumbersome to write out the axioms. The criterion for a definition of entailment is therefore whether it makes it easy to write out axiomatizations which obtain the right model sets. This is the claim that is tentatively made for chronological minimization of discontinuities. [3, p. 896].

Sandewall's claim would thus appear to be roughly the following: that although it might well be *possible* to formulate (and presumably also solve) problems of this kind in classical logic, it is nonetheless *simpler* to do so in CMD. This claim is far more modest than those made above by Shoham and McDermott, and is consequently by no means as easy to refute. Nonetheless, by examining one of Sandewall's own examples, we shall show that he is standing on distinctly shaky ground.

The idealized scenario shown in Fig. 5 is taken from [2]. The problem is formulated as follows:

---

[3] All page references in this section are to [2] unless otherwise stated.

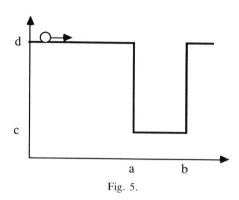

Fig. 5.

A ball is moving along a horizontal "plane" (actually a horizontal
line) towards a shaft with vertical sides and a horizontal bottom.
Idealized physical laws are assumed: the ball has zero size; there is
no drag so the ball's horizontal velocity is constant until it reaches
an obstacle, and when the ball reaches the pit its vertical acceleration changes instantly from zero to −9.81. The ball bounces
perfectly against the walls of the pit, so that its vertical velocity
does not change and its horizontal velocity reverses its sign but
keeps the magnitude. Also the bottom of the shaft absorbs impact
perfectly, so that the ball stops its vertical movement without
bounces when it reaches the bottom. (p. 415)

The problem is to justify the intuitive conclusion that the ball will eventually
end up at the bottom of the shaft. Before examining the formal description of
the problem, it will first be helpful to look a little more closely at the way in
which CMD defines entailment. The basic idea (as the name would suggest) is
closely related to Shoham's logic of chronological minimization [4]: as in
Shoham's approach there is a *preference relation* between models, and only
maximally preferred models are considered when computing entailment. Sandewall gives the following informal definition and motivation of the preference
relation (it is defined formally elsewhere in the paper):

> . . . If there is some way of satisfying the axioms without discon-
> tinuity then such an interpretation is preferred. If discontinuities
> are necessary i.e. no interpretation without discontinuity satisfies all
> the axioms, then the definition prefers to have the discontinuities as
> late as possible, and secondarily it minimizes the set of discon-
> tinuities which do occur.

> . . . For example by this definition of entailment, the axioms charac-
> terizing the ball-and-shaft scenario will entail that the temperature
> of the ball is continuous as the ball begins going into the shaft, since

there is no axiom that forces the temperature to be discontinuous there.

The reason for having continuity as a default is not only to deal with other, independent parameters for the same object, such as temperature, but also and perhaps more importantly to deal with multiple objects whose discontinuities occur independently. (p. 417)

This all sounds very good. If Sandewall's system really had the attractive properties claimed here, then there would obviously be a fair case to be made for using nonmonotonic logic; but as we shall soon see, things in fact work out rather less smoothly. This will become apparent when we now examine Sandewall's formalization of the problem, which we reproduce below. We have the following axioms:

(1) $\text{Supp}(x_b, y_b) \rightarrow \partial^2 y_b^r = 0$
    ;The ball has no vertical acceleration when supported
(2) $\text{Wall}(x_b, y_b) \rightarrow \partial x_b^l = -\partial x_b^r$
    ;The ball bounces perfectly at the wall
(3) $\partial^2 x_b = 0$
    ;The ball has no horizontal acceleration
(4) $\neg\text{Supp}(x_b, y_b) \rightarrow \partial^2 y_b = -g$
    ;The ball has vertical acceleration $-g$ when unsupported
(5) $C(y_b) \,\&\, C(y_b)$
    ;The ball's spatial position is continuous
(6) $\neg\text{Wall}(x_b, y_b) \rightarrow C(\partial x_b)$
    ;The ball's horizontal velocity is continuous except at the wall

(There are also some axioms defining the predicates Supp and Wall)

Now even in Sandewall's tiny example, things are already starting to go wrong. This becomes plain when we consider the justification for including axiom (6): as explained on p. 418, it is needed if we are to make the right prediction about what will happen when the ball reaches the edge of the shaft. There has to be a "breakpoint" here: either the ball's horizontal velocity or its vertical acceleration will change discontinuously. However, CMD is unable to prefer to keep the velocity continuous without an additional axiom which explicitly removes the other possibility; this is what axiom (6) is for. Without it, there will be a model where the ball spontaneously reverses direction and starts moving left again on reaching the edge.

This analysis of the rationale behind axiom (6) reveals that the problem it is intended to solve is, unfortunately enough, an extremely general one; in fact, it becomes natural to wonder why there is no need for a further axiom, which will explicitly restrict the situations in which the vertical velocity component

358   *M. Rayner*

can change discontinuously. On closer consideration, it turns out that is more or less an accident: it just so happens in our particular scenario that vertical motion can never carry the ball over a boundary where some other parameter undergoes discontinuous change.

A small alteration in the problem will be quite enough to remove this fortuitous circumstance. Suppose (just as Sandewall suggests in the passage from p. 417 quoted above) that we also want to think about the ball's temperature. We will assume the modified scenario illustrated in Fig. 6: when the ball's y-coordinate is greater than e, it loses heat by radiation at a rate proportional to the fourth power of its absolute temperature, but when it is below e it is also warmed by an infra-red beam which heats it at a constant rate w. Calling the ball's temperature Θ_b, we have the additional axioms

(7) $\neg\text{inbeam}(x_b, y_b) \rightarrow \partial\Theta_b = -k\Theta_b^4$
       ;Radiation cooling
(8) $\text{inbeam}(x_b, y_b) \rightarrow \partial\theta_b = w - k\Theta_b^4$
       ;Radiation cooling plus warming from beam
(9) $\text{inbeam}(x_b, y_b) \leftrightarrow 0 < y_b < e \ \& \ a \leqslant x_b \leqslant b$

Things have thus been set up so that there will a discontinuous change in $\partial\Theta_b$ when the ball falls into the beam, and now we get exactly the same problem with the vertical velocity component as we did previously with the horizontal one. As things stand, there will be valid models in which the ball, on reaching the beam, spontaneously begins moving upwards so as to stay out of it (Fig. 7); the only obvious way to block them will be to add another formula analogous to axiom (6), like for example (6a):

(6a) $\neg\text{Supp}(x_b, y_b) \rightarrow C(\partial y_b)$
       ;The ball's vertical velocity is continuous except on hitting the floor

What is really disquieting about the example is that it completely violates the intuitive assumption that the rate of change of the ball's temperature cannot

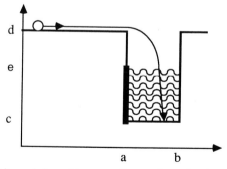

Fig. 6. The ball is warmed by an infra-red beam on its way down, but its trajectory should be the same.

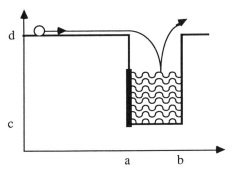

Fig. 7. An unintended model: the ball reverses direction spontaneously, to stay out of the beam.

affect its velocity. In general, it seems to show that a *global* analysis of the problem will be necessary if we are to know whether we can dispense with a "continuity" axiom like (6) or (6a): this negates the potential utility of the whole framework, since it would normally be simpler just to add all the continuity axioms immediately and work within classical logic. The obvious moral is that nonmonotonic entailment is buying us very little—far less than would justify abandoning the well-understood framework like classical logic.

6. Conclusions

In summary, I believe I have shown that there is so far no strong case for using nonmonotonic logic in the continuous-time temporal reasoning domain. Shoham and McDermott attempt to demonstrate the insufficiency of classical logic, but their arguments are quite simply incorrect. Sandewall, in a rather more restrained vein, suggests that nonmonotonic logic is possibly superior in terms of compactness of notation, since it can be used to obviate the necessity of explicitly specifying the regions in which parameters are continuous. However, the drawback with this approach is that it is difficult to ascertain precisely when it is possible to dispense with "continuity" axioms without performing a global classical-logic analysis of the problem; since this is precisely what nonmonotonic logic is supposed to avoid, it is hard to see that it will in fact help. Naturally, it is quite conceivable that some other way of using non-monotonic logic may turn out to offer concrete advantages, and it is indeed impossible in principle to refute such a statement. At the moment, though, it seems clear that the onus of proof is firmly on the nonmonotonic logicians.

There is one final question I would like to examine briefly before concluding. Sandewall (personal communication) has recently criticized the arguments offered above on the grounds that I nowhere consider in detail the treatment in classical logic of physical systems involving discontinuous change: the example in Section 4 above only involves proving that such a change will occur, not what will happen after it has done so. From this, he implies that there it is still possible to argue for the potential superiority of CMD as a framework for describing such processes.

Basically, I have two answers to this objection. Firstly, one can if necessary import the left and right limit notation used by Sandewall himself, adding explicit continuity conditions as outlined in the previous section. The point is that this really has nothing to do with CMD: it is equally possible in classical logic to describe discontinuous change simply by giving axioms relating the left and right limits at points of discontinuity. Proofs carried out in such a framework will be similar to those given by Sandewall, with *reductio ad sbsurdum* replacing nonmonotonic inference in the way shown in Section 4. However, it seems to me that it may be possible to do better. Working with limits is unattractive from a computational viewpoint, and a tempting alternative is to use the methods of nonstandard analysis [1]: thus instead of talking about "the left limit of f at t", we would have "$f(t - \varepsilon)$" for a positive infinitesimal ε. Weld [7] has recently demonstrated that use of such constructs is certainly feasible in some contexts, but I will postpone further discussion of the issues raised to a later paper.

Acknowledgement

I would very much like to state my appreciation of the unfailingly courteous and correct attitude which both Yoav Shoham and Erik Sandewall have displayed in the face of hostile criticism of their work. The comparison between the EPP and Zeno's paradox at the end of Section 4 is due to Rune Gustavsson, and the paper as a whole benefited immensely from numerous discussions with Annika Wærn.

References

[1] A. Robinson, *Non-standard Analysis* (North-Holland, Amsterdam, 1966).
[2] E. Sandewall, Combining logic and differential equations for describing real-world systems, in: R.J. Brachmann, H. Levesque and R. Reiter, eds., *Proceedings First International Conference on Principles of Knowledge Representation and Reasoning* (Morgan Kaufman, Los Altos, CA, 1989) 412–420.
[3] E. Sandewall, Filter preferential entailment for the logic of action in almost continuous worlds, in: *Proceedings IJCAI-89*, Detroit, MI (1989) 894–899.
[4] Y. Shoham, Chronological ignorance: experiments in nonmonotonic temporal reasoning, *Artif. Intell.* **36** (1988) 279–331.
[5] Y. Shoham and D. McDermott, Problems in formal temporal reasoning, *Artif. Intell.* **36** (1988) 49–61.
[6] J. van Benthem, *The Logic of Time* (Reidel, Dordrecht, 1983).
[7] D.S. Weld, Exaggeration, *Artif. Intell.* **43** (1990) 311–368.

Artificial Intelligence 49 (1991) 361–395
Elsevier

Principles of metareasoning

Stuart Russell and Eric Wefald

Computer Science Division, University of California, Berkeley, CA 94720, USA

Received November 1989
Revised June 1990

Abstract

Russell, S. and E. Wefald, Principles of metareasoning, Artificial Intelligence 49 (1991) 361–395.

In this paper we outline a general approach to the study of metareasoning, not in the sense of explicating the semantics of explicitly specified meta-level control policies, but in the sense of providing a basis for selecting and justifying computational actions. This research contributes to a developing attack on the problem of resource-bounded rationality, by providing a means for analyzing and generating optimal computational strategies. Because reasoning about a computation without doing it necessarily involves uncertainty as to its outcome, probability and decision theory will be our main tools. We develop a general formula for the utility of computations, this utility being derived directly from the ability of computations to affect an agent's external actions. We address some philosophical difficulties that arise in specifying this formula, given our assumption of *limited* rationality. We also describe a methodology for applying the theory to particular problem-solving systems, and provide a brief sketch of the resulting algorithms and their performance.

This paper is dedicated to the memory of Eric Wefald

1. Introduction

> Blot out vain pomp; check impulse; quench appetite;
> keep reason under its own control.
>
> *Marcus Aurelius Antoninus*

The study of resource-bounded intelligent systems promises to be a major area of research in AI in the near future, with the potential for drastic revision of our understanding of learning, inference and representation. One reason for this is practical: few people believe that classical, normative models can scale up. A second, and more fundamental, reason is that existing

0004-3702/91/$03.50 © 1991—Elsevier Science Publishers B.V.

formal models, by neglecting the fact of limited resources for computation, fail to provide an adequate *theoretical* basis on which to build a science of artificial intelligence. The "logicist" approach to AI, exemplified by Mc-Carthy's Advice Taker proposal [37], emphasizes the ability to reach correct conclusions from correct premises. The "rational agent" approach, derived from philosophical and economic notions of rational behaviour, emphasizes maximal achievement of goals via decisions to act. When resource bounds come into play, direct implementation of either approach results in subopti-mal performance. Instead, what we want is an optimal design for a *limited* rational agent. A view of artificial intelligence as a *constrained* optimization problem may therefore be more profitable. The solutions to such a con-strained design problem may look very different from those provided by the deductive and decision-theoretic models for the unconstrained problem.

Our long-term project is the design of robust software architectures for goal-driven, resource-limited intelligent systems (also known as *ralphs* [1]). Our approach has been to address the design problem with the finitude of resources as a *starting point*, rather than trying to lop corners off the deductive model. A major tool of this research is a normative meta-level theory for the value of computations, since this allows an agent to allocate scarce computational resources optimally; alternatively, it allows the AI researcher to show the optimality of a nonoptimizing algorithm for decision-making, and to design such algorithms constructively. Progress on developing and applying such a theory forms the main subject matter of this paper. Given the absence of a satisfactory axiomatic system for computationally limited agents, our results have only a heuristic basis, strictly speaking. However, the general methodology and the structure of the theory should remain in place even when an axiomatic approach is found, and by taking the development all the way to practical implementations we have shown that there are no fundamental limitations to the realization of a theory of metareasoning.

We begin in Section 2 by defining the notion of real-time problem-solving, and discuss the various approaches that have been taken to the problem of boundedness in this context. We see that metareasoning has a vital role to play, along with meta-level learning and compilation. Section 3 introduces the idea of *rational* metareasoning, wherein computations are treated as actions to be selected among on the basis of their expected utilities. In turn, these utilities are derived from the expected effects of the computations, chief among which are the consumption of time and/or space and the possible revision of the agent's intended actions in the real world. We define three levels of analysis, specifying the performance system at increasing levels

---

[1] Ralphs inhabit the RALPH (Rational Agents with Limited Performance Hardware) project at Berkeley.

of detail. Section 4 sets up the equations for the most general level, and Section 5 covers the case of bounded agents that use utility estimates to decide on actions. Along the way, we also examine certain ways in which the assumption of limits on the agent's rationality forces us to depart from the standard axiomatic framework for decision theory. Section 6 outlines a methodology for applying the theory to specific classes of decision-making systems, and mentions the results we have obtained for search applications. While the framework we have developed allows the analysis and construction of a variety of bounded rational systems, we do not deal with rational selection of all types of computation; for example, learning by induction and compilation is not covered explicitly. Section 7 discusses these and other directions for future research.

2. Approaches to bounded rationality

Two conditions conspire to create what has been called the "finitary predicament" [6]: first, real agents have only finite computational power; second, they don't have all the time in the world. One characterization of a "real-time" problem situation is the following: the utility of performing a given action varies significantly over the time necessary for a complete solution to the decision problem. Typically, the utility of an action will be a decreasing function of time. Since the time at which an action can be carried out depends on the amount of deliberation required to choose the action to be performed, there is often a tradeoff between the *intrinsic utility* of the action chosen and the *time cost* of the deliberation (see Section 5.2 below). As AI problems are scaled up towards reality, virtually all situations will become "real-time". As a result, system designs will have to be sufficiently flexible to manage such tradeoffs. One aim of this paper is to develop a methodology for constructing real-time algorithms that can be used as the "building blocks" for more complex systems. The composition problem for real-time systems is discussed in Section 7.

Standard algorithms in computer science either maximize intrinsic utility with little regard for the time cost, or minimize the time cost for achieving some fixed level of intrinsic utility. Work in *real-time AI* has traditionally followed a variant of the latter approach, focusing on delivering AI capabilities in applications demanding high performance and negligible response times. As a result, designers typically choose a fixed level of output quality, and then perform the necessary precompilation and optimization to achieve that level within a fixed time limit. Laffey et al. [31] survey a large number of application programs for real-time AI, and note, somewhat despairingly, that "Currently, ad hoc techniques are used for making a system produce a response within a specified time interval".

The inappropriateness of solution optimality as a criterion for success has been recognized in theoretical computer science. As exact methods have been shown to be intractable for a wide range of problems, theorists have looked at algorithms with one of two properties:

(1) A guarantee that the solution returned will be within some ε (either relative or absolute) of the optimal solution. This is called *approximation*.

(2) A probability of at least $1 - \delta$ that the algorithm will return the correct or optimal solution. These are often called *probably correct* algorithms.

Some researchers, notably Valiant and others in the field of inductive learning [22,46] have studied "probably approximately correct" algorithms, combining the above properties in the obvious way. However, as Horvitz [25] and Hansson and Mayer [19] have pointed out, what is needed is a theory of algorithms that maximize the *comprehensive value* of computation. In other words, since the utility of a computation and resulting action is a function of both the quality of the resulting solution and the time taken to choose it, we would like methods for designing algorithms that maximize this combined utility. A suitable generalization of complexity theory has not yet been developed.

A somewhat longer tradition of considering the effects of boundedness on decision-making exists in economics and the decision sciences, where human characteristics must sometimes be considered. Since the 1960s, Good [16] has emphasized the conceptual distinction between classical or "type I" rationality, and what he called "type II" rationality, or the maximization of expected utility *taking into account deliberation costs*. Researchers in decision analysis, especially Howard [27], have studied the problem of the *value of information*. Although the theory given below was developed independently, there is a strong parallel with Howard's approach. In the field of economics, Simon [45] made clear the distinction between systems that compute the rational thing to do (procedural rationality), and systems that simply do the rational thing (substantive rationality). He pointed out that procedurally rational systems, whose execution architectures are based on explicit use of declarative knowledge to reach decisions to act, seem to suffer from a good deal of overhead, both in terms of time and extra cognitive machinery.

A notion popularized by Brooks [5] and by Agre and Chapman [2] is that all this deliberation is a waste of time—why don't we just build agents that "do the right thing"? Substantive rationality, however, does not come for free. Although it means that an agent can be perfectly rational despite limited computational resources, it can only arise by prior design or adaptation. In nontrivial environments, particularly those with significant variation, it will be the case that exact solutions to the decision problem are intractable for the designer and unreachable by simple adaptation. With situation-dependent allocation of resources by the agent, on the other hand, it may be possible to approximate rationality to some degree.

We therefore believe that flexible, autonomous systems in complex environments require the ability to reason about the appropriate resources to allocate to computation at any point, and about which computations will be most effective. This premise is shared by several other researchers in AI, and has been the source of a number of projects that have, until recently, developed more or less independently. Doyle's "rational psychology" project [10,11] is based on the idea that computations, or internal state changes, are actions to be chosen like any other actions. He has applied this idea to clarify the notions of belief, intention and learning. Horvitz [24,26] was also an early AI contributor to the study of rational choice of computation, recognizing its potential to provide a new foundation for the design of intelligent systems. His work on the control of probabilistic inference in medical decision-making parallels our own on the control of search. Heckerman and Jimison [23] have also used medical decision-making as an example domain, showing how to vary the depth of analysis of a therapy problem according to its expected benefits. A third independent project was started in 1986 by Hansson and Mayer [18–21], who proposed the use of information value as a means of controlling heuristic search, which in turn is implemented as probabilistic inference using information from the heuristic function as evidence. Dean's work on real-time planning [7,9] assumes a known variation of the intrinsic utility of the results of a computation method with the amount of resources allocated to that method, and hence allocates resources optimally in various resource-bounded scenarios. His survey paper [8] provides a good summary of much of the technical work on decision-theoretic control of inference. Fehling and Breese [13] have applied a decision-theoretic approach to the control of information-gathering actions in a mobile robot domain. Agogino [1] has investigated the use of decision-theoretic modelling of computation in the control of mechanical systems. Bratman, Israel and Pollack [4] sketch a system design combining decision theory with AI planning techniques, using plans to limit the set of actions to be considered. Lesser and his group have studied real-time problem-solving in the context of a distributed vehicle-tracking application [34], modulating approximate problem-solving to achieve robust performance.

3. A framework for metareasoning

By *metareasoning* we mean deliberation concerning possible changes to the *computational* state of the agent. Our analysis in this paper is aimed primarily at *episodic* decisions at the base level; that is, we are most concerned with changes to the internal state that are made in the service of selecting the next action in the real world. Other computational actions, such as inductive learning and compilation, should be covered in any general theory of metareasoning (cf. Doyle's analysis [11]). In principle, their utility can be defined in terms of their effect on the complete sequence of future actions, and by replacing single actions by sequences in our analysis we can evaluate this utility; but to attempt to derive practical consequences from such an analysis appears premature at this stage.[2] In the context of episodic decision-making, there are two vital, and complementary, roles for metareasoning: first, it allows us as designers to reason about the computational strategies we implement, and to discuss their rationality in a bounded context; second, when implemented explicitly in an agent, it allows that agent to allocate flexibly its limited computational resources depending on the decision situation and to design and compile its own substantively rational decision procedures. In this latter role the justifications for employing explicit metareasoning are the same, in effect, as those for declarative base-level systems, with the additional argument that the knowledge required—knowledge of the agent's own computational structure—can be made introspectively available with little difficulty.

All meta-level systems share a common methodology for implementation: the base-level problem-solver operates via the explicit formulation and solution of meta-level problems. For example, the base-level problem-solver in Genesereth's MRS [14,39] is essentially a theorem-prover, but one that takes the user's goal and, instead of simply running a resolution algorithm, sets up its own goal of finding a way to prove the user's goal. This new goal is a theorem-proving task in its own right, and is solved using meta-level knowledge.

In a *uniform* meta-level architecture, the meta-level problems are formulated using the same language as the base-level problems, and solved using the same mechanism—that is, a meta-meta-level problem is set up to decide how to solve a meta-level goal. The uniformity of language enables the meta-level rules to apply to meta-meta-level goals, and so on. This produces very flexible systems, but introduces the possibility of infinite regress. Regress is particularly problematic when we try to define a constructive notion of the optimal design for a limited rational agent, since the metareasoning done

---

[2]The formal treatment of computations that change the agent's utility function lies outside the framework of this paper. As in classical decision theory, we assume that the agent's actual utility function is fixed, although estimates of its value may change with further computation. Rational changes to utility functions are not well understood. Ultimately, it seems that an autonomous agent does not in general know its own utility function exactly, since this must be induced from specific experiences, such as pain, pleasure or death, whose interpretation as utility data points is definitional. Revisions to the utility function, then, should be seen primarily as attempts to bring one's predictions of "happiness" into line with reality.

to control problem-solving optimally itself has costs, and therefore needs to be controlled. In other words, no computation can be executed until a computation has been executed to decide on it. Regress has been mentioned by many researchers concerned with bounded rationality [3,11,13,33] but so far only Lipman [35] has claimed any progress on the problem. Clearly we must back off from insisting on optimal control of *all* reasoning, just as we back off from insisting on optimal decisions to act. Some actions, whether computational or external, will have to be taken without being the *immediate* results of deliberation. Decisions at various points in the hierarchy can be hardwired or made by default, approximate decision methods can be used, and so on. However, if an action (including a computational action) is taken by an agent purporting to be an optimal limited rational agent, then unless the agent is extremely fortunate in its selections the action must be the result of prior deliberation or adaptation which has constructed a policy for an intentionally defined class of situations. For the above reasons, among others, two important topics in the RALPH project are inductive learning of meta-level policies and compilation of reasoning. Meta-level learning is discussed briefly in Section 5.4.1, and at greater length in [49]. On compilation of decision-making see [40].

We now turn to the topic of how an agent can select its computations optimally without knowing their outcome—the topic of rational metareasoning.

3.1. Rational metareasoning

The construction of a system capable of rational metareasoning rests on two basic principles:

(1) Computations are to be treated as actions, and are therefore to be selected among on the basis of their expected utilities.
(2) The utility of a computation is derived from its expected effects, consisting of:
    (a) the passage of time (and associated changes in the external environment);
    (b) the possible revision of the agent's intended actions in the real world.

The ability of a computation to cause the agent to take a different course of action, that has been revealed by the computation to be superior to the agent's original intention, is the fundamental source of positive utility for computations.[3]

---

[3]As mentioned above, the value of computations that change the agent's utility function is problematic. Not so problematic is the question of whether a computation is valuable if it increases the agent's confidence that it is taking the right course of action, rather than offering

It is important to emphasize the obvious fact that the choice of which computation to make, and whether to continue computing, must be made in the absence of exact and immediately available knowledge of the outcome of the computation (else the computation would be pointless). Therefore it will only be possible at best to perform optimally on average, by computing an *expected value* of the computation. That is, computations are treated as if they were stochastic experiments, even when their outcomes are completely deterministic. Note that this already goes against the classical Bayesian assumption that the agent's probabilities and expectations are conditioned upon the sum total of his "knowledge", which is assumed to be deductively closed. For a philosophical discussion of this point which supports our view, see Hacking [17]. Therefore, from a formal standpoint, the results in Sections 5 and 6 have as yet only a heuristic justification, borne out by practical results. We expect, however, that the structure of the theory will be retained when it is put on a firmer footing.

We assume in this paper that the outcome of each base-level action is known. The equations to be set forth here can be extended to cover the case of uncertainty about action outcomes, at some cost in terms of the complexity of the exposition. On the other hand, we consider the *utility* of each outcome to be uncertain in most cases. The utilities of a certain perhaps small set of possible states, such as game-ending positions or goal states, may be fully known, but the utilities of other states are defined as an expectation of a distribution over the known states. Again, the classical theory holds that the utility of a game position, for example, is logically determined by the utility of the game-ending positions via the minimax criterion, and hence accessible to the agent's knowledge—although in this case our approach of treating the exact utility of most positions as an inherently unknowable, random variable is more familiar to AI researchers. Just how the standard axioms of probability and utility theory [38,47] should be revised to allow for the limited rationality of real agents without making them vulnerable to a charge of incoherence is an important open philosophical problem, which we shall not attempt to tackle here. However, we will suggest some of the goals that such a re-axiomatization should accomplish.

3.2. Models of deliberation

There are many types of computations that may be used in refining a decision to act. In this section, we introduce three progressively more specific models of deliberation.

---

the possibility of revising that course of action. Clearly, if an as yet undone computation can increase the agent's confidence in a course of action, then it can also decrease it (else the optimality of the action must already be guaranteed). Hence there can be no utility to computations whose sole possible outcome is to increase confidence.

(1) *External model.* At the most general level, we can analyze a system as an external observer, by ascribing utilities and probabilities to the system's actions and internal states. The formal discussion of Section 4 applies to any computation for deciding on an action, as long as there is at any given time a *default action* or "current best action", which we denote by α, that the agent would take if it ceased computing at that time. (It is important to emphasize that this is the action which *appears best* to the agent given its deliberations so far, not necessarily the action which would be truly best for the agent.) The goal of any further computation prior to action is then to refine the choice of default action. Note that *any* algorithm for deciding how to act can be assimilated to this model by assuming that the initial default action consists of a uniform random choice from the available options, which would be taken if the algorithm were interrupted before it produced any useful output.

(2) *Estimated utility model.* One way the agent might select its current best action is by making explicit numerical estimates of the utilities of action outcomes. The agent's best action α at any given time is then the action whose current utility *estimate* is a maximum (we assume ties are broken somehow, perhaps randomly). In the AI literature, such utility estimation functions are often called evaluation functions. Deliberation then proceeds by revising and refining the utility estimates. This model will be discussed in Section 5. The principal theoretical problem introduced in this model is the dependence of the utility estimates on the computations that are done. This results in a potential ambiguity in defining a rational course of computation.

(3) *Concrete model.* At the concrete level, the decision algorithm is specified as far as the way in which the results of a computation step revise the agent's intended action. In the class of estimated utility systems, this means updating one or more of the action utility estimates. In our applications work [41,44], we have concentrated on metareasoning in forward search programs—programs that revise the utility estimates for outcome states by generating and evaluating their successors. Analysis at the this concrete level is discussed briefly in Section 6.

3.3. Notation

We will use the following notation throughout the paper:

- A_i: one of a set of possible external actions available to the agent in the current state. (To streamline the notation, reference to a context-dependent "current state" is always implicit.)

- S_j: one of a set of possible computational actions available to the agent.
- W_k: a world state. This includes both external aspects and the internal state of the agent.
- $[X]$: the world state that results from taking action X in the current state, where the action can be internal (a computational action) or external. For simplicity, we consider the case in which each action has a deterministic outcome.
- $[X, W_k]$: the result of taking action X in world state W_k.
- $U(W_k)$: the agent's utility in the state W_k. Typically, U will depend only on the *external* portion of the world state.
- S: a sequence of computational actions; typically, the sequence carried out between the previous external action and the current state. We will use T to refer to a potential future sequence of computational actions, particularly one ended by an external action.
- $S.S_j$: the sequence of actions consisting of sequence S followed by action S_j.
- $\hat{Q}^S$: the agent's *estimate* of a quantity Q, where the estimate results from a computation S.
- α: the agent's current default "intention"; typically, the external action considered so far to have the highest utility.
- α_T: the external action recommended by a computation T.
- $\beta_1, \beta_2, \ldots$: the external actions currently ranked second-best, third-best, etc.

4. The meta-level decision problem

In order for the concept of resource allocation to make sense, the system in question must have a choice of computations available to it, each of which can return a decision or can affect the ultimate decision made. The computations may vary along dimensions such as the amount of time used, the quality of the solution returned, the certainty that an adequate solution will be returned, and the usefulness of a partial computation if the process is interrupted. For our purposes, the amount of time used and the quality of solution returned will be the most significant aspects. Figure 1 illustrates the choice situation in which the agent finds itself. At any given time, the agent can either decide to continue computing, by performing one of $S_1, \ldots, S_k$, or to stop computing and take the current best external action α.[4] If the

---

[4]It is important to recall that, at this stage, we are considering the meta-level choice from the viewpoint of an external observer, without suggesting that the agent itself must explicitly set up and solve the decision problem for every computation. In particular, we do not assume that the agent has access to the exact utility function U.

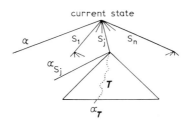

Fig. 1. The meta-level decision situation.

agent takes a computation step, then thereafter any sequence of steps may be taken, including the empty sequence, followed by an external action α_T, where T is the complete sequence of computation steps undertaken before acting. For example, a president faced with a difficult and potentially unpopular economic policy choice might request a coarse-grained simulation model to be run; if the results are still equivocal, a more detailed model might be run, but eventually the bullet will have to be bitten and taxes will have to be raised.

According to decision theory, an optimal action is one which maximizes the agent's expected utility, given by

$$E[U([A_i])] = \sum_k P(W_k)U([A_i, W_k]) \tag{1}$$

where $P(W_k)$ is the probability that the agent is currently in state W_k. The value of a computation step S_j is therefore defined in terms of the resulting state $[S_j]$. Computations, however, directly affect the system's internal state, and only indirectly the external world (except by consuming time), whereas a utility function usually refers only to aspects of the total situation that are external to the agent, such as budget deficits. We must therefore define $U([S_j])$ in terms of the changes that take place in the world while the computation occurs, *and the possible change in the agent's future action as a result of the computation*. The next section makes this more precise.

4.1. The value of computation

We define the *net value* of a computational action S_j to be the resulting increase in utility, compared to the utility of the default external action α that would be taken instead:

$$V(S_j) = U([S_j]) - U([\alpha]). \tag{2}$$

A major distinction that needs to be made in specifying $U([S_j])$ is between *partial* and *complete* computations. A partial computation is one that does not result in a commitment to external action; whereas a complete computation does.

If S_j is a complete computation, then the utility of S_j is just the utility of the action α_{S_j} chosen as a result of the computation, given that the action is carried out *after* S_j is completed. That is, $U([S_j]) = U([\alpha_{S_j}, [S_j]])$. Hence,

$$V(S_j) = U([\alpha_{S_j}, [S_j]]) - U([\alpha]). \tag{3}$$

For example, if the aforementioned economic simulation takes a week, then its value will be the difference between doing α (cutting spending, perhaps) now and raising taxes a week later.

In the general (partial) case, the computational action will bring about changes in the internal state of the agent that will affect the value of possible further computational actions. In this case, we want to assess the utility of the internal state in terms of its effect on the agent's ultimate choice of action. Hence the utility of the internal state is the *expected* utility of the base-level action which the agent will ultimately take, given that it is in that internal state. This expectation is defined by summing over all possible ways of completing the deliberation from the given internal state. That is, letting T range over all possible complete computation sequences following S_j, α_T representing the action chosen by computation sequence T, we have

$$U([S_j]) = \sum_T P(T) U([\alpha_T, [S_j.T]]) \tag{4}$$

where $P(T)$ is the probability that the agent will perform the computation sequence T.

If the agent has a perfectly rational meta-level, then the computation sequence selected will be the one maximizing $U([\alpha_T, [T]])$, and this sequence will have probability 1 in the above equation.[5] In other words, the agent would carry out next the computation step at the beginning of the most valuable computation sequence. This leads to the standard minimax or "expecti-max" approach of decision analysis (see Pearl [38, Chapter 6]). However, an agent with only limited rationality might not have any good reason to assume that she will actually succeed in taking the action with highest expected utility. Much less is such an assumption warranted when modelling an agent from the outside. Approaches that avoid this requirement of perfection are discussed in Section 5.4.

4.2. Ideal and approximate control

According to decision theory, the ideal solution to the meta-level decision problem is simply to perform whichever action from the set $\{\alpha, S_1, \ldots, S_k\}$

---

[5]If several completion sequences have the same maximal utility, the probability of each occurring might be less than 1, but the result of the summation would be the same.

has the maximum expected utility. Equivalently, in terms of the net value of computation defined above, the *ideal control algorithm* is as follows:

Step 1. Keep performing the available computation with highest expected net value, until none has positive expected net value.

Step 2. Commit to the action α that is preferred according to the internal state resulting from Step 1.

This algorithm, and the intuitive notion of the value of computation which we have defined precisely above, were also proposed by Good [15].

Obviously, the calculation of the expected values of the various possible computations cannot be instantaneous; in fact, as we describe below, it can be arbitrarily hard. It is, however, possible to *approximate* the ideal algorithm by making simplifying assumptions. In particular, we will show how it is possible to use the agent's own utility estimation function to estimate the expected net value of computations.

5. The value of utility estimate revisions

In this section, we will spell out transformations on the equations given in the previous section, which render them more useful to a less-than-omniscient designer or to a limited rational agent that is explicitly reasoning about its own problem-solving. This will correspond to the second level of analysis defined in Section 3.

Our first job is to replace the function U by the function $\hat{U}$, since we are assuming that the former is unknowable, and the agent is able to calculate only in terms of the latter. This will require some care, because the function $\hat{U}$ depends on the stage of the computation. For reasons that we discuss below, we choose to replace U in equation (4) by utility estimates for actions made in the state after the computation in question has been done. Then the estimated net value of computation S_j, from equation (2), is given by

$$\hat{V}(S_j) = \hat{U}^{S.S_j}([S_j]) - \hat{U}^{S.S_j}([\alpha]).$$ (5)

If we now assume that the agent will take whatever action appears best at the time it decides to act,[6] then equation (4) becomes

$$\hat{U}^{S.S_j}([S_j]) = \sum_T \hat{P}^{S.S_j}(T) \max_i \hat{U}^{S.S_j.T}([A_i, [S_j.T]]).$$ (6)

---

[6]Note how this assumption differs from the more dubious assumption of classical decision theory that the agent will choose the action whose *true* utility is highest.

Of course, before the computation S_j is performed, $\hat{V}(S_j)$ is a random variable. The agent can't know ahead of time what the exact value of $\hat{V}(S_j)$ will be, but given sufficient statistical knowledge of the distribution of $\hat{V}$ for similar actions in past situations, the agent can estimate its *expectation*,

$$E[\hat{V}(S_j)] = E[\hat{U}^{S.S_j}([S_j]) - \hat{U}^{S.S_j}([\alpha])]. \tag{7}$$

The next three subsections deal with the problem of estimating equation (7) for *complete* computations. Section 5.4 discusses the problem of estimating the expected value of partial computations, for which we have not yet found a fully satisfactory solution. The section concludes with a generic description of rational behaviour with respect to decisions between computation and action.

5.1. Analysis for complete computations

Suppose we know or assume that the agent will act after the computation step S_j in question (if it does not act immediately); i.e., suppose it is only choosing among complete computations. Then the utility of S_j will be equal to the utility of the action α_{S_j} believed by the agent to be optimal after S_j has been carried out, given that the action is carried out *after* S_j is completed. That is,

$$\hat{U}^{S.S_j}([S_j]) = \hat{U}^{S.S_j}([\alpha_{S_j}, [S_j]]). \tag{8}$$

The net value of S_j is therefore given by

$$\hat{V}(S_j) = \hat{U}^{S.S_j}([\alpha_{S_j}, [S_j]]) - \hat{U}^{S.S_j}([\alpha]) \tag{9}$$

and its expectation in the current state is given by

$$E[\hat{V}(S_j)] = E[\hat{U}^{S.S_j}([\alpha_{S_j}, [S_j]]) - \hat{U}^{S.S_j}([\alpha])]. \tag{10}$$

From this equation, it is clear that the knowledge necessary to assign values to computations resides in the probability distribution for the future utility estimates of the top-level actions. A computation step S_j can in general affect the utility estimates for any of the actions A_i. Thus, let $\boldsymbol{u} = \langle u_1, \ldots, u_n \rangle$, and let $p_j(\boldsymbol{u})$ be the joint distribution for the probability that the actions A_1 through A_n get new utility estimates u_1 through u_n respectively. Let $p_{\alpha j}$ be the projection of this distribution for the current best action α—that is, the probability distribution for the random variable $\hat{U}^{S.S_j}([\alpha])$. Finally, let $\max(\boldsymbol{u}) = \max\{u_1, \ldots, u_n\}$. Then, by equation (10), we have

$$E[\hat{V}(S_j)] = \int_{\boldsymbol{u}} \max(\boldsymbol{u}) p_j(\boldsymbol{u}) \, d\boldsymbol{u} - \int_{-\infty}^{\infty} u \, p_{\alpha j}(u) \, du. \tag{11}$$

The probability distributions can be obtained by gathering statistics on past computations or, in the case of computations yielding exact values, simply by using the agent's current probability distribution for the variable in question. In either case, the computation S_j is characterized as belonging to a given *class* of computations, such as an economic forecast provided by a certain model, or an additional ply of search in an iterative-deepening algorithm. The computation will also be characterized by some pre-determined set of features describing the situation in which it is carried out. Then we can characterize the distribution of the random variable $\hat{V}(S_j)$ by computing post hoc the net increase $\hat{U}([\alpha_{S_j}, [S_j]]) - \hat{U}([\alpha])$ for a large sample of computations in similar situations drawn from the same class.[7] If the sampling is done off-line, and the results stored in parameterized form, then the cost of applying equation (9) to estimate the expected net value of computation S_j can be orders of magnitude cheaper than carrying out S_j itself. In that case, the expected value calculation will be well worth doing, since it allows one to select among computations, to prune pointless branches, and to terminate deliberation in such a way as to maximize the overall utility of the agent.

This crude approach will fail when the value of the computation depends on more than a few aspects of the current state; either too much data will be needed to provide accurate statistical estimates, or some aspects will have to be ignored, resulting in large errors. To do better, we need to know the process by which the computation actually revises the utility estimates for external actions. Section 6 describes such improvements.

5.1.1. Discussion

Some deep issues arise from the fact that the agents we are dealing with have only limited rationality. They manifest themselves particularly in questions about the theoretical status of utility estimates. The majority of work on limited rationality has been done in the context of probability estimates; since utility estimates can be viewed as estimating the probability of obtaining some exact rewards, the issues are the same. Put simply, the problem is that probability estimates, made by a particular computation sequence, do not obey the axioms of probability. For example, one axiom of probability states that the probability of a tautology is 1. Thus if, say, P-K4 is a winning opening move in chess, then the implication relationship between the rules of chess and this fact is tautologous. However, any probability estimate we can arrive at for the win will be less than 1. This is one reason why we adopted the superscript notation for the computation used to arrive

---

[7]This provides the *performance profiles* for the available computations, as used by Dean [7]; his *deliberation scheduling* algorithm follows from equation (10) with each S_j consisting of running one of the available decision procedures for a small increment of time.

at a utility estimate. Fehling and Breese [13] simply write the computation as additional conditioning in the conditional probabilities used to make decisions. While this seems natural, it is perhaps misleading since one is no longer dealing in probabilities.

The lack of a coherent theoretical basis for probability and utility estimates results in some tricky problems in formulating our approach to controlling computation. Note that in the above equations we use the later estimate $\hat{U}^{S.S_j}$ to evaluate both α_{S_j} and α, the new and the old best moves. The reason for this is most obvious if we consider the case where $\alpha_{S_j} = \alpha$, but $\hat{U}^{S.S_j}([\alpha_{S_j}]) > \hat{U}^S([\alpha])$; i.e., S_j simply revises upward the estimated utility of α but does not alter the choice of move. Then the net value of S_j should depend only on the passage of time spent in deliberation, since the real intrinsic utility is of course constant. This would not be the case if we used the later utility estimate for the new best move and the current utility estimate for the current best move. [8]

Examining Howard's Information Value Theory [27] we find a formula which, in the above context, would amount to defining the *expected* net value of S_j as

$$E[\hat{V}(S_j)] = E[\hat{U}^{S.S_j}([\alpha_{S_j}, [S_j]])] - \hat{U}^S([\alpha]). \tag{12}$$

This will only be equivalent to our formula, given in equation (10), *provided* we have, in the current state $[S]$, $E[\hat{U}^{S.S_j}([\alpha])] = \hat{U}^S([\alpha])$. This *coherence condition* will hold true of a perfectly rational agent, since any expected increase or decrease in its expected utility estimate due to further deliberation should already be reflected in the current estimate.

For an agent with only limited rationality, for instance an agent who relies on a fixed, easily computed evaluation function, it may not be safe to assume that the utility estimate is rational in this sense. In fact, it may not be the case that the coherence condition holds even for an *optimal* limited rational agent, since any evaluation function which satisfies the coherence condition might be complicated and expensive to compute. The underlying principle that must, however, be respected is that the real utility of carrying out a given action at a given time will not be changed just by thinking about it. This principle is even more important in *inductive meta-level learning*, wherein the agent evaluates computational actions post hoc in order to learn statistical distributions and a predictive function for the value of computation (see Section 5.4.1). Here, we do not want to use the formula

$$\hat{V}(S_j) = \hat{U}^{S.S_j}([\alpha_{S_j}, [S_j]]) - \hat{U}^S([\alpha]) \tag{13}$$

---

[8]Of course, the desired effect would be obtained if we used the current estimates for both moves. But then every computation would have nonpositive utility, since by definition α has a higher current utility estimate than the other moves.

whose expectation is taken in (12), since this will lead to erroneous evaluations. In particular, in the case where $\alpha_{S_j} = \alpha$, we ought to have $V(S_j) \leq 0$, since in this case the only external effect of the computation is to delay action. Equation (9) will be in agreement with this condition, but equation (13) need not be.

This gives a second reason not to employ the Bayesian conditional subjective expectation notation $E[U(A_i)|\boldsymbol{S}]$ for our concept $\hat{U}^{\boldsymbol{S}}(A_i)$, since the former denotes the expected utility of A_i, given all knowledge logically deducible by the agent from state $[\boldsymbol{S}]$, and trivially obeys the identity

$$E[E[U(A_i)|\boldsymbol{S}.S_j]|\boldsymbol{S}] = E[U(A_i)|\boldsymbol{S}]. \tag{14}$$

In fact, our use of the expectation symbol $E[\cdot]$ in equation (10) must also be interpreted with some caution. Recall that we wish to view computations as if they were stochastic experiments whose outcomes are drawn from some perhaps unknown probability distribution. Given this assumption, equation (10) refers to the expectation in the objective or frequency sense.

5.2. Time and its cost

Thus far we have captured the real-time nature of the environment by explicitly including the situation in which an action is taken in the argument to the utility function. Such a comprehensive function of the total state of affairs captures all constraints and trade offs; in particular, any form of time constraint can be expressed in this way. However, the inclusion of this dependence on the overall state significantly complicates the analysis. Under certain assumptions, it is possible to capture the dependence of utility on time in a separate notion of the *cost of time*, so that the consideration of the quality of an action can be separated from considerations of time pressure.

For many estimated utility functions $\hat{U}$, we can define a related function, the estimated *intrinsic utility*, denoted by $\hat{U}_I$, along with a cost function C, that expresses the difference between total and intrinsic utility:[9]

$$\hat{U}([A_i, [S_j]]) = \hat{U}_I([A_i]) - C(A_i, S_j) \tag{15}$$

where $\hat{U}_I([A_i]) = \hat{U}([A_i])$.[10]

Of course there will always exist a function C which will satisfy equation (15), if only trivially. In order for $\hat{U}_I$ to qualify as an intrinsic utility, it must satisfy a further constraint. Namely, once the state $[S_j]$ has become

---

[9]Often in AI applications, we begin with an intrinsic utility function (such as a static evaluation function), and C is then defined to yield an accurate estimate of the true utility of an action under various time pressures. Only $\hat{U}$ is in fact independently definable from empirical observations of outcomes.

[10]We define intrinsic utility with reference to the current situation only for convenience; in fact, utility is well-defined only up to an arbitrary positive linear transformation.

the new current state, the agent's optimal action *at that time* should always be the one with highest intrinsic utility, independently of the cost C. A sufficient condition for this is that the cost of the computation be independent of the action being evaluated: [11]

$$\hat{U}([A_i, [S_j]]) = \hat{U}_I([A_i]) - C(S_j). \tag{16}$$

Moreover, in the cases we are considering the change in actual utility of an action that occurs during some computation S_j will depend only on $|S_j|$, the length (in elapsed time) of S_j, and on the course of events in the outside world during that time. Since, by definition, computations alter only internal state, S_j will not affect that course of events, so we can let C, and thus $\hat{U}$, depend on the length of the computation rather than the computation itself. Thus the cost function, which we will in this case call TC or "time cost", gives the loss in utility to the agent due to the temporal delay in performing any given action:

$$\hat{U}([A_i, [S_j]]) = \hat{U}_I([A_i]) - TC(|S_j|). \tag{17}$$

If such a function TC exists, then we can separate out the cost and benefit of a computation. We can therefore rewrite equation (9) as follows:

$$\begin{aligned} \hat{V}([S_j]) &= \hat{U}^{S.S_j}([\alpha_{S_j}, [S_j]]) - \hat{U}^{S.S_j}([\alpha]) \\ &= \hat{U}_I^{S.S_j}([\alpha_{S_j}]) - \hat{U}_I^{S.S_j}([\alpha]) - TC(|S_j|) \\ &= \Delta(S_j) - TC(|S_j|) \end{aligned} \tag{18}$$

where

$$\Delta(S_j) = \hat{U}_I^{S.S_j}([\alpha_{S_j}]) - \hat{U}_I^{S.S_j}([\alpha]) \tag{19}$$

denotes the *estimated benefit* of the computation. That is, Δ is the estimated increase in intrinsic utility of the new best action over the old best action.

5.3. Simplifying assumptions

Ideally, at any given point in a computation we would like to be able to assess the expected value of all immediate continuations of the computation, without making any assumptions about what we would do afterward. But since computations can in general be arbitrarily long, such a complete analysis is infeasible. Moreover, it is difficult to estimate the value that computations provide by making further computations possible or more

[11] This is approximately true in many AI domains such as game-playing or path-planning in a fixed or slowly changing environment. It will not be true in domains such as hunting or war, where different possible actions will gain or lose value at very different rates over time. Even in chess this condition can sometimes fail, since as time is used up more complex positions become less valuable.

valuable. Thus, it is necessary to employ simplifying assumptions or approx-imations. Here we present two such simplifications. They are closely related to what Pearl [38] has called a "myopic policy". They can be validated only by consideration of the domain of application. Our experiments show that the resulting selection of computations is far better than random; in fact, better than any algorithm designed "by hand", under certain conditions.

5.3.1. Meta-greedy algorithms

If explicit consideration of all possible complete sequences of computation steps is intractable, then an obvious simplification is to consider *single* primitive steps and to estimate their ultimate effect; we then choose the step appearing to have the highest immediate benefit. We call such algorithms *meta-greedy algorithms*. We get different variants depending on how we estimate the ultimate effect of the computation (see below). A meta-greedy algorithm, then, is one that effectively has a fixed meta-meta-level policy of a depth limit of 1 on the meta-level decision problem. An analysis based on such an approach will be said to employ the "meta-greedy assumption"; i.e., the assumption that employing such a restricted horizon for the meta-level decision problem will provide an adequate framework for meta-level control. This should be compared with the corresponding assumption made in game-playing research, that limited-depth search is an adequate method for choosing moves.

A weaker form of this approach is to consider, for purposes of the meta-level analysis, some, but not all, finite sequences of computation steps. For instance, in the context of single-agent heuristic search [48], we consider the expansion of all leaf nodes to any given finite depth, up to some fixed depth horizon. This analysis is incomplete because it does not consider the possibility of expanding different nodes to different depths; since that would involve exponentially many possibilities in the number of leaf nodes, it would not lead to a tractable policy. However, by considering a simple subset of the possible computation sequences, up to a given finite size, we can provide a tractable approximation to the complete policy.

5.3.2. Single-step assumption

As we discuss in more detail in the next section, even when we restrict our attention to a limited set of possible computations, it can be very difficult to assess all ways in which a computation can increase utility. In particular, it is difficult to take account of the impact of a computation in making further computations possible or more valuable. On the other hand, it is not difficult to write down simple closed-form expressions for the expected value of *complete* computations, as we have seen. Thus, an obvious simplification is to use these equations to evaluate partial computations. That is, to assume that a computation's value as a complete computation is a useful approximation to its true value as a *possibly* partial computation. This assumption is tantamount to acting as if we had time for at most one more complete computation step; hence we call it the "single-step assumption". The assumption can cause underestimation of the value of some computations; in the case of game-playing, for trees that have grown to a certain size, there will be many node expansions that are valuable as partial computations but have no value as complete computations. This effectively limits the depth to which a meta-greedy algorithm employing the single-step assumption can search a game tree. In the case of single-agent search, however, this phenomenon does not occur, and there is no such restriction on search depth.

It is worth emphasizing here that if either the meta-greedy or single-step assumptions were completely relaxed, the other would become completely true. That is, if it were possible to consider all possible sequences of computations, thus completely relaxing the meta-greedy assumption, then it would be no restriction to consider those sequences as complete computations, assuming the process of deliberation must eventually terminate, so the single-step assumption would be exactly correct. On the other hand, if we could accurately compute the full expected value of single computation steps considered as possibly partial computations which could be followed by further computations, then we would not need to consider all possible computation sequences. Thus, the simplification lies in employing the two assumptions jointly; neither alone would be a restriction.

5.4. Partial computations

When we can assume that the agent will necessarily take the action α_{S_j} after performing computational action S_j, then the methods of Sections 5.1 and 5.2 will suffice. However, in general this is not the case, since, as long as the agent does not arrive at complete certainty about its utility function—which we assume our agents almost never attain—in state $[S_j]$ the agent will still have a choice between taking action α_{S_j}, and continuing to deliberate. (Assume, for simplicity, that there is only one course of computational action open to the agent at each juncture.) Thus the value of the computation S_j will be the value of having this choice. In this section, we will discuss possible ways of attempting to relax the single-step assumption and evaluate S_j accurately as a partial computation; our discussion will be preliminary, as the general problem remains unsolved. There are at least two ways to model the utility of being in the state of having a choice between actions, which we discuss below.

To see the *practical* effect of ignoring partial computation values, consider a computation S_1 which increases the utility estimate of the current second-best action β_1 to a point roughly midway between the current value of

$\hat{U}_1(\beta_1)$ and that of $\hat{U}_1(\alpha)$. Since it does not change the choice of current best move, S_1 has no positive benefit as a complete computation. However, suppose that S_1 is followed by a further computation S_2 which decreases the utility estimate of α below that of β_1. In this case, the complete *sequence* $S_1.S_2$ has net benefit $\Delta(S_1.S_2) = \hat{U}_1^{S_1.S_2}(\alpha_{S_2}) - \hat{U}_1^{S_1.S_2}(\alpha)$, where $\alpha_{S_2} = \beta_1$. If we evaluate the two computations S_1, S_2 separately using the single-step assumption, we will decide that $\Delta(S_1) = 0$ while $\Delta(S_2) = \hat{U}_1^{S_1.S_2}(\alpha_{S_2}) - \hat{U}_1^{S_1.S_2}(\alpha)$. But intuitively it is clear that some of this benefit should be ascribed to S_1, since it made it possible for S_2 to have its effect. Just as in ordinary decision-making, it is best to consider "plans", or action sequences, that do have some easily identifiable benefit.

5.4.1. An adaptive approach

If we assume that the agent will be able, when faced with a choice, to choose the best option, then the utility of having a choice between two actions is just the maximum of the utilities of the two actions. This is a standard approach taken in decision analysis; see for instance, Pearl [38]. Let S_k be the action of continuing to compute in state $[S_j]$. Then on this model, the utility of computational action S_j in the current state is given by

$$E[U([S_j])] = E[\max\{U([\alpha_{S_j}, [S_j]]), U([S_k, [S_j]])\}]. \quad (20)$$

One difficulty with this formula is that it defines the value of a present computation in terms of the value of a possible future computation. Moreover, it is usually unreasonable for the agent to assume that a *limited* agent without perfect knowledge of its utility function will necessarily choose the action with maximum utility in state $[S_j]$.

On the other hand, if we replace U by $\hat{U}$ in equation (20), we obtain the following:

$$E[\hat{U}([S_j])] = E[\max\{\hat{U}([\alpha_{S_j}, [S_j]]), \hat{U}([S_k, [S_j]])\}]. \quad (21)$$

It might be argued that equation (21) is indeed a principle of rationality, in the sense that it imposes a constraint on any *extension* of $\hat{U}$ from base-level actions to computational actions. For it is true almost by definition that the agent will pick the action with maximum $\hat{U}$, and hence in a sense equation (21) says that the agent should value an action the same as it values the computation that recommended the action.[12] As far as possible, then, the function $\hat{U}$ should obey this equation.

---

[12]Against this it might be argued that if the agent *knows* that its estimated-utility function is error-prone, it needn't think that the right-hand side of equation (21) gives the true expected utility of the computational action S_j. We have found it very difficult to settle the sorts of philosophical questions raised by such considerations, and will not attempt to do so here. But we hope the dilemma raised here might convince the reader, as it has us, that the questions raised here are very deep.

However, equation (21) still cannot define a *unique* extension of $\hat{U}$ to computational actions because it is "ungrounded"; i.e. it does not specify how the recursion bottoms out. One possible way of overcoming the nonuniqueness involves specifying a *conservative extension* of $\hat{U}$ from base-level to computational actions. In fact, all we need is a method for arriving at a reasonable post hoc evaluation of a given computational action, in order to gain knowledge about the distribution of values by statistical sampling. Note that at the time we are collecting our sample data, we can have available to us the complete outcome of any given decision-making event. Thus, if we are willing to assume, solely for the purpose of evaluating sample computations, that our current agent's decisions between action and computation are correct, then we can arrive at justifiable numerical values by evaluating completed computations using equation (18), and backing up the values obtained to determine the values of partial computations. These values can then be used as data points to induce an intentional characterization of the utility of computations. A more detailed description of this procedure is given in [43,49].

Data derived in the above way will of course be error-prone, since the whole point of doing the analysis is that we think that the agent often makes incorrect judgments concerning when to stop and when to continue computing. But once we have done our sampling and equipped the agent with decision-theoretic search control knowledge, it will no longer be the same agent, since it will make different, and we hope better, choices in the same sorts of situations. But once an initial set of distributions is obtained, it would be a simple matter for the agent to revise those distributions incrementally as it gains more decision-making experience. In this way, the agent might adaptively converge on a state in which it would possess accurate knowledge of the value of its own computational procedures. If this knowledge can be applied with negligible overhead, then the system will have achieved a state of bounded optimality.

5.4.2. Probabilistic self-modelling

If we do not wish to assume that the agent will always be able to choose the best action in state $[S_j]$, we may assume instead that the agent has a certain probability of taking any given action. This probability may be directly related to the utility of the action; in an extreme case, if we assume that the probability is 1 for the action with highest utility, and 0 for other actions, we arrive at the model of equation (20). The better the agent's utility estimator $\hat{U}$ as an approximation to U, the closer will these probabilities come to this extreme case, but as long as $\hat{U}$ remains error-prone, the probabilities will lie in the open interval $(0,1)$.

Let $p(\alpha_{S_j}|S_j)$, $p(S_k|S_j)$ be respectively the probabilities that in state $[S_j]$ the agent will immediately take the new best action α_{S_j}, and that it will continue deliberation with computational action S_k. Then on this model the expected utility of the computational action S_j is given by

$$E[U([S_j])] = E[p(\alpha_{S_j}|S_j)U([\alpha_{S_j}, [S_j]]) \\ + p(S_k|S_j)U([S_k, [S_j]])].$$ (22)

Like equation (20), this formula gives the value of a current computational action in terms of the value of a future one. If we expand the action S_k recursively in a similar way to the expansion of S_j, and so on, we develop a decision tree as is usual for sequential decisions, except for the fact that all and only the peripheral branches represent external actions (see Fig. 1). The right-hand side of equation (22) then becomes the expectation of a sum of terms of the form

$$p(\alpha_{S_j}|S_j)U([\alpha_{S_j}, [S_j]]) \\ + p(\alpha_{S_j S_k}|S_j S_k)p(S_k|S_j)U([\alpha_{S_j S_k}, [S_j S_k]]) \\ + p(\alpha_{S_j S_k S_l}|S_j S_k S_l)p(S_k|S_j) \\ p(S_l|S_j S_k)U([\alpha_{S_j S_k S_l}, [S_j S_k S_l]]) + \dots.$$

This expression thus averages over all possible complete computations (see equation (4)).

If we then combine terms corresponding to situations in which the same action is chosen, we get an expression of the form

$$p(A_1)U(A_1) + \dots + p(A_n)U(A_n),$$

where now $p(A_i)$ represents the *probability that action A_i is eventually chosen* after completing the computation. Thus, after transforming the equation in this way, we can then drop the expectation sign on the right-hand side to obtain the following constraint on $\hat{U}$:

$$\hat{U}([S_j]) = \sum_i p(A_i)\hat{U}^S([A_i]|A_i \text{ chosen})$$ (23)

where we use the conditional notation to denote informally that the fact that an action will be chosen influences our estimate of its utility, and that the action's utility will depend on the time at which it is taken, and hence on the computation that ends in its being recommended. We believe it should be possible in practice to estimate the various probabilities and conditional expected utilities involved in this equation, although we have not yet attempted an implementation.

5.5. *Qualitative behaviour*

Before looking at specific implementations, we can describe the *qualitative* behaviour of any algorithm based on our approach. Clearly, an agent will tend to forego further consideration of an action whenever its current

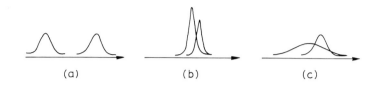

Fig. 2. Three basic situations: (a) terminate; (b) terminate; (c) continue.

estimated value and that of the best candidate are too far apart; in this case, it is unlikely that further computation will provide useful information, since the probability of changing action preference with any reasonable amount of extra computation is negligible. But deliberation may also be pointless if the current estimated utilities of two actions are too close together, and the variance of the difference in values is small; in that case, it may be unlikely that further computation will reveal a *significant* difference between them. In an extreme case, the two actions may actually be symmetric, or nearly so, so that no amount of computation will differentiate significantly between them. This case has received scant attention in the literature, since many algorithm designers erroneously assume that the goal of deliberation is to identify the best action, rather than to maximize net expected utility. Lastly, if there is considerable uncertainty as to the values of the available actions, and considerable overlap, further computation is recommended. We illustrate the three major situations graphically in Fig. 2.

6. Applications—the concrete level

Up to this point, we have been working at a very general level, making few assumptions about the nature of the base-level decision-making mechanism. Naturally, there are some attributes of certain mechanisms that make them amenable to meta-level control. The overall computation should be modular, in the sense that it can be divided into "steps" that can be chosen between; the steps must be capable of being carried out in varying orders. Also, systems that use estimated action utilities in their decision-making are more amenable to analysis, as discussed in Section 5. In this section, we give a brief description of our methodology and results in analyzing and implementing limited rational systems at the concrete level described in Section 3.2.

As mentioned in Section 5, decision-theoretic control of reasoning can be carried out using statistical knowledge of the probability distributions for the future utility estimates of external actions, as those estimates are changed by the computation in question. The crude approach, based on data giving these distributions directly, can be refined using knowledge of the base level decision-making methods of the agent. Essentially, the principle is this:

(1) Typically, a computation under consideration is known to affect only *certain components* of the agent's internal structure; for example, running a query about proposition p through a belief network will affect the probability that the agent assigns to p.

(2) Changes in those components affect the agent's choice of action in known ways; for example, if the base-level is decision-theoretic, then a change in the probability assigned to some action outcome would affect the expected utility for that action, and hence the choice of action, in the manner prescribed by equation (1).

The empirical component of evaluating computations arises only in the first of these two stages; the more specific we can be about the structure of the base level, the easier it will be to focus on a well-defined, homogeneous population of computation episodes and the more accurate our value estimates will become.

The basic technique to achieve localization of the stochastic effect of the computation is to write the value of the top-level action as a function of the immediate output of the computation. For example, in a search algorithm, the immediate outcome when a node is expanded is the new backed-up value of the node. Recall that $p_j(\boldsymbol{u})$ is the probability density function for the vector of new values of the top-level actions following computation S_j. This is composed of a probability density function $p_{ij}(u)$ for each top-level action A_i. If the immediate outcome of computation S_j is to change the value of a node j in the tree, then we can model the effect of the computation with a density function $p_{jj}(u)$ for the new value of j.

Now we can define the *propagation function* f that transmits the new value of the node j to produce the new value of each top-level action:

$$\hat{U}_{\mathrm{I}}^{S.S_j}([A_i]) = f(\hat{U}_{\mathrm{I}}^{S.S_j}[j]).$$

Thus we have a case of one random variable being defined as a function of another. We can therefore use a standard theorem to rewrite the density function p_{ij} in terms of the density function p_{jj}:

$$p_{ij}(x) = p_{jj}(f^{-1}(x)) \left| \frac{\mathrm{d}}{\mathrm{d}x}(f^{-1}(x)) \right|. \tag{24}$$

This transformation can be applied for any base-level decision-making algorithm. Each algorithm will have a characteristic propagation function, that will depend in characteristic ways on the current state of the computation. The main effort involved in applying our theory consists of identifying the function f for the decision algorithm and proving simplifying theorems for

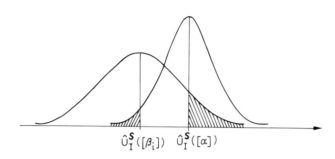

Fig. 3. Revision of action preference under subtree independence.

the value of computation formula. For an extended example of this process, see [41].

6.1. Subtree independence

Many base-level decision-making algorithms satisfy the general condition that a given computation affects the utility estimate of only one action. This is the case of *subtree independence*, and it enables us to obtain a further simplification of equation (11). In many domains, such as standard game-playing programs using minimax as a back-up method, the independence assumption will be straightforwardly true, if we consider individual node expansions as single computational steps. [13] Formally, subtree independence holds if and only if for all actions A_i except at most the one action whose utility estimate is affected,

$$\hat{U}_I^{S.S_j}([A_i]) = \hat{U}_I^S([A_i]). \tag{25}$$

In this case, examining equation (18), we see that there are essentially two distinct cases in which a computation can have positive benefit, by changing the agent's intention. Either further computation about some currently nonpreferred move β_i causes its utility estimate to be raised above that of α, or computation on α causes its utility estimate to be lowered below that of β_1, the current second-best move. Let us call two such computations S_j and S_k respectively (see Fig. 3).

---

[13]However, if the search space is treated as a graph rather than a tree, as in some chess and go programs, then the analysis becomes slightly more complicated. In certain problem-solving systems the full analysis must be used. For example, if a computation involves refining a probability estimate used in an influence diagram, the new value may affect the utility of all the top-level actions. In the worst case, the meta-level may have to resort to simulating the computation in question.

Suppose we are considering the computation S_j, which affects only the estimated utility of action β_i. The search action will only change our preferred move if

$$\hat{U}_1^{\mathbf{S}.S_j}([\beta_i]) > \hat{U}_1^{\mathbf{S}.S_j}([\alpha]),$$

or equivalently, given equation (25), only if

$$\hat{U}_1^{\mathbf{S}.S_j}([\beta_i]) > \hat{U}_1^{\mathbf{S}}([\alpha])$$

(the shaded region to the right of $\hat{U}_1^{\mathbf{S}}([\alpha])$ in Fig. 3). If this happens, we expect to be better off by an amount

$$\hat{U}_1^{\mathbf{S}.S_j}([\beta_i]) - \hat{U}_1^{\mathbf{S}}([\alpha]).$$

If not, there is no gain since our move preference remains unchanged. Thus in this case

$$E[\hat{V}(S_j)] = \int_{\hat{U}_1^{\mathbf{S}}([\alpha])}^{\infty} p_{ij}(x)(x - \hat{U}_1^{\mathbf{S}}([\alpha]))\,\mathrm{d}x - \mathrm{TC}(S_j). \tag{26}$$

Similarly, if we perform a computation S_k that affects only the utility estimate of the current best action α, our action preference is changed only if $\hat{U}_1^{\prime \mathbf{S}.S_k}([\alpha])$, the new expected value of our current preferred move, is less than $\hat{U}_1^{\mathbf{S}}([\beta_1])$. In that case β_1 will become the new best action. (Although the new estimated utility of the new preferred action would be less than the current estimated utility of the current preferred action, the agent would still be *better off than it was*, since the computation will have revealed that α is a blunder.) Hence

$$E[\hat{V}(S_k)] = \int_{-\infty}^{\hat{U}_1^{\mathbf{S}}([\beta_1])} p_{\alpha k}(x)(\hat{U}^{\mathbf{S}}(\beta_1) - x)\,\mathrm{d}x - \mathrm{TC}(S_k) \tag{27}$$

where $p_{\alpha k}(x)$ is the probability density function for $\hat{U}_1^{\prime \mathbf{S}.S_k}([\alpha])$.

All the quantities in equations (26) and (27) are well-defined and are either directly available to the agent or can be estimated statistically. Further simplification and greater accuracy can be obtained by applying the transformation given in equation (24).

6.2. Results for search applications

In a search program, computation typically proceeds by expanding "frontier nodes" of the partially-grown search tree. The value estimates for actions are calculated by backing up values from the new leaf nodes through their parents. The propagation function f therefore depends on the type of backing up that is used, and will typically involve examining the values of some "critical" nodes adjacent to the path between the leaf node and the root. The density functions p_{jj} for the immediate effect of the computation depend on the nature of the node being expanded, and the nature of the expansion computation. Statistical information on the probability distribution can therefore be acquired by induction on a large sample of similar states using the same type of expansion computation. Here we only sketch the the nature of the applications and their performance. Details appear in the various papers cited below.

For single-agent search with an admissible heuristic, we have shown [48] that only nodes in the subtree of the current best move should be expanded; derived a computable formula for the expected benefit for expanding a set of such nodes; shown that a best-first search (such as A*) is in fact the best policy given only the heuristic function; and derived an optimal stopping criterion for real-time search. Two common applications of this type of search are the familiar Eight Puzzle, and path-planning through an environment containing randomly-shaped polygonal obstacles. If we model the cost of computation by assuming a fixed cost-ratio between the cost of generating an edge in the search graph and the cost of the corresponding motion in the external world, we arrive at a figure for the total cost of a solution to such a problem, as a weighted sum of the cost of the solution path taken and the cost of the search employed to find it. We have constructed an algorithm, called DTA* for "decision-theoretic A*", which attempts to minimize the expected total solution cost using the ideas discussed here. We have tested DTA*, for which the cost-ratio is a given parameter, against both A*, which always finds shortest paths regardless of search cost, and RTA* [30], which uses a limited search horizon. [14] For each algorithm, the total solution cost is found for various values of the "rate of exchange" between computation cost and solution path length. Typical results for the Eight Puzzle, and for two-dimensional path-planning problems with twenty random polygons, are shown in Fig. 4. Regardless of the rate of exchange, it seems that DTA* outperforms the other algorithms, and as the cost of computation tends to zero, its behaviour tends to that of A*, as we would expect.

For game-playing, we have derived a formula for the value of expanding a leaf node that can be computed with very little overhead, given the simplifying assumptions outlined above [44]. We implemented a search algorithm, MGSS*, using this formula and played five 32-game tournaments against an alpha-beta algorithm with depth limits from two to six; both algorithms used the same evaluation function. The results, in terms of games

---

[14]It should be noted that the depth limit for RTA* is an additional parameter chosen by the user, and that for many problem instances the best performance was obtained with the limit set to 1, i.e., hill-climbing.

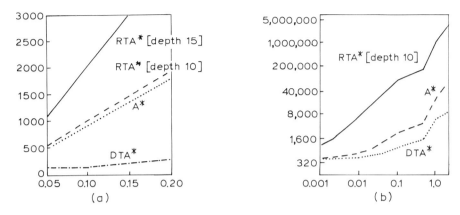

Fig. 4. (a) Eight Puzzle results. (b) Path-planning results.

won, nodes searched and CPU time used, are given in Table 1. Decision-theoretic search control is shown to be up to thirteen times more effective than alpha-beta pruning. The results of the more refined search control method in [41], though preliminary, show a factor of 59 improvement. We do not, however, expect this performance trend to persist against deeper-searching alpha-beta programs. As the MGSS* search tree grows larger it is highly likely to reach a situation in which no *single* node expansion can alter the best move choice; at that point, given our meta-greedy and single-step assumptions, the algorithm must conclude that no further search can be worthwhile. We call this phenomenon the "meta-greedy barrier". A promising approach in the short term is to use a two-stage search, consisting of, say, a depth-8 alpha-beta search extended by an MGSS* search, yielding an effective search depth of about 14. We are actively pursuing this line

Table 1
Summary of results for Othello

Algorithm	Wins	Nodes/game	Seconds/game
MGSS*	24.5	3,666	40
α-β[2]	7.5	2,501	23
MGSS*	22	6,132	68
α-β[3]	10	9,104	82
MGSS*	20	12,237	170
α-β[4]	12	42,977	403
MGSS*	16.5	21,155	435
α-β[5]	15.5	133,100	1,356
MGSS*	17	45,120	1,590
α-β[6]	15	581,433	6,863

in collaboration with Hans Berliner. The theory has also been applied to probabilistic games, such as backgammon, where deep alpha-beta searches are not feasible in backgammon due to the enormous branching factor. We expect very significant performance improvements as a result.

7. Further work

Future research topics can be divided into two classes: those concerning the construction of a completely general framework for metareasoning, and those concerning the improvement and generalization of the methods that arise from the framework in its current state.

Before we can be said to have a satisfactory formal theory of metareasoning, the scope of the theory must be extended to govern any kind of computational action.[15] Computations such as learning and compilation result in long-term internal state changes rather than contributing to immediate decisions. Hence to include them in the framework we need to consider utility over lifetimes, rather than instantaneous states. Although this, and the resulting need to consider complete action sequences, pose no theoretical difficulty for a framework-builder, it remains to be seen whether useful simplifications can be found that yield practical insights.

The place of metareasoning in a general theory of bounded optimality must also be ascertained. Instantaneous metareasoning yields bounded optimality when it is available, but when it has costs itself, the picture muddies. The problem of infinite regress, mentioned in Section 3, illustrates the complexities. One route to clarity may lie through the construction of feedback constraints for a learning procedure that can be shown to converge to bounded optimality even in an architecture with arbitrary levels of metareasoning.

Within the framework already established, we plan to extend the analysis from evaluation search to other forms of decision-making computations, and to construct a general problem-solving architecture that employs "normative" control over all its activities. The concept of *universal subgoaling* [32,33] is intended to capture the notion of a complete decision model, by making every aspect of the agent's deliberation recursively open to metareasoning. In the Soar system [33], however, the basic deliberation mode is goal-directed search. We intend to construct a problem-solving architecture in which decision-theoretic deliberation and its various possible compilations [40]

---

[15]Obtaining a satisfactory definition of computational action, as distinct from action in general, is nontrivial. Doyle [11] simply posits a division of the total world state into internal and external portions. The addition of time into such a framework is reasonably straightforward. Actions such as information-gathering experiments are problematic, since the rules governing their rationality are isomorphic to those for computations rather than ordinary external actions.

are the basic modes of computation, and in which metareasoning is carried out in the principled fashion outlined above, rather than through hand-generated condition–action rules.

One can also consider the possibility of applying these ideas to control search in theorem-provers. However, in order to do this one needs something amounting to a "current best move". As currently implemented, theorem-provers have no partial information about the success of the branch under consideration (but see [12] for an application of conspiracy numbers to theorem-proving search). The notions of "guaranteed solution" and "proof" must be replaced by *tentative/abstract/partial solution* and *justification*. Algorithms using defaults, abstraction hierarchies and island-driving strategies thus seem more amenable to meta-level control and therefore much more robust in the face of complexity.

In addition to trying to relax the meta-greedy and single-step assumptions to obtain still better search control, there are some algorithmic extensions that would yield better performance. We can improve the efficiency of real-time interleaving of computation and action by preserving and extending the partial search tree developed by previous deliberations. Our current implementations successfully alternate deliberation and action, but do not retain any information between deliberations. By keeping and extending that part of the search tree that involves the action that is actually chosen, the system will approach standard optimizing algorithms in the limit of unbounded computation. In highly time-bounded situations, the system's behaviour would essentially become that of a reactive system adapting a dynamically-constructed plan to violations of its expectations at the look-ahead horizon.

We can also improve the space-efficiency of selective-search algorithms (and, by extension, any recursively-defined decision-making system). The selective search paradigm has come under criticism because of the need to keep a significant portion of the search tree in memory. A recursive, or problem-reduction algorithm can be implemented that still employs the metareasoning methods described above yet only keeps a small number of nodes in memory. The approach is based on *iterative expansion*, a generalization of iterative deepening. The algorithm is given a current state and a resource limit (say K nodes of search), and calls itself on the state's successors with resource allocations $k_1, \ldots, k_n$. Depending on the results of the initial search, the algorithm can increase the resource allocation of some successor by a constant factor α. In this way the algorithm uses only linear space, and in the limit wastes a negligible amount of time in repeated subtree expansions. Furthermore, the use of information returned from each subtree to select the direction for further search gives the scheme a clear advantage over IDA* [29].

The decision-theoretic meta-level can be seen as a means to construct a near-optimal anytime algorithm, in Dean's sense [7], from atomic computation steps. Given several such anytime algorithms, together with their *performance profiles*—mappings from time allocation to output quality—one may wish to construct a more complex real-time system by applying simple composition operators, without having to explicitly specify time allocations among the subsystems. This is a natural generalization of the task of a compiler for a language with procedural abstraction—that is, subroutines. The "contract specification" between caller and callee now has an additional degree of freedom. Consider, for example, the following definition of a treatment system:

```
(defun treat (x) (repair (diagnose x)))
```

Given the performance profiles of the two subsystems, it is mathematically straightforward to construct the optimal apportionment of resources for a given total allocation, and hence to construct the optimal anytime algorithm for the whole problem. We are currently investigating the extent to which programming constructs other than simple functional composition can be generalized in the same way.

8. Summary

We see computational resource limitations as a major influence on the design of optimal agents. This influence has been neglected in classical theories of normative behaviour, with the result that practical AI systems for nontrivial domains are constructed in an ad hoc fashion. A theory of the value of computation will play a central role in the design of optimal limited rational agents.

The basic insight behind normative control reasoning is that computations are actions. Choosing good actions involves reasoning about outcomes and utilities. The utility of a computational action *must be derived from its effect on the agent's ultimate choice of action in the real world.* When the computational action effects changes in internal state that amount to learning or compilation, the relevant effect will be on the long-term sequence of actions. The next problem is to assess this effect without actually performing the computation. Our method can be viewed as an extension and revision of information value theory to cover computations in resource-bounded agents. When the base-level problem-solver operates using value estimates for the real-world actions, the effects of computations can be assessed by using prior statistical knowledge of the distribution of the new value after the computation in question. The required distributions can be induced from direct observation of actual computations. Estimates of the value of computations can then be used to optimize a system's overall behaviour in real-time situations. We can also derive some general qualitative insights into principles of resource allocation, pruning and termination.

We formalized the notion of real-time problem-solving in our framework, and identified time cost as a useful abstraction enabling significant simplifications in the theory. We have applied the theory to analyze both single-agent problem-solving and competitive game-playing, in each case using knowledge of the decision-making algorithm to derive an efficiently-computable formula for the value of computation. The resulting algorithms exhibit significantly better performance than standard methods with negligible meta-level overhead. We indicated some areas for further research in this vein.

Underlying the idea of decision-theoretic control is a distinct approach to dealing with complexity in AI systems. A view prevalent in the inference community, and eloquently described by Kautz [28], has it that intractable problem classes must be avoided, and progress can be made by concentrating on finding polynomial-time subclasses that are as general as possible. Instead, we propose that systems should simply select the computations that will yield the highest return in the shortest time, using as much knowledge of the domain as possible to carry out the selection. The above theory identifies and utilizes one source of appropriate knowledge. Only in domains that have very few identifiable regularities will the formal intractability results apply.

A decision-theoretic, meta-level architecture, particularly one endowed with a varied set of forms of compiled knowledge, generates a rich space of possible agent configurations. Ideally, we would like such a system to converge to a state of bounded optimality. Full development of the theory of metareasoning should provide a set of "regulative principles" to define and guide this convergence process, replacing the standard axioms of perfect rationality.

Acknowledgement

This research has been supported by an equipment grant from the AT&T Foundation, and by funding from the Lockheed AI Center, California MICRO Program, and the National Science Foundation under grant no. IRI-8903146. Eric Wefald was supported by a GE Foundation Fellowship and more recently by a Shell Foundation Doctoral Fellowship. We gratefully acknowledge this assistance. In addition, we would like to thank Steve Bradley, Jack Breese, Murray Campbell, Jon Doyle, Michael Fehling, Michael Genesereth, Eric Horvitz, Maurice Karnaugh, Richard Karp, David McAllester, Devika Subramanian, Michael Wellman and two reviewers for their valuable comments and suggestions.

References

[1] A.M. Agogino, Real-time reasoning about time constraints and model precision in complex, distributed mechanical systems, in: *Proceedings AAAI Spring Symposium on AI and Limited Rationality*, Stanford, CA (1989).

[2] P. Agre and D. Chapman, Pengo: an implementation of a theory of activity, in: *Proceedings AAAI-87*, Seattle, WA (1987).

[3] J. Batali, A computational theory of rational action (draft), MIT AI Lab, Cambridge, MA (1985).

[4] M. Bratman, D. Israel and M. Pollack, Plans and resource-bounded practical reasoning, *Comput. Intell.* **4** (1988) 349–355.

[5] R.A. Brooks, A robust, layered control system for a mobile robot, *IEEE J. Rob. Autom.* **2** (1986) 14–23.

[6] C. Cherniak, *Minimal Rationality* (MIT Press, Cambridge, MA, 1986).

[7] T. Dean, Intractability and time-dependent planning, in: M.P. Georgeff and A.L. Lansky, eds., *The 1986 Workshop on Reasoning about Actions and Plans* (Morgan Kaufmann, Los Altos, CA, 1987) 245–266.

[8] T. Dean, Decision-theoretic control of inference for time-critical applications, *Int. J. Intell. Syst.* (to appear).

[9] T. Dean and M. Boddy, An analysis of time-dependent planning, in: *Proceedings AAAI-88*, St. Paul, MN (1988) 49–54.

[10] J. Doyle, What is rational psychology? Toward a modern mental philosophy, *AI Mag.* **4** (3) (1983) 50–53.

[11] J. Doyle, Artificial intelligence and rational self-government, Tech. Report No. CMU-CS-88-124, Computer Science Department, Carnegie-Mellon University, Pittsburgh, PA (1988).

[12] C. Elkan, Conspiracy numbers and caching for searching and/or trees and theorem-proving, in: *Proceedings IJCAI-89*, Detroit, MI (1989).

[13] M.R. Fehling and J.S. Breese, A computational model for decision-theoretic control of problem-solving under uncertainty, in: *Proceedings Fourth Workshop on Uncertainty in Artificial Intelligence*, Minneapolis, MN (1988).

[14] M.R. Genesereth and D. Smith, Meta-level architecture, Stanford Heuristic Programming Project, Memo HPP-81-6, Stanford University, Stanford, CA (1981).

[15] I.J. Good, A five year plan for automatic chess, in: E. Dale and D. Michie, eds., *Machine Intelligence* **2** (Olivier & Boyd, Edinburgh, 1968).

[16] I.J. Good, Twenty-seven principles of rationality, in: V.P. Godambe and D.A. Sprott, eds., *Foundations of Statistical Inference* (Holt, Rinehart, Winston, Toronto, Ont. 1971) 108–141.

[17] I. Hacking, Slightly more realistic personal probability, *Philos. Sci.* **34** (1967) 311–325.

[18] O. Hansson, G. Holt and A. Mayer, The comparison and optimization of search algorithm performance, Unpublished manuscript, Columbia University, Computer Science Department, New York (1986).

[19] O. Hansson and A. Mayer, The optimality of satisficing solutions, in: *Proceedings Fourth Workshop on Uncertainty in Artificial Intelligence*, Minneapolis, MN (1988).

[20] O. Hansson and A. Mayer, Heuristic search as evidential reasoning, in: *Proceedings Fifth Workshop on Uncertainty in Artificial Intelligence*, Windsor, Ont. (1989).

[21] O. Hansson and A. Mayer, Probabilistic heuristic estimates, *Ann. Math. Artif. Intell.* **2** (1990) 209–220.

[22] D. Haussler, Quantifying inductive bias: AI learning algorithms and Valiant's learning framework, *Artif. Intell.* **36** (1988) 177–221.

[23] D. Heckerman and H. Jimison, A perspective on confidence and its use in focusing attention during knowledge acquisition, in: *Proceedings Third Workshop on Uncertainty in AI*, Seattle, WA (1987) 123–131.

[24] E.J. Horvitz, Problem-solving design: reasoning about computational value, trade-offs, and resources, in: *Proceedings Second Annual NASA Research Forum*, Moffett Field, CA (1987) 26–43.

[25] E.J. Horvitz, Reasoning under varying and uncertain resource constraints, in: *Proceedings AAAI-88*, St. Paul, MN (1988) 139–144.

[26] E.J. Horvitz, Reasoning about beliefs and actions under computational resource constraints, in: L.N. Kanal, T.S. Levitt and J.F. Lemmer, eds., *Uncertainty in Artificial Intelligence* 3 (North-Holland, Amsterdam, 1989) 301–324.

[27] R.A. Howard, Information value theory, *IEEE Trans. Syst. Sci. Cybern.* 2 (1) (1966) 22–26.

[28] H. Kautz, Computers and Thought Lecture, IJCAI-89, Detroit, MI (1989).

[29] R.E. Korf, Depth-first iterative deepening: an optimal admissible tree search, *Artif. Intell.* 27 (1985) 97–109.

[30] R.E. Korf, Real-time heuristic search: first results, in: *Proceedings AAAI-87*, Seattle, WA (1987) 133–138.

[31] T.J. Laffey, P.A. Cox, J.L. Schmidt, S.M. Kao and J.Y. Read, Real-time knowledge-based systems, *AI Mag.* 9 (1) (1988) 27–45.

[32] J.E. Laird, Universal subgoaling, Doctoral Dissertation, Computer Science Department, Carnegie-Mellon University, Pittsburgh, PA (1984).

[33] J.E. Laird, A. Newell and P.S. Rosenbloom, SOAR: an architecture for general intelligence, *Artif. Intell.* 33 (1987) 1–64.

[34] V. Lesser, J. Pavlin and E. Durfee, Approximate processing in real-time problem-solving, *AI Mag.* 9 (1) (1988) 49–61.

[35] B. Lipman, How to decide how to decide how to …: limited rationality in decisions and games, in: *Proceedings AAAI Symposium on AI and Limited Rationality*, Stanford, CA (1989).

[36] D.A. McAllester, Conspiracy numbers for min-max search, *Artif. Intell.* 35 (1989) 287–310.

[37] J. McCarthy, Programs with common sense, in: R.J. Brachman and H.J. Levesque, eds., *Readings in Knowledge Representation* (Morgan Kaufmann, Los Altos, 1985) 300–307.

[38] J. Pearl, *Probabilistic Reasoning in Intelligent Systems: Networks of Plausible Inference* (Morgan Kaufmann, San Mateo, CA, 1988).

[39] S.J. Russell, The compleat guide to MRS, Tech. Report No. STAN-CS-85-1080, Computer Science Department, Stanford University, Stanford, CA (1985).

[40] S.J. Russell, Execution architectures and compilation, in: *Proceedings IJCAI-89*, Detroit, MI (1989).

[41] S.J. Russell, Fine-grained decision-theoretic search control, in: *Proceedings Sixth Workshop on Uncertainty in Artificial Intelligence*, Cambridge, MA (1990).

[42] S.J. Russell and E.H. Wefald, Multi-level decision-theoretic search, in: *Proceedings AAAI Spring Symposium Series on Computer Game-Playing*, Stanford, CA (1988).

[43] S.J. Russell and E.H. Wefald, Decision-theoretic control of search: general theory and an application to game-playing, Tech. Report UCB/CSD 88/435, Computer Science Division, University of California, Berkeley, CA (1988).

[44] S.J. Russell and E.H. Wefald, On optimal game-tree search using rational metareasoning, in: *Proceedings IJCAI-89*, Detroit, MI (1989).

[45] H.A. Simon, *Models of Bounded Rationality* 2 (MIT Press, Cambridge, MA, 1982).

[46] L.G. Valiant, A theory of the learnable, *Commun. ACM* 18 (1984) 1134–1142.

[47] J. von Neumann and O. Morgenstern, *Theory of Games and Economic Behavior* (Princeton University Press, Princeton, NJ, 1947).

[48] E.H. Wefald and S.J. Russell, Estimating the vaue of computation: the case of real-time search, in: *Proceedings AAAI Spring Symposium on AI and Limited Rationality*, Stanford, CA (1989).

[49] E.H. Wefald and S.J. Russell, Adaptive learning of decision-theoretic search control knowledge, in: *Proceedings Sixth International Workshop on Machine Learning*, Ithaca, NY (1989).

Artificial Intelligence 49 (1991) 397–398
Elsevier

Author Index—Volume 49 (1991)

Elsevier Science Publishers B.V.

Subject Index